THE FATE OF THE BOLSHEVIK REVOLUTION

Library of Modern Russia

Advisory Board:

Jeffrey Brooks, Professor at Johns Hopkins University, USA
Michael David-Fox, Professor at Georgetown University, USA
Lucien Frary, Associate Professor at Rider University, USA
James Harris, Professor at the University of Leeds, UK
Robert Hornsby, Senior Lecturer at the University of Leeds, UK
Ekaterina Pravilova, Professor of History at Princeton University, USA
Geoffrey Swain, Emeritus Professor of Central and East European Studies at the University of Glasgow, UK
Vera Tolz-Zilitinkevic, Sir William Mather Professor of Russian Studies at the University of Manchester, UK
Vladislav Zubok, Professor of International History at the London School of Economics, UK

Building on Bloomsbury Academic's established record of publishing Russian studies titles, the *Library of Modern Russia* will showcase the work of emerging and established writers who are setting new agendas in the field.

At a time when potentially dangerous misconceptions and misunderstandings about Russia abound, titles in the series will shed fresh light and nuance on Russian history. Volumes will take the idea of 'Russia' in its broadest cultural sense and cover the entirety of the multi-ethnic lands that made up imperial Russia and the Soviet Union. Ranging in chronological scope from the Romanovs to today, the books will:

- Reconsider Russia's history from a variety of inter-disciplinary perspectives.
- Explore Russia in its various international contexts, rather than as exceptional or in isolation.
- Examine the complex, divisive and ever-shifting notions of 'Russia'.
- Contribute to a deeper understanding of Russia's rich social and cultural history.
- Critically reassess the Soviet period and its legacy today.
- Interrogate the traditional periodizations of the post-Stalin Soviet Union.
- Unearth continuities, or otherwise, among the tsarist, Soviet and post-Soviet periods.
- Reappraise Russia's complex relationship with Eastern Europe, both historically and today.
- Analyse the politics of history and memory in post-Soviet Russia.
- Promote new archival revelations and innovative research methodologies.
- Foster a community of scholars and readers devoted to a sharper understanding of the Russian experience, past and present.

Books in the series will join our list in being marketed globally, including at conferences – such as the BASEES and ASEEES conventions. Each will be subjected to a rigorous peer-review process and will be published in hardback and, simultaneously, as an e-book. We also anticipate a second release in paperback for the general reader and student markets.

For more information, or to submit a proposal for inclusion in the series, please contact: Rhodri Mogford, Publisher, History (Rhodri.Mogford@bloomsbury.com).

New and forthcoming:

Fascism in Manchuria: The Soviet-China Encounter in the 1930s, Susanne Hohler

The Idea of Russia: The Life and Work of Dmitry Likhachev, Vladislav Zubok

The Tsar's Armenians: A Minority in Late Imperial Russia, Onur Onol

Myth Making in the Soviet Union and Modern Russia: Remembering World War II in Brezhnev's Hero City, Vicky Davis

Building Stalinism: The Moscow Canal and the Creation of Soviet Space, Cynthia Ruder

Russia in the Time of Cholera: Disease and the Environment under Romanovs and Soviets, John Davis

Soviet Americana: A Cultural History of Russian and Ukrainian Americanists, Sergei Zhuk

Stalin's Economic Advisors: The Varga Institute and the Making of Soviet Foreign Policy, Ken Roh

Ideology and the Arts in the Soviet Union: The Establishment of Censorship and Control, Steven Richmond

Nomads and Soviet Rule: Central Asia under Lenin and Stalin, Alun Thomas

The Russian State and the People: Power, Corruption and the Individual in Putin's Russia, Geir Hønneland et al. (eds)

The Communist Party in the Russian Civil War: A Political History, Gayle Lonergan

Criminal Subculture in the Gulag: Prisoner Society in the Stalinist Labour Camps, Mark Vincent

Power and Politics in Modern Chechnya: Ramzan Kadyrov and the New Digital Authoritarianism, Karena Avedissian

Russian Pilgrimage to the Holy Land: Piety and Travel from the Middle Ages to the Revolution, Nikolaos Chrissidis

The Fate of the Bolshevik Revolution, Lara Douds, James Harris and Peter Whitewood (eds)

Writing History in Late Imperial Russia, Frances Nethercott

Translating England into Russian, Elena Goodwin

THE FATE OF THE BOLSHEVIK REVOLUTION

ILLIBERAL LIBERATION, 1917–41

Edited by Lara Douds, James Harris and Peter Whitewood

BLOOMSBURY ACADEMIC
LONDON • NEW YORK • OXFORD • NEW DELHI • SYDNEY

BLOOMSBURY ACADEMIC
Bloomsbury Publishing Plc
50 Bedford Square, London, WC1B 3DP, UK
1385 Broadway, New York, NY 10018, USA

BLOOMSBURY, BLOOMSBURY ACADEMIC and the Diana logo are
trademarks of Bloomsbury Publishing Plc

First published in Great Britain 2020

Copyright © Lara Douds, James Harris, and Peter Whitewood, 2020

Lara Douds, James Harris, and Peter Whitewood have asserted their right under the
Copyright, Designs and Patents Act, 1988, to be identified as Editors of this work.

Cover design by Tjaša Krivec
Cover image: Soviet poster commemorating the October Revolution of 1917,
showing a worker shattering his chains. The poster also shows symbols of democracy,
socialism and freedom. (© Photo by Michael Nicholson/Corbis via Getty Images)

All rights reserved. No part of this publication may be reproduced or transmitted
in any form or by any means, electronic or mechanical, including photocopying,
recording, or any information storage or retrieval system, without prior permission
in writing from the publishers.

Bloomsbury Publishing Plc does not have any control over, or responsibility for,
any third-party websites referred to or in this book. All internet addresses given in this
book were correct at the time of going to press. The author and publisher regret
any inconvenience caused if addresses have changed or sites have ceased to exist,
but can accept no responsibility for any such changes.

A catalogue record for this book is available from the British Library.

A catalog record for this book is available from the Library of Congress.

ISBN: HB: 978-1-3501-1790-7
       PB: 978-1-3501-1789-1
       ePDF: 978-1-3501-1791-4
       eBook: 978-1-3501-1792-1

Typeset by Integra Software Services Pvt Ltd.
Printed and bound in Great Britain

To find out more about our authors and books visit www.bloomsbury.com
and sign up for our newsletters.

CONTENTS

Contributors		ix
Introduction: Illiberal Liberation, 1917–41 *Lara Douds, James Harris and Peter Whitewood*		1
Part I Bolshevik Ideology and Practice		**15**
1	Dictatorship Unlimited: Lenin on the State, March–November 1917 *Erik van Ree*	17
2	The Permanent Campaign and the Fate of Political Freedom in Russia *Lars T. Lih*	31
Part II Workers' Democracy and Soviet State-Building		**47**
3	Local Government, Disorder and the Origins of the Soviet State, 1917–18 *Dakota Irvin*	49
4	Lenin's 'Living Link'? Petitioning the Ruler across the Revolutionary Divide *Lara Douds*	63
5	The Communist Party and the Late 1930s Soviet Democracy Campaigns: Origins and Outcomes *Yiannis Kokosalakis*	77
Part III Internal Party Democracy		**93**
6	Trotsky and the Questions of Agency, Democracy and Dictatorship in the USSR, 1917–40 *Ian D. Thatcher*	95
7	Discipline versus Democracy: The 1923 Party Controversy *James Harris*	109

Contents

Part IV Repression and Moderation	125
8 Democracy and Violence, 1917–37 J. Arch Getty	127
9 Stalinist Moderation and the Turn to Repression: Utopianism and Realpolitik in the Mid-1930s Olga Velikanova	141
Part V National Tensions and International Threats	155
10 Debating the Early Soviet Nationalities Policy: The Case of Soviet Ukraine Olena Palko	157
11 The International Situation: Fear of Invasion and Growing Authoritarianism Peter Whitewood	173
Part VI Culture and Society: Experimentation and Control	187
12 Bolshevik Revolution and the Enlightenment of the People Sheila Fitzpatrick	189
13 Walking the Razor's Edge: The Origins of Soviet Censorship Polly Corrigan	201
14 Revolutionary Participation, Youthful Civic-Mindedness Andy Willimott	215
15 Liberation and Authoritarianism in the Early Soviet Campaign to 'Struggle with Prostitution' Siobhán Hearne	231
16 Soviet Canteens in Pre-War USSR, 1917–41: Promises of Emancipation and Everyday Violence François-Xavier Nérard	245
Notes	256
Select Bibliography	307
Index	309

CONTRIBUTORS

Polly Corrigan is a PhD candidate at King's College London. Her thesis examines the NKVD and the repression of writers in the Soviet Union in the 1930s.

Lara Douds is Vice Chancellor's Research Fellow in History at Northumbria University and is the author of *Inside Lenin's Government: Ideology, Power and Practice in the Early Soviet State*. She has published in *Historical Research* and *Revolutionary Russia*.

Sheila Fitzpatrick is a Professor of History at the University of Sydney. She is the author of *The Commissariat of Enlightenment: Soviet Organization of Education and the Arts under Lunacharsky, 1917–1921; Education and Social Mobility in the Soviet Union, 1921–1932; Stalin's Peasants: Resistance and Survival in the Russian Village after Collectivization; Everyday Stalinism: Ordinary Life in Extraordinary Times: Soviet Russia in the 1930s; On Stalin's Team: The Years of Living Dangerously in Soviet Politics*.

J. Arch Getty is a Distinguished Professor of History at the University of California, Los Angeles. He is the author of *Practicing Stalinism: Boyars, Bolsheviks, and the Persistence of Political Tradition; The Road to Terror: Stalin and the Self-Destruction of the Bolsheviks, 1932–1939; Yezhov: The Rise of Stalin's 'Iron Fist'; Origins of the Great Purges: The Soviet Communist Party Reconsidered, 1933–1938* and editor of *Stalinist Terror: New Perspectives* (with Roberta T. Manning).

James Harris is a Professor of Modern European History at the University of Leeds. He is the author of *The Great Fear: Stalin's Terror of the 1930s; The Great Urals: Regionalism and the Evolution of the Soviet System; Stalin's World: Dictating the Soviet Order* (with Sarah Davies). He was editor of *The Anatomy of Terror: Political Violence under Stalin* and *Stalin: A New History* (with Sarah Davies).

Siobhán Hearne is a Leverhulme Early Career Fellow at Durham University. Her PhD thesis examined prostitution in Russia between 1900 and 1930. She has published in the *Journal of Social History* and *Revolutionary Russia*.

Dakota Irvin is a PhD candidate in History at the University of North Carolina at Chapel Hill. His thesis is titled 'Revolving Doors of Power: How Revolutionary Ekaterinburg Became Sverdlovsk, 1917–1924' and has published in *Revolutionary Russia* and *Novyi istoricheskii vestnik*.

Yiannis Kokosalakis is a Marie Skłodowska Curie Fellow at the University College Dublin Centre for War Studies. He has published in *Revolutionary Russia*.

Contributors

Lars T. Lih is a scholar who lives in Montreal. He is the author of *Bread and Authority in Russia, 1914–1921; Lenin; Lenin Rediscovered: What Is to Be Done? in Context*.

François-Xavier Nérard is an Associate Professor in History at the University of Paris 1 Pantheon-Sorbonne. He is the author of *Cinq pour cent de vérité: La dénonciation dans l'URSS de Staline* and editor of *Commémorer les victimes en Europe: XVIe-XXIe siècles* (with David El Kenz).

Olena Palko is a Leverhulme Early Career Fellow at Birkbeck, University of London. Her PhD thesis examined cultural sovietization of Ukraine in the 1920s–1930s. She has published in the *Journal of Contemporary Central and Eastern Europe* and *Jahrbücher für Geschichte Osteuropas*.

Ian D. Thatcher is a Professor of History at Ulster University. He is the author of *Trotsky; Leon Trotsky and World War One: August 1914 to February 1917* and editor of *Late Imperial Russia: Problems and Prospects; Regime and Society in Twentieth-Century Russia; Reinterpreting Revolutionary Russia*.

Erik van Ree is an Assistant Professor in European Studies at the University of Amsterdam. He is the author of *The Political Thought of Joseph Stalin: A Study in Twentieth-Century Revolutionary Patriotism; Boundaries of Utopia: Imagining Communism from Plato to Stalin*.

Olga Velikanova is a Professor at the University of North Texas. She is the author of *Popular Perceptions of Soviet Politics: Disenchantment of the Dreamers* and *Mass Political Culture Under Stalinism: Popular Discussion of the Soviet Constitution of 1936*.

Peter Whitewood is a Senior Lecturer in History at York St John University. He is the author of *The Red Army and the Great Terror: Stalin's Purge of the Soviet Military*.

Andy Willimott is a Lecturer in Modern Russian History at Queen Mary University of London. He is author of *Living the Revolution: Urban Communes and Soviet Socialism, 1917–1932* (OUP, 2017) and co-editor (with Matthias Neumann) of *Rethinking the Russian Revolution as Historical Divide* (Routledge, 2018).

INTRODUCTION: ILLIBERAL LIBERATION, 1917–41

Lara Douds, James Harris and Peter Whitewood

In 1917, the Bolsheviks promised to liberate the working masses of the Russian Empire from a repressive and exploitative system. Within two decades, they had established a system that was even more dictatorial and coercive than the one they had overthrown. The question of how a regime that promised ultimate liberation ended up delivering a violent dictatorship has been at the core of Soviet studies since its emergence as a discipline. The earliest literature, which coalesced around Carl Friedrich and Zbigniew Brzezinski's 'totalitarian model' asserted that the drive to dictatorship was in the Bolshevik DNA and that the Bolsheviks, a small, unrepresentative and already or embryonically totalitarian party, usurped power and imposed itself by force on the population in October 1917. From that moment on, Soviet politics and society were determined by the totalitarian dynamics of the monolithic Communist Party, with its dictatorial nature, ruthlessness, ideological orthodoxy, programmatic dogmatism, ultra-discipline and centralized bureaucratic organization.[1] In the hostile climate of the Cold War, American democracy in the United States was presented as 'government by the will of the people' in contrast to 'government against the will of the people' in the USSR.

Since the 1970s, various challenges to the totalitarian canon have rejected the deterministic view of a dictatorial dogma shaping post-revolutionary politics, state building and society. Early 'revisionists' like Robert Tucker and Stephen Cohen recognized an initial democratic, idealistic impulse and argued that Leninism and Stalinism were different political phenomena and that one did not lead inevitably to the other.[2] Other revisionists identified principled democrats among the Bolsheviks, but saw them as peripheral, oppositionist figures, and enumerated the circumstances that favoured those seeking to establish an authoritarian order – principally Stalin.[3] Studies of 1917 challenged the notion of a coup d'état led by a hyper-centralized party and identified elements of popular support.[4] Then a second wave of revisionists from among social historians variously attributed the origins of communist party-state dictatorship to Russian backwardness and the impact of the civil war.[5] Though revisionism consciously rejected the prevailing orthodoxy, it nevertheless reproduced the old Cold War dichotomy of democracy versus totalitarianism in seeing the movement as divided between 'good, democratic-Bolsheviks and bad, authoritarian Bolsheviks'. It was not open to the idea that the Bolsheviks had real democratic intent that they did not deliberately or consciously abandon.

Even now, twenty-five years after gaining access to the archival sources necessary to rethink this question, much historiography remains locked in these patterns of thought characteristic of the Cold War. To move beyond the Cold War paradigm, it is helpful to set Bolshevik dilemmas in the context of the broader European hesitations and concerns about democratic progress and the weaknesses of actual democratic development in early twentieth-century Europe. Post-revisionist scholars of the 'modernity school' have begun to situate the interwar Soviet Union in the framework of modern European development in terms of mass politics, progressive social interventionism, industrialization and urbanization, literacy campaigns, and scientific and technological change.[6] But further exploration of the fragility of contemporary European democracy and the challenges of building a democratic order serves as context for a re-examination of the situation in revolutionary Russia, where the obstacles to democratic development were significantly greater. The Bolshevik vision of an alternative political order that would give real power to the working masses was at once related to, but also reacting against, the political forms of its European neighbours.

The Cold War-era scholarship posits that the Bolsheviks had a choice of opting for democracy and they chose authoritarianism instead – but not only was democracy underdeveloped and seriously biased towards the possessing classes and old elites, democracy was collapsing across Europe in the interwar. Its reputation was in tatters. Even where it survived, it was perceived as weak and corrupt and exacerbating social and political tensions rather than calming them. The real core of the historical amnesia of the Cold War scholarship is that the extension of the suffrage to the working class was tremendously controversial.[7] Were they ready for the vote? Would they be susceptible to demagoguery? And yet the Bolsheviks were not allowed to have the same doubts and seek to educate the largely illiterate population first.

This volume reconsiders the binary notion of an intentional choice between authoritarianism and democracy. The Soviet experiment was inherently and self-consciously 'anti-Liberal', yet strove to emancipate the broad masses and offer them a superior form of class-based democracy. A form of 'illiberal liberation', revolutionary democracy was to be very different than democracy in liberal, rule-of-law states with freedom of speech, civil society and limits on rulers through constitutions. 'Liberal democracy' in the modern United States and in Western Europe combines two constituent parts, a democratic element and a liberal element. 'Democracy' is derived from a Greek word meaning rule by the people, while 'liberal' and 'liberalism' derive from a Latin word meaning free. Today, however, democracy often is used as shorthand for liberal democracy and thus is thought also to incorporate the protection of individual freedom. Democracy and liberalism may be understood as addressing different questions. Democracy answers the question of who rules. It requires that the people be sovereign. Liberalism, by contrast, speaks not to how rulers are chosen but what the limits to their power are once in office to protect the rights of the individual. Although democracy was typically paired with liberalism in the twentieth-century West, the two are not inseparably linked. Premodern democracies were not liberal, and in nineteenth-century Europe there existed constitutional monarchies that were not governed democratically.

Yet, the definition of democracy is often assumed to be settled. It is generally characterized as a system in which everyone has a vote and the opportunity periodically

Introduction: Illiberal Liberation, 1917–41

to elect representatives to a national legislative assembly or parliament. These representatives are members of multiple political parties and the one that wins the most votes acts to form a government which will set national policy for the term of the parliament. In the main, this was the sort of political system that emerged across Europe throughout the nineteenth century, but it was not universally accepted as the only form that democracy could take and the only way the 'will of the people' might be represented. More significantly, at the turn of the twentieth century, the political systems in Europe fell far short this definition. Nowhere in Europe did every adult have the vote. There were significant restrictions on the suffrage based on property ownership, wealth, naturalization status, education and/or geography, though these were being gradually reduced by successive acts of electoral reform. Still, at the time of the Bolshevik revolution, fewer than six out of ten men had the vote in Britain.[8] France and Germany were ahead of Britain in granting full suffrage to the male population, but there were other significant limitations on the significance of that suffrage.

All three of these European powers had bicameral legislatures, but while the parliaments were gaining independent power, they were still far from being in a position to dictate policy. In fact, in each case, their powers were carefully circumscribed to limit the influence of the lower houses elected by those outside the privileged elite.

There were, of course many groups and individuals across Europe exerting pressure for further democratic reform, though well into the twentieth century the idea of allowing the full expression of the one person one vote principle was controversial. The working masses constituted a clear majority of the population and giving them the vote effectively meant giving them the dominant voice in politics. Before the advent of universal literacy towards the turn of the twentieth century, the arguments against extending the suffrage were more obvious. Participation in democratic politics was supposed to require an informed electorate and it was largely taken for granted that illiteracy disqualified the masses. Yet the fact of universal literacy alone did not overcome general class prejudice or specific fears about how the masses might vote.[9] The scaremongering did not ultimately halt the gradual extension of the suffrage, because it did not show signs of destabilizing the existing political order. The working masses were not obviously susceptible to calls for revolution. In their millions, they patriotically fought and died in the trenches of the First World War. But there was another factor that served to break resistance to the extension of the suffrage. Parties of the establishment were coming to understand the conservative inclinations of the working-class voter. They were willing to extend the suffrage because workers would vote for them.[10]

In the years leading up to the October Revolution, progress towards universal suffrage in Europe was consistent though controversial, but the establishment had considerable 'safeguards' to protect itself against unwelcome initiatives from the working masses. In this context, what was the Bolshevik attitude to democracy? Their critique of European liberal democracy or 'bourgeois democracy', as they called it, was clear and consistent: the promises of universal suffrage and of popular (*obshchenarodnaia*) power were a deception because real power was exercised behind the scenes by the capitalist bourgeoisie. This analysis set them apart from other Social Democratic groups in Russia, such as the Mensheviks, who embraced a republican Russia in which Social Democratic parties would represent the interests of the masses as the basis for a peaceful transition to socialism.

In the months before the October seizure of power, Lenin wrote the pamphlet *State and Revolution*, which was at once a polemical attack on the Mensheviks and Socialist Revolutionaries (SRs), a restatement of his pessimism about the potential of a Russian liberal democracy and an exposition of his alternative vision of 'democracy' and the political future towards which the Bolsheviks would work. The pamphlet opens with an argument that the Mensheviks' and SRs' support for a liberal democratic Russia was rooted in a misreading of Marx. For Lenin, the state is an organ for the repression of one class by another. It cannot reconcile the conflicting interests of classes. To accept 'bourgeois' democracy for Russia, as the Mensheviks and SRs were doing, was to betray the interests of the masses. Lenin was thus addressing himself to Social Democrats and other participants in the political struggle in an effort to gain support for the Bolsheviks and the seizure of power.

At the same time, the pamphlet was more than merely an attack on rivals and an appeal for support. When Lenin was writing *State and Revolution* in the autumn of 1917, he was anticipating the seizure of power and thinking not only about how it would be accomplished, but what form of rule the Bolsheviks would establish. The seizure of power would be violent, he warned. The bourgeois state must be smashed and the bourgeoisie dispossessed, before socialism could be achieved. Previous attempts at revolution had failed because they did not suppress the bourgeoisie and crush their resistance with sufficient determination. Yet Lenin balanced warnings about the impending violence of the seizure of power with the rather optimistic promise that it will end the basis of oppression altogether and bring 'the withering away of the state.'[11] Lenin asserted that this was no abstraction, but something that could readily be achieved once the bourgeoisie had been expropriated and the private ownership of the economy had been transformed into social ownership:

> Capitalist culture has created large scale production, factories, railways, the postal service, telephones etc., and on this basis, the great majority of the functions of the old 'state power' have become so simplified and can be reduced to such exceedingly simple operations of registration, filing and checking that they can be easily performed by every literate person.[12]

Lenin's ultimate goal was neither dictatorship nor democracy, but the end of rulership altogether and the emergence of a cooperative, consensual, self-administered society – communism. Communism was a realistic aim, he insisted, but the transition would take a long time. So, what form would the state take in the process of the transition – in the period after the revolution? Following Marx and Engels' work on the Paris Commune, Lenin agreed that the state remained absolutely necessary in the transition from capitalism to communism: 'The special coercive force for the suppression of the proletariat by the bourgeoisie must give way to a special coercive force for the suppression of the bourgeoisie by the proletariat – i.e. the dictatorship of the proletariat.'[13] The proletarian dictatorship was necessary to smash the bourgeois state, dispossess the bourgeoisie and defend against counter-revolution. Lenin argued that the dictatorship of the proletariat was wholly democratic, though he never quite resolved the tensions between the two. Following Marx, he accepted that the period of transition would involve 'winning the battle of democracy,' though not in the sense that the Bolsheviks would compete for power with other parties in a democracy of a parliamentary type. His criticisms of parliamentary democracy were similar to those voiced by many on the contemporary European left. He observed that parliaments have their 'professional cabinet ministers and parliamentarians,' who are divorced from the people. The people may have a vote, but that does not in itself confer power because parliaments have their 'hidden chancelleries and departments' where the real business of government was done.[14]

In *State and Revolution*, Lenin did not commit to any specific alternative institutions. He wrote that the 'transition from capitalism to communism is [...] bound to yield a tremendous abundance and variety of political forms.' Nevertheless, there appeared to be a place for voting and elections: 'The way out of parliamentarism is not, of course, the abolition of representative institutions and the elective principle, but the conversion of representative institutions from talking shops into "working bodies".' Here Lenin associated his vision with Marx's writing on the Paris Commune, but at the same time seemed to take it further. Marx saw in the Commune a decentralized, representative democracy based on elected local councils.[15] By contrast, Lenin proposed the election of 'all officials without exception.'[16] This suggested that he imagined a more radical form of decentralization that hinted at the 'self-administered' society that was to be characteristic of communism. Elsewhere in the text he indicated that the decentralization and electoral element would not come immediately after the revolution. For example, Lenin noted that smashing the bourgeois state would require an 'undivided power directly backed by the armed force of the people.'[17] He also implicitly acknowledged the relative backwardness of the working masses in the Russian Empire. The task of the dictatorship was to organize the proletariat 'into a ruling class', but that required an education in Marxism and:

> [a] vanguard of the proletariat, capable of assuming power and leading the whole people to socialism, of directing and organising the new system, of being the teacher, the guide, the leader of the working and exploited people in organising their social life without the bourgeoisie and against the bourgeoisie.[18]

Lenin did not explain when and by what steps this centralized and armed vanguard would subsequently cede power to the people. One can infer that what he saw was no reason to rush. Previous revolutions had failed because they were not adequately organized to defend against the inevitable counter-revolution. Armed and 'undivided' power would be needed until the threat had subsided. Besides, in Lenin's view the dictatorship of the proletariat would already be more 'democratic' than any European parliamentary democracy because it would rule in the interests of the overwhelming majority where European democracies ruled in the interests of the bourgeoisie.

Lenin had not yet finished *State and Revolution* when the decision to seize power was made. After October 1917, theory and practice would be inseparably intertwined. In his first public speeches, Lenin emphasized the democratic thrust of the seizure of power not merely in that the new regime was committed to rule in the interests of the workers and peasants, but also in defending the electoral principle that applied to local soviets. In these existing soviet structures that had worked in parallel with the Provisional Government in 1917, there was the basis of a sort of representative democracy. Local soviets sent delegates to periodic Congresses of Soviets and they in turn appointed a Central Executive Committee to act as a legislature, with the Council of Peoples' Commissars serving as an executive. Bolsheviks dominated these bodies, but they were not the only party to contest elections or to be represented on them.

The Bolsheviks were committed to 'smashing the bourgeois state' but that too was not straightforward. The 'bourgeois' Provisional Government had been eliminated on day one, but dispossessing the bourgeoisie was held up by the danger it posed to the functioning of the economy. 'Bourgeois' experts, officials and managers were also retained in government, industry and the army in the interests of preventing the collapse of the functions of these institutions.[19] If the revolution was to succeed, first and foremost it had to survive. The beginning of the civil war in the spring of 1918 focused minds further still. The emergent workers' control in factories was replaced with one-man management and the militarization of labour. The Red Guards – voluntary paramilitary forces that had emerged in defence of the revolution – were transformed into the conscripted, centralized, Red Army. The political police (Cheka) was expanded dramatically. Lenin had anticipated counter-revolutionary resistance and he was determined to be in a position to confront it.

In the course of the civil war, Bolshevik pragmatism did not exclude 'revolutionary dreaming' and concrete efforts to work towards a new kind of state, economy and society. There were substantial advances towards gender equality.[20] The mass Proletkult movement set about to encourage the working masses to create a wholly new proletarian culture.[21] The Commissariat of Justice instituted wide-ranging progressive reforms reducing sentences and emphasizing the importance of rehabilitation.[22] Lenin's government established a plan for the electrification of Russia and the reorganization of industry on the basis of the most advanced modern technologies. But the background of these dreams, plans and actions was a brutal military conflict that left Soviet power hanging by a thread. The Red Army's grip on European Russia was not at all certain until well into 1920. Political violence on both sides was ferocious and arbitrary. The food supply was barely sufficient to feed the front lines of the war let alone to satisfy the needs of the home front and industry lurched from crisis to crisis.

The end of the civil war did not immediately usher in conditions conducive to democratic change. The destruction wrought by more than six years of war was immense. Infrastructure was in ruins. Industry was running at barely more than 10 per cent of its pre-war capacity. Unemployment was at catastrophic levels. Famine was raging through towns and countryside. Unsurprisingly, people were desperate and angry. The situation was worse in Russia than in contemporary Western and Central

Introduction: Illiberal Liberation, 1917–41

Europe, but there too economic crisis, unemployment and low living standards were provoking anger and political instability. As parliamentary government failed to address the crises, European democracies slipped towards authoritarianism. First the fledgling democracies of Bulgaria, Romania and Hungary fell, then Mussolini formed a Fascist government in Italy in 1922 after years of social and political disorder; Miguel Primo de Rivera overthrew the parliamentary government in Spain and established a military dictatorship in 1923 and Poland followed suit in 1926. Even in those countries where democracy survived, the staunchest defenders of the parliamentary system were tepid in their praise. More seriously, contemporary commentators on the left complained that the extension of the suffrage had failed to deliver political equality and pass real power to the masses. On the right, there were calls once again to restrict the suffrage, arguing that mass participation in the political process had a deleterious effect on the quality of policy-making. But both sides commonly agreed that political leaders were often venal and incompetent and that the parliamentary system was poorly equipped to address the crises of the day.

Given the depths of Russia's crisis, Lenin was conscious that weakening central control was fraught with risks and he fought those groups pressing for immediate democratic change. As soon as the tide of the civil war shifted in the Bolsheviks' favour, the Democratic Centralists argued that War Communism had fed an excessive and 'bureaucratic' concentration of power in the centre, preferring a radical decentralization of power and the 'popular participation of the workers in government and economic administration as the most vital precondition of socialist construction.'[23] The Workers' Opposition, led by Aleksandr Shliapnikov, picked up their mantle in the early 1920s, again railing against centralization and proposing that workers should elect councils that would direct the economy. In a sense, they were only paraphrasing Lenin's own words, from *State and Revolution*, about establishing the 'working bodies' that would form the basis of the 'self-administered society'. Lenin's response was also consistent with that work: it would take time to educate workers and prepare them for these new roles. It was the same logic applied by the conservative critics of the extension of the suffrage in Western European democracies: the masses were not yet ready.

Between 1917 and the early 1920s, Lenin had become notably more pessimistic on this issue. In *State and Revolution* he asserted that the 'great majority of the functions of the old "state power" [...] can be easily performed by every literate person'. Setting aside the obvious problem of illiteracy in Russia, he tempered this optimism slightly in the contemporaneous brochure 'Can the Bolsheviks retain state power?' (October 1917):

> We are not utopians. We know that an unskilled labourer or a scullery maid cannot immediately get on with the job of state administration [...] We demand that [...] a beginning be made at once in training all the working people, all the poor, for this work.[24]

By 1923, Lenin was coming to terms with the complexity of the tasks the new regime faced. He accepted that for all the Bolsheviks' efforts since the revolution, the state apparatus was 'deplorable' and that improving it would require intensive study by the brightest of minds.[25] The ambitions were the same, but the time frame for establishing this new kind of state was getting longer. Progress was, nevertheless, being made. Campaigns to 'liquidate' illiteracy in the young and older population began shortly after the revolution and were conducted through the workplace, trades unions and the Communist Youth League, by means of short courses and through the supply of free reading and teaching materials in specially allocated and well-advertised mini-libraries the length and breadth of the country. There were also efforts to get working-class men and women into higher education. Yet, for all the effort and investment, only 51 per cent of the population over the age of ten had achieved basic literacy by 1926.[26]

There were other related and equally fundamental problems in creating the sort of political order envisaged at the time of the revolution. Chief among them was the problem of scale. The Bolsheviks had seized power in the core of European Russia in 1917, but by the early 1920s they controlled most of what had been the Russian Empire, covering half the Eurasian continent: eleven time zones and in excess of 150 million people. Even the most basic governance required colossal manpower. Partly for this reason, the Bolshevik Party was expanded from a few tens of thousands before the revolution to a mass party of half a million by 1924. In that process, the average educational level of party members plummeted. To establish competent public administration across that immensity of territory with a semi-literate cadre was a near-impossible task. Preventing the collapse of industry, sustaining the supply of food and enforcing basic public order were first priority. Establishing a more participatory and democratic order had to wait.

Lenin's death and the struggle to succeed him complicated things further still. Just as local organizations were beginning to make progress in adapting to the New Economic Policy, factional squabbling in the centre threatened to reignite local infighting. This also sowed confusion when most organizations wanted clear and unambiguous instructions. They were focused on the bread and butter issues of local government: economic reconstruction, employment and the food supply. The disagreements among party leaders in the Kremlin were for the most party an unwelcome distraction. The leaders of the various 'oppositions' demanded that the principles of inner-party democracy should be observed not only as a matter of political principle, but also so that they could disseminate their policy alternatives. Some party organizations supported the oppositions, but the majority were only dimly capable of grasping the issues at stake. They resented the distraction from the concrete tasks at hand. They tended to be unenthusiastic about promoting a public discussion or debate within their organizations. Some prevented the spread of opposition documents, but mostly, they waited for a clear policy line to emerge at the top so that they could rally their organizations to it.

Stalin did not speak out against party democracy as such, but at the 13th Party Conference in January 1924, he warned that '[it] is not something appropriate to all times and places [...] Democracy demands a certain minimum of culture ["*kultur'nost*'"] from the members of [party] cells and organizations as a whole.' He insisted that what Leon Trotsky was promoting was not democracy, but a 'freedom of group struggle' (*svoboda gruppirovok*) that would be fatal in the 'current conditions'.[27] Stalin did not directly challenge Trotsky's right or that of the subsequent United Opposition to challenge the political line of the majority, though the polemics in the press had their effect. Every time the oppositions put forward their views in the press, they were rebutted as anti-Leninist, muddled, pessimistic and a threat to the progress that was being made. Neither side showed a particular inclination to compromise, which more than anything else served to discredit the role of discussion and debate in formulation of policy. As the slanging matches persisted through the mid-1920s, the majority could point to real successes, particularly in economic policy. The idea that debating policy alternatives got in the way of progress resonated down the party hierarchy and took hold. This echoed contemporary events in Europe where parliaments pitched left against right, where governments rose and fell in quick succession, at times provoking political paralysis that discredited democracy itself.

Unlike Europe, though, where the defence of democracy became hushed and embarrassed and forms of authoritarian rule were openly mooted and sometimes embraced, in the Soviet context, 'democracy' retained its positive connotation, but its meaning shifted to notions of bringing the people into government. Education, not just in the sense of making progress with basic literacy, but also higher education, technical education and 'political' education were the foundation. The task was then to bring the people and particularly factory workers, into trades unions, into the soviets and into the party. That element had a clear Leninist heritage. But at the same time, what was lost was the connection Lenin drew between the emergent 'self-administered' society and the withering away of the state as an instrument of coercion. Lenin had failed, or was unwilling, to explain how the dictatorship of the proletariat would ultimately cede power to the people and Stalin showed no inclination to do so either. In the mid to late 1920s, this drawing of the masses into the state was not about preparing them to rule. Their role was to assist the party in checking the fulfilment of decisions, fighting 'bureaucratism', improving the efficiency of production, preventing the embourgeoisement of officials. They were very much encouraged to 'discuss' policy and though it was not said in so many words, it was perfectly clear that they were not meant to challenge it. Soviet democracy in its Stalinist variant was meant to be perfectly compatible with unity and discipline.

Lenin had warned that the dictatorship of the proletariat would be necessary for a long time and Stalin was not about to disagree. He made it clear that while the USSR was surrounded by hostile capitalist powers and while there existed a threat of invasion the further development of democracy was unthinkable. The dictatorship was also still needed to steer the immense state apparatus that, without adequate oversight, would not exercise power effectively and in the interests of the masses. Raising the cultural level of the masses was needed and that would take time.[28] For that reason, Stalin and the party leadership devoted immense energy and resources to achieve a 'cultural revolution'. But in the process, they should have confronted a fundamental flaw in Lenin's thought. Lenin had been grossly optimistic in asserting that the scullery maid could be taught to administer the state. Lenin had plainly been wrong that the functions of state power could be 'easily performed by every literate person.' Indeed the 'functions of state power' became ever more complex, especially as the leadership undertook to accelerate economic growth in the Great Break. That required a further sharpening of hierarchy and central control. Improvements in educational levels did not keep pace with the growing complexity of administration, such that state administration seemed to get ever more 'bureaucratic' and less reliable. The international situation of the USSR worsened sharply in the mid-1930s as ever more liberal democracies gave way to fascist dictatorships overtly hostile to Soviet 'communism'. Rather than underpinning advances towards a cooperative and consensual society, the immense pressures of the five-year plans provoked new tensions, conflict and anger.

Democratic transitions often begin with the best of intentions, but are immensely complicated. The end of the confrontation between the authoritarian, communist East and the liberal democratic capitalist West in 1991 did not bring the 'end of history', and the universal triumph of liberal democracy. Indeed, the past few decades have seen the rise of new illiberal, authoritarian, populist and nationalist governments where there had been great hopes for democratic transition: the failure of the Arab Spring, of post-colonial transitions in Africa and Asia, the rise of populism in Europe and America. In contexts of economic crisis, ethnic and class divisions and weak traditions of constitutionalism, transparency, consensus-building and compromise, democracy can, and frequently does, fail. The Bolsheviks wanted to create a completely new kind of democratic state, society and economy amidst the ruin of war and revolution where the educational levels of cadres and the population at large were appallingly low. While Stalin personally played a role in the failure of the Soviet democratic transition, to date, explanations have relied far too heavily on the story of his purported personal ambition to accumulate personal power, often taking their led from the polemical writings of his political rival Leon Trotsky.

This volume examines the efforts of Soviet leaders to realize their vision of a new kind of state, the variety of obstacles that stood in their way and the reasons for the persistence of the 'transitional' dictatorship. It is clear that there were a range of contingent factors which contributed to the rise of authoritarian rule as well as flaws in the ideological basis which underpinned the whole project. Ideology was important, but more in how it narrowed options rather than laid out an authoritarian blueprint. Various chapters deal with how the Bolsheviks were initially over-optimistic, even naïve and only gradually realized how monumental was their task in establishing some kind of participatory political order. Experiments failed and compromises were made. The demands of rapid industrialization, the fear of war, concerns about wreckers and spies, persistently low levels of education and concerns about popular legitimacy convinced the leadership that the extension of political participation from below was premature. The chapters here explore different aspects of this process, not only in politics and state-building, but also in terms of society, culture and the national question.

The volume opens with a pair of chapters which deliver fresh readings of Bolshevik ideology's emancipatory and authoritarian potentialities. Van Ree examines Lenin's writings in the months March to November 1917, when he was preparing his party to overthrow the Provisional Government and to seize power for itself, asking whether the

Introduction: Illiberal Liberation, 1917–41

rise of an authoritarian system was a case of broadly democratic intent that, given highly unfavourable circumstances, just could not be effected. He concludes that although practical circumstances played a part, Lenin's ideas on the state as they crystallized in the course of 1917 were themselves flawed and conducive to authoritarian forms. Lih's chapter then demonstrates how the logic of 'campaignism', the employment of a panoply of agitational techniques focused on a particular goal and limited in time, contributed to the development of Soviet authoritarianism. He highlights the passionate but paradoxical relationship between the permanent campaign and political freedom, but points out that 'campaignism' was not a uniquely Soviet or Stalinist instrument. Both the thinking behind the 'permanent campaign' and its essential techniques had their roots in the pre-revolutionary and Western European past.

Next, three chapters consider how ideas of 'proletarian' democracy were put into practice via Soviet state-building. Irvin's local case study of the Bolsheviks in revolutionary Ekaterinburg emphasizes the exigencies and practicalities at the expense of revolutionary transformation and ideological commitment in shaping state-building and political culture. Continuities in practices and methods of rule between the Whites and the Reds suggest that Bolshevik rule was not uniquely authoritarian or 'antidemocratic', but rather a product of a particular political, social and cultural environment of a country devastated by violence and fratricidal war. Douds examines the Soviet government's 'Reception' which early Soviet state-builders imagined as an innovative tool of legitimacy for their responsive proletarian-democracy, but actually replicated traditional tsarist paternalism. Douds considers how and why the revolutionary leadership reinvigorated a tool of supplication which at first glance appears antithetical to their values of revolution, class struggle and proletarian-democratic rule. While the Soviet government accommodated popular expectations in doing so, it also rationalized the practice in its own ideological framework of openness and responsiveness of 'proletarian democracy', reconceptualizing its role as a 'living link' and a means of a popular check on the accountability of government officials. Next, Kokosalakis takes a fresh look at the 1930s democracy campaigns surrounding the new Stalin constitution, traditionally regarded as a propaganda move on the part of the Soviet leadership, arguing that the decision to introduce a new constitution, as well as the attendant party and trade-union initiatives, is best seen as a return to the institutional experimentation of the early years of Soviet power. Much as in the immediate post-revolutionary period, the party leadership attempted to develop political structures within which popular participation in the running of the state had always been a central goal. Considerations of stability drove the leadership to moderate its agenda but retreats were followed by attempts to promote political participation amongst the party rank and file, as a substitute for the more ambitious goal of involving the whole people in the business of government.

Moving to internal party democracy, chapters by Thatcher and Harris seek to expunge Trotsky's long enduring sway over interpretations of the rise of the Stalinist dictatorship. Thatcher's chapter critiques the perception of Trotsky's concern for democracy compared to Stalin's ruthless determination to establish a personal dictatorship. Thatcher questions the traditional picture of a nobler, more intelligent and more decent communist beaten by an unscrupulous backroom manager by taking a close look at the question of how Trotsky conceived of democracy in the Russian Revolution post-1917. He highlights several weaknesses in Trotsky's analysis of party bureaucratization. First, there was no profound definition of what was meant by 'bureaucracy' and 'democratization'; second, there was little attention paid to the forces that produce 'bureaucratization' or 'democratization'; and third, there was no clear political strategy of how to battle against 'bureaucracy' and how to achieve 'party democracy' if the Secretariat, for example, was unwilling to cede power voluntarily. Ultimately, Thatcher's Trotsky had limited room for political manoeuvre as he remained tied to the one-party state and agreed that factionalism in the party was unacceptable, while his recommendations for the restoration of a healthy party regime were vague and unconvincing. Putting this theory into practice, Harris's study of regional politics and internal party democracy in the early years after the revolution focuses on the first major confrontation between Trotsky's Left Opposition and the Politburo majority in the autumn of 1923. He argues that rather than Stalin employing underhand organizational methods to defeat Trotsky, instead Trotsky simply picked a fight he was extremely unlikely to win. Trotsky appears as largely ignorant of the mood in regional party organizations and why they would have a decisive role in the outcome of the confrontation. Harris finds that regional party leaders were hostile to the thrust of Trotsky's platform and did not need to be pushed, directed or cajoled by the Politburo majority to take action against the Opposition.

Next, Getty and Velikanova address the cycles of violent repression followed by more peaceful moderation in the decades after the October Revolution. Getty considers how centre-periphery relations shaped repression across the twenty years after 1917, arguing that the bloody mass operation of 1937–8 was the third instance (after the civil war of 1918–21 and the enforcement of collectivization in 1928–33) in which central Bolshevik authorities unleashed whirlwinds of local, class-based bloodletting and the settling of personal, political and class scores. In these three crises, the central Bolshevik leadership did not have the means to defend itself from real or imagined enemies without turning violence over to their local and regional agents. But those local authorities were inclined to violence of their own that often displeased the centre which, while licensing local violence, tried to control it. The interludes between these three events saw restricted repression controlled by central authorities, combined with some kind of legality. Velikanova argues that what looks like the moderation of policy in the period 1933–5 was sometimes a reactive correction after 'excesses' and at other times, a relaxation motivated by the expectation of the advent of socialism. Government expectations of relaxation belonged to a master narrative of socialism's victory through the five-year plan and the elimination of 'enemies'. Moderation evolved on two levels: utopian and realpolitik. As Stalinists manoeuvred between paradigmal expectations of a triumphant socialism and realpolitik on the ground, they failed to pursue a coherent policy and radical changes of policy resulted from the incompatibility of the utopian ambitions of the Bolsheviks with the pressure of reality and the resistance of human nature.

Next, Palko and Whitewood consider how the context of national tensions and international threats shaped the theory and practice of party and Soviet democracy.

Introduction: Illiberal Liberation, 1917–41

Palko considers early Soviet nationalities policy in relation to Ukraine, examining the change of the central party leadership's views in this sphere as various local challenges forced them to adjust their universal objectives. She argues that the process of elaborating and implementing the nationalities policy was not linear and, in the case of Ukraine, the civil war and the *korenizatsiia* policy became important instances when Bolshevik theory and practice diverged over the issues of centralization and perceived security problems. Whitewood then demonstrates how a perceived Polish menace contributed to an understanding within the Bolshevik Party that a new war was a real and existential threat to the state in the 1920s which in turn encouraged the formation of a state based on a monolithic party. From the early 1920s, the Bolsheviks attentively watched the international situation looking for any hint of a new intervention by the capitalist world. Poland, as a hostile country on the border viewed by the Bolsheviks as a tool of capitalist powers, stimulated a genuine fear of invasion which produced an environment that helped closed down party discussion.

Finally, five chapters on culture and society demonstrate the Bolshevik impulses towards both experimentation and control in the areas of education, censorship, popular civic-mindedness especially among the youth, regulation of prostitution and provision of collective canteens. Fitzpatrick considers whether the enlightenment of the people really mattered to Lenin and whether, if so, he conceived of it as something instilled by the revolutionary party from above or generated through popular participation from below. She demonstrates that the degree of Lenin's expressed concern about popular education and work at the grassroots varied over time, but in the last years of his life became one of his central and persistent concerns. Before 1910, he was impatient when such concerns looked to him like bourgeois philanthropy or populist sentimentalism, but between 1910 and 1917, in response to both disappointment of revolutionary hopes and Krupskaia's current theoretical work, he paid much more attention to education. As leader of the Soviet government after the Bolshevik revolution, he insisted on the priority of education and gave consistent support to Narkompros on educational questions, and in his last illness a grassroots 'cultural revolution' and the dangers of 'bureaucratism' in the Soviet administration were uppermost in his mind.

Willimott's chapter explores early Soviet *obshchestvennost'* as a bridge to the commune-state imagined in Lenin's *State and Revolution*. Despite conditions of limited democracy during the civil war, the Bolsheviks nevertheless clung to idealized visions of Soviet society and sought to make room for autonomous action – for the earliest shoots of the commune-state. In this regard, the Komsomol and its broader membership became purveyors of an emergent Soviet *obshchestvennost'*. The cultural activities overseen by the Komsomol, as well as their explicit or implicit support of various mass organizations formed part of a wider ambition to integrate a fragmented population into an ideologically coherent Soviet society. From an idealistic standpoint, mass organizations and volunteer activities were seen as the germs of revolutionary society. From a practical standpoint, such developments were seen as a means of gaining mass support and providing the new state with legitimacy. Towards the end of 1920s, the party was increasingly concerned to ensure that the Komsomol did not function as a rival political organization or an ungovernable source of influence and sought to bring it into alignment with party-state priorities. The leadership still desired voluntarism, but they were also afraid of it.

Hearne's chapter focuses on the Soviet campaign against prostitution, examining the competing narratives of liberation and limitation evident in social policy. Rather than a marked break between the emancipatory ideals of the early 1920s and the repression characteristic of the 1930s, this chapter illuminates the complex and overlapping discourses of multiple government bodies to demonstrate how narratives of liberation and limitation ran alongside each other from the outset of Bolshevik power right up until the mid-1930s. This lack of resolution and the urgent need to build a functioning state amplified the voices that called for repression, yet discourses of liberation did not completely disappear during, and even after, the First Five-Year Plan.

Corrigan's chapter presents early Soviet censorship as a unique synthesis of classic censorship assisted by the political police and the banning of texts, but also educational censorship or 'speech regulation', working to uphold the values of the new Soviet state. Examining the work of Glavlit Corrigan argues that censorship became a complicated fusion of different approaches, all finding their roots in the specific context of the years of revolution, the Bolshevik programme of mass literacy and Lenin's conception of a revolutionary censorship that would serve the proletariat. The state could not become what the Bolsheviks wanted without citizens learning to read and also being kept away from what might damage the future of the Soviet state; they were one and the same aim. Finally, Nérard's chapter considers how Soviet collective catering aimed to create a *novyi byt*, but the actual system and resulting repression and violence observed in canteens were formed by contingencies of time, urgency and the discrepancy between the objectives set by the authorities and the reality of the scarcity of food and the lack of trained personnel.

Rather than viewing the fate of the revolution as a journey from liberation to tyranny, many of the contributions present both emancipatory and authoritarian tendencies coexisting from the Soviet experiment's inception, waxing and waning through changing circumstances of political, social and economic dislocation, the threat of foreign invasion, lack of qualified and educated cadres, and growing from pre-existing Russian political culture and the wider European political context. Instead of looking for and failing to find hallmarks of liberal parliamentary democracy, such as multi-party elections, separation of powers and civil society in the Western model, chapters consider features which Soviet leaders intended as tools of an alternative 'proletarian', Soviet democracy. A number of chapters draw attention (Douds, Willimott, Kokosalakis and Nérard), to the processes of consultation and communion with the masses, in the form of government receptions, *obshchestvennost'*, complaint-books and public letter writing to the press and attempts to solicit public opinion on the 1936 Constitution which suggests an alternative kind of interface between government and governed, which previous interpretations have failed to acknowledge. We can see here too how the cultivation of Soviet 'public opinion' via Willimott's *obshchestvennost'*, Corrigan's censorship as 'speech regulation' and Fitzpatrick's educational Soviets could aid the cultural transformation necessary as a stage in preparing the proletarian masses to 'govern' themselves in the future communist society.

PART I
BOLSHEVIK IDEOLOGY AND PRACTICE

CHAPTER 1
DICTATORSHIP UNLIMITED: LENIN ON THE STATE, MARCH–NOVEMBER 1917
Erik van Ree

Today few would deny that, whatever their original intentions, the Bolsheviks ended up creating an autocratic power. Much less clear, however, is the relative weight of the factor of circumstance – socio-economic backwardness, isolation, civil war and so on – and of the Leninist frame of mind and mentality. Was this a case of broadly democratic intent that, given highly unfavourable circumstances, just could not be effected, or was Lenin's radical democracy flawed to begin with?

This chapter hopes to contribute to the latter reading of the events, but it is not my intention to deny the significance of circumstance. My point is that Lenin's ideas on the state as they crystallized in the course of 1917 were conducive to the autocratic formation of the Soviet Union. This chapter focuses on Lenin's writings in the months March to November 1917, when he was preparing his party to overthrow the Provisional Government and to seize power for itself.[1]

Lenin imagined the proletarian state as a radical democracy of soviets underpinned by workers' control and workers' militia. He wrote his most systematic exposé on *State and Revolution* in August–September, when he was hiding in Finland from the Provisional Government that had issued a warrant for his arrest. The text, which was published only after the Bolshevik takeover, announced the 'most extensive democracy'.[2] The population would have to participate in '*day-today administration*'[3] as well as in the 'governing (*upravlenii*) of the state'.[4]

The existing literature offers a wide range of interpretations of Lenin's plans. Neil Harding suggests that Marx and Engels bequeathed not one but *two* views of the state to him. Whereas prior to 1871 Marx would have advocated proletarian state centralization, the Paris Commune allowed him to reframe the revolutionary state as radically decentralized workers' autonomy. In Harding's reading, what Lenin wrote in 1917 was indebted to Marx's democratic model. After 1917 he returned to Marx's state centralism. In this interpretation, his early speculations about the proletarian state were in no way responsible for the Bolshevik autocracy that followed. On the contrary, this unfortunate turn of events came about only because these speculations were being discarded.[5] Kevin Anderson likewise casts Lenin as an adherent of 'direct mass self-rule' and 'direct, or council, democracy'.[6]

But it has long been established in the scholarly literature that the Lenin of *State and Revolution* was no crystal-pure proletarian democrat. Christopher Read characterizes his 1917 model as an 'ultra-democratic' structure geared towards protecting the common people against oppression.⁷ Read points however to flaws in Lenin's argumentation, mainly that he regarded workers not following his guidelines as a bourgeois force.⁸ According to James Ryan, *State and Revolution* advocated a 'direct democracy of proletarian self-rule.' But Lenin also advocated leadership by the 'vanguard party' and, in advocating strict control, coercion and violence he to some extent expressed 'the ideological and cultural bases in embryo of dictatorial rule.'⁹

Even before he assumed the chairmanship of the Council of People's Commissars, Lenin understood the need of a proper administrative state machinery. His armed workers could do only so much. Christopher Hill pointed out in 1947 that the Bolshevik leader did not fully accept Marx's call to smash the old state apparatus: he exempted the economic state bureaucracy from that fate. The administrative machinery of the banks and syndicates would have to be taken over by the soviets rather than be dismantled.[10] According to Alain Besançon, Lenin advocated that the state 'not be reduced but rather immeasurably extended'.[11]

Several authors point to the influence of Rudolf Hilferding and Nikolai Bukharin on Lenin. These fellow-Social Democrats suggested that the new administrative structures of trusts, syndicates and banks would allow a smoother transition to planned, socialist regulation.[12] Lars Lih argues that Lenin did not advocate the smashing of the bourgeois state machinery, but only that it be 'thoroughly democratized'. Lenin hoped to copy and perfect the bourgeois 'wartime state' as a 'ready-made tool'. According to Lih, he especially admired Germany's *Waffen- und Munitionsbeschaffungsamt*. 'Lenin's vision of socialist revolution can be paraphrased as "WUMBA for the people"'.[13] This is as far as we can possibly get from Lenin the workers' democrat.

Another important contribution focused on the one-sidedly administrative as opposed to political orientation of Lenin's conception of the proletarian state. A. J. Polan argues that, for all the ink he wasted on workers' control and workers' militia, Lenin had nothing like a political democracy in mind – not even for the workers. He was uninterested in creating a political structure that would allow them free deliberation and decision-making. Lenin identified workers' participation with 'a right to partake in the monitoring of administrative processes'. His was a technocratic conception, with politics collapsing into administration.[14]

Recently, Tamás Krausz staged a powerful defence of Lenin's radical-democratic credentials. In Krausz's reading, the latter was motivated by the obvious defects of bourgeois parliamentarism in the early twentieth century, which he regarded as inevitably tied up with this form of democracy.[15] Krausz flatly denies that Lenin's alternative democratic model suffered from any sort of authoritarian or violent leanings.[16] He defended hierarchical, state-capitalist arrangements only for a short transitional period.[17]

Most importantly, Krausz finds Polan and other liberal critics of Lenin's alleged democratic deficit to be ahistorical and 'presentist': in his eyes such critics are retrospectively imposing their own present-day political views upon history.[18]

It seems to me that this critique is misguided. Undeniably, Lenin's taste for dictatorship stands out more starkly against present-day realities than against those of his own days, when Krausz points out much of Europe's adult population still was excluded from the vote. But the values of equal rights for all were widely available even at that time. International Social Democracy, the party Lenin officially still adhered to, defended these values; they were not the only ones to do so. No doubt, critical analysis of historical personalities must be tied in with contemporary perspectives available to them. It wouldn't make much sense to accuse Lenin of not having taken LGBT identities into account in *State and Revolution*. But I see nothing ahistorical in exploring the Bolshevik leader's views from a perspective of liberal universalism, if he was perfectly acquainted with that perspective and was even polemicizing against it himself.

Lenin regarded himself as a radical democrat, and measured against a definition of democracy narrowly centring on popular participation that is what he was. But I will argue that, for all his overwrought and feverish infatuation with armed workers monitoring the state, his thinking was fundamentally anti-democratic. Lenin's outlines of the Soviet state foreshadowed the autocratic pattern of the Bolshevik dictatorship in all important respects. Nobody who would have been in a position carefully to study what this man was writing could have doubted that, if he ever came to power, the only remaining sensible thing to do was to board the first train north from Finland Station.

Social democratic thinking on the state

Lenin's interest in the question of the state was triggered in 1915, when Bukharin submitted an article called 'Toward a Theory of the Imperialist State' for publication in *Sbornik sotsial-demokrata*.[19] Lenin as journal editor rejected the piece.[20] A shorter version, 'The Imperialist Robber State', was however allowed to appear in the journal *Jugend-Internationale* the next year.[21]

In December 1916 Lenin, the exile in Zürich, wrote that Bukharin was mistaken in assuming that socialists want to 'blow up' the state. On the contrary, they want to capture and use it for their own purposes. The proletarian dictatorship would be subjected to a process of gradual 'withering away' only after its task of creating a classless society would be fulfilled.[22]

This would have been incomprehensible for readers unacquainted with the subtleties of Marxist thought. Bukharin and Lenin were referring to certain key passages in the works of Marx and Engels.

The two fathers of modern communism began their political careers as democratic republicans, an ideal they never abandoned. The *Communist Manifesto* defined the 'establishment of democracy' as the first goal of the proletarian revolution – not altogether unreasonable at a time when the workers were mostly excluded from the vote.[23] Marx and Engels expected the newly established democracy to expropriate the means of production, thus ushering in communism.

When the revolutions of 1848 ended in defeat and in France ended in Emperor Louis Bonaparte, Marx concluded in 1852 that the bureaucratic state machineries and standing armies functioned as bulwarks of the counter-revolution. Victorious revolutionaries must not simply capture these institutions and set them to work but 'smash [*brechen*]' them.[24] Later, the experience of the Paris Commune of 1871 suggested to him that workers' governments need only a small apparatus of elected civil servants close to the people, subject to recall at all times and working for workers' wages.[25]

Marx and Engels furthermore defined states in terms of class and as instruments of violent repression of particular classes.[26] Upon the disappearance of class differences, the state logically would lose its *raison d'être*. In the formulation of the *Communist Manifesto*, it then 'loses [...] its political character'.[27] As Engels wrote in 1874, only 'simple administrative functions' will remain.[28] It was also Engels who concluded that, once government will be reduced to 'the administration of things and the management of production processes', the state *'withers away'*.[29]

In early 1917 Lenin would tie these scattered observations made over a number of decades together into one simple sequence: the triumphant proletariat will first smash the bourgeois state machinery; then create a state of its own that is at once repressive and radically democratic; and then, finally, allow that new proletarian state to wither away as the classless society is realized.

But in December 1916 Lenin did not yet see things in this light. Marx's and Engels's views on the state had not been self-evidently accepted in the international Social Democratic movement. For Karl Kautsky, the main German party ideologue and a man deeply admired by Lenin until they fell out over the issue of the war, the proletarian renovation of the state apparatus would essentially mean bringing it under parliamentary control.[30] In 1912, Kautsky argued against the Dutch Social Democrat Anton Pannekoek that it was in the nature of modern production to fall under a 'bureaucratic organization'. Bureaucracies must be controlled, not reduced, let alone destroyed.[31]

Obviously, Lenin was still in sympathy with Kautsky when he berated Bukharin for anarchism in December 1916. But apparently he was not sure of his case. He plunged himself into an intense reading programme. His January–February 1917 notebooks with excerpts from and comments on works by Marx, Engels and Kautsky testify to a fundamental change of mind. He now came to accept that the bourgeois state-apparatus could not be set to work but would have to be destroyed.[32] He admitted to Aleksandra Kollontai and Inessa Armand that Bukharin had been closer to the truth than Kautsky.[33]

To smash or not to smash, that's the question

When the tsar was overthrown, Lenin immediately recognized the potential of the soviets to evolve into a new government. But it would not have been a foregone conclusion that the revolutionaries must dismantle the existing bureaucracies.

Lenin's reading programme had immersed him in Marx's radical-democratic formulas, which clearly thrilled and exhilarated him. But once a transition to socialism of sorts actually began to look feasible for the relatively near future, he was sober enough to recognize that 'smashing the state apparatus' alone could not bring him very far. Russia's bureaucratic realities could not be ignored.

Lenin was faced with a peculiar dilemma that he shared with all Social Democrats of the time. In his very authoritative *Anti-Dühring*, Engels had noted that the scale of capitalist production was all the time increasing and that establishments such as railways, post and telegraph could only be properly managed by the state. Engels believed nationalizations by the capitalist state would facilitate the transition to socialism.[34] In 1891 he observed that joint-stock companies and trusts, monopolizing whole branches of industry, effectively put an end to the *'absence of planning* [Planlosigkeit]'.[35] Shortly before his death Engels concluded that the transition to socialism had become so much easier that it could be effected 'overnight'.[36] The celebrated Austrian economist and Social Democratic Party ideologue Hilferding concluded in 1910 that the banking sector's planning machinery was available for socialists to use and made the transition to socialism 'extraordinarily' easier.[37]

The Great War only contributed further to the processes of centralization and state intervention, not only in Germany but also in Britain and other countries at war. Influential right-wing German Social Democrats such as Paul Lensch now began to argue that 'organized' modern capitalism essentially already constituted socialism.[38]

Russia took part in these international trends. Even though industry comprised a relatively modest share of the country's national product, Russian industry was even more highly concentrated than its American and German counterparts. Around the turn of the century, Finance Minister Sergei Witte's industrialization programme had been strongly state-backed. Early in the century, 'various monopolistic devices for regulating production and sales', mainly branch-organized syndicates, had become widespread. During the war the Russian state obtained a strong grip on the economy through procurement agencies, government orders and powers of intervention in the management of industries.[39]

The ultra-revolutionary Lenin of 1917 had much more in common with German Social Democrats of the right than is commonly assumed. To be sure, he violently disagreed with Lensch that state intervention by bourgeois governments represented a variety of socialism and he rejected the latter's use of the term 'war socialism' out of hand. According to Lenin, the socialist implications of such measures could only be realized under a workers' government.[40] But he did agree wholeheartedly that trustification, concentration of the bank sector and government intervention effectively *prepared the ground* for socialization. Lenin's enthusiasm about what he called 'state monopoly capitalism' and 'state capitalism' was strong, consistent and sincere.[41]

That Russia shared in this state-capitalist pattern was precisely why Lenin believed that, for all its backwardness, his country was ripe for the socialist transition. In his 12 May speech at the Seventh Party Conference he insisted that 'state-monopoly capitalism', 'social regulation of production and distribution' and the 'militarised [*voennoe*] state' added up to make Engels's observations about the new, more plan-friendly character of capitalism come true. *That is why*, Lenin concluded, Russia too was ripe for socialism, even though only for the socialization of its industries; agriculture continued to lag behind.[42]

This was, then, Lenin's dilemma: he had just recently come to agree with Bukharin that existing bureaucratic institutions would have to be smashed. But the new organizational potential of capitalism depended on its state, banking and corporative institutions.

According to the argumentation pioneered by Engels and enthusiastically embraced by Lenin, the socialist prospects of Russia depended precisely on those state-capitalist institutions that he hoped to see dismantled.

Socialism as efficient hierarchy

State and Revolution testifies to Lenin's wrestling with this dilemma. He directly announced the thorough 'smashing' of the 'bureaucratic-military state machine'.[43] Following the example of the Paris Commune, new-style officials would be paid workers' wages and be subjected to election and recall. Lenin did not hesitate to admit that what he had in mind amounted to a return to '"primitive" democratism'.[44]

The Bolshevik party leader's anti-bureaucratic sentiments were however far from consistent. On occasion he indeed announced the complete abolishment of 'officialdom'.[45] But if you read him closely, he was really thinking of replacing existing administrative institutions by new ones, which he again referred to as 'institutions', a 'machine', an 'apparatus' or even a 'bureaucracy'. These new institutions would continue to be staffed by 'officials'.[46]

'Smashing' was in fact another word for radical organization. Lenin hoped that management could be restaffed with 'talented organizers' from among the workers whom the proletarian state would 'advance (*vydvinut'*) from below' to leading positions.[47] But he did not regard Marx's famous strictures to be cast in iron. Specialists would be hired rather than elected.[48] It might even be wise to allow them higher wages.[49]

The point is that Lenin never seriously considered breaking with the bureaucratic principle, which he understood as well as Kautsky was indispensable in the modern world. In one of the most revealing passages of *State and Revolution*, he admitted that large-scale institutions need '"bureaucratic" organization'; modern production requires this kind of discipline and accuracy, without which the 'mechanism' fails. The victorious workers must smash the 'bureaucratic apparatus' and leave no stone upon the other, but all the same they will 'replace it with a new one'.[50]

Lenin did not hesitate to advocate the adoption of existing state-capitalist mechanisms by the proletarian state. He famously regarded the '*post-office* (pochtu)' as the 'model (*obraztsom*) of the socialist economy'. In his eyes the postal services represented a sophisticated management mechanism that was 'ready-made (*uzhe gotov*)'.[51] Also, all citizens would become employees and workers of '*one* nationwide state "syndicate"'.[52] In late September he wrote that 'socialism is nothing but a state-capitalist monopoly, *set to work to benefit of the whole people* and insofar ceasing to be a capitalist monopoly'.[53] The next month he finally and solemnly proclaimed that the part of the apparatus tied to the banks and syndicates 'must not and need not be smashed'.[54]

Krausz suggests that Lenin advocated the adoption of these institutions only as a mere transitional arrangement on the way to a future democratized socialist order. But that misses the point entirely. Lenin only found use for centralistic state-capitalist apparatuses because the future socialist economy would be even more centralistic.

In the same text in which he waxed lyrical about armed workers, Lenin offered his image of socialism as an efficient hierarchical order. Under socialism, 'All of society will be one office and one factory'. 'Accounting and control' was *'the main thing* required' for the proper functioning of the socialist society.⁵⁵ In October he defined accurate *'accounting* (uchetom) of production and distribution' as the 'main task of the proletarian, i.e. socialist revolution'. One huge state bank encompassing the whole economy would effectively represent 'nine tenth of the *socialist* apparatus'. And 'state-wide *accounting* (*obshchegosudarstvennoe* schetovodstvo)' represented the *'skeleton* of the socialist society'.⁵⁶

All this sharply ran counter to the proletarian discourse in letter and spirit. The idea Lenin drew from Marx's 1852 and 1871 musings was that the existing bureaucratic-capitalist apparatuses would have to be dismantled. But he balanced this with the alternative discourse pioneered by Engels and Hilferding that socialism, on the contrary, depended precisely on *adopting* the existing systems of capitalist management and regulation.

Workers' control

All this is not to deny that Lenin took workers' control over the economy very seriously. He regarded this mechanism as an effective response to Russia's catastrophic state of near-collapse. The Provisional Government never managed to return the war-shattered Russian economy to order. Production went into catastrophic decline, provisions plummeted and inflation soared. Russia fell into a state of *razrukha* – ruin or collapse. When owners attempted to close their factories, threatening the workers with unemployment, the latter responded by organizing 'factory committees' to monitor and keep in check the management. 'Workers' control' was primarily intended to keep imperilled companies afloat. Soaring urban crime rates were one of the reasons why citizens organized militias. Workers organized their own militia units.⁵⁷

Lenin enthusiastically cheered the emergence of workers' control. He attributed the chaos and the ruination of the country to the capitalists' self-serving sabotage of production and distribution. In the Bolshevik leader's eyes only the workers could put an end to the country's sorry state of affairs by taking factory management in hand and monitoring and punishing the capitalists-saboteurs.⁵⁸

Workers' control was in the first place just that – a form of control, a powerful order-creating machine. As Lenin wrote in State and Revolution, armed workers were no 'sentimental *intelligentiki*'; they were quick to mete out punishments and wouldn't let anybody trifle with them.⁵⁹ He noted with obvious relish that for every single bourgeois specialist or capitalist dozens or hundreds of workers would make themselves available to breathe down his neck.⁶⁰ Strikingly, Lenin wanted *armed* workers to control the factories. As far as he was concerned, the militias' tasks would not remain confined to patrolling the streets.⁶¹

In Lih's apt characterization, Lenin responded to a realization shared by many Russians, 'that only a *tverdaia vlast*, a strong and tough-minded sovereign authority, could effectively respond to the multiple crisis buffeting Russian society'.⁶²

In the longer run, workers' control anticipated Lenin's utopian scheme to make *all* workers in one way or other participate in economic administration.[63] He famously argued that common workers were ready to monitor and administer the factories because modern capitalism immensely simplified administration, reducing it to simple arithmetic and book-keeping within the grasp of any literate person. He was confident enough to state that the proletarian makeover of administration in principle could be effected immediately, overnight.[64] Lenin admitted ('We are not utopians') that not every unskilled labourer and every cook was ready, but he saw no fundamental obstacles on the road towards all-encompassing popular administration.[65]

Ironically, however, Lenin's commitment to workers' control only deepened the problem of socialist bureaucracy, for the very simple reason that many more people would become involved in it. Essentially, the workers' organs for Lenin represented a huge reservoir of administrators.

As Besançon points out, Lenin's scheme was bound to *upsize* the administrative apparatus. Lenin realized this very well: he announced that the new apparatus would become '*even bigger*, even more democratic, even more comprehensive'.[66] The Bolshevik leader acknowledged that large-scale involvement of the workers in monitoring the economy was bound to inflate rather than shrink the administrative machinery. Millions would be engaged in the 'state apparatus' and its size would increase at least tenfold.[67]

Ultimately, comprehensive participation was part of the Marxist project of the 'withering away of the state' under communism. The involvement of the population in the administrative apparatuses of state and economy would be instrumental in bringing this utopian scheme to fruition: if all citizens become bureaucrats, bureaucracy imperceptibly shades off into collective self-administration.[68] What will remain is one vast, centralized but self-administered productive organism.

Whether communist participatory self-administration would add up to democracy is quite another matter, however.[69] Following Marx and Engels, Lenin assumed that communist government would lose its political character and be reduced to the management of things.[70] The point of maximum participation was not to establish direct democracy or self-government, but to allow technical production decisions to be made by all and in the most comprehensive, all-round way.

Soviet democracy

Lenin envisioned the proletarian state as a pyramid of soviets.[71] There are at least two reasons why he came to embrace these councils as building blocks of the state of the future. First of all, when he saw them in action in 1905 he was sufficiently impressed to conclude that they had the potential to evolve into a revolutionary government.[72] He never let go of this enticing vision.[73] When the soviets snapped back to life he immediately understood that the perspective of their supremacy might help to attract radical workers to his cause. He was also, secondly, following Marx and his definition of the Paris Commune as a '*government of the working class*'.[74] The parallels between the

Soviet and the Commune as forms of radical democracy were obvious enough. Lenin referred to the Soviet state as a 'commune-state'.[75]

Like Marx's idealized Commune, the Soviet represented a radical variety of the representative model rather than a direct democracy.[76] This seems to be at odds with the Bolshevik leader's own definition of the proletarian state as '*the proletariat organised as a ruling class*'[77] and as a 'state *of the armed workers*'.[78] Standing army and professional police would be replaced by the militia.[79] But the militia would fall under the sovereign control of the elected soviets.[80] Lenin accepted as a matter of course that the proletariat could not do without 'representative institutions'.[81]

Lenin was also enthusiastic about Marx's idea of the Commune as a 'working' rather than a 'parliamentary' body.[82] He appreciated the soviets more in their capacity of powerful administrative machinery than as arenas of political deliberation. Following Marx, Lenin announced that parliamentarism as a 'separate system' would be abolished. The Soviet delegates would combine legislative work, associated with 'opinion and discussion' by Lenin, with executive work. He clearly prioritized the latter aspect: his main concern was to prevent the soviets as 'working institutions' from degenerating into 'talking shops'.[83]

Obviously, Marx and Engels had never been democrats pure and simple. They had worked under the assumption that the exploiting classes would not accept their expropriation. These 'slave owners', as they used to call them, were bound to rebel as soon as the democracy resorted to intervention against their property rights. The workers would then have to respond; the radical democracy would be forced to take recourse to campaigns of repression.[84]

Marx and Engels indicated that the proletarian democracy would have to establish a 'dictatorship of the proletariat', a form of rule to be maintained not only for the time of the revolution but for the whole period leading up to the final demise of classes. Marx used the term for the first time in 1850.[85] He and Engels did not use it very often, but often and insistently enough to show that it was more than a casual slip of the tongue on their part.[86] Obviously, in referring to proletarian dictatorship Marx and Engels had some form of repression in mind. The term 'dictatorship' classically referred to the suspension of the constitutional order and the establishment of a temporary state of emergency.

That Marx and Engels meant business is also suggested by the fact that they regarded states as instruments of violence to hold down particular classes in the first place. The class interpretation of the state implied that the state, as long as it exists, never serves all but always only some to the exclusion of others. In the language of political philosophy, the state is no social contract but, precisely to the opposite, proof that social conflict and social war *cannot* be reconciled. The state cannot avoid becoming an instrument of either one of the warring parties; in Marxism, the state does in other words not represent the overcoming of the state of nature but its continuation with other means.

But what the proletarian dictatorship concretely would look like remained almost completely undefined in Marx's and Engels's works. They never cared to elaborate. The latter directly associated it with a 'democratic republic'[87] and with the Paris Commune.[88]

The Fate of the Bolshevik Revolution

In the *Communist Manifesto*, he and Marx had however indicated that the democracy of workers would initiate 'despotic' measures against the owners.[89]

Lenin too conceptualized state power as 'the centralised organisation of force (*sily*), the organisation of violence (*nasiliia*)'.[90] And just like Marx and Engels he supposed that the state would be exercising the violence in its capacity as an 'organ of class *rule* (gospodstva), an organ of the *repression* (ugneteniia) of one class by another'.[91]

What remained undefined with Marx and Engels hardened in Lenin's thought to an idea never encountered in their works, that is that democracy, as such, is something reserved exclusively for one segment of the population while other parts are formally excluded from it and are being reduced to the status of outcasts. Even if they expected the workers' state to have to resort to dictatorial actions, Marx and Engels never advocated formal exclusion from democracy of the bourgeois section of the citizenry. With Lenin democracy became a mere variety of dictatorship, that is the one in which the majority puts down the minority instead of the other way around.

In *State and Revolution* Lenin gave the following indication of the state he hoped his party one day would come to lead: 'Democracy for the gigantic majority of the people and suppression by force, i.e. the exclusion of the exploiters from the democracy'.[92] While he mostly referred to democracy as majority 'rule (*gospodstvo*)',[93] he might also horrifically define it as the 'absolute power (*vsevlastiiu*)'[94] or even the 'autocracy (*samoderzhavie*)'[95] of the majority over the minority. He was at his most horrific when he defined democracy as the 'subjection (*podchineniem*) of the minority to the majority' through the 'organisation of systematic *violence* [...] of one part of the population over another'.[96] In this reading, nothing remained of equality of rights and rights for the minority – denial of the rights of the minority was the whole point of democracy.

Dictatorship unlimited

Whereas all this reflected an undoubtedly crass and unbalanced reading of Marx and Engels on Lenin's part, he seemed to remain loyal to their basic idea insofar as the Soviet state would be run by the class as a whole, not by radical political minorities. In the many definitions of democracy that he provided it was always the workers, 'the majority', who would be holding the power.

However, class dictatorship was in fact not what Lenin had in mind. He did not trust the workers to exercise their power wisely, but was preoccupied with securing a free hand for future dictators operating in the workers' name.

Lenin operated with a very peculiar definition of dictatorship, which he had worked out at the time of the first Russian Revolution. Hal Draper has pointed attention to this definition of Lenin's, which he calls 'unique' and which Draper believes 'came out of his own head.'[97] The Marxist Draper regarded it as a 'theoretical disaster, first-class'.[98] It made nonsense of the whole Marxist notion of class power.

In a report to the Third Party Congress in May 1905, Lenin referred to dictatorship as a state on a war footing. The revolutionary state 'can be only a dictatorship, i.e., not an organisation of "order", but an organisation of war'. The dictatorship would remain in place after the revolution: 'Whoever intends to storm a fortress cannot refuse to continue the war even after he has taken the fortress.'[99] The next year he indicated that the soviets represented an embryonic workers' dictatorship because

> this power (*vlast'*) recognised neither *any* other power, nor *any* law, nor *any* norm, no matter by whom established. Unlimited power outside the law, based on force (*silu*) in the most direct sense of the word – precisely that constitutes dictatorship.[100]

Several paragraphs further on we are informed of the following:

> The scientific concept of dictatorship means only this: a power limited by nothing, untrammelled by any laws or by any rule whatever and based directly on force.[101]

These were outrageous thoughts from a Marxist as well as a humanist perspective. Essentially, to be a dictator meant to have unlimited power, not to have to take anybody's wishes into account but to be absolutely free. Logically, even such standards as established by the proletariat would lack all legitimate force.

Lenin seemed to withdraw from this extreme standpoint when he admitted that the soviets represented 'the power of the people, workers and peasants, over the minority'.[102] He sketched an accidentally congregated 'people' freely meting out punishments and establishing 'new revolutionary justice (*pravo*)'. But he immediately retraced his steps to assert that the Soviet dictatorship would in fact *not* emerge from the 'whole people'. Many people were after all morally degraded 'philistines'; they are simply too terrified to engage in the necessary 'intense struggle'. Power would therefore fall to a particular segment of the people Lenin referred to as 'the *revolutionary* people'.[103] Obviously, this dictator could overrule the Soviet.

According to Draper, Lenin thus defined the revolutionary state as a 'dictatorship wielded by *revolutionary* activists. [...] The entire construct has led to the transmogrification of the class dictatorship into a party dictatorship.'[104]

In 1917 Lenin returned to these thoughts about dictatorship with full force, to the point of obsession. On 9 April he indicated that in a 'revolutionary dictatorship' such as the Paris Commune, 'the source of power is not law discussed and promulgated beforehand by parliament but the direct initiative of the popular mass [...], direct "usurpation (*zakhvat*)".'[105] The next day he referred to revolutionary dictatorship as 'a power based neither on law nor on prior expression of the popular will, but on usurpation by force, while this usurpation is realised (*osushchestvlen*) by a particular class'.[106] Again, in his 7 May speech at the Seventh Party Conference, he indicated that a Paris-Commune type of state is 'a dictatorship, i.e. it is not based on law, not on the formal will of the majority, but directly, immediately on violence.'[107] On 21 June he indicated that dictatorship is 'a power based neither on law nor on elections, but directly on the armed force of some particular segment of the population.'[108]

Class sovereignty became invisible in these formulations. Class would remain significant only insofar as the revolutionary dictators in their own minds would be representing the workers.[109] But, as the will formulated by any segment of the population counted for nothing, they would be justified to ignore the actual wishes of the workers as it pleased them.[110] *State and Revolution* delivered further, final evidence that its author was intending to concentrate power in the hands not of the class but of his own people: its author famously referred to the 'workers' party' as the 'vanguard of the proletariat, capable of seizing power and *leading the whole people* to socialism'.[111]

It is hard to avoid the conclusion that even before he seized power Lenin had already made up his mind that he would not let the Soviets tie his hands. Otherwise put, he was determined never to allow the Soviet state to fall into the hands of the soviets.

Concluding remarks

Lenin's vision of the proletarian state represented a curious compound of three dialectically entangled sentiments. At basis, his conception of socialism was straightforwardly bureaucratic and technocratic. He complemented and balanced these preferences with an element of radical-democratic utopianism, but that was, again, overshadowed by powerful dictatorial, even tyrannical instincts.

Lenin's dream of the orderly socialist economy run by efficient hierarchies was not essentially different from what Kautsky, Hilferding or Lensch envisioned. Had it been realized, Soviet Russia would have turned out the same ultra-centralized syndicate it later became. Perhaps even more so: Lenin's 'single post-office' was a chilling, nightmarish construction that later, messier Soviet realities could never match.

All the same, Lenin added a militant, workerist element to the new order. Government bureaucracies, factory management and the specialists running them would come under the watchful eye of ubiquitous armed workers; the workers and employees of factories and state departments would be involved in administering these establishments on a daily basis. Lenin however followed Marx and Engels in importantly reducing government under communism to technical management. The focus of comprehensive participation was not on involving the workers in a deliberative, political process but on turning them into competent monitoring agents of production processes and state agencies.

Lenin's idea about the Soviet state was for an elected radical democracy to represent the workers and the classes allied to them, but those belonging to enemy classes would be completely excluded from it. He intended to turn the bourgeois strata into utterly subjected and terrorized outcasts.

Finally, Lenin was prepared to ride roughshod even over the workers' representative organs. Whatever formal, constitutional arrangements would be adopted in the name of the proletariat or of the majority, the unlimited dictator would *not* be bound by the expressed will of that majority. This conception effectively nullified the Marxist idea of class sovereignty and reduced the armed workers to the state's enforcers from below.

Lenin did, of course, believe that proletarian dictators were bound by the proletarian class interest as their guiding principle. But what the proletarian interest was, again, only for the dictator to decide. If it clashes with the will of the dictator, the will of the actual workers will be overruled. The proletarian class interest will limit the dictator only to the degree that it is being reflected in the dictator's own understanding of that interest. The drift of Lenin's theory of unlimited dictatorship was essentially, then, to accept only the dictator's self-limitation and to deny any *external* limitation on his power. The *only* institution effectively to restrain and rein in the dictator is the dictator himself.

To my knowledge, no one else in the history of political thought ever formally stated the despotic principle in Lenin's outrageous form of a state power limited by *absolutely nothing* and *exclusively* based on force.

The original model, the classical Roman dictatorship, *was* rule-bound and based on law. The dictator did not come to power through usurpation but was appointed by the existing state organs. His rule was bound to a maximum period and he was not allowed to make changes in the institutional order.[112] The power of traditional monarchs was limited by established traditions and rituals; estate privileges set boundaries to their actions in theory and practice.

The closest to Lenin's view comes the Nazi philosopher Carl Schmitt with his concept of the state of emergency, but even his exceptional dictatorship was not totally unlimited insofar as it remained answerable to 'the acclamation of plebiscitary moments'.[113]

Lenin's principle of unlimited government had a unique nihilistic quality and a sheer weirdness that is difficult to fathom. Perhaps Draper's analysis of its origin is the best one: the theory 'came out of Lenin's own head'.

Acknowledgements

The author wants to thank Hans Schoots for his critical remarks, James Harris for our discussion and David Brandenberger for convincing me that I had been (just a tiny bit) too harsh in my judgement of Lenin.

CHAPTER 2
THE PERMANENT CAMPAIGN AND THE FATE OF POLITICAL FREEDOM IN RUSSIA
Lars T. Lih

The agitation campaign, with its standard repertoire of techniques – the mass demonstration with banners flying, the door-to-door petition drive, the flyers, the newspaper editorials, the speeches from whatever tribune is available, all focused on one message and one goal – is such a familiar and inherent part of the life of the Left, yesterday, today and presumably tomorrow, that we forget that it too has its history.

A political campaign – the label is based on a military metaphor – can be defined as the employment of a *panoply* of agitational techniques *focused* on a particular goal (a message or a desired action) and *limited* in time. The 'permanent campaign' does not mean a single campaign that never ends, but rather an unceasing series of campaigns undertaken as an essential activity of a party or state. Although the permanent campaign was a pervasive feature of the Soviet Union (and of all communist regimes), we have not really examined it historically. The permanent campaign was not invented by the Bolsheviks: both the thinking behind the permanent campaign and its component techniques stem from basic features of Marxism and pre-war European Social Democracy.

Most crucially, there is a passionate but paradoxical relation between the permanent campaign and political freedom. One of the most important political facts about the late nineteenth and early twentieth centuries was that the most orthodox and militant advocates of revolutionary Marxism were staunch fighters for political freedom, precisely because of their commitment to revolutionary Marxism. One of the most important political facts about the rest of the twentieth century was that the most orthodox and militant advocates of revolutionary Marxism were devoted to regimes that crushed political freedom to an unprecedented degree. The logic of campaignism lies behind both these developments.

One core feature of the mission of 'revolutionary social democracy' before the First World War was spreading the message through the various techniques of the permanent campaign. The Bolsheviks remained true to this sense of mission before and after the conquest of power, but with radically different policy consequences. Before the revolution, the Bolsheviks were determined fighters for the political freedom that would allow them to create the campaigns, rallies, agitational pamphlets, press and cultural societies employed by European Social Democracy to spread the message in a hostile environment.

The Fate of the Bolshevik Revolution

After the conquest of power, the Bolsheviks relied on the same techniques as before, but now backed up with all the resources of the state. One of these resources was coercive prohibition of any messages perceived as hostile. The same old goal of spreading the good word now turned the Bolsheviks into champions of what can be called state monopoly campaignism – and, as such, enemies of political freedom. Much of what we associate with a totalitarian 'propaganda state' – the incessant campaigns, the ubiquitous 'agitprop' – had its roots in the innovative practice of pre-war social democracy, but now applied without any limit or rival.[1]

Some central features of high Stalinism can only be traced back to the massive dislocation of the early thirties, particularly collectivization; other features can be traced back to the civil war or to the Bolshevik revolution in October 1917. In this essay we look at a feature that can be traced to pre-revolutionary roots shared by all the socialist parties, but also one whose implications changed drastically when the Bolsheviks took power. Campaignism became a permanent fixture of the Soviet system that weathered all other changes in the political system.

Marxist origins

The heart of the Marxist project is the world-historical mission of the proletariat. Marx succinctly defined the proletariat's great task in a late interview (1871): 'The economical emancipation of the working class by the conquest of political power. The use of that political power to the attainment of social ends.' The historical impact of this vision of the world-historical mission of the proletariat derives in large part from the drive to prepare the working class for its great task. Precisely because the workers themselves were the only ones who could carry out their own emancipation, a huge amount of preparation was required: the workers had to *understand* and *accept* their mission and then had to *organize* themselves to be able to carry it out. Enlightenment and organization: these concepts form the leitmotif of Marx and Engels from the 1840s to the end of their lives, whatever the exact words (Marx in 1864: 'united by combination and led by knowledge'; Engels in 1890: 'united action and discussion').

John Rae, a British economic historian writing a year after Marx's death, describes the crucial implications for socialist politics. In Marx's conception, those who aimed at a true social revolution could no longer use the methods of 'the old political conspirators and secret societies':

> A social revolution needed other and larger preparation; it needed to have the whole population first thoroughly leavened with its principles [...] [revolutionary socialists] ought to make use of all the abundant means of popular agitation and intercommunication which modern society allowed. No more secret societies in holes and corners, no more small risings and petty plots, but a great broad organization working in open day, and working restlessly by tongue and pen to stir the masses of all European countries to a common international revolution.[2]

The specifically Marxist commitment to using 'all the abundant means of popular agitation and intercommunication which modern society allowed' meant that a large and growing section of the socialist movement had a vital interest in political freedom (free press, right of assembly, etc.) and therefore in the anti-absolutist revolutions needed to acquire them. The logic behind this development can already be seen in Marx and Engels. At first, the two friends expected that the task of introducing political freedom could be left to the bourgeoisie, but bitter experience both in France and Germany convinced them otherwise.

'Bourgeois freedom' was too important simply to be left to the bourgeoisie. Responding to the situation in Prussia in the mid-1860s, Engels told the workers that even if the bourgeoisie itself was too frightened to fight for 'its own principles', 'the worker party would have no choice but, notwithstanding the bourgeoisie, to continue its campaign for bourgeois freedom—freedom of the press and rights of assembly and association—which the bourgeoisie had betrayed. Without these freedoms the worker party will be unable to move freely itself; in this struggle it is fighting to establish the environment necessary for its existence, for the air it needs to breathe.'[3]

Engels says here that political freedom is an urgent priority for the proletariat and that the proletariat is now the principal champion of political freedom in Germany and France – and yet he still refers to political freedom as 'bourgeois freedom'. The air of paradox – the proletariat fighting for bourgeois principles – is still present in the debates among Russian Social Democrats a half-century later.

The elective affinity between Marxism and campaignism can also be viewed from the other direction. The aim of campaignism is to make people feel and act as part of a greater whole, and so, in order to justify itself, campaignism needs a narrative of world-historical mission of some kind. Indeed, it might be that this feeling of belonging to a greater whole is really an end in itself, rather than a means to carry out a particular programme.

Ferdinand Lassalle and the SPD: The permanent campaign

The agitation campaign was developed empirically in the first half of the nineteenth century by people with specific and limited political goals in mind. A successful and highly influential example was the campaign mounted in the early 1830s by middle-class reformers to repeal the Corn Laws in Great Britain. By the end of 1848, many of the component techniques such as petitions and demonstrations had become familiar to working-class activists.

The move from scattered campaigns to campaignism – that is, to the explicit justification of agitation campaigns as a central and continuing activity – was made by Ferdinand Lassalle. In my view, the huge historical importance of Lassalle's innovation has been overlooked. His great idea was to transform the campaign from an ad hoc tool to a permanent ongoing institution and to envision a new type of party which would make this permanent campaign its central activity. In Lassalle's words:

Found and publish newspapers, to make this demand [universal suffrage] daily and to prove the reasons for it from the state of society. With the same funds circulate pamphlets for the same purpose. Pay agents out of the Union's funds to carry this insight into every corner of the country, to thrill the heart of every worker, every house-servant, every farm-labourer, with this cry [...] Propagate this cry in every workshop, every village, every hut. May the workers of the towns let their higher insight and education overflow on to the workers of the country. Debate, discuss, everywhere, every day, without pausing, without ending.[4]

Lassalle's vision was a stimulant to the empirical search for improved agitation techniques by several generations of primarily Social Democratic activists. The result of these discoveries and innovations is described in books such as Vernon Lidtke's *The Alternative Culture* and Kevin Callahan's *Demonstration Culture*.[5] The permanent campaign was an essential item in the institutional DNA transmitted from the Second International to the post-war Third International. In *Left-Wing Communism,* his pamphlet written for the Second Comintern Congress in 1920, Lenin's exhortation is startlingly similar to that of Lassalle:

The Communist Parties must issue their slogans; real proletarians, with the help of the unorganized and downtrodden poor, should scatter and distribute leaflets, canvass workers' houses and the cottage of the rural proletarians and peasants in the remote villages [...] they should go into casual meetings where the common people gather, and talk to the people, not in scientific (and not in very parliamentary) language, they should not at all strive to 'get seats' in parliament, but should everywhere strive to rouse the minds of the masses and to draw them into the struggle, to catch the bourgeoisie on their own statements, to utilize the apparatus they have set up, the elections they have appointed, the appeals to the country they have made, and to tell the people what Bolshevism is in a way that has never been possible (under bourgeois rule) outside of election times.[6]

Lenin's parenthetical qualification – 'under bourgeois rule' – points to the crucial contrast between campaignism conducted by an opposition party that remained one among many versus campaignism conducted by a party in power. But of this, more later.

Lassalle also understood that above and beyond any particular concrete aim, the permanent campaign contributes to a sense of belonging to a greater whole. The idea inherent in Marxism of a great historical mission – a noble task that one has an obligation to accept – provided a solid basis for campaignism. As Lassalle put it, 'we may congratulate ourselves, gentlemen, that we have been born at a time which is destined to witness this the most glorious work of history, and that we are permitted to take a part in accomplishing it.'

Lassalle's call for a permanent campaign was turned into an imposing edifice by the *Sozialdemokratische Partei Deutschlands* (SPD), the flagship party of social democracy. In order to bring Lassalle's idea of a permanent campaign into existence, the German

SPD created a remarkable agitation machine. The single most impressive feature of this machine was the party press. In 1895 there were seventy-five socialist newspapers, of which thirty-nine were issued six times a week. These newspapers catered to a broad variety of workers. There were newspapers for worker cyclists and worker gymnasts, for abstinent workers and even for innkeepers. By 1909 the total circulation was over 1 million, a figure that implies a great many more actual readers. But the printed word was embedded in a wider context of the face-to-face spoken word: public meetings, smaller conferences for the party militants and agitation by individual members.

Nor did the SPD confine itself to political propaganda and agitation. The Social Democratic movement in Germany attempted to cover every facet of life. Party or party-associated institutions included trade unions, clubs dedicated to activities ranging from cycling to hiking to choral singing, theatres and celebratory festivals. The broad scope of the movement's ambitions justifies the title of Vernon Lidtke's classic study *The Alternative Culture*. Looking just at Lidtke's index under the letter 'W,' we find the following: workers' athletic clubs, workers' chess societies, workers' consumer societies, workers' cycling clubs, workers' educational societies, workers' gymnastic clubs, workers' libraries, workers' rowing clubs, workers' Samaritan associations, workers' singing societies, workers' swimming clubs, workers' temperance associations, workers' theatrical clubs and workers' youth clubs.[7] These institutions should be considered part of campaignism.

The permanent campaign became the most distinctive and innovative feature of the SPD and the other European parties that followed its lead. For example, Jules Guesde, founder of the *Parti Ouvrier Français*, called for 'a propaganda that is both vigorous and unrelenting [*aussi active que continue*]' that would result in a 'proletariat conscient et organisé'.[8] Guesde himself was very popular among Russian Marxists and his many pamphlets translated into Russian constituted another channel for the diffusion of the SPD model.

Thus the SPD fully deserves the label 'party of a new type'. All European Social Democratic parties were vanguard parties in the sense that they saw their mission, not as simply reflecting the opinions of the working class as a whole, but rather as spreading the socialist message. Thus they recruited into the party only those whom they considered to be the elite of the working class, that is workers who consciously accepted the socialist message and were willing to propagate it to their less enlightened comrades.

International Social Democracy also inherited Lassalle's goal of instilling confidence and a sense of belonging to a greater whole. Sometimes the International seems a vast exercise in boosting self-esteem – or, to use the more flowery language of Viktor Adler, urging the working class 'to throw off the debilitating dream of its impotence.'[9] This self-confidence was visible in the body language and even clothing of participants in socialist demonstrations. As an observer noted in the case of a huge demonstration through the streets of London in 1896:

> It was curious to notice how a vivid sense of their own importance in taking part in such a demonstration and of marching along to the strains of the 'Marseillaise'

had given even the most wretched of the Jewish tailors an air of proud distinction. They stepped along with their heads and chests well thrown back, as if compelling the attention of the sightseers on either side.[10]

The cult of leaders that always marked the Social Democratic movement was yet another device, not for crushing the rank and file into insignificance, but rather to make the party leader a symbol for 'the noblest virtues of the International', as Kevin Callahan well puts it.[11] He quotes a speech about August Bebel given by Emile Vandervelde (Bebel was ill and could not attend.) After describing Bebel as 'the purest embodiment of our socialist ideals […] the most beautiful realization of socialist intellectualism,' Vandervelde sums up by calling Bebel 'the most typical expression for the fighting and victorious proletariat […] By the fact that you applaud the name Bebel, you are celebrating the international workers movement of the socialist proletariat.'[12]

The prestige of social democracy's permanent campaign made it a source of inspiration for Russian socialists searching for a new path after the collapse of *Narodnaia volia* and its strategy of terror. But the SPD model did more than inspire Russian socialists – it ensured that they would become fighters for political freedom.

Russian social democracy: Campaignism and political freedom

When activists in one country are inspired by a prestigious political institution in another country, they usually obtain their sense of the foreign institution through literary sources. French supporters of the Enlightenment in pre-Revolutionary France obtained their sense of the English parliamentary system from Montesquieu. For the newly fledged Social Democrats in the Russian Empire in the late nineteenth century, the role of Montesquieu was filled by Karl Kautsky, the main theoretician of 'revolutionary social democracy' and a man whose influence on Russian Social Democracy is impossible to overestimate.

In his seminal textbook of social democracy, *The Erfurt Program* (1891), as well as other early writings such as *Parliamentarianism* (1893), Kautsky set forth the umbilical connection between campaignism and political freedom.[13] As Kautsky put it, 'the task of Social Democracy is to make the proletariat aware of its task.' This self-appointed task was crippled at the outset if political freedom was absent. The achievements of German Social Democracy were only possible because of the relative political freedom of the German Empire. Kautsky explains why:

> To bring these masses into contact with one another, to awaken their awareness of their broad community of interests and to win them over for organizations capable of protecting their interests – this implies the possibility of speaking freely to the great masses, this implies freedom of assembly and the press […] Without the help of the press, it is absolutely impossible to unite the huge masses of today's wage labour into organizations and to get them to the level of unified action.

For all these reasons and more, there was no worse sin from a Social Democratic point of view than to disparage the crucial role of political freedom:

> Where the working class bestirs itself, where it makes the first attempts to elevate its economic position, it puts political demands next to purely economic ones – namely, demands for freedom of association, of assembly, of the press. These freedoms have the greatest significance for the working class: they are among the conditions that makes its life possible and to which it unconditionally owes its development. They are light and air for the proletariat; he who lets them wither or withholds them – he who keeps the proletariat from the struggle to win these freedoms and to extend them – that person is one of the proletariat's worst enemies.

Kautsky's insistence on the need to fight for political freedom was constitutive for Russian Social Democracy and gave it a *raison d'être* in backward Russia. The founding congress of the Russian Social Democratic Worker Party in 1898 issued an influential Manifesto drafted by Petr Struve, the first official programmatic document of the new party. Here we read – in words clearly taken from Kautsky – that 'political liberty is as necessary to the Russian proletariat as fresh air is to healthy breathing. It is the fundamental condition for its free development and for a successful struggle for both partial improvements and final emancipation.'[14]

This nexus of ideas was central for the *Iskra* group out of which both Menshevism and Bolshevism emerged. As Iulii Martov, a later leader of Menshevism, put it in the late 1890s:

> The liberation of the workers can only be the job of the workers themselves. In order to attain the final goal of the worker movement – the triumph of socialism – it is necessary beforehand to enjoy broad political freedom, which is the one thing that will allow the proletariat to develop its strength and its self-awareness to the extent needed to take social production into its own hand. Therefore, the task of the Russian worker party is to develop in the worker masses, despite all political constraints, an awareness of the necessity of attaining political struggle and to organise them for the struggle with the Russian autocracy.[15]

In contrast, the Russian critics of the *Iskra* group all explicitly rejected the SPD model and therefore rejected political freedom as a priority goal. Elena Kuskova, the author of the famous 'economist' *Credo*, was blasé about the usefulness of political freedom for worker struggle and did not hide her opinion that a constitutional system was no big prize. She pointed out that the reactionary bourgeoisie in the constitutional West forced workers to fight even for their established rights. Since the Russian bourgeoisie would certainly follow their example, 'it is utopian to think the overthrow of the autocracy would cause the Russian bourgeoisie to change the political position of the workers [...] One must not expect anything from a constitution in Russia.'[16]

Accordingly, Kuskova soundly rejected the SPD model itself: 'Any talk about an independent worker party is in essence nothing more than the product of the transfer of alien tasks, alien results, onto our soil.' Similarly, another 'economist' critic, K. M. Takhtarev, recalled that in conversations with Lenin in London in the early years of the century, the root of their disagreements was that Lenin regarded 'the German Social Democratic party as a model working-class party.'[17]

Even prior to the party split in 1903, Lenin propagandized the link between the SPD model and the need for a revolutionary conquest of political freedom. His thoughts on this issue are best seen in a publication of 1903 entitled *To the Rural Poor*. This short book is in fact one of the very few works in which Lenin sets forth in systematic fashion what he sees as basic principles of social democracy. Lenin answers his own question 'what do the Social Democrats want?' by energetically asserting that 'the Russian Social Democrats are first and foremost striving to win *political freedom*. They need political freedom in order to unite all the Russian workers extensively and openly in the struggle for a new and better socialist order of society.'[18]

The following extensive quotation from Lenin's book brings out the central importance of Social Democratic campaignism as a real-world proof of the Social Democratic call for an anti-tsarist revolution to acquire political freedom:

> In all European countries where the people have won political liberty, the workers began to unite long ago [...] 'Workers of all countries, unite!' – during the past fifty years these words have circled the whole globe, are repeated at tens and hundreds of thousands of workers' meetings, and can be read in millions of Social-Democratic pamphlets and newspapers in every language [...]
>
> Everything is done to prevent the workers from uniting: either by means of direct and brutal violence, as in countries like Russia where there is no political freedom, or by refusing to employ workers who preach the doctrines of socialism, or, lastly, by means of deceit and bribery. But no violence or persecution can stop the proletarian workers from fighting for the great cause of the emancipation of all working people from poverty and oppression. The number of Social-Democratic workers is constantly growing.
>
> Take our neighbouring country, Germany; there they have elective government. Formerly, in Germany, too, there was an unlimited, autocratic, monarchist government. But long ago, over fifty years ago, the German people destroyed the autocracy and won political freedom by force.[19]

I pause here to note that this passage hardly fits the stereotype of Lenin who 'worried about workers' because he was convinced that they were inherently unrevolutionary. On the contrary, Lenin's consistent view of workers was that 'no violence or persecution can stop the proletarian workers from fighting for the great cause of the emancipation of all working people from poverty and oppression.'

The goal of political freedom continued to be a central point of contention between 'revolutionary Social Democrats' and 'opportunists'. Indeed, of the two wings in Russian

The Permanent Campaign

Social Democracy – Mensheviks and Bolsheviks – the Bolsheviks were the ones for whom the revolutionary conquest of political freedom was the most urgent priority. Lenin's fight against 'liquidationism' (a political current within Menshevism from 1910 to 1914) can serve as an example. The 'liquidationists' (at least as described by Lenin) argued that, even though more political freedom was always welcome, there now existed enough of it in tsarist Russia to be getting on, so that an illegal underground party was now only a hindrance.

Lenin responded that the underground remained the only space for true political freedom in Stolypin's Russia, that is, the only space where a socialist could say what he or she really thought about the necessity of a democratic republic and about socialism. Furthermore, the abandonment of anti-tsarist revolution as an urgent goal was an unacceptable betrayal of political freedom:

> It is extremely important to point out that freedom of the press, association, assembly and strikes are [indeed] *absolutely* necessary for the workers, but precisely in order to implement [these freedoms] we must understand the *inseparable connection* between them and the general foundations of political freedom, between them and a *radical* change in the entire political system. Not the liberal utopia of [obtaining meaningful] freedom of association under [Stolypin's] Third of June regime, but a struggle *for the sake* of freedom in general, and for freedom of association in particular, *against this regime* all along the line, against the *foundations* of this regime.[20]

Was campaignism only a distant goal for Russia or was there any opportunity to apply it immediately in absolutist Russia? Many dispiriting contrasts between the situation in Western Europe and the situation faced by the Russian Social Democrats were painfully evident. The Western European Social Democratic parties operated legally and enjoyed sufficient political freedom (freedom of speech, press, assembly) to carry out impressive agitational campaigns and to sustain a flourishing socialist press. In tsarist Russia, no political parties were legal before 1905 and the socialist parties were never legalized. Forced underground, they could only dream of sending spokesmen to address huge rallies and of someday publishing the kind of high-circulation newspapers that were commonplace in Western Europe. For the time being, they were forced to use badly printed leaflets and newspapers smuggled in from abroad, while trying to preserve minimal organizational continuity under repressive police persecution.

No wonder that the attitude of Russian Social Democratic *praktiki* towards the massive rallies, parades, newspapers and congresses of the Western parties was something like that of children with their noses pressed against the glass of an inaccessible candy store. Memoirs written by these *praktiki*, both Menshevik and Bolshevik, often contain an episode where the author goes abroad, sees a massive parade or protest rally and wonders if he or she will ever live to see such things in Russia.

We can best understand the organizational arguments of Lenin's *What Is to Be Done?* when we realize that he was idealizing and propagandizing a new type of underground, one that had already been laboriously built up by underground activists in order to apply campaignism to the extent possible in absolutist Russia. The old type of underground had tried to wall itself off from society in order to carry out assassination plots and the like. The aim of the new underground formed in the 1890s was to connect party organizations to the workers by as many threads as possible (to use the image of the Bolshevik *praktik* M. Liadov) while still maintaining security from police repression.

The techniques developed to pull off this daunting task were collectively called *konspiratsia*, a word that certainly cannot be translated as 'conspiracy'. For this reason, I have labelled this new type of underground 'the *konspiratsia* underground,' although perhaps a better name would be 'Erfurtian underground'. 'Erfurtian' refers to the European Social Democracy parties inspired by the *Musterpartei* SPD, especially as presented in idealized form by Karl Kautsky in *Das Erfurter Programm*.[21]

The *praktiki* for whom Lenin wrote dreamed of an underground that could put the permanent campaign into practice even in repressive Russia. In 1906, in his famous novel *Mother*, the left-wing writer Maksim Gorkii gave narrative form to this collective dream so effectively that his book later became a Soviet icon and was acclaimed as the precursor of 'socialist realism'. In 1917, on the eve of the Bolshevik revolution, Gorkii's novel was summarized for American readers by Moissaye Olgin, an émigré with personal experience in the Russian underground. Olgin's summary reveals not so much what the underground was as what it wanted to be. Olgin describes the impact of socialist 'papers' (*listki*, leaflets) – or rather, he describes the ambitious aims of the *konspiratsia* underground:

> Soon the streets of the suburb are strewn with 'papers' written with blue ink (hectographically reproduced proclamations). The 'papers' venomously criticize the system in the factory, they tell about labour strikes in Petersburg and Southern Russia, they call the workingmen to unite in defence of their interests. The 'papers' are read and commented upon. The older folks are morose, the younger are delighted, the majority have no confidence in the strength of the workingmen, yet they know the 'papers' are well meant; the papers speak about the sufferings of the working people; they are telling 'the truth.'
>
> A bond of sympathy is established between the secret organization and the bulk of the toilers. The 'papers' appear regularly; they have become necessary to the population. When they fail to appear for a whole week, people are uneasy. None of the 'rank and file' knows the address or the members of the organization, yet its influence grows.[22]

'Yet its influence grows.' This affirmation sums up the perhaps romantic confidence in the inspirational power of campaigns that lies behind the creation of state monopoly campaignism.

From the permanent campaign to state monopoly campaignism

As soon as the Bolsheviks took power in October 1917, there commenced a very rapid transition from the permanent campaign conducted by one party among others to state monopoly campaignism conducted by a party with a monopoly of power. The continuities with pre-war campaignism are striking: the ambitious hopes placed on campaign methods; the same basic repertoire of techniques, from rallies to posters to attention-grabbing slogans; the coordination of different channels into a single-party-dominated campaign. Yet state monopoly campaignism is something new: by eliminating all competition and by mobilizing resources by fiat, the state discovers that it can put on campaigns on an inconceivably grander scale than previously. The result is recognizably akin to the SPD's permanent campaign, but it has metastasized to fill up all the available space. Pre-war campaignism motivated socialists to fight for political freedom. State monopoly campaignism motivated socialists to stamp it out completely.

The rapid installation of state monopoly campaignism presents a paradox. On the one hand, there was no pre-revolutionary call for any such system. To the contrary, as we have seen, the Bolsheviks put the drive for political freedom in Russia at the centre of their revolutionary strategy. On the other hand, the project of installing state monopoly campaignism was adopted almost instantaneously, with no sense of misgiving, compromise or improvised response to events. Ideological justifications were quickly produced and the machinery of state monopoly campaignism got down to work without delay. As the control of the new political system spread over the country, so did state monopoly campaignism.

An article by Lenin from 1905 brings out this paradox but also helps to explain it. 'Party Organisation and Party Literature' has often been cited to show that Lenin was already looking forward to totalitarian control of the media.[23] In actuality, Lenin's article documents the link between the SPD model and the drive for political freedom in Russia. He wrote it during the 'days of freedom' in late 1905 when hopes were high that censorship and political repression would soon be abolished. Lenin was eagerly looking forward to the party's full legalization, so that it would be able finally to move past the wretched compromises of underground existence and to adopt the SPD model in all its glory. Lenin certainly does not argue that all 'literature should be party literature' nor that 'the literature of the proletariat' should be under the exclusive control of the Russian Social Democratic party.[24] His stated aim is to ensure that any publication that advertises itself as Social Democratic should be duly authorized by the party. This straightforward goal, taken for granted by parties in Western Europe, will be possible in Russia only when and if political freedom made the stultifying underground obsolete.

Lenin's defence of the party-dominated permanent campaign in 1905 is based squarely on the logic of political freedom: a private association has the right and even the duty to control the integrity of its message.

Calm down, gentlemen! In the first place, we're talking about *party* literature and its subordination to *party* control [emphasis added]. Everybody is free to write and say anything they want, without the slightest limitation. But every free association (and this includes the party) is also free to throw out members who use the party brand to propagate non-party views. Freedom of word and of press must be complete. But then, freedom of association must also be complete.[25]

Nevertheless, those who see a connection to post-revolutionary state monopoly campaignism are not wrong, precisely because Lenin speaks here as an orthodox Social Democrat who envies the coordinated party campaigns of the German and French parties: 'Literary production should be one part of the general proletarian cause, the "cog-wheels and bolts" of a single, unified, and mighty Social Democratic mechanism, put into movement by the entire purposive advance-guard of the whole working class.' In 1905, Lenin still assumed that only political freedom made such a permanent campaign possible. After 1917, he and the Bolsheviks learned different.

Therefore, the previous tight link in Bolshevik thinking connecting campaignism and political freedom now had to be broken. Bukharin stepped up to this task in early 1918 when he wrote in *Program of the Communists*:

> Another question may be put to us: why did the Bolsheviks never before speak of the complete destruction of the freedom of the bourgeois press? [...] The reason is very simple. The working class at that time was not yet powerful enough to storm the bourgeois fortress. It needs time to prepare, to gather strength, to enlighten the masses, to organize [...] It could not come to the capitalists and their government and demand: 'close your newspapers, Messrs. Capitalists, and start newspapers for us workers.' They would have been laughed at [...] And that is why the working class (and our party) said 'long live freedom of the press (the whole press, the bourgeois press included)!' [...] Now times have changed.[26]

Hal Draper comments on this argument: 'Bukharin claimed that the movement had lied in the past, and he was telling the truth now: but in fact, of course, no such absurd conspiracy had ever existed – Bukharin was lying *now*, to cover up a 180° turn in his view of democracy.'[27] Draper is correct that Bukharin misrepresents the conscious intentions of pre-war social democracy, including Lenin. And yet, Bukharin's comment reminds us that the central rationale for Social Democratic support of political freedom was to enable the permanent campaign. Given this rationale, Bukharin's justification of state monopoly campaignism in the new context of a Social Democratic party in power makes a good deal of sense. 'Now times have changed.'

If one mark of an SPD-type party was the massive effort to inculcate an alternative culture, then certainly one possible path for an SPD-type party in power was to carry out the same task on an even more grandiose scale. In 1920, Grigorii Zinoviev explained why the Bolsheviks chose this path:

> As long the bourgeoisie holds power, as long as it controls the press, education parliament and art, a large part of the working class will be corrupted by the propaganda of the bourgeoisie and its agents and driven into the bourgeois camp [...] But as soon as there is freedom of the press for the working class, as soon as we gain control of the schools and the press, the time will come – it is not very far off – when gradually day by day, large groups of the working class will come into the party until, one day, we have won the majority of the working class to our ranks.[28]

Alongside this ideological rationale came the rapid creation of state monopoly campaignism in practice. We have many useful monographs on particular facets of state monopoly campaignism in Soviet Russia: festivals, posters, cinema, newspaper and book publishing, agitation theatre, among others.[29] Yet one general criticism must be levelled at these studies by academic specialists in Soviet history: by focusing entirely on Russia, they overlook the principal source of the themes, methods and aims of all their individual topics, namely the permanent campaign of European Social Democracy. Historians are more likely to look at Russian saints' lives than at the parties that served as essential inspiration for all Russian socialists, including both Social Democrats and Socialist Revolutionaries. As a consequence, historians overestimate the inventiveness of the Bolsheviks and underestimate the receptivity of the Soviet constituency: campaignism was not just a set of Bolshevik techniques, but an integral and long-standing part of the culture of the socialist working class. State monopoly campaignism was a new phenomenon with unexpected consequences, but we cannot understand it if we do not realize that campaignism itself was familiar to all participants.

Campaigns were already an integral part of mass politics in 1917. One of the outstanding episodes of the early months of the revolution was the mass funeral parade to honour the victims of the revolution. This extremely impressive event descended directly from similar mass demonstrations carried out by European Social Democratic parties before the war. Like the pre-war demonstrations of European Social Democracy, the funeral parade manifested not only solidarity but also the ability of the workers to impose their own discipline and order on events. But this early mass demonstration pointed to another reality: the real possibility of domination exercised by the *narod* over the elite. In the early days of Soviet power, agitation techniques inherited from social democracy were an indispensable tool for the Bolsheviks simply because the collapse of state power deprived them of more traditional levers of governance. Indeed, the party's familiarity with campaign techniques undoubtedly gave it a great advantage over its rivals in the daunting environment of a *smuta* or 'time of troubles'.

The erection of state monopoly campaignism as a long-standing integrated system occurred along three mutually reinforcing tracks: the elimination of political freedom by suppressing all independent political life; the assertion of control over *all* 'publishers and warehouses, shops and reading spaces, libraries and various kinds of book retail' (in 1905, Lenin merely wanted the party to control its own 'shops and reading spaces')[30]; the energetic application of campaignism as a tool of political rule. The contours of state monopoly campaignism are already apparent in the First of May celebrations in 1918. Anatolii Lunacharskii spent the day walking around Petrograd and was thrilled to report, not only on the enthusiasm of the participants, but also on the projection of state power:

> Yes, the celebration of the First of May was an official one. The state celebrated it. The power of the state came through in many ways. But isn't the very idea intoxicating: the state, up to now our most vicious enemy, is now ours, and it celebrates the First of May as its own great holiday?[31]

The Fate of the Bolshevik Revolution

The installation of state monopoly campaignism had been long completed when the second congress of the Third International was held in July–August 1920. This congress allows us to look back at similar congresses held during the pre-war Second International and to observe both continuity and contrast. Among the continuities: careful choice of location; mass demonstrations and rallies replete with slogan-bearing banners; celebration of party leaders/heroes; memorializing earlier martyrs to the cause. The pre-war socialist congresses had organized mass demonstrations and rallies with the participation of the local worker population, with the aim of creating 'a proletarian public, a counter-public to the state-bourgeois public'.[32] The Second Congress in 1920 also organized a mass demonstration, with thousands of worker participants and culminating in a piece of mass theatre, the *Spectacle of Two Worlds*. One delegate described his reaction to this early example of mass theatre: 'it was like a dream. As the sailors' armoured car drove up, we delegates stood, shouting, waving our arms, so enthusiastic we were quite overcome.'[33]

Despite these similarities, there remains a crucial difference between the two congresses. The demonstrations engineered by pre-war socialist leaders were meant to establish a legitimate claim to participate in a public space controlled by others. In Russia in 1920, the organizers of the congress themselves controlled the public space. On the one hand, this control allowed ever more grandiose efforts at campaignism such as the *Spectacle of Two Worlds*. On the other hand, the genuine drama of actual contestation with independent forces was absent.

Campaignism and the rhythm of life in the Soviet Union

The permanent campaign in its state monopoly form became perhaps the most striking permanent feature of life in the Soviet Union. Such a vast topic can only be sketched in the broadest of terms. Some idea of what it is like to live under state monopoly campaignism is provided by a first-hand account of the Stakhanovite campaign in the mid-1930s by an apolitical outside observer (American mining engineer John Littlepage) who spent a decade in the Soviet Union working in the top ranks of Soviet gold-mining. Littlepage describes the 'evangelistic enthusiasm' of the intense but short-lived 'universal promotion' of the Stakhanov movement. His vivid account bears close comparison to the dreams of Lasalle and Lenin cited earlier:

> It is difficult for an outsider to imagine what the propaganda machine in Russia can do when it is turned loose on a single subject. American advertising men or press agents must turn green with envy at the thought of it. The Bolsheviks control every newspaper, every magazine, every publishing house, every hoarding, every motion-picture and legitimate theatre, every film-producing company, every school and university, every club and social organization.
>
> When the Communist General Staff gives orders for universal promotion, as they did in the case of the Stakhanoff movement, the country simply hears

of nothing else for days or even weeks on end [...] Inside Russia whole libraries began to spring up describing various phases of the Stakhanoff movement, and Soviet publishing houses hurried into print with dozens of books and pamphlets which showed more evangelistic enthusiasm than genuine comprehension of the aims and principles of the movement. For several weeks Soviet newspapers gave up most of their space to this movement, and new magazines were started dealing with nothing else. During this period I saw railway-station bookstalls whose entire stock-in-trade dealt with 'Stakhanovism' [...]

The papers reported that [Stakhanovite methods] had been successfully organized by workers who cremate dead bodies. Pamphlets were put out to show how book-keepers and school-teachers and farmers and even housewives could adapt the movement to their own work. But after a few weeks most nonsense of this sort was quietly dropped, as the Russians usually do after such spells.[34]

The permanent campaign dominated the rhythm of life throughout the Soviet era on a number of levels. Campaigns were central to *sacred time*, that is, the holidays, festivals, leader cults and other assertions of the sacred nature of the Soviet mission. They were central to *daily life*: the 'planned economy' was essentially based on campaigns to meet specific targets, thus giving a peculiar rhythm to economic life. Finally, campaigns were central to *historic time*: a history of the Soviet Union could be written around the various mass campaigns from literacy to collectivization to the Virgin Lands and on to glasnost (the campaign to end state monopoly campaignism).[35] The essential activity of a leader such as Stalin consisted of devising and carrying out campaigns. This method of ruling also imposed its own rhythm, seen most strikingly in the various campaigns to undo the excesses of previous campaigns ('dizzy with success' in 1930, the 1938 campaign against over-enthusiastic purging).

One more impact of state monopoly campaignism should be mentioned: the *anekdot*, the Soviet joke, whose special flavour comes from subverting the grandly inspirational scenarios that had been inherent in socialist campaigns from the days of Lasalle onward – scenarios that were now often seen by Soviet citizens as a pompous but inescapable source of irritation.

To conclude, the SPD was a party of a new type that served as a model for all other parties in pre-war social democracy. It pioneered the innovative techniques of the permanent campaign and the alternative culture in order to spread the socialist message. Lenin and the Bolsheviks were champions of political freedom in tsarist Russia because they saw freedom of speech and assembly as light and air in their efforts to emulate the German model. When the Bolsheviks came to power, the Bolshevik party no longer looked up to the German SPD as a model party, but instead presented itself as the model party for revolutionary socialists world-wide. Now the logic of campaignism morphed into state monopoly campaignism and made the Bolsheviks enemies of political freedom. They realized they could conduct the permanent campaign and inculcate the alternative culture much more efficiently if they eliminated the political freedom of everybody else.

PART II
WORKERS' DEMOCRACY AND SOVIET STATE-BUILDING

CHAPTER 3
LOCAL GOVERNMENT, DISORDER AND THE ORIGINS OF THE SOVIET STATE, 1917-18
Dakota Irvin

The question of the authoritarian foundations of Bolshevism and the rejection of liberal democracy has long been the subject of scholarly and polemical tracts endeavouring to understand the origins and consequences of the October Revolution. One of the key stumbling blocks for Bolsheviks in the capital and in the provinces in realizing their transformative revolutionary agenda lay in the question of what to do with institutions and structures of the 'bourgeois state', which Lenin had called for in *The State and Revolution* to be 'smashed' after seizing power. As the editors of the volume note in the introduction, this task proved to be more complicated and contingent than had been expected, not least due to the destruction the country had faced after years of total mobilization, world war and economic collapse. The state structures the Bolsheviks' inherited from the Provisional Government were weakened, ineffective and unpopular, especially on the local level, where the February Revolution had vested local governments more freedom to act independently, but less financial support to do so. Lenin and the Bolsheviks had famously called for 'All Power to the Soviets!' in the lead up until the October Revolution and it seemed logical that in the new Soviet state, workers' and peasants' institutions would serve as the administrative and political centres of local life.

However, as the following chapter will show through a case study of the city of Ekaterinburg before and after the October Revolution, local Bolsheviks there sought, for a time, to utilize existing 'bourgeois' structures of local government for their rule. It challenges arguments about the Bolsheviks' 'authoritarian DNA' by showing that, when viewed from the local level, the Bolsheviks emerged from a particular constellation of extant conditions, including administrative, economic and social collapse. Far from immediately giving way to authoritarian predilections, they strove to achieve political legitimacy by working within traditional municipal institutions to improve public services and to reconstitute a functioning administration, both of which enjoyed widespread public support.

Known as the 'capital of the Urals', Ekaterinburg was an industrial and railroad centre that by 1917 had a population of almost 80,000, not including 35,000 garrisoned soldiers.[1] The challenges of rising crime, breakdown in food supply and deterioration of sanitary conditions during the First World War and after the February Revolution of 1917 shook the foundations of the City Duma, Ekaterinburg's municipal government. The February Revolution ushered in a new era of 'democratic' politics and governance, especially on the local level, where authorities gained more ability to shape their own policies. However, this also meant that Ekaterinburg's city government assumed more direct responsibility of city affairs and scrutiny from an emboldened public. At the same time, monetary support from the central government increasingly disappeared, leaving local institutions underfunded, unpopular and unable to provide the state services expected by the local population.

The First World War's total mobilization put tremendous strains on the country's ability to feed its population, leading tsarist administrators to introduce a centralized food supply system, continued by the Provisional Government's introduction of the grain monopoly in March 1917.[2] Ekaterinburg and most of the Urals were designated as 'food purchasing' areas, meaning that they needed to import food from surrounding agricultural regions.[3] The threat of starvation, a prospect already raised by the City Duma in July 1917, most concerned local authorities.[4] However, the prospect of 'disorder' (*besporiadok*) that food shortages would cause also troubled officials; one City Duma official warned, 'We are threatened by starvation and unrest on the grounds of hunger, that is, the same that preceded the revolution.'[5]

The degradation of public services is perhaps best illustrated through the example of the city militia, created by the City Duma and the Committee for Public Safety (KOB) to replace the derided Police after the Ministry of Internal Affairs dissolved the national force on 10 March 1917. The former police chief told the City Duma that in the first days after the revolution, local policemen were subjected to insults, spitting in the face and forced removal of epaulettes, a highly symbolic act.[6] However, one KOB member noted, 'it is impossible to immediately demolish the old mechanism' while simultaneously creating a replacement and in the meantime soldiers from the local garrison policed the city.[7] The city militia was officially formed in April 1917, although it suffered from severe underfunding, given that the Provisional Government shifted the cost of policing to the cities, making recruitment of militiamen nearly impossible. By October 1917 the situation deteriorated even further, with a report to the City Duma describing the 'total collapse of the people's militia', where officers arrested each other, conducted illegal searches and were drunk on duty. Ekaterinburg's mayor grimly concluded, 'The people's militia in its current form is worse than the former police.'[8]

The dissolution of the tsarist police and the failure to establish the militia resulted in a drastic rise in crime and the disappearance of law and order. As Tsuyoshi Hasegawa shows in his recent work on mob violence in Petrograd, the increase in crime after the February Revolution contributed to widespread social disintegration that 'emasculated' the Provisional Government and paved the way for the Bolsheviks to exploit the lawlessness.[9] Ekaterinburg's newspapers reported daily about crime, frequent robberies on the street and apartment break-ins, but there were many more serious instances of physical violence, murder and most troubling, vigilante justice (*samosud*).[10] With public services including the militia poorly functioning, and in some cases not at all, *samosud* contributed to the febrile atmosphere in Ekaterinburg and exposed the weaknesses of the Provisional Government's structural reform of local administration. The rise in crime placed major pressures on the city administration and fuelled widespread dissatisfaction among the local population.

Furthermore, as Hasegawa shows, in Petrograd, workers' militias formed to fill the vacuum created by the abolition of the tsarist police, but in Ekaterinburg the task of instilling order largely fell to the soldiers of the local garrison, with the City Duma declaring on 4 March that the garrison would provide security for 'robbery, violence, and disorder.'[11] However, soldiers themselves represented a major source of disorder and during the spring and summer of 1917, they engaged in a wave of crime, including illegal searches and seizures, armed robbery and murders.[12] On 25 April, an echelon of soldiers heading from Siberia passed through Ekaterinburg and after making their way to the city's central square held a rally to discuss the 'food supply question' and the ineffectiveness of local food supply.[13] The meeting included speeches from members of the City Soviet, who implored the soldiers not to cause 'disorder' and argued that mass demonstrations were not the solution to shortages and high prices.[14] While this gathering was largely peaceful, the following day crowds poured onto the streets and descended into an orgy of destruction of symbols of the old regime. The soldiers destroyed several prominent statues of Catherine I and Peter I and broke into buildings of the *Uprava* and District Court, where they tore down Romanov family portraits and frightened employees.[15]

Traditional institutions in Ekaterinburg proved largely unable to prevent the destruction and therefore appeared powerless to many residents. The KOB received appeals from citizens requesting they be allowed to bear arms, while one resident excoriated them for not understanding their duties to protect the revolution and 'support its peaceful development.'[16] The City Soviet proved to be the most decisive actor among municipal institutions and introduced compulsory registration of all food reserves in the city, partly to reassure public opinion and partly to collect crucial information on the dwindling food supplies.[17] While rumours and incidences of 'imposter' searches and theft carried out by soldiers proliferated,[18] the City Soviet's position strengthened as it laid out plans to overhaul the food supply situation by imposing limits on exports of food out of the city. The leader of Ekaterinburg's Bolsheviks, Lev Sosnovskii, urged the Soviet to go further and provide for the 'just distribution' of supplies to the poorest population and the establishment of a food supply department of the City Soviet.[19] The City Soviet used the riots of 26–27 April to increase their standing with the population by taking actions to alleviate food shortages, while the City Duma and KOB stood paralysed.

In addition to the food supply question, the deterioration of sanitary conditions and the rise of infectious diseases such as typhus presented a major challenge to local authorities. Although often not featured in scholarly narratives on the revolutionary period, sanitation and waste removal touched the lives of every person. For Ekaterinburg, and many other provincial cities, waste removal was carried out with horses, barrels and manual labour, and construction of a city-wide sewage system would not begin until 1927.[20] The presence of the city garrison put tremendous strains on waste removal services, especially given that the military was often unwilling to pay for upkeep of its soldiers.[21] While the issue of waste removal might evoke a grimace or seem trivial in the kaleidoscope of revolutionary events, it was central for local authorities in Ekaterinburg and deeply entangled with questions of public safety and order, as well as political legitimacy of the municipal government. The February Revolution exacerbated the crisis of these public services, as funding from the centre dried up at the same time as a rise in inflation. The build-up of excrement in the city's public squares, many of which served as stables for the garrison's horses, presented a major threat to the city's public health and in April 1917 city authorities faced an outbreak of typhus.[22] Because the City *Uprava* was unable to prevent the proliferation of waste, illegal dumps began popping up in central districts of the city, threatening to contaminate the drinking water.[23] After appeals for individual citizens to clean up courtyards and public spaces went largely unheeded, the *Uprava* turned to the City Militia to enforce mandatory cleaning.[24]

It was within this matrix of collapsing public services, rising crime and the inability of the municipal government to provide basic services that Ekaterinburg's Bolsheviks developed their political agenda. Scholars often point to the February Revolution as a democratic awakening in Russia, a time of unlimited possibilities for ordinary people with 'radiant joy on all of their faces' to take their future into their own hands and build a new society upon the wreckages of the tsarist autocracy.[25] As Sarah Badcock notes in her study of Kazan and Nizhnii Novogorod, 'For ordinary people, the February Revolution offered great hopes, and the promise of social and political change.'[26] While I do not seek to downplay the enthusiasm and utopianism of the halcyon days after February 1917, I seek to reorient the discussion away from what 'ordinary people' wanted out of their ideal government to what was generally expected of a functioning administrative state. For ordinary people after the February Revolution, in nearly every measureable category, standards of living decreased drastically, as the state's ability to provide food, sanitation, safety and a myriad of other services ebbed away.

That is not to say that the emergence of possibilities for participation in local government did not represent an important development. Following the wave of 'democratization' that spread across the country after the February Revolution, the City Duma came under increasing pressure to 'democratize' itself and conform to the new political landscape. However, 'democratization' in this context did not necessarily mean broad popular participation in city politics, but rather the replacement of old officials appointed or elected under the tsarist regime with representatives from 'democratic elements' from social organizations and political parties, even if elections did not occur, similar to the later concept of lustration after the fall of communism in Europe. Furthermore, the ethos of bureaucratism and strict adherence to arcane procedural rules did not disappear with the February Revolution and both liberals and moderate socialists in the municipal government and even in the Soviet remained hesitant to take the necessary decisive actions to improve conditions, which the Bolsheviks would capitalize on when they assumed power.

Russia's first free municipal elections scheduled for 30 July 1917 provided the opportunity for citizens to elect their leaders and for those leaders to bolster their democratic credentials. Despite the transformation in the political climate, the City Duma initially attempted to avoid elections by adding thirty representatives from 'democratic elements' to the sixty-one seats Duma, which the KOB roundly rejected. Furthermore, while nearly all members from different political parties within the KOB supported the 'democratization' process of city institutions, several members warned of the problems of new Duma members not understanding the complexities of 'city management' and that new 'democrats' needed to comprehend their administrative 'responsibilities'. Presciently, left-leaning Kadet L. A. Krol' cautioned that 'when the changes to the Duma take place [...] [we] must first of all take not to discredit democracy.' Public finances and administration were in a 'poor state' and in some cases, there was nothing that could be done.[27]

Ekaterinburg's political parties began preparations for City Duma elections after the February Revolution, with parties developing platforms on major issues, selecting candidate lists and helping to compile voter registry lists. The Bolsheviks actively took part in these elections and fielded a full slate of candidates, with the local party building on Lenin's May publication on elections to district dumas in Petrograd, where 'the party of the proletariat clearly, openly and wholeheartedly took part in the elections.'[28] Parties framed the election around local government and its importance to the Revolution and the lives of residents. The City Soviet's newspaper, *Bor'ba*, told supporters not to let bourgeois parties continue their 'decay' of city management, while the Mensheviks warned voting for the Bolsheviks would turn the City Duma into a place of 'constant squabbles and divisions, disorder and anarchy.'[29] An election flier from the Popular Socialists succinctly attacked the previous administration's 'evilness' for inadequate schools and hospitals, lack of water supply and the overall failure to develop the poorest districts on the outskirts of the city.[30]

Furthermore, each political party developed its own 'municipal platform', which addressed Ekaterinburg's specific needs and outlined competing visions for local government. The foundation of all the parties' municipal platforms was the failure of the tsarist city administration to adequately provide state and city services. Both the Socialist Revolutionaries (SRs) and Bolsheviks proposed overhauls of the tax code, including the imposition of 'progressive taxes' and new taxes on property and income for wealthier residents. Both parties advocated the 'municipalization' of 'city enterprises' that served a public good, such as the electrical station, transport, water and food production, as well as the direction of city services towards the poor.[31] The transfer of enterprises and utilities from private to state hands was not exclusively a socialist position and as one Duma member noted, all political parties supported municipalization of key industries with a 'public purpose'.[32] The Bolshevik platform demanded 'full autonomy' of the local government from 'state power', including the ability for municipal government to pass mandatory acts and regulations, as well as full control over the militia.[33] In addition, the Bolsheviks supported free speech and a climate of openness and chastised supporters for destroying Kadet election posters instead of openly debating their opponents.[34] Far from demanding centralization and the primacy of the City Soviet, Ekaterinburg's Bolsheviks recognized the significance of the municipal administration and through it the potential to realize their political goals.

Voter turnout in the elections was relatively high at 56 per cent, with 27,136 citizens casting votes out of a total urban electorate of 48,891. Following national trends, the SRs dominated and secured an outright majority with forty-four out of eighty-five total seats, with major support coming from soldiers, although the Bolsheviks performed well in districts with soldiers as well. The Bolsheviks came in second with eighteen seats, the Kadets third with ten seats and the Mensheviks and Union of Homeowners each with three.[35] The elections themselves were chaotic and filled with irregularities, most prominently election-day agitation and campaigning the Provisional Government had banned. The newly elected Ekaterinburg City Duma reflected the triumph of socialist parties over liberals and conservatives, a not unsurprising result for an industrial city with large numbers of workers and soldiers. However, the 'People's Duma' would never sit because the Perm' *Guberniia* Commissar invalidated the results of the election, primarily on the grounds of same-day electoral agitation and violations in voting procedures. An investigation found that agitators (believed to be Bolshevik supporters) engaged in ballot stuffing, handing out filled out ballots to illiterate voters and generally disrupting public order on election day.[36] As a result, the *guberniia* administration mandated new elections be held, although given the logistical challenges combined with feet dragging in Ekaterinburg, new elections would not be held until after the October Revolution.

The invalidated City Duma elections created a crisis of legitimacy in Ekaterinburg, as the 'limited franchise' (*tsenzovaia*) Duma held power without a democratic mandate and remained in control of the municipal administration. City Duma members themselves prevaricated on whether they were still legally in charge and some members advocated dissolving the old Duma and transferring the responsibilities to the newly elected intake. This was impossible, given that local parties refused to participate in convening the new assembly and therefore the old City Duma members would stay in power until new elections were held.[37] While the Duma was paralysed to act decisively, the KOB was dissolving itself and the City Soviet remained occupied with factional debates. May reelections to the City Soviet, demanded by soldiers loyal to the SRs, returned a big majority for the party and removed Bolsheviks from key positions in the Soviet.[38] For a variety of reasons, the City Soviet under SR leadership did not play a leading role in Ekaterinburg, reflecting broader trends across the country as the SRs and moderate socialist parties haemorrhaged popular support.[39] Reelections to the Soviet in October 1917, on the eve of the seizure of power in Petrograd, returned a majority for the Bolsheviks and positioned the Soviet to play a decisive role in the struggle for political and administrative control in Ekaterinburg.[40]

The first meeting of the newly elected Ekaterinburg City Soviet took place on 25 October, the same day of the opening of the All-Russian Congress of Soviets in Petrograd and the beginning of the October Revolution, as rumours swirled about preparations for an armed seizure of power in the capital.[41] The meeting of the Soviet addressed basic organizational matters, but after midnight on 26 October, telegrams about the seizure of power in Petrograd began to trickle in, although the Bolsheviks in Ekaterinburg waited until the next day to acknowledge the revolution.[42] An emergency meeting of the City Soviet and the District and Oblast Soviets on 26 October resulted in the dismissal of the Ekaterinburg County Commissar, the highest authority of the Provisional Government in the city and the *Ispolkom* declaring itself 'the only authority (*vlast'*) in the city,' meeting no resistance.[43]

In stark contrast to the bloody events in Petrograd, Moscow and some other cities across the country, where outright conflict and violence broke out, Ekaterinburg experienced no violence or conflict after the October Revolution; according to local Bolshevik M.V. Nagorskii, 'the city did not lose its usual life. On that day, the residents quietly went to bed.'[44] *Bor'ba*, the City Soviet's press organ, reported that the change in power was 'met calmly by the population […] and did not cause any shadow of unrest,' while at an extraordinary session of the City Duma, Ekaterinburg's old authorities did not even discuss a report on the events of Petrograd and released no official position, with some suggesting that the coup had occurred only in Petrograd.[45] Vladimir Anichkov, a local banker and City Duma member, noted that 'the first days of the transfer of political power to the communists was not especially noticeable.' He argued that since the 'real' power had already been in the hands of the City Soviet, Ekaterinburg's conservatives and opponents of the October Revolution would not follow 'Moscow's example' and take up arms against the Bolsheviks.[46]

At 7 pm on 26 October, the City Soviet held an extraordinary meeting at the City Theatre, the largest public hall in the city, attended by representatives of all major political parties, as well as hundreds of members of the public. The meeting opened with a fiery speech from the chairman of the *Ispolkom*, Lev Sosnovskii, who spoke about the need to defend the gains of 'democracy' and the 'unavoidable civil war' that led the Petrograd Soviet to take up arms against the Provisional Government. Sosnovskii acknowledged since the City Soviet itself had just undergone elections unity among all socialist parties was necessary, as the time demanded 'all constructive forces of democracy' to 'be able to exercise the power received' from the revolution.[47] He urged socialist parties to 'forget their previous discord' and unite with the Bolsheviks to fight for the interest of workers and peasants 'under the banner of the 3rd International.' Sosnovskii's overtures received an enthusiastic response and representatives from the SRs, anarchists and non-party delegates pledged their support of the new Soviet government, particularly their policies on bread and food supply, which received 'thunderous applause'. Sosnovskii closed the meeting by stating the Soviet's first goal was to 'preserve social calm and safety,' and would not hesitate to take 'decisive measures' to stop those who wanted to sow 'disorder'.[48]

While Ekaterinburg's Bolsheviks utilized the same language deployed by the central party, emphasizing class warfare, an end to the imperialist conflict and the dictatorship of the proletariat, they also made direct appeals to other parties to solve the major crises facing the city. The Bolsheviks translated these words into deeds several days later, when plagued by a strike of telegraph workers and swirling rumours of pogroms, they accepted a proposal from the SRs to invite socialist parties to form a 'Revolutionary Salvation Committee' (*Revkom*) entrusted with 'the administration of the city and its defense against counterrevolution.'[49] On 31 October, the Soviet established the *Revkom* as city administrator and promised to use the armed forces of the Soviet against 'hooligans' and those spreading 'disorder'.[50] The coalition *Revkom* existed only for several 'anxious days' after the October Revolution before being replaced by the Bolshevik Military-Revolutionary Committee, but it highlighted the local Bolshevik leadership's willingness (if only temporary) to work with other parties on administrative and security issues.[51]

Despite Bolshevik party leaders in Petrograd and elsewhere promising a radical transformation not only of Russian society, but also of the collapsing administrative state, in Ekaterinburg the new city authorities utilized, rather than dismantled, the 'bourgeois' administrative apparatus for the first months after the October Revolution. Even though the Urals Oblast' Soviet, the organ representing the individual soviets of the Urals region first formed in May 1917, took political control as the 'temporary representative of the new government in the Urals', all municipal services still resided with the City Duma, while the City Soviet exercised its new power primarily through armed security and maintenance of 'order'.[52] Even after coming to power and declaring that they 'could not be restricted to the simple replacement' of the old system, the Bolsheviks remained committed to holding elections to the City Duma.[53]

Before the October Revolution, newspapers reported that the contest for control of the City Duma was essentially a two-way race between the Bolsheviks and the Kadets, with the SRs having lost their influence among the workers due to their 'tactical blunders' in the summer and fall of 1917.[54] The Bolshevik platform, developed before the October Revolution, contained the usual language of opposition to capitalists and support for confiscation of the land, while promising major reforms for the city, including 'real' workers' control over production and trade in order to alleviate food supply problems, control over banks to stop speculation, 'full independence of the city government,' and conducting 'all urban affairs in the interests of the poor'.[55] The Bolsheviks' approach to elections to the City Duma underlined the party's understanding that the municipal centre remained the Duma despite the transfer of all political power to the City Soviet. Moreover, from the available evidence Ekaterinburg's Bolsheviks chose not to use force to sway the City Duma elections, or even dissolve the institution itself and replace it with the City Soviet.

In the 5 November 1917 City Duma elections, Ekaterinburg's Bolsheviks nearly won an outright majority, taking 40 out of the available 85 seats, with the SRs (20) and Kadets (15) finishing a distant second and third. Voter turnout in the election was down about a quarter, with around 20,000 casting votes, still a considerable percentage of the city's eligible voters.[56] The major newspaper, *Ural'skaia zhizn'*, formerly broadly sympathetic, declared that the elections 'felt the influence of legality and law, freed from the misinterpretations of absolutism, creating a new free life on the basis of democratic principles'.[57] Bolshevik representatives took up elected positions in the *Uprava*, an institution that in many ways resembled the *Ispolkom*, with the seasoned Ural Bolshevik Sergei Chutskaev ironically assuming the position of 'mayor', a title strongly associated with the city government under the tsarist regime.[58] Chutskaev and the new Bolshevik members of the *Uprava* even requested help from the previous mayor to 'familiarize' them with the intricacies of 'city management'.[59] The first meeting of the Bolshevik City Duma proceeded more or less by the old procedures and although the Kadets and Right SRs gave speeches protesting the Bolshevik seizure of power, they ultimately remained in the Duma.[60]

Ekaterinburg's Bolsheviks were on the whole no less radical than other party organizations throughout the country. Moreover, the Urals Bolsheviks operated independently from the central party apparatus and the Central Committee was forced to send their own representative to oversee the transfer of the Romanov family from Tobol'sk to Ekaterinburg in the spring of 1918, in large part because they feared the Ekaterinburg Bolsheviks would shoot the former tsar in transit.[61] Ekaterinburg Kadet Krol' observed in 1921 that the Urals Bolsheviks had created their own 'autonomous *Sovnarkom*' that worked 'in contact' with Moscow while remaining independent until May 1918, when they ran out of money.[62]

Given the deep roots of Bolshevism and the natural support base of workers in the Urals, as well as the total lack of armed opposition to Soviet power in Ekaterinburg, why did the city's Bolsheviks pursue a moderate, if not cooperative, track in practical matters of governance and municipal administration? The answer to this question, I argue, can be found in the extant social and economic conditions that they inherited when they took the reins of power in October 1917. The effects of the First World War and the brief rule of the Provisional Government had created an environment of social atrophy, collapse of public services, rising crime, food shortages, degradation of sanitary conditions and many others that seriously weakened the foundations of state power. The City Soviet, the political centre of Ekaterinburg, became the headquarters for the fight against 'disorder', broadly defined, while the City Duma remained as the administrative centre. From their very first proclamations on 26 October 1917, Ekaterinburg's Bolsheviks considered one of their primary tasks to be the 'struggle against disorder'. The first declarations from the City Soviet after the October Revolution concerned 'disorder', the need to suppress 'hooligans' in the 'most severe way'.[63]

Although Hasegawa argues that the Bolsheviks were ambivalent to, if not supportive of, crime and disorder, the experience in Ekaterinburg shows that focus on national leadership can obscure the nuances of the Revolution outside of the capitals. Hasegawa points to the 'alcohol pogroms' of 1917–18 as the pivotal moment when the Bolsheviks recognized the threats to the 'legitimacy of the nascent regime'.[64] In contrast, the Ekaterinburg *Revkom* ordered the destruction of the city's alcohol warehouses by pouring the spirits into a pond, leading to a tense showdown between Red Guards and soldiers assigned to guard the stores.[65] However, as the leader of the mission to destroy the alcohol Iurovskii recalled, the ice on the pond did not melt when the alcohol was dumped out and a comic scene unfolded with soldiers and city residents using teapots to scoop up and drink the alcohol right from the ice. Ultimately Iurovskii and an armed detachment were able to dispose of the alcohol even though the drunkenness reached 'menacing proportions', although the slow formation of the Soviet militia meant that Red Guards performed policing functions instead of a professional force.[66]

The Bolshevik City Duma also took several measures to improve the sanitary conditions in Ekaterinburg, including an ambitious programme to reorganize medical institutions, as the confusing overlapping of responsibilities and jurisdictions between institutions prevented the enactment of necessary measures. City leaders also moved quickly to alleviate the situation and given the lack of workers and resources for the city's waste removal service (the city possessed 50 barrels for waste removal and needed 350), they shifted the burden to society.[67] In January 1918, the Bolshevik *Uprava* released 'compulsory regulations' that banned the dumping of any waste on the streets and made residents responsible for the upkeep of sidewalks, streets and ditches; those who did not fulfil their public duty would be sent to the Revolutionary Tribunal.[68] The Bolsheviks also mandated free typhus vaccinations for the city's poor, organized free medical services and compelled doctors to serve shifts at public clinics, while keeping in place the city's experienced professional medical personnel.[69]

Perhaps more than any sector of the municipal administration, Ekaterinburg's Food Supply Committee faced the most serious challenges and suffered from the breakdown of the Perm' *Guberniia* distribution network due to the chaos of revolutionary events. Keenly aware of the threat of starvation and popular unrest over food shortages, Ekaterinburg's Bolsheviks proceeded cautiously in their reforms and did not immediately make any radical changes, other than providing more food to the poor. In many cases, fundamental restructuring of the municipal administration was not necessary, as the administration already oversaw a vast network of enterprises and the new Duma simply reoriented their activities towards mass production for the poor.[70] In an ironic twist of fate, the Kadet Krol' found himself attacking the Bolsheviks for their preservation of the bread monopoly, initially introduced by the Kadets in the Provisional Government, while the socialists defended its ability to control prices.[71] Moreover, at the first meeting of the enlarged City Food Supply Committee in January 1918, the Left SR chairman called for the introduction of a meat monopoly due to shortages, but acceded to a 'privatized monopoly' where the state would be the primary purchaser and seller of meat from private companies, due to the practical challenges of implementing the monopoly. The committee devolved major questions about changes to the ration card system and the creation of district food supply committees to special commissions, reflecting the leaders' awareness that major administrative reforms could not be achieved overnight.[72]

Among the most surprising aspects of the Bolsheviks' pragmatic approach to municipal administration was their supervision of the public finances, which by October 1917 were on the verge of collapse with the city facing millions of rubles in short-term debt obligations.[73] Historians do not usually associate the Bolsheviks with prudent fiscal management and balanced budgets, but the Bolshevik City Duma and *Uprava* under mayor Chutskaev adopted a cautious approach to city administration, including working side-by-side with some of Ekaterinburg's most conservative Kadets on the City Theatre Commission.[74] One of the first steps taken by the Bolshevik City Duma and its financial-budget commission, led by mayor Sergei Chutskaev, was to appeal to local capitalists for an emergency loan to keep the government solvent.[75] The City *Uprava* initiated extensive negotiations over the length of the deal and interests with wealthy local residents, whose signatures were needed to approve the credit and whose money would be loaned.[76] In mid-January 1918, the City *Uprava* received 500,000 rubles in donation from the 'commercial-industrial class [...] in light of the critical state of city finances'.[77] Thus, paradoxically, Ekaterinburg's local capitalists and merchants provided a direct monetary lifeline to the struggling Bolshevik municipal government, whose leaders had publicly demonized those very groups since the February Revolution. At a further meeting of the *Uprava*'s Budget-Finance Committee on 28 January 1918, Chutskaev lamented the state of the city's finances by noting that, among other upsurges, the annual cost of upkeep for the Militia had risen from 43,000 rubles to 800,000 rubles. As a partial solution to the city's spiralling deficits, Chutskaev proposed the 'municipalization' of homes, not for ideological purposes and the Bolsheviks' vision of communal living, but so the city could receive additional revenue from renting the buildings.[78] The Oblast' Soviet eventually enacted this decree and ordered the municipalization of private housing, although it did not mention the plight of the poor and homeless, but rather the administration's 'need for money, need for space, and need for immediate help in all forms.'[79]

As memoirist Vladimir Andronnikov noted, after the October Revolution, in Ekaterinburg, 'the city administration directed all of its money to settling the industrial question.'[80] Many factories and industries in Ekaterinburg were 'municipalized' rather than 'nationalized', and the Bolshevik administration continued a process begun during the First World War of extending municipal control over the means of production. This meant the allocation of huge outflows of public money to keep city industries open, while simultaneously maintaining existing services with heightened costs. These fiscal constraints led Chutskaev personally to reject an appeal from the city's Union of Chefs to build a cheap cafeteria in the centre of the city, because he had already allocated the building for the expansion of the city pawnshop.[81] Moreover, after an order from the People's Commissariat of Internal Affairs from January 1918 calling for 'immediate, merciless taxation of the propertied classes'[82] Chutskaev and the committee conducted negotiations over the 'commercial terms' of a million ruble 'loan' from a group of 'citizens who were subsidising the city.'[83]

When the Bolshevik administration began to nationalize banking in late 1917, a drawn-out process where private and public banking existed uneasily side-by-side until March 1918, banker Vladimir Anichkov noted with surprise the 'calmness and even indifference' to the nationalization of private deposits and assets and there were no protests or complaints during the process. Anichkov speculated that this was the result of two factors: on the one hand, many of Ekaterinburg's wealthy residents believed the nationalization, as well as Bolshevik rule, would be temporary, and on the other hand, that they had 'grown accustomed' to the idea of losing their capital due to the unstable financial situation of the country since the First World War. Anichkov clearly believed the latter to be the true cause of the peaceful capitulation of capital, which he attributed to 'a characteristic trait of the Russian man, namely humility.'[84] The fiscal management pursued by the Bolshevik City Duma starkly contrasted with ideological proclamations emanating from the national leadership of the party and demonstrated their recognition of the elevated importance of municipal services during a time of disorder, social breakdown and countless other deprivations. The first months of Soviet power in Ekaterinburg also underlined the relative competence of the Bolsheviks as administrators in contrast to their predecessors, a key factor in establishing legitimacy that is often overlooked in favour of high politics and ideology.

At a meeting of the *Ispolkom* on 25 February 1918, Ekaterinburg's leaders approved the abolition of the structures of 'local self-government' and the transfer of all affairs of 'city management' to newly created commissariats under the Soviet. The proposal was developed by the *Uprava* and its members would assume analogous positions within the commissariat system, thus smoothing the transition of administrative control.[85] Although these reforms loosely followed instructions from the centre on the structure of the commissariats, in particular an order from the People's Commissariat of Internal Affairs from January 1918 declaring the 'liquidation' of institutions of local self-government,[86] the changes in Ekaterinburg's were largely cosmetic and often involved nothing more than jurisdictional and name changes. The commissariat system in Ekaterinburg directly mirrored the structure of the City Duma administration, with the new commissariats built on the foundations of sub-commissions of the *Uprava* introduced in the early twentieth century, including the Food Supply, Technical-Management, Medical-Sanitary and others.[87] In the case of the Commissariat of Health, Ekaterinburg's professional doctors participated in the creation of the institution, allowing them to realize their long-standing goal of creating a unified medical institution that could centralize the city's sprawling public health organizations.[88]

The Bolsheviks' reorganization of local self-government into the commissariat system in Ekaterinburg did not represent a radical break with the liberal or tsarist past, nor a fundamental reconceptualization of municipal institutions. After 'seizing' power peacefully in the city and demonstrating a willingness, however fleeting, to work with other political parties to overcome disorder and chaos, Bolshevik leaders pursued a pragmatic approach to municipal administration and provision of public services, reflecting not only local conditions, but also their sensitivity to the failures of their predecessors to provide for the city's residents. The first months of the 'dictatorship of the proletariat' in Ekaterinburg's city administration were marked by fiscal prudence, increased attention to public order and sanitation, the continuation of food supply policies instituted by the Provisional Government and an overall slow progression towards the radical transformations of state and society espoused by Lenin and others in Petrograd.

The pragmatic approach to governance by Ekaterinburg's Bolsheviks for the first months after the October Revolution did not survive the civil war, which began in earnest in the Urals in December 1917, with the uprising of Ataman Aleksandr Dutov placing the city in direct military threat. Many of Ekaterinburg's most influential Bolshevik leaders personally organized detachments of Red Guards units to campaign against the Cossacks and their deaths in combat deprived the party of its most experienced members.[89] Even though Dutov was momentarily defeated, Ekaterinburg's leaders continued to worry about a counter-revolutionary uprising, fears which were confirmed when the Czechoslovak Legion rose up in nearby Cheliabinsk in May 1918. Throughout this time, arrests and repression of political enemies by the Bolshevik regime increased, and the focus of the local administration shifted from improving municipal services to combat the real danger of counter-revolution. The Ekaterinburg Cheka, formed in February 1918, emerged as one of the most powerful institutions in the region and engaged in a wide range of repressive activities against political enemies as well as ordinary criminals. The use of coercion and violence by local authorities reached the point of no return in early June 1918 when a meeting of frontline soldiers turned violent after demonstrators began calling for the end of Soviet power and the reestablishment of the Constituent Assembly, with Red Guards brutally suppressing the gathering and executing the ringleaders.[90] After this event, the Oblast' War Commissariat banned any unsanctioned gatherings and declared any resistance to Soviet power 'traitorous' and punishable by shooting.[91] The threat of armed uprisings in the Urals pushed the local government's priorities towards security and away from public services, simultaneously marginalizing both Ekaterinburg's municipal administration and its leaders, with food supply transferred to Oblast authorities and control over the Soviet militia to the Red Army.[92] On the eve of the fall of Ekaterinburg to anti-Bolshevik forces, administrative control had been effectively removed from the city's municipal government.

An examination of the Bolsheviks' brief time in power after the October Revolution in Ekaterinburg sheds new light not only about how the party approached practical matters of governance, but also about the nature of state power on the local level and the importance of provision of public services in establishing political legitimacy. After the February Revolution, Ekaterinburg's Bolsheviks developed a municipal platform to address the catastrophic state of the public services, combining elements of the party's ideological doctrine with a response to the mismanagement of municipal administration under the tsarist regime and the Provisional Government. Far from being a radical outlier, Sosnovskii's party was firmly integrated into the local political environment along with moderate socialists, liberals and conservatives and concerned themselves with issues central to all parties. They actively participated in democratic elections to improve Ekaterinburg by working within 'bourgeois' structures of local self-government. The bungling efforts of tsarist and Provisional Government city leaders led to widespread dissatisfaction and social breakdown among the local population, which the Bolsheviks capitalized on to peacefully, using Alexander Rabinowitch's famous formulation, 'come to power'.[93] At a time dominated by the struggle to establish political legitimacy and power, Bolsheviks in Ekaterinburg turned to the revitalization of municipal institutions and public services in the service of their larger transformative agenda.

Above all, the concerns of Ekaterinburg's Bolsheviks were local and to improve the urban environment they followed directives from the centre when suitable and eschewed them when extant conditions demanded a different approach. Whatever Vladimir Lenin and the Bolsheviks' leadership intended the proletarian state to look like after seizing power, Ekaterinburg after the October Revolution did not resemble any of the vague prescriptions outlined in *The State and Revolution*. Authoritarian valences and a lack of understanding of Western-style democracy prevailed across a wide range of political parties and movements before and after the fall of the autocracy in 1917, although the Bolsheviks' demand for results would pay fateful dividends when class conflict turned into civil war in the spring of 1918. The idea of the civil war as a transformational experience for the Bolsheviks is not a new one, though one must distinguish between discursive shifts in describing enemies or political arrests and the direct threat of an approaching front. In Ekaterinburg, the proximity to the front lines of civil war and loss of many of the most capable leaders contributed to an abandonment of administrative state building and its replacement with coercion and violence.

CHAPTER 4
LENIN'S 'LIVING LINK'? PETITIONING THE RULER ACROSS THE REVOLUTIONARY DIVIDE
Lara Douds

Each year in June President Vladimir Putin conducts a multi-hour telethon on Russian television where ordinary people are invited to call in and 'ask him anything.' Calls often involve Russian citizens telling Putin about local grievances in dealing with the government's vast, indifferent bureaucracy. In these cases, Putin takes note and acts swiftly to rectify the caller's problem. In the most recent episode, in June 2018, for example, one Natalia Zhurova from Tomsk, expressing her joy and gratitude in speaking to Mr Putin, appealed to the president:

> I have three children. My question has to do with the allocation of free land to large families. This law does not work very well in our region [...] At present, regional authorities are responsible for allocating free land to large families. In 2010, I signed up and was placed on the waiting list. I was number 735 at the time. This year, I have moved up half the list to 300 something [...] Mr President, my question is this. How much longer will I have to wait – eight years or maybe ten – with three children, two of them boys? You see, we want to teach them, to show them how to work, we want each one of them to grow up to be someone and to love the Russian soil [...]. When I went to our regional authorities, I was told that I should get on the waiting list, that is, I have no right to get land now, because in our region, it only goes to families with four children or more. And with three children, you have to wait in line. But, as I know this law, I think that the regional government is most likely violating it.[1]

Acting decisively, live on air, Putin immediately called Tomsk governor Sergei Zhvachkin to account. The governor claimed: 'It looks as if officials have failed to inform her of her rights. We will definitely settle her problem soon, and I will meet with her and subsequently update you on progress in her case, Mr President.' Putin reiterated his concern for the loyal citizen, Mrs Zhurova, admonishing governor Zhvachkin:

> You said that some officials seem to misunderstand. We must know which officials these are, and they must not be guided by any formal considerations but try to act in the interests of the people who live on the territory these officials have been entrusted to manage. Of course, if there are instructions in your region that free land can only be issued to families with four children, you should take a closer

look at them. Raising three children is a challenging task in modern conditions […], hence you should help these people. I ask you to settle this.²

While technological developments have allowed for a new form of virtual 'personal audience', the supplicatory tone and emotional plea of this oral petition to the ruler are startlingly similar to that of the 'proshenie' or 'khodataistvo' of the tsarist era, and indeed petitions to rulers in many pre-modern societies more broadly. Putin's response to the appeal is strongly reminiscent of the paternalist 'batiushka myth' explored by Perrie and Field in their studies of tsarist era 'naïve' or 'popular monarchism'.³ As part of the 'little-father' motif, faithful subjects brought to the tsar's attention the abuses of local leaders and he reprimanded them for corruption or incompetence and offered direct intervention to take care of the petitioner's needs.

In many parts of nineteenth-century Europe, with the rise of liberal, representative ideas and structures, the petition was transmuted from an individual, supplicatory and emotional plea for assistance to a collective demand in formal, rights-based language with an agenda to effect reform to wider policy. This chapter asks why in Russia the traditional form was preserved, and even expanded, in the twentieth century, and how this instrument of political engagement helped to shape the fate of the Bolshevik revolution by maintaining paternalist and authoritarian forms of interaction between government and people. Of course, an obvious answer is that Russia did not follow the liberal, representative path of constitutional development, with the Duma, its weak quasi-parliament from 1906, failing to limit the power of the tsar. Soon after, the Bolshevik socialist revolution interrupted any development of Western liberal democratic forms promised by the February Revolution of 1917. Yet, the Bolsheviks themselves aspired to construct a radical, alternative form of democracy, one superior to the 'bourgeois' liberal model. They came to power with a vision to transform political structures and practices, destroy the old state and bring to life new, genuinely democratic ways of governing and administering.⁴ While the Bolsheviks possessed a transformational, emancipatory agenda, certainly not a conservative one, elements of tsarist paternalist political culture continued across the revolutionary divide.⁵

Recently J. Arch Getty argued that 'ancient' and 'archaic' Russian practices of patrimonial politics such as personalized notions of power, clan politics rather than strong institutions and leader cults predated Stalin and outlived him, transcending regime change. Getty rejected previous explanations for this continuity such as Rieber's 'persistent factors' determining coevolution of different political systems towards similar practices, as well as the argument that the Soviet government – and especially Stalin personally – consciously invoked traditional methods in a strategic, even cynical manner to summon the obedience of the wider population.⁶ In Getty's view, 'At some point in time, this form of traditional rule ceased being conscious […] and became habit, familiar practice and therefore culture […] Other political strategies or forms of organization might be more utilitarian or functional, but the old ones persist'.⁷ Getty's focus on the 1930s, by which time these political forms were a fait accompli and his argument that these practices became 'embedded somehow', invites closer examination of the mechanics of how paternalist practice was carried over, whether there was an element of conscious choice, where the impetus arose and how revolutionary leaders rationalized their institutional choices for the new Soviet government.

Over the last few decades scholars have mined Russian archives to make use of letters sent to the tsarist and Soviet governments in the form of petitions or denunciations to explore the fabric of everyday life, to examine separate events such as the 1905 Revolution or distinct issues such as divorce, and examine popular conceptions of authority.[8] This chapter is a preliminary attempt to consider the persistence of the actual medium (rather than the individual content or subject matter) of receiving and responding to petitions, and how and why the revolutionary leadership preserved and even expanded a supplicatory political tool which at first glance appears antithetical to their firmly-held values of revolution, class struggle and proletarian-democratic rule.

As the introduction to this volume makes clear, the Bolshevik vision of democracy explicitly rejected the contemporary parliamentary, representative model as a smokescreen to deceive the working masses. All political parties accepted the capitalist order and thus the exploitation of the masses by the owners of the means of production. In that sense, 'bourgeois' democracy offered no real choice for the majority. Instead the Bolsheviks imagined democracy as rule by the masses and in the interests of the masses and the end of exploitation, class conflict and private ownership of the economy. In the context of autocratic Russia, the Bolsheviks perceived that they, as the 'vanguard' of the working masses, needed to seize control and destroy existing power structures before they could begin to establish their new democracy. As outlined in the introduction, Lenin envisioned Soviet administration as being profoundly democratic and accountable to the broad masses of the proletariat. The Bolshevik state builders sought alternative levers of responsiveness and participation, although they were not at first clear about how and when new democratic institutions would emerge and what forms they would take.

One problem confronting revolutionary state-builders was how to accommodate popular expectations of the forms and duties of state power, including accepting petitions. It was not only the Bolsheviks who had no regard for 'bourgeois' parliamentary democracy. Besides a small pool of liberal intellectuals, neither was there a clear popular conception of, nor appetite for, parliamentary-style democratic institutions in the Western model.[9] Scholarship on nineteenth- and early twentieth-century rural schools, the army and the peasant experience in the city have shown how villagers 'peasantized' the very institutions that were supposed to transform them.[10] Thus, peasants had influenced the way in which tsarist institutions and policy planned from the centre were played out in practice. Could the political expectations of the majority rural population have shaped the institutional choices of the 'proletarian' revolutionary government's leaders while its structures were in their nascent, most malleable phase?

Petitioning, alongside violent protest, was the most significant form of popular political agency in Muscovite and Imperial Russia, following a long tradition dating back to the Middle Ages. The system of autocratic rule and the rudimentary and generally corrupt nature of lower-level administrative institutions in Russia meant that throughout much of its history, appeals, complaints and denunciations were often directed to the very top as well as at the local level. In the sixteenth century a special chancellery, the *chelobitnyi prikaz*, was created to deal with the petitions and complaints addressed to the tsar. It was dissolved in the late seventeenth century, but the practice of sending petitions did not cease. Russian serfdom was exceptional among types of unfreedom because serfs possessed the right to petition the highest level of authority, as well as local elites. This outlet of legal agency was not subversive. It allowed the state to interact with and placate the vast population of serfs that may have otherwise threatened the established structure of power. Moreover, the serfs' petitions were not grand requests for legal reform or emancipation. Instead, they aired everyday grievances and levelled individual complaints. Petitions circulated through the government bureaucracy and it was not uncommon for serfs' complaints to prompt official investigations.[11]

In attempt to improve effective functioning of government, Peter the Great first attempted to curb the volume of individual, personal petitions which flowed directly to the tsar. His 1718 edict informed petitioners who 'pestered' the tsar 'what a multitude there is of them, whereas it is only one person they petition, and he is surrounded by so much military business and other burdensome work … even if he did not have such a lot of work, how would it be possible for one man to look after so many? In truth it would be impossible either for a man or an angel.'[12] From then on, the tsarist 'Petitions Office' experienced a series of reincarnations between 1720 and 1917, from Peter the Great's foreign-inspired 'Kantseliariia reketmeisterskikh del' or (1720–1810), then the 'Komissiia proshenii' (1810–84), to the 'Kantseliariia po priniatiiu proshenii' or Chancellery for the Receipt of Petitions (1884–1917).[13] During the eighteenth and nineteenth centuries Russian rulers' attitudes towards petitioning ebbed and flowed. 'Enlightened' Westerniser Catherine the Great attempted, again, to curb serf petitions to the tsar, causing discontent over the breaking of the traditional connection. Despite her best efforts at modernization, serfs creatively misunderstood legislation which curtailed petitioning the monarch directly, exploiting legal contradictions.[14] The 'direct link' between tsar and peasants via petitioning was then enthusiastically reinvigorated by her conservative son, Paul I. Paul invited citizens to submit petitions and requests at the beginning of his reign by placing them in a 'yellow box' by the gates of the palace. Paul would personally open the box each morning and his replies were posted in St Petersburg newspapers. Paul's experiment came to grief because obscene verse and caricature found their way into the box, but nevertheless, he had revived the official promotion of petitioning.[15]

Petitioning suffered again under the 'Great Reforms' which aimed to modernize paternalistic principles and forms of government into a more rational, bureaucratic system. But problems in Alexander II's reforms to rural administration which attempted to introduce rational institutions of peasant self-rule led conservatives at court to argue that peasants wanted not more foreign-inspired laws and procedures, but justice that corresponded to their ostensibly patriarchal way of life and deeply embedded customs. Calls for the reaffirmation of autocratic principles emphasized the paternalistic, personal nature of government authority and this vision gained the upper hand under Alexander III in the 1890s with the creation of the Land Captain. Alexander III and later Nicholas

II sought to reaffirm the affinity between the tsar and the peasantry in order to build national unity between government and governed.[16] This effort included ceremonial expressions of the familial ties that bound the father-tsar to his peasant-children as well as the practice of direct petitioning of the monarch.[17] The Petitions Chancellery helped 'to maintain the illusion of an autocracy resting directly on the people' and to sustain in the 'common people' their faith on monarchical justice.[18] By 1908 the tsarist government's petitions chancellery was receiving 65,000 petitions annually.[19]

Meanwhile, petitioning had expanded not just to the ruler, but the entire hierarchy of tsarist administration. The tsars' subjects were keen to make use of opportunities for redress or assistance whenever and wherever it was on offer.[20] Appeals and complaints were so ubiquitous by the late nineteenth century, even at the lower levels, that Chekhov was inspired to write his comic short story 'A Defenceless Creature' (1887) mocking the practice. In this tale, a woman visits a bank, pleading for aid on behalf of her sick husband who had lost his job. Despite the best efforts of staff to convince her she is petitioning at the wrong place, she refuses to take no for an answer. Her persistent, hysterical pleas lead, in the end, to the exhausted bank manager giving her the money from his own pocket. The next day she returns with a further petition requesting employment for her husband. In this case, it is not the petitioner who is the 'defenceless creature', but the petitionee.[21]

Thus, petitioning was deeply ingrained in the political culture of the late tsarist empire, but there was an especial quality to the petition directed to the ruler. By the early twentieth century, Russia's tsars had cultivated this act as a central pillar of the 'batiushka' or tsar-father myth. It is ironic, in light of the subsequent co-opting of the practice by his own government after 1917, that Lenin had complained of the 'naïve patriarchal faith in the tsar' expressed via petitioning and predicted its 'death agony' in wake of the 1905 Revolution's 'Bloody Sunday', where a peaceful procession to present a petition to the tsar was violently suppressed. In an article for the Bolshevik newspaper *Vpered* in January 1905 he wrote of: 'millions of Russian workers and peasants who until now could believe naively and blindly in the Tsar Father and seek alleviation of their unbearable lot from "Our Father the Tsar" himself, who put the blame for all the atrocities and outrages, the tyranny and plunder, *only* on the officials that were deceiving the tsar.' He linked supplicatory petitioning to the backwardness of the rural population, 'Generation after generation of downtrodden, half-civilised, rustic existence cut off from the world tended to strengthen this faith', and foresaw that while the growth of the 'new, urban, industrial, literate Russia' was destroying this faith, behind these 'scores of thousands (of politically conscious workers) stood … millions, of toiling and exploited people, proletarians and semi-proletarians, suffering every insult and indignity, in whom this faith could still survive. They were not ready for revolt, they could only beg and plead.'[22]

Yet, when the new Bolshevik leaders were inundated, from the earliest days of the revolution, with petitions, appeals and complaints in person and by letter they fell into the same, traditional posture in response to this 'pleading'. It is clear that this practice of receiving and responding to petitions was not consciously planned and imposed by

Lenin's government of its own initiative, but was a reactive response to a wave of popular pressure. The Bolsheviks could have chosen to reject the practice of petitioning outright as a traditional tool of tsarist, paternalist rule, but their nebulous conceptions of the institutional forms of revolutionary state power meant that they were able to rationalize it in their own ideological language. They renamed the new government's engagement with this 'pleading' as the '*Priemnaia*' or 'Reception', a less supplicatory sounding term and reimagined the practice as a de-bureaucratizing tool of openness, responsiveness and accountability for a revolutionary government. Yet despite Lenin's vision of popular petitioning as a responsive dialogue between government and governed and check on abuses of officialdom, what resulted was the perpetuation of a paternalist, authoritarian dynamic.

The impetus for the establishment of the main Soviet government petitions office, or '*Priemnaia*', came from below, its creation an ad hoc response on the part of the Bolshevik leadership to the deluge of expectant petitioners. As one of the institution's secretaries described, the early weeks of the revolution were 'a time of uncontrollable pilgrimage to Lenin. Every day from morning till night I found dozens of people who came to see Vladimir Ilich from their localities. They sat for hours in the waiting room of the Council of People's Commissars, patiently waiting for the reception. Despite all persuasion, the delegates did not want to return home without seeing Lenin.'[23] Revolutionary upheaval and instability intensified popular desire to petition the centre and a huge quantity of letters, petitions and requests, as well as visits from delegations, arrived at the Soviet government's headquarters.[24]

Alexandra Kollontai, the first People's Commissar for Social Welfare, recalled that her first act in this role was 'to compensate a small peasant for his requisitioned horse'. Her testimony reveals the persistence with which visitors approached the new government with petitions:

> The man was determined to receive compensation for his horse. He had travelled from his distant village to the capital and had knocked patiently on the doors of all of the ministries. Always with no results. Then the Bolshevik revolution broke out. The man had heard that *the Bolsheviks were in favour of the workers and peasants*. So he went to the Smolny Institute, to Lenin, who had to pay out the compensation. As a result of the conversation [...] the man came to me with a small page torn from Lenin's notebook on which I was requested to settle the matter somehow since at that moment the People's Commissariat for Social Welfare had the greatest amount of cash at its disposal.[25]

It is clear from Kollontai's recollection that although the formula was the same, petitioners were quick to learn the new discourse required to push the correct buttons of the authorities and thus receive the desired relief. Although the tone and structure tended to echo the tsarist-era model 'proshenie', the language of petitions was quickly adapted to reflect the Soviet government's self-perception as superior to its forerunners in serving the needs of the poorest workers and peasants.[26]

The initial, make-shift 'Reception' was hastily put together by Lenin's staff during the first weeks of Soviet power in the government's first headquarters at the Smolny Institute to accommodate the groups of workers, soldiers and peasants who descended daily.[27] Peasant petitioners, or '*khodoki*', brought with them instructions worked out at village gatherings, listing issues to be resolved in Petrograd, by Lenin himself, most relating, at this stage, to implementing the Decree on Land.[28] Having received numerous peasant delegations in the first week of the revolution, at a meeting of the Petrograd Soviet on 4 November 1917, Lenin remarked 'the peasants refuse to believe that all power belongs to the Soviets, they are still waiting for something from the government.'[29] On 5 November 1917 he drafted, 'An Answer to the Requests of the Peasants,' in response to numerous questions submitted by peasant petitioners to his government. Subsequently, each of the *khodoki* got a typewritten copy bearing Lenin's personal signature which read:

> In reply to numerous questions from peasants, be it known that all power in the country henceforth belongs wholly to the Soviets of Workers', Soldiers' and Peasants' Deputies [...] Landed proprietorship has been abolished by the Second All-Russia Congress of Soviets.[30]

From all over Russia, peasants, nominated by their local community and travelling on funds assembled by the village communes, came to meet with the 'head Bolshevik', to discuss peasant affairs. Lenin received delegations either in his office or behind a round table in the Soviet cabinet's main office if the party was too large.[31] The ritualized behaviour of the peasant petitioners is clear from the testimony of Sovnarkom Reception staff, who recalled:

> Despite all persuasion peasant delegates did not want to return to the localities without having seen Lenin. Some, after visiting the reception, asked the secretary to give them a note. In this note they demanded to write that so and so had really been received by Lenin. Very often we had to issue such papers. The peasant envoys took these documents and like a sacred object carefully placed it to their bosom, having wrapped it in a clean rag. Peasant envoys, having seen Lenin and heard his advice were then considered the 'first' person in the village.[32]

The Sovnarkom Reception was open from 12 noon on Tuesdays and Thursdays in the first year after the move to the Kremlin for visitors to deliver petitions.[33] Reception staff heard the requests and complaints of all petitioners and noted them down.[34] After the day's work the staff were obliged to report to Lenin on all 'interesting and socially important visits.' He read the written reports prepared by Reception staff, gave directions on tasks arising and demanded the tracing of their implementation.[35] The Reception secretary also passed notes to Lenin every morning and reported to him on who asked for receptions with him personally and what they wanted to discuss.[36]

According to the Reception manager, 'In the course of close to six months we received more than 6000 people, each of whom was a representative of a large group of the population.'³⁷ Indeed, the number of visitors was so large that in early 1919, a year after the government moved to Moscow, an 'external reception' was established. Bonch-Bruevich recommended that because peasant visitors were appearing in increasing numbers, it was necessary to transfer the Reception just outside the Kremlin where it would be fully accessible to all wishing to visit. He complained that many peasant visitors 'are not allowed to enter (the Kremlin) as they cannot explain why they have come and our Commandant is very concerned by the many strange persons entering the government building.'³⁸ Clearly the assassination attempt on Lenin months earlier had raised security concerns. The Reception was transferred to Mokhovaia Ulitsa, where visitors could sit and drink tea while they wrote down their petitions or if illiterate, were assisted in doing so.³⁹ In March 1921 the external Soviet Government main Reception was united with that of the Central Executive Committee of Soviets, under its Chairman and Soviet 'head of state' Mikhail Kalinin.⁴⁰ He was presented in the Bolshevik press as 'The All-Russian Village Headman,' which reinforced the notion of a personal link between the Reception and the peasant masses.⁴¹ He led a very busy Reception, receiving more than 1.5 million written and oral petitions over the years 1923–35.⁴²

What made the Soviet government's receiving of petitions distinct, in theory at least, from its tsarist predecessor, was the aspiration that it could be employed as a tool of popular '*kontrol*'' over state institutions to create a form of accountable, responsive 'proletarian democracy'. The 'Outline of the rules of management of Soviet institutions' of December 1918 declared:

> In order to combat red tape and successfully expose abuses, as well as to eliminate dishonest officials who have penetrated Soviet institutions [...] in every Soviet institution the days and hours of reception of the public should be hung not only inside the building, but outside so that they are accessible to all without any passes. The premises for reception must be arranged so that admission is free, without any omissions. In every Soviet institution a book should be opened for recording [...] the name of the petitioner, the essence of his application and the direction of the case [...]. Officials from State Control are given the right to be present at all receptions and are obliged from time to time to attend receptions, check the visitors' book and draw up a record of visiting, examining the book and polling the public.⁴³

Reception hours were established in the People's Commissariats and even in the Cheka headquarters.⁴⁴ The Commissariat of Justice, for example, located a short walk from the Kremlin, at 21 Ilinka St, held its receptions on Mondays, Wednesdays and Fridays. The People's Commissar Stuchka was available for visits 12–1 pm on all these days and two further members of the collegium received people: comrade Kurskii on Mondays and Wednesdays, 12–2 pm and comrade Kozlovskii on Wednesdays and Fridays, 1.30–2.30 pm.⁴⁵

As well as receiving visitors in person, the Soviet government Reception also accepted written petitions. By 1921 the main Soviet Government Reception received more than 9,000 complaints and petitions annually. Of these, most were varied requests (1,529), complaints on the activity of local power (977), applications for help (927), on the taking of allotted property and food tax (296), on land questions (235).[46] The Secretary of the Reception was responsible for processing all written petitions and reporting fortnightly to Lenin on the general sum.

The Sovnarkom Reception functioned as an instrument of 'illiberal liberation' in three main ways. First, public accessibility of government buildings seems to have been an important element of conceptions of Soviet democracy. In his critique of parliamentary democracy in *State and Revolution*, Lenin highlighted the principle that 'public buildings are not for "paupers"!' as a 'restriction upon democracy'. He complained that:

> These restrictions, exceptions, exclusions, obstacles for the poor seem slight, especially in the eyes of one who has never known want himself and has never been in close contact with the oppressed classes in their life (and nine out of 10, if not 99 out of 100, bourgeois publicists and politicians come under this category); but in their sum total these restrictions exclude and squeeze out the poor from politics, from active participation in democracy.[47]

Thus, public access to government administrators was part and parcel of the new, revolutionary system, from the local level to the highest state offices.

Second, petitioning offered the Soviet government a means of gathering information about the situation 'on the ground' throughout the country and hearing the views of the masses: the 'authentic voice of the land', as Lenin described it.[48] Lenin's colleagues noted that he drew useful information from thousands of peasants and workers who came to see him and through these meetings he claimed to 'perceive the pulse of life' across the Soviet Republic.[49] In some sense, the petitions represented an informal kind of consultation or polling of the population, albeit a rather arbitrary one and without any compulsion to respond in terms of broader policy direction to the views aired to the authorities.

Third, the serious attention devoted to the government's responses to petitions suggests a further purpose beyond accessibility and gathering information. The leaders of the new Soviet government imagined the Sovnarkom Reception as a 'living link' to the 'labouring masses', a lever of democracy and legitimacy for their government. According to Lenin, this 'living link' was a vital tool of his revolutionary proletarian-democratic government.[50] In a letter of 3 December 1921 to state officials who dealt with complaints from petitioners to the Soviet government main Reception, Lenin wrote: 'From the work of the Sovnarkom Reception in handling complaints and petitions, it is clear that serious and urgent cases have demonstrated the usefulness of the Reception as a living link.'[51] (*zhivaia sviaz'*).

As part of his 'living link' mechanism, Lenin demanded a personal response to all citizens' letters reporting that 'their affair had been directed somewhere'[52] and also pressed for 'careful surveillance over the execution of my resolutions on these complaints.'[53] In a special instruction to the Administration Department of Sovnarkom of 18 January 1919 Lenin insisted that the secretaries report to him on all complaints arriving in written form within twenty-four hours and on oral complaints in forty-eight hours and, crucially, demanded careful checking of the execution of decisions on citizen's complaints.[54] One occasion, for example, when Reception Secretary Brichkina failed to follow through the checking of the response to a petition, resulted in a reprimand from Lenin. In January 1920 the peasant V. Iushin from the village of Osht in Olonets Gubernia sent a telegram to the Soviet government, in which he complained that local powers had taken, as part of *razverstka*, one of his three cows. Iushin reported that his large family consisted of nine people and one son was a Red Army soldier and requested compensation to help them survive. Brichkina sent a copy of this telegram to the People's Commissar of Foodstuffs, Alexander Tsiurupa, but she did not trace the reply sent to Iushin outlining which measures were to be taken on his behalf. As a result of this lapse, Lenin sent her the following note: 'To Brichkina, this is impossible. It is not enough to send it to Tsiurupa. It is necessary to check and to note what answer was sent, and when.'[55]

Lenin frequently expressed his concern to provide responses to petitions and reprimanded state officials dragging their feet in these tasks. This extra workload was not appreciated by Commissariat officials and there were repeated complaints that the Reception overloaded the commissariats with petitions. Lenin, though, was convinced of the importance of this work to de-bureaucratize Soviet democracy, remarking acerbically that 'Our own bureaucrats are already bureaucratized to such a degree that they are dissatisfied that the population, by whom they govern, try, on behalf of their needs, to lodge complaints and requests [...] We created the state apparatus, really, for this PURPOSE.'[56]

When in December 1921 Lenin discovered that complaints and statements of workers sent by the Sovnarkom Reception to commissariats for solution had remained unanswered, he reprimanded the leaders of these institutions:

> Once and for all it is necessary to put an end to the outrage of Red Tape and '*kantseliarshchina*' in your institutions. Important and urgent tasks sent to you by the Sovnarkom Reception in solving numerous complaints [...] remain completely unanswered and unfulfilled. I propose to pull together the machine of Soviet administration immediately [...] From its slackness not only do the interests of individual people suffer, but the whole business of administration takes on a sham, illusory character.[57]

Again, on 3 December 1921, Lenin wrote a letter on this problem to several state officials, including head of the Cheka, F. E. Dzerzhinskii and editor of *Bednota* newspaper, V. A. Karpinskii who, in the positions they occupied, most often had to deal with the complaints of working people, stressing the usefulness of the Reception as a 'living link'.[58]

In another case, two peasants (one from Iaroslavl, the other from the Moscow province) appealed to Lenin as Chairman of the Soviet government about the illegal requisition of their horses. The Reception sent their complaints to a special commission in charge of resolving such issues. An official of the commission, Romanov, having received these petitions, wrote on the envelope: 'There are so many jobs, and there is no time to deal with trifles.' When Lenin learned of this 'bureaucratic, soulless rejection' he gave an order to bring this 'official' to criminal liability.[59]

From 1919 the Reception became ever more closely intertwined with the concept of state '*kontrol*'' as a participatory, democratic lever. *Kontrol'*, meaning 'checking' or 'supervision' in a general sense, like the English term 'controller' or 'comptroller' was intended to enable the 'labouring masses' to monitor bureaucrats' work, until such time as sufficient members of the proletariat gained the skills to allow them take over the work of administration themselves. The decree on the reorganization of state *kontrol'* of April 1919 expanded the commissariat's duties to include receiving and investigating complaints from ordinary people. The decree formally established a reorganized Complaints Bureau in order that the 'formalistic methods' of the old state *kontrol'* commissariat were replaced by methods of 'factual' *kontrol'* carried out by the 'broad strata of workers and peasants'. Outgoing commissar Karl Lander greeted the decree as bringing about an 'October Revolution' in *kontrol'* because it directed the commissariat's activity to 'political *kontrol'*' of the broadest kind.[60] This commissariat soon became one of the key points of extra-bureaucratic authority to which citizens could address petitions and complaints. The largest number of complaints was received from peasants about food requisitions, then the Chekas and the next most common were complaints about government housing and other agencies. In the month of December 1919 alone, the Central Complaints Bureau examined about 700 cases and its local bureaus another 1,300.[61]

This system attracted criticism from party oppositionists that despite the party's concern with making *kontrol'* effective and non-bureaucratic, *kontrol'* organs had become self-enclosed and autonomous of Soviet authorities. Instead of becoming more accountable and less bureaucratic, the regime was turning into, some observed, not the power of the Soviets (*vlast' Sovetov*), but power of control organs (*vlast' kontrolia*).[62] Nevertheless, Lenin's preoccupation with engagement with popular petitions and complaints as a tool to combat red tape and bureaucracy and hold officials to account only intensified further, such as in the decree 'On the Elimination of Red Tape' of 30 December 1919.[63]

Thus the 'living link' which the Soviet leadership conceived of as a tool of their anti-bureaucratic, revolutionary democracy inadvertently reinforced traditional customs and 'manual control' from the top down. Instead of finding representative institutional solutions, they attempted to connect state and society through receptions and through making sure things got done for those individuals who contacted the government directly. While, like the Rabkrin, the Reception was envisaged as a way to draw the masses into holding government officials to account and participating in observation of their activities, there were negative side effects. First, the petitioning system made for inefficient administration and overloaded the state departments with mountains of minor complaints and appeals to handle, disrupting the rational flow of normal government business. Second, receiving these petitions gave the Bolsheviks a potentially misleading sense that the legitimacy of their 'open and responsive' government had been accepted by a large section of the population.

A letter from Lenin to the Commissariat of Foodstuffs in 1922 regarding one petition demonstrates how he imagined constructing a link between government and people by responding to petitions. Lenin wrote:

> I ask you to show assistance to the peasant Sergei Frolov, in buying bread for his village Alakaevka, Samara Gubernia [...] Because I was personally acquainted with this village, I consider that it would be politically useful if the peasant does not leave without any help for sure. I ask you to try to help and to report to me on what is achieved.[64]

Having received bread, the peasants replied: 'We, those authorized, returning home to Samara Gubernia, attest that the centre really does offer special care to overcome great hunger and calamity and that our great leader Lenin took close to his heart all the needs of the suffering peasantry.'[65] As regards the traditional supplicatory and emotional rhetoric of this response, it is unclear how far Soviet leaders were able to deal critically with this form of positive popular feedback. Surely this sort of discourse was intoxicating for a nascent regime clinging to recently won power. The act of petitioning, on the surface at least, is an integrative act, a celebration of power, acknowledging the government's authority in its ability and duty to respond, and presented an impression of popular acceptance when help was granted. This perception, on the part of the leaders at least, perhaps reduced the pressure on them to gain legitimacy through other methods such as representative Soviet assemblies.

Yet the difficulty lies in ascertaining how authentic these expressions of gratitude and loyalty were, whether Lenin's 'living link' was reality or illusion. In his critical analysis of naive monarchism, James C. Scott argued that contact between the powerless and powerful is laden with deception. The powerless feign deference as a mechanism to realize their objectives without summoning the wrath of the authorities through open resistance or criticism. Subordinates construct public (loyal) transcripts in dialogues with power, and hidden (disloyal) transcripts 'spoken behind the back of the dominant'.[66] Was the system of petitioning a genuine connection between government and governed, a safety valve which shored-up the stability of the tsarist and Soviet governments, a shared discourse to alleviate grievances or a superficial and disingenuous mirage which made for a brittle and deceptive kind of ballast? Perhaps the Soviet subjectivities school would offer a more optimistic interpretation of the performance of 'speaking Bolshevik' found in petitions.[67]

Either way, petitioning as a significant form of political participation continued to expand throughout the remainder of the Soviet period. Petitions to Nikita Khrushchev and Leonid Brezhnev were relatively 'more direct and critical, but contained the same elements: beliefs in an impartial ruler and complaints about unlawful local officials.'[68] Indeed, the tradition of popular petitioning surely lay beneath the explosion of public opinion under Gorbachev's glasnost and survived the collapse of the USSR, remaining a key feature of authoritarian state-society dynamics in Russia's 'managed democracy' today.[69]

Thus, the explanation of the emergence of Soviet authoritarianism is more complex than the simple ill-intentions of any power-hungry leader or the direct and inevitable result of an inherently repressive ideological dogma, or even solely due to the tumultuous context of civil war and dislocation in this period. While practical circumstances mattered, elements of traditional Russian political culture, such as petitioning helped shape the way modern socialist ambitions, rooted in a flexible Marxist philosophy, played out in practice. Interesting to explore would be the dynamic of how the traditional supplicatory, individual 'proshenie' developed into, on occasion, the assertive, collective demands of the rarer 'trebovanie' or 'petitsiia', in 1905 for example, or when the unresponsiveness of the Soviet authorities to dissidents' quiet and direct personal appeals led to their penning of open protest letters and petitions in support of arrested intellectuals. Only much wider investigation of the wealth of archival material relating to petitioning in Imperial and Soviet Russia, and indeed in the Provisional Government period, over the long duree, could offer fresh answers to the larger questions of state–society relations raised in this chapter.

CHAPTER 5
THE COMMUNIST PARTY AND THE LATE 1930s SOVIET DEMOCRACY CAMPAIGNS: ORIGINS AND OUTCOMES
Yiannis Kokosalakis

In February 1935, the Central Committee (TsK) of the All-Union Communist Party issued a statement announcing that it had instructed its prominent member and head of government V. N. Molotov to address the Seventh Congress of Soviets with some recommendations regarding necessary amendments to the country's constitution. These would be directed at democratizing the Soviet electoral system and reforming the USSR's institutions to reflect the social transformations it had undergone since the initiation of the First Five-Year Plan (FYP). Over the following months, a commission composed of the party's greatest luminaries and headed personally by Stalin drafted an entirely new constitution extending the suffrage to previously disenfranchised groups and providing for secret, multi-candidate elections. At the same time, in 1936 a public discussion campaign unfolded through all major press outlets, encouraging Soviet citizens to read, discuss and comment on the draft. Nevertheless, in December 1937, a mere week before the first elections to be held under the new constitution, *Pravda* announced that communist candidates would run in the elections in a single bloc with non-partyists, effectively reneging on the party's earlier commitment to contestability. Moreover, instead of a turning point for socialist democracy, the year 1937 has since become synonymous with political violence as the campaign of repression initiated in the end of the preceding year reached its crescendo in the mass NKVD operations of late 1937.

Because of the combination of these facts, traditional scholarship regarded the introduction of a new constitution as a propaganda move on the part of the Soviet leadership, intended to present a more positive image to its own people and the public opinion of foreign democratic states, within the context of a deteriorating international environment.[1] Revisionist historiography offered an alternative interpretation, which nevertheless still posited ulterior motives behind the campaigns. Highlighting the amount of effort put in by party leaders in developing the draft constitution, as well as the fact that democratization campaigns were initiated along similar lines within the trade-union and Communist Party apparatuses, revisionist scholars argued that promoting public participation was amongst the genuine intentions of the Soviet leadership. Democratization was pursued by the centre with the intention of channelling popular anger against powerful regional officials or oppositionists lurking within the state and party apparatus. It was only after losing control of the process that the leadership applied the brakes on the campaign and reverted to the status quo ante.[2]

This chapter ultimately offers a different interpretation arguing that the decision to introduce a new constitution, as well as the attendant party and trade-union initiatives, is best seen as a return to the institutional experimentation of the early years of Soviet power. Much as in the immediate post-revolutionary period, the party leadership attempted to develop political structures consistent with its communist ideological worldview, within which popular participation in the running of the state had always been a central goal. In both cases, considerations of security and political stability drove the leadership to moderate its reform agenda. It will be shown that these retreats were followed by inward-focused attempts to promote political participation amongst the party rank and file, as a substitute for the more ambitious goal of involving the whole people in the business of government.

The argument will proceed in three parts. First, an account will be given of Lenin's early reflections and subsequent discussions amongst the Bolsheviks regarding the appropriate relationship between party, state and society, with a focus on the role played therein by the concept of democracy. It will be shown that the settlement on the one-party system was followed by an attempt to make the party more closely linked and more representative of the Soviet citizenry. Second, the framing and conduct of the campaigns of the late 1930s will be examined in order to demonstrate their connection to earlier attempts at institutional development. Finally, it will be shown that while the soviet campaign fizzled out, attempts to reform the functioning of the party apparatus continued. In 1939, the 18th Party Congress adopted new Rules, strengthening the institutional standing of primary party organizations (PPOs) and maintaining the commitment to multi-candidate elections. Significantly, these did take place and continued thereafter until the German invasion in 1941.

Origins: From commune-state to party-state

Written in hiding, Lenin's pamphlet on *The State and Revolution* engaged with the ideas of Marx and Engels to consider the role of the state during the course of and after the victory of a socialist revolution, thus addressing an important gap in Marxist theory. The essence of Lenin's argument was that state power was an organized form of coercion serving to enforce the rule of one social class over another. In bourgeois society, the state guaranteed the exploitative power of capitalists over the working class. Thus, in liberal democracies, working people may be free to elect representatives, but ultimately policy will be determined by the interests of the owners of capital.

Denouncing liberal constitutionalism as a sham, the Bolshevik leader outlined his vision of a polity modelled on the Paris Commune, where working people would run their own affairs according to a simple system of elected and recallable delegates. Although to establish this system it would be necessary to employ coercive measures against members and agents of the capitalist class, the victory of the socialist revolution would eventually render state power obsolete, by abolishing the rule of the few over the many.[3]

The State and Revolution proposed a system of direct democracy that largely dismissed the necessity of organized bureaucracies as a relic of the era of class exploitation. Lenin insisted that in order to achieve this enormous social transformation, the existing state apparatus would have to be 'smashed' rather than simply taken over by the proletariat. Nevertheless, he argued, the modern state performed a number of administrative and accounting functions that the new revolutionary authority would have to reproduce and in that respect, it would be possible for workers to make limited use of the existing institutional structures of governance. To support this claim, Lenin relied on a distinction, drawn by Marx, between a lower and a higher phase of communism.[4]

In the first phase, the task of the proletariat was to destroy the power of the capitalist class by smashing the core of its state apparatus in the form of the army, police and the upper echelons of the civil service. At the same time, workers would have to further develop the administrative-accounting functions of state power, democratizing them through the active involvement of the broad masses in the daily business of public administration and accounting over the production and distribution of goods. It was only after 'the vast majority' of society had successfully assumed the tasks of 'governing the state' that the highest phase of communism could begin. There would no longer be a need for a distinct apparatus to make and enforce decisions, these powers having been dispersed amongst the population as a whole. The state would thus 'wither away'.[5]

In writing *State and Revolution*, Lenin established two fundamental principles in Soviet political thought. First, state power was defined as inherently coercive and class-based. To the extent then that the working class would maintain a state apparatus after coming to power, it would be to repress social elements that undermined its rule. Second, democracy was conceived as being central to the revolutionary process. However, Lenin's vision of democracy had little to do with the notion of individual citizens choosing between proposed political alternatives. Instead, Lenin understood democracy as the ability of citizens to collectively supervise and exercise state power. These ideas would exert strong influence over the conduct of the democratization campaigns of the late 1930s.

The proletariat as a class remains the chief political subject throughout *State and Revolution*. Lenin remained silent on the place of specific political formations in the new order, including that of his own Bolshevik Party. The issue was first seriously broached in an article titled *Will the Bolsheviks Hold State Power?* written weeks before the October uprising. Responding to critics suggesting that the Bolshevik programme was mere posturing in the context of the crisis gripping the Russian Republic, Lenin restated his views on the soviets as the kernel of the workers' state.[6] But in a crucial passage, he argued the following:

> We know that every unskilled labourer, every kitchen-maid cannot right now join in state governance. In this we agree [with other parties]. But we differ [...] in that we demand an immediate break with the prejudice that only the rich and

bureaucrats from rich families can run the state. [...] *Conscious workers must lead*, but they are able to draw into the task of governance the masses of toilers and the oppressed.[7]

Several pages later, Lenin added that 'workers have formed a party of a quarter million people to take control and set in motion the state apparatus in a planned manner.'[8] He thus qualified the argument set out in *State and Revolution* with the idea that the transition to the kind of participatory governance envisioned therein would have to be led by the most politically conscious of workers organized as a party, that is the Bolsheviks. The key task of this leadership would be to 'demonstrate to [toilers] in practice that they themselves need to set about [...] distributing bread, all food, milk, clothing, accommodation.'[9]

Lenin's article foreshadowed two fundamental traits of the Soviet political system: leadership by the Communist Party and a social conception of citizenship emphasizing the provision of welfare rights as a fundamental aspect of the Soviet social contract. These principles underlay one of Lenin's most candid statements on the increasingly authoritarian direction taken by the early Soviet state after the October Revolution.

His pamphlet on *The Immediate Tasks of Soviet Power* was published in April 1918, a month after the signing of a peace treaty with Imperial Germany, as the civil war was rapidly gathering pace. Asserting that having 'conquered Russia from the rich for the poor' workers had to 'learn how to govern Russia', Lenin went on to argue that the pressing task facing the Soviet state was the elementary 'maintaining of sociality' by providing for public order and rudimentary economic growth in the disintegrating country. He declared 'accounting, no skiving, economizing, no stealing, being disciplined' to be the slogans of the day, denouncing those who opposed them as 'lackeys of the bourgeoisie' who 'thrive on destruction and brutalization'.[10]

The significance of the *Tasks* lies in the recognition of the need for organized hierarchies and coercion as tools of governance beyond the suppression of the 'tiny minority of exploiters' outlined in *State and Revolution*, thus marking a considerable retreat from the commune-state ideal described in this earlier work. 'The construction of socialism requires orderly organization, but this requires coercion in the form of dictatorship. There is no plausible outcome for Russia other than a dictatorship by [White general] Kornilov or the proletariat.'[11] Lenin went on to define dictatorship as 'iron authority [...] ruthless in its suppression of exploiters as well as hooligans', thus recognizing in the state a tool of public order as well as class struggle.[12] It was the task of the communist party to grasp this necessity: 'take leadership of the exhausted masses and lead them on the [...] path of labour discipline.'[13]

Lenin thus laid the intellectual groundwork for the subsequent institutional form of the Soviet state. At the same time however, Lenin warned against the dangers of 'bureaucratism', arguing that it would be necessary to complement the 'dictatorship' with comprehensive development of Soviet democracy in the sense of the 'harshest of controls from below', as well as his earlier recommendations for recallable deputies and popular involvement in the affairs of state.[14]

The common thread running through Lenin's writings is a social conception of citizenship that consisted in the right to have one's needs met and participate in the process by which this is achieved. Although the election of representatives had a place in Lenin's vision, it was only one component of his concept of democracy, which did not permit political alternatives to the construction of socialism. These principles found their legal expression in the Constitution of the Russian Soviet Federative Socialist Republic (RSFSR) adopted by the Fifth All-Russian Congress of Soviets in July 1918. Incorporating a Declaration of the Rights of the Labouring and Exploited Peoples, the constitution introduced social provisions such as access to education and equal civil rights for all nationalities, while explicitly depriving 'all individuals and groups of rights which could be used to the detriment of the revolution'.[15]

Although the 1918 Constitution did not provide for single-party rule, this became a fact following the failed coup launched by the Left Socialist Revolutionaries in July. Having ruled in coalition with the Bolsheviks until March 1918, the Left SRs had been the only other all-Russian party supporting Soviet power after October. Their dissolution following the suppression of their attempt to seize control of Moscow left the Bolsheviks in sole charge of the Soviet state apparatus. Over the next few years, Lenin's party extended its power over the former empire by routing its enemies on the battlefield and employing a combination of coercion and co-optation to neutralize the splintered groups supporting the Soviets in the periphery.[16]

In the extreme conditions of total war and without a legal opposition to act as a check on their power, the Bolsheviks were able to ignore the constitution's provisions for accountability, establishing a long-lasting pattern of untrammelled executive power. Nevertheless, the Bolsheviks also made sustained efforts to attract workers and peasants to the soviets as a means for the resolution of local conflicts and the provision of services. This policy allowed the Bolsheviks to build a coalition of poor peasants and ethnic minorities that gave the Red Army an edge over its enemies in the countryside, deciding the civil war in its favour.[17]

Single-party rule over a state apparatus accommodating public participation in its structures thus proved to be a winning strategy for Bolshevism. It is unsurprising therefore that the institutional architecture of the Soviet state was never seriously challenged from within the party's ranks. Despite the emergence of no less than four internal oppositions during the 1920s, none of the challengers disputed the party's monopoly on state power. What was at stake in these struggles was the way the party related to its working class and peasant constituencies.

The first of these conflicts reached a head in the party's Tenth Congress in 1921, when delegates from the Workers' Opposition and Democratic Centralist factions argued that the lack of separation between state and party was threatening to depoliticize the latter by transforming it into an appendage of the administrative apparatus. According to the oppositionists, communists should avoid relating to the broader masses by administrative channels, seeking instead to attract them to the socialist project by sharing their concerns and addressing their needs in practice. They did not however consider the legal existence of other parties as a desirable alternative. What vexed the oppositionists was the perceived distance that separated the Bolsheviks from the masses.[18]

Subsequent attempts to oppose the party leadership launched by Trotsky, Zinoviev and Bukharin were centred on economic policy and the extent to which this strengthened or undermined the party's relationship with workers and by extension, the prospects of socialism in the USSR. Although arguments around democracy were raised in the polemics exchanged during these power struggles, they remained within the boundaries of social citizenship and participatory administration set by Lenin and did not challenge single-party rule.[19]

Similarly, oppositionists criticized bureaucratic practices like the broad powers of appointment and co-optation enjoyed by local and central secretaries, as well as their ability to suppress dissent by controlling meeting agendas and access to the press. Nevertheless, none of the opposition leaders succeeded in articulating a political alternative consistent with the institutional limitations of the emerging party-state. At the same time, they hesitated to reject these outright, thus becoming vulnerable to accusations of recklessness and political dishonesty. Throughout the decade, Stalin and the central leadership were able to argue that the conditions that had led the party to its current mode of operation – including security threats and the low educational levels of members – were still in place. Aware of this, the opposition was thus acting in bad faith and threatened the very prospects of the full democratization it promoted.[20]

What is more, the leadership seemed to share many of the democratic instincts of their opponents in so far as these did not threaten the stability of the party apparatus. The idea of being closer to the masses was reflected in the mass recruitment campaign launched by the party in 1924. The 'Lenin Levy' swelled the party's ranks with industrial workers and succeeded in re-establishing its presence amongst the country's proletariat after the civil war.[21] The leadership launched several initiatives to provide new recruits with the skills necessary to participate in party life, including literacy classes and political education activities. Over the same period, attempts were made to provide channels for participation in public affairs by the broader masses, with 'production conferences' and factory newspapers becoming regular features of daily life in industrial enterprises throughout the country.[22]

Thus, the leadership could reasonably claim that its policies were laying the ground for the future democratization of the party and state apparatuses, albeit not at the speed demanded by oppositionists. This view was eloquently argued by district party secretary Martemian Riutin in a substantial *Pravda* article on 'The Party and internal party-democracy.' Riutin argued that the party's careful approach was yielding results, reflected in increased percentages of workers in responsible posts following recent elections at Moscow's party-cells. In his view, this demonstrated the following:

> Our internal party democracy rests on party unity and grows out of this unity. The more monolithic our party is, the more boldly we will implement […] internal party democracy. In contrast, the more attempts there are to shake the unity of our party ranks the more obstacles will be placed in the path of internal party

democracy. In practice [the] opposition leads not to internal party democracy, but to its weakening and debasement.[23]

The first years of Soviet power therefore saw the Bolsheviks retreat from Lenin's early vision of a self-governing commune-state, first to the idea of the need for some sort of tutelage and subsequently to a hard-headed acceptance of the reality of dictatorial power. Following victory in the civil war, concerns regarding the bureaucratization of the party and its separation from the class it claimed to represent were addressed by broadly successful campaigns to attract large numbers of workers to the ranks and train the new recruits in the principles of Bolshevism. The following decade, the party leadership would re-examine the constitutional foundations of the USSR under very different conditions.

Process: Mass discussion, elections, repression

In the years between the end of the power struggle within the party and the launching of the democratization campaigns in the mid-1930s, the USSR was transformed from an agrarian economy with rudimentary industry and an extensive private sector to an industrial power where the state owned and directed most economic activity. The sheer scale of the industrialization process as well as the violent repression of recalcitrant officials and peasants who resisted collectivization gave the First FYP the character of a military campaign, with one historian of the period describing it as 'the march for metal'.[24]

With the party leadership facing a series of acute crises culminating in the famine of 1932–3, the First FYP was not a period conducive to theoretical reflection and institutional experimentation. However, by the time the 17th Party Congress convened in January 1934, conditions in the country had begun to improve, with agriculture recovering and the Second FYP already under way committing significant resources to the production of consumer goods. The leadership had weathered the storm and Stalin was able to address Congress delegates in a tone that was both triumphant and conciliatory. In his report on behalf of the TsK, the General Secretary announced that the First FYP had made the socialist state-sector dominant in the economy, eliminating private capital and leaving co-operative collectivized agriculture as the only major economic activity not under state control.[25] This, he argued, had demonstrated in practice the correctness of the leadership line, leading most former oppositionists to repudiate their views and become loyal to the TsK. The party was 'united like never before.'[26] Its primary task from now on would be to overcome the 'remnants of capitalism' in the economy and in the 'conscience of people'.[27]

Molotov's address to the February 1935 Congress of Soviets regarding the need to amend the USSR's constitution was therefore made against the backdrop of the successful construction of the foundations of a socialist economy and society proclaimed the year before. Shortly after Molotov's announcement, *Pod Znamenem Marksizma (PZM)*, the country's main philosophical journal, led with an editorial on 'The New Era in the Development of Soviet Democracy.' The article linked the plans for constitutional revision with the successful completion of the substance of the tasks set by the 1918 Constitution of the RSFSR, namely the elimination of classes and the suppression of exploiters.[28] Citing Lenin's articles on the nature of revolutionary state power, the unnamed author went on to argue that the distinguishing trait of the Soviet state was that unlike states in the capitalist world, it was not a force alienated from society and standing in opposition to it. 'The Soviet apparatus does not stand above the masses, but merges with them.'[29]

To be sure, any resident of the Soviet countryside who had experienced collectivization knew that this merging was not a bloodless process. However, in addition to using state repression to pursue its objectives in the countryside, the party had also employed a combination of methods to rally the rural poor to its cause.[30] Thus, the message of the editorial was that having successfully wielded state power as a weapon to eliminate exploitative classes, the popular masses could now turn it into a channel of participation in public affairs. Similarly, an article on 'Legislation in conditions of proletarian democracy' appearing the same year in the jurisprudential review *Sovetskoe Gosudarstvo* (*SG*) highlighted the convocation of conferences of collective farmers and industrial workers to offer feedback on the implementation of laws. According to the author, public consultation was a fundamental element of the socialist legislative process, a manifestation of the diffusion of state power amongst the people Lenin had advocated in his revolutionary writings.[31]

At the same time as Soviet intellectuals were reintroducing the subject of socialist democracy into public discourse after a decade-long hiatus, the party leadership was developing a draft of the constitution that would give the appropriate legal form to the core institutions of the socialist state. Scholars who have studied the drafting process have stressed the time devoted to it as a sign of the seriousness with which the leadership viewed the project. From its first meeting in June 1935 to the release of the final Draft Constitution for public discussion on 12 June 1936, the drafting commission produced five drafts meticulously examined and edited personally by Stalin.[32] The topics considered by the commission covered standard constitutional provisions such as the separation of powers and delineation of jurisdictions, but also a number of issues arising from the Bolsheviks' social conception of citizenship, including a broad range of welfare rights that were eventually incorporated into the final draft.[33] Significantly, the drafting process also saw the first attempt to establish a legal basis for the party's ubiquitous social presence. Like the 1924 Constitution then in force, the first working drafts included no mention of the Bolsheviks or any other party. It was by Stalin's personal edit that an article mentioning the party was included in the Soviet fundamental law.

Article 126 guaranteed citizens' rights to voluntary association in, among others, trade unions, youth organizations and sports clubs, in the interests of promoting the 'organisational initiative and political activity of the popular masses.' It continued as follows: 'The most active and conscientious people amongst workers and toilers unite in the communist party, the vanguard of toilers in their struggle for the victory of communism and the leading force of all toilers' organizations in the USSR.'[34] Stalin thus came up with a legal formula which captured all of the basic parameters of Lenin's thinking and Bolshevik practice regarding the relationship between state, society and the party in socialism. The state was constitutionally obliged to promote various forms of activism, leadership of which was assigned to the Communist Party, which was thus established as a mediating institution between society and the state. In the final draft released for public consultation, the slightly indeterminate term 'Communist Party' was dropped for the official name All-Union Communist Party (Bolsheviks) and the segment on its leadership edited to extend to 'state as well as social organizations', thus formally transforming the country's ruling party into an essential feature of its institutional architecture.[35]

Despite being a significant development in law, the formalization of one-party rule attracted little attention in the mass discussion that followed the publication of the Draft Constitution of the USSR in June 1936. Instead, both in press coverage and the thousands of public meetings organized by party and other organizations, the main theme of the campaign was the extensive democratization of the Soviet state made possible by the successful construction of socialism.[36] This was reflected in the electoral system set out in Chapter XI of the Constitution, which provided for secret, direct and universal elections to the soviets, rescinding the exclusion from suffrage of priests, former white officers, kulaks and other hostile classes in force since 1918.

Stalin publicly indicated the importance he attached to electoral reform on several occasions. In an interview with the American journalist Roy Howard, he predicted that competitive elections would lead to very 'lively' campaigns. Multi-candidate elections would place a weapon in the hands of the people against incompetent and corrupt officials. 'Have you improved housing conditions? Are you a bureaucrat? Have you helped to make [...] our lives more cultured?' would be only some of the criteria by which the General Secretary expected the Soviet people to judge their candidates.[37] Several months later, Stalin addressed the 8th Congress of Soviets stressing the strength of socialism in the USSR and dismissing reservations about the introduction of universal suffrage. Former kulaks and Whites were now too weak to threaten Soviet power and any gains they might make were certain to be due to the party's own failures.[38]

In his interventions Stalin was essentially arguing directly from Lenin, framing elections as a form of participation in administration and provision of services, rather than contests between competing political projects. Similarly, his insistence that former class enemies had been rendered powerless echoed Lenin's prediction that the need for coercive measures would recede as the first phase of communism progressed.

The following year, party intellectuals picked up this line of argument, further elaborating on the significance of the coming elections. Throughout 1937, major journals carried several articles extolling the virtues of the Soviet political system over bourgeois parliamentarism. Writing for *SG*, the legal scholar R. Vol'skii argued that the new constitution represented the realization of the universalist aspirations expressed in the 1776 Virginia Declaration of Rights and the 1789 French revolutionary Declaration of the Rights of Man and the Citizen. In contrast to the capitalist world, where democracy was limited in practice by exclusion from the suffrage based on race, sex and property qualifications, the USSR was argued to be the first country to extend full, substantive political rights to the entirety of its population.[39] Along similar lines, an editorial of *PZM* provided a broad review of undemocratic practices in parliamentary systems ranging from the United States to Japan, including gerrymandering, aristocrat-dominated upper chambers and colonial exploitation. According to the editorial, the formal abolition of all democratic rights by fascist dictatorships was but the extension of these practices to their logical conclusion.[40]

The electoral dimension of democratic politics was therefore a central element of the way in which the constitution campaign was framed by the party leadership. It is on this stark contradiction between the public commitment of the leadership to extensive democratization of the Soviet political system and the ultimate decision to conduct uncontested elections that the interpretation of the constitution as a propaganda exercise has been based. There is, however, no documentary evidence to support this view. Instead, as J. Arch Getty has demonstrated, the archival record suggests that Stalin was personally committed to the elections as a way to streamline the state apparatus and curb the power of regional leaders. The General Secretary sprung the prospect of contested elections on local party bosses at the June 1936 TsK Plenum which met to discuss the constitution draft. The document appears to have shocked TsK members so much that Stalin's speech on the draft was met with dumbfounded silence.[41] Over the next months, the regions showered the centre with reports of reenergized political activity by kulaks and other counter-revolutionaries seeing the coming elections as an opportunity to strike against Soviet power. Stalin insisted on going through with the elections and the conflict reached a head in the February–March 1937 TsK Plenum.

Famous as a prelude to the third Moscow Trial due to its condemnation of Nikolai Bukharin, the plenum was equally remarkable for the stark way in which it demonstrated the breakdown in the relationship between the centre and the regions. Rather than walking-back from its elections goals, the leadership doubled down on the offensive, with Leningrad regional secretary and close Stalin ally Andrei Zhdanov announcing that the principle of multi-candidate, secret-ballot elections would be extended to the party, in order to break-up 'family-circles' of corrupt officials.[42] Apparently spontaneously, trade-union head Nikolai Shvernik suggested that a similar democratization campaign be extended to the Soviet trade-union apparatus.[43]

By the summer of 1937, a combination of international developments, NKVD reports and regional leaders' manoeuvring appears to have convinced Stalin that the Soviet Union was facing a grave security threat. The mass operations unleashed against former kulaks and foreign nationals led to hundreds of thousands of arrests and executions, a scale of violence reminiscent of the civil war and dekulakization.[44] At the same time, the party, soviet and trade-union democratization campaigns were exposing large networks of corruption that implicated most of the country's regional leadership. By the time mass repression was wound up in early 1938, almost all of the party's regional secretaries had been arrested.[45]

There is no space here to examine the full range of factors behind the violence of 1937–8. It is worth remembering however that a decade earlier, Stalin and his allies had shielded regional leaders from the opposition's scathing critiques of their methods of rule. That Stalin was now responding to similar accusations from the base with violence against local party bosses suggests that he believed their power was no longer serving the interests of the Soviet system.

There is much to recommend the interpretation of the democratization campaigns as an attempt by Stalin to reassert control over the party-state apparatus. Nevertheless, had power dynamics been Stalin's only motivation for the campaigns, we would expect these to fizzle out after the regional cliques had been destroyed. Indeed, it was during this period that the decision to conduct the Soviet elections as single-candidate confirmation affairs was made.[46] This, however, was not the end of the story.

Outcomes: The 18th Congress and new party rules

On 19 January 1938, *Pravda* published a TsK resolution bearing the wordy title 'On the mistakes of party organisations regarding expulsions of communists from the party, on the formal-bureaucratic treatment towards the expelled from VKP (b), and on measures for the elimination of these faults.' The directive attacked 'false vigilance' as 'counter-revolutionary in substance', an enemy tactic intended to spread panic and destroy honest cadres. Denouncing 'slander' and 'mass expulsions' as a form of 'wrecking in party organizations,' the resolution issued a three-month deadline for the completion of all outstanding appeals and listed ten measures to be immediately taken against 'over-vigilance', including the provision that none of the expelled should lose their jobs before their appeal process was over.[47]

Viewed against the backdrop of the mass repression unleashed the previous year, the TsK resolution was a signal that the leadership was applying the brakes on the campaign. At the same time, the condemnation of 'over-vigilance' increased the pressure on incumbent functionaries, for whom false accusations had been a reliable means of deflecting criticism.[48] Although the leadership was careful not to indicate that the hunt for enemies was over, criticism of slander remained a central theme in *Pravda* editorials and reporting throughout the year, with the second-page column on 'party life' carrying almost daily reports of individual cases of honest communists wrongfully denounced by careerist bureaucrats.[49] Another round of party elections announced in late March ushered in a renewed torrent of critical articles in *Pravda* and the regional press, this time regarding the failure of local organizations to organize electoral contests in line with the provisions set by the TsK in its February–March plenum the previous year, while at the same time ensuring the meaningful participation of the rank and file in the entire process.[50]

The following year, electoral accountability and members' rights became the main pillars of a new phase in the party democratization campaign. In January 1939, a TsK plenary session finalized the agenda for the party's 18th Congress held in March. Among the main items was a report by Andrei Zhdanov on the updating of the party's governing statues, the Party Rules. Published in *Pravda* in early February, Zhdanov's theses proposed a range of changes to the Rules, framed as a response to far-reaching transformations in Soviet social structure. Key among these was the strengthening of the status of PPOs, the return to the principle of electability of all responsible posts, the abolition of differential recruitment procedures depending on social origin and most strikingly, the declaration that mass party purges were no longer acceptable practice.[51]

Following the publication of Zhdanov's proposed amendments to the Rules, the TsK initiated an extensive discussion on the text. District committees were instructed to organize meetings and return detailed reports of the recommendations made by the rank and file.[52] Regional and central party press outlets reported closely on the progress of the consultation amongst the grassroots, often attacking local organizers who failed to elicit sufficient engagement.[53]

Articles published in *Pravda*'s pre-Congress bulletins indicate that members responded actively to the TsK initiative. Several pieces were published recommending concrete measures to safeguard members' rights, including making the unjust application of disciplinary measures a disciplinary offense in itself.[54] Many contributors also offered suggestions for a further clarification of the powers of PPOs vis-à-vis state administration.[55] Nevertheless, despite the customary praise heaped upon the leadership in many of the contributions, most pieces took issue with at least some aspect of the proposals.

Although entrenching members' rights and democratizing the apparatus were invariably applauded as political goals of the utmost importance, the relaxation of recruitment standards proposed in Zhdanov's theses attracted the suspicions of several communists. Opposition to the abolition of differential recruitment was strong enough that three Leningrad party secretaries had to pen a joint article defending it.[56] A worker from a Kiev factory suggested that recommendations for new members should come from communists with at least five years in the party, rather than the three stipulated in the draft. One Klimovich wrote against the amendment of the definition of a member from someone who has 'mastered the Party programme' to someone who accepts it.[57] On a similar note, V. Shelomovich, head of the Moscow City Party Committee agitprop department, argued that the Rules should mandate that cadres in elected posts be well versed in theory, strong knowledge of Marxism–Leninism making the difference between good leaders and petty bureaucrats.[58] At the same time, other contributors offered a diametrically opposite view, recommending even more drastic relaxations in recruitment practices, such as shorter candidacy periods and the abolition of the category of 'sympathizers' in favour of an expanded candidate membership.[59]

The discussion of Zhdanov's theses was the most extensive public self-reflection the party had engaged in since the debates of the 1920s. Communists from all over the USSR were writing to *Pravda* to weigh in on a debate that was substantially similar to those of more than a decade earlier. Underlying the public dialogue was the old theme of the appropriate relationship between the party and broader Soviet society. The leadership had proposed a reduction of the distance between the vanguard and the masses, eliciting apprehension amongst some communists while being viewed as insufficiently bold by others.

Party leaders underscored the deep significance of the proposed Rules changes in their speeches at the 18th Congress, explicitly linking the amendments with the social transformations reflected in the 1936 Constitution. Stalin began the delivery of the TsK report with a grim assessment of international affairs in the context of the 'second imperialist war already in progress,' stating bluntly that war was 'in the order of the day.'[60] The grave security threat facing the USSR was thus introduced as the backdrop of the General Secretary's address. This lends particular significance to the fact that, in addition to a detailed overview of the country' economic progress during the Second FYP, Stalin devoted a large part of his report to 'theoretical questions'. First amongst these was the question of the state and its purpose in socialism.

Stalin declared that it was now time for the party to engage with the fundamental questions posed by Lenin in *State and Revolution* and continue the theoretical work that the venerated leader had left unfinished. He offered an overview of the history of the Soviet state which he divided into two phases. First, from the October Revolution to the 'liquidation of exploitative classes,' when the main function of the socialist state was to defend against imperialist aggression and to put down the resistance of the dispossessed bourgeoisie and its allies. The second phase of Stalin's schema was that initiated by the successful completion of the First FYP and crowned by the adoption of the 1936 Constitution. State power in the second phase was chiefly applied to the organization of the socialist economy and national defence. 'The function of military repression within the country' had already 'withered away', with imperialist encirclement being the only factor preventing the rest of the state apparatus from following suit. The repressive arm of the state was now turned primarily outwards rather than inwards, even though agents of hostile foreign powers could be recruited amongst the remnants of the liquidated exploiter classes.[61]

Given Stalin's close involvement with the mass operations of the previous years, the extent to which he was truly convinced that threats to the Soviet state were now mainly external is questionable, although it is possible he believed that the last round of repression had finally broken the back of home-grown counter-revolution. Whatever the case, the significance of Stalin's speech lies in that it provided an overarching theoretical framework for the institutional experimentation the leadership had engaged in since the constitution drafting process. Reaching back to the founding text of Marxist-Leninist state theory, Stalin essentially argued that the first phase of communism identified in the *State and Revolution* was coterminous with the construction of socialism, achieved in the USSR after the success of the First FYP. With exploiting classes liquidated and the lines between workers, collectivized peasants and highly skilled personnel ('intellectuals') becoming blurred, the objective conditions had been put in place for the transition to a classless society even though the ultimate prize of the withering away of the state remained some way off.

Stalin thus placed all of the political campaigns of the previous years within a single narrative. The constitution, democratization and the campaign against 'over-vigilance' were nothing less than aspects of the maturation of communism in the USSR. These themes were further expanded on by responses to Stalin's speech by other party luminaries, including secret police chief Lavrentii Beria who railed against the habit of misperceiving incompetence as sabotage.[62]

One week later, Andrei Zhdanov delivered his report on the 'changes to the Rules of VKP (b),' grounding his argument on the same premises as Stalin. According to the Leningrad secretary, the successful completion of 'the world-historical tasks of the construction of socialism and the defence of the gains of victorious socialism from capitalist encirclement and its agents in the USSR demanded from the Party a radical restructuring of party-political and organisational work.' Zhdanov went on to remind Congress delegates that changes in the Rules had always accompanied radical developments in the country's political life, such as the introduction of NEP, the beginning of industrialization and its successful completion.[63] All of the major changes proposed were dictated by the progress of Soviet society towards communism.

Thus, Zhdanov argued, the abolition of differential recruitment reflected the fact that there were no longer any classes hostile to socialism in the USSR. It would be absurd for the party to put so much effort to liberate the working class, only to penalize those of its members who had risen to prominent positions in industry. Similarly, party purges were to be forbidden in the future because those hostile elements that did exist within the party were no longer representatives of a broader social challenge to working-class power, but rather petty traitors and foreign agents who had to be individually discovered and prosecuted.[64]

The full democratization advocated by Zhdanov's theses was similarly grounded in the social transformations of the past few years. The introduction of direct, secret and equal elections to the soviets was a step in the greater involvement of the masses in the running of the state. However, Zhdanov went on to add that in order for the party to lead this process it was necessary that its organizations themselves would first:

> [I]mplement fully in their internal affairs the fundamentals of democratic centralism, that all Party organs become electable, that criticism and self-criticism are developed [...] to their full extent, that accountability of Party organisations before the Party rank-and-file becomes fully activated.[65]

Zhdanov thus framed the party democratization campaign as both an extension of its soviet precedent and a precondition for its successful long-term implementation. He then went on to remind Congress delegates of the February–March 1937 TsK plenum, which had exposed the fact that regional leaders had been 'violating Party Rules with impunity' to avoid accountability before their organizations. The leadership had initiated the party democratization campaign precisely to remedy this situation. According to Zhdanov, the success of the campaign had been demonstrated by the fact that the renewal rate in the composition of party committees after the internal elections of 1938 ranged from 35 per cent to 60 per cent.[66]

The political signal of Zhdanov's speech could not have been missed by the members of the party elite in attendance. The senior Bolshevik was indicating that the leadership had no intention to restore the status quo following the decimation of the preceding two years. To be sure, the abolition of the purge suggested a more predictable manner of conducting disciplinary affairs in the future, but Zhdanov's insistence on accountability before the rank and file was a sign that the leadership remained unwilling to shield its subordinates from grassroots pressure. Instead of a one-off strike to debilitate specific regional power networks, the campaign was an attempt to permanently recast the internal dynamics of the apparatus.

Perhaps the strongest evidence of the seriousness with which Stalin and his allies regarded the campaign lies in the fact that they never backtracked on their commitment to multi-candidate elections. Archival records from Zhdanov's own Leningrad region indicate that contests took place shortly after their announcement at the February–March 1937 Plenum and continued doing so until the German invasion of 1941.[67] In some of the smaller organizations, such as those on the ships of the Baltic Fleet, finding enough candidates often turned out to be a challenge, with nominees ending up on the ballot against their will in order to comply with the multi-candidate rule.[68] In very large organizations, elections were much more complicated affairs. As per the new Rules, these held their own delegated conferences to elect their leading organs, thus having to conduct multi-tier contests. The 3,000-member strong PPO of the enormous Kirov machine-building plant conducted three such conferences in the period 1938–41, in which all leading posts were elected individually in contested elections.[69]

Conclusion

In the introduction to his monograph on the political thought of Joseph Stalin, Erik van Ree made a rather counterintuitive point for a Western audience. When, in his various pronouncements, Stalin described the USSR as the most democratic country in the world, he was not only being honest, but also factually correct. This is because Stalin's concept of democracy was derived from the Marxist–Leninist ideological canon and therefore encompassed a variety of conditions not usually associated with the term in Western liberal thought, but present in the Soviet Union.[70] The preceding pages have offered an interpretation of the democratization campaigns launched in the mid-1930s that is in line with this view.

The contours of Bolshevik thought on socialist state–society relations were set by Lenin in 1917, when he developed a notion of citizenship as welfare and democracy as participation. Single-party rule was not inherent in this framework, but it was incipient in the notion of communists as the most politically advanced workers guiding society through an objective world-historical transition. After the Bolshevik monopoly of power had become a fact during the civil war, none among themselves challenged this outcome. The party, it was assumed, would have to lead the fight against counter-revolution and keep the economy running until society matured into the commune envisioned by Lenin.

Introducing a new constitution in 1936 was an attempt to pick up again the thread of institutional experimentation and do away with some of the more embarrassing practices of Soviet public administration while revitalizing the bonds between party, state and society. Stalin's decision to codify in law the party's control over the state indicates that he believed that the conditions that had led to one-party rule were still in place. It seemed possible however to take some steps towards the commune ideal by reforming the state. Just like the civil war had forced Lenin to retreat from some of his more utopian views in favour of authoritarian rule, a combination of security concerns and regional recalcitrance led Stalin to decide against pushing through with the most substantial of the proposed reforms, contested elections to state organs.

Instead, the leadership launched a campaign of violence against counter-revolutionaries in the country and competing power centres within the apparatus. At the same time, Andrei Zhdanov headed a campaign to democratize the party mirroring that of the constitution. In this case, the reforms were more substantial than cosmetic, with elections taking place on several occasions and the party attempting to make itself more representative of Soviet society by abolishing class-based recruitment barriers. Once again, the leadership responded to the frustration of its revolutionary plans by reforming the party itself.

This is not necessarily inconsistent with previous scholarly interpretations of Stalin's motivations for the campaigns. However, these must be seen as contingent, rather than necessary. Having initiated the project, Stalin plausibly tried to use the constitution to gain good will abroad. It is nevertheless difficult to sustain the argument that diplomacy was his main motivation, given that the party campaign offered little advantages in that direction and the Soviet press continued to denounce liberalism as the antechamber to fascism. Similarly, there can be no doubt that democratization was used as a cudgel with which to crush regional elites but again, the continuation of the party campaign after 1938 is harder to explain on this basis alone.

Instead, the democratization campaigns are best viewed as an ambitious political project inspired by Marxist–Leninist ideology, a major aspect of which foundered on security threats and perceptions thereof. What this chapter has shown is that although not spectacular, the campaigns did have some appreciable effects on the functioning of the Soviet party-state.

PART III
INTERNAL PARTY DEMOCRACY

CHAPTER 6
TROTSKY AND THE QUESTIONS OF AGENCY, DEMOCRACY AND DICTATORSHIP IN THE USSR, 1917–40
Ian D. Thatcher

Trotsky more than any other Russian communist is famous as participant and political analyst and historian of the October Revolution and its aftermath. In the history of the USSR and in the emergence of Stalin's rule, Trotsky enjoys the reputation of honesty against his rival's intrigue and of a concern for democracy compared to Stalin's ruthless determination to establish a personal dictatorship. The picture of a more noble, more intelligent and more decent communist beaten by an unscrupulous backroom manager was central to Isaac Deutscher's famous trilogy.[1] The combined impact of Trotsky and Deutscher's work, both born out of political commitment and passion, on subsequent scholarship cannot be underestimated.[2] This is especially so in considerations of Stalin and Stalinism.

This chapter will examine several inter-linked questions. First, how did Trotsky conceive democracy in the Russian Revolution post-1917? When did democracy first become a pressing issue for him? Was this largely within the context of the party or did he have a broader conception of pluralism that included wider societal rights and freedoms? Second, what did Trotsky identify as the agents of democracy and democratization? This could be partly a question of class – in the Preface to the *History of the Russian Revolution*, for example, he wrote of revolution as the 'forcible entry of the masses in the realm of rulership over their own destiny'.[3] But this leaves the important issue of how would the workers' democratic will be expressed institutionally and procedurally? Third, how does Trotsky understand the rise and continuing rule of Stalin? Is it a failing of the working class that proved itself incapable of fulfilling its liberating mission? Is it a failure of the international revolution without which Trotsky's theory of permanent revolution had since its first inception at the time of the first Russian Revolution stated that an isolated revolution would degenerate?[4] Is there ever an acknowledgement of the personal factor, of Stalin? At key points in his writings, after all, Trotsky points to the role of the individual and lends this a prominence above all other considerations. In a diary entry of the mid-1930s for example, he makes the October Revolution conditional upon Lenin's presence.[5]

Above all this chapter contributes to the volume's central thesis that the themes of democracy and dictatorship coexisted in Bolshevik thought from the Revolution's inception. Trotsky was a passionate advocate of the dictatorship of the proletariat, arguing that it offered opportunities to the workers that encapsulated key democratic gains. It was a higher form of democracy as a dictatorship. Trotsky was also aware of the fragile nature of communist rule. It could degenerate by factors such as the failure of the revolution to internationalize. He worried about the impact of Russian backwardness. In the First World War he cautioned against taking power in a country ravaged by conflict. Yet, in 1917, his revolutionary optimism prevailed, but success was far from guaranteed. Should the correlation of forces turn negative, dictatorship could triumph over democracy, and the struggle for communism would begin afresh.

Dictatorship and democracy in the Soviet State, 1917–22

Russian politics after the fall of Nicholas II is largely interpreted as a crisis of state power.[6] The Provisional Government's failure to govern effectively, for example, is explained by its lack of authority.[7] The Bolsheviks, in contrast, are often acknowledged as the force that could and did re-establish a central executive power or *vlast'*.[8] If this was the pressing issue of the Russian Revolution, then we can say that in the early stages of this state-building project Trotsky was the advocate of centralization *par excellence*. He championed the class dictatorship of the proletariat as superior to the workings of formal democracy, that is rule by majority vote in contested elections, a free press, freedom of assembly, freedom of association and so on. Here we must take into account Trotsky's governmental portfolios and his career as a revolutionary. He was defending a process of change in which he had invested his political life. Nevertheless, this was not simply self-justification. Trotsky deserves our attention as theoretician and practitioner of revolution. He formulated the case for proletarian dictatorship against formal democracy in several ways.

First, for Trotsky, a revolution could not be carried out peacefully, via the ballot box. This was because Trotsky saw formal democracy as a mask for the class rule of the bourgeoisie. The capitalist class was expert at limiting choice to the advantage of the capitalist exploiters in so-called free elections. According to Trotsky, Marxists should well understand that at most parliamentary elections are only one aspect of a broader class conflict; they can never replace or neutralize the class struggle. There was zero possibility, on Trotsky's calculation, that the bourgeoisie would simply concede its class rule and privileges to a proletarian majority in an election, if such an outcome were possible. Given these definitions and assumptions, the defence of democracy undertaken by Second International socialists like Karl Kautsky had to be, for Trotsky, nothing less than a sell-out to the exploiters. Socialists who argued for the overthrow of capitalism via elections were in fact backing reactionary imperialism. They were, on Trotsky's understanding, social imperialists.[9]

Second, a revolution then was a violent overturn of the old order, a transfer of power from one class to another, in which the correlation of class forces would be decisive. The deciding factor would be which side could muster the most physical force. The key constituencies on the communist side, for Trotsky, were the advanced workers and their political leaders in the party vanguard. The correctness of the tactics of the communist revolutionaries could not be questioned at or held accountable to 'free elections', if for no other reason that it would be impossible to convene these in the conditions of the civil war that inevitably accompanies the power struggle between the proletariat and the bourgeoisie in a revolution. Thus, for example, in the midst of the Russian Civil War it would be foolish to demand of the communist authorities that they lay down arms and offer the opportunity of publicity and propaganda to counter-revolutionaries in competitive elections. All groups and forces deemed to be counter-revolutionary were to be suppressed by the class dictatorship of the proletariat, in which only workers and their allies would have electoral rights in elections to class-based institutions, the soviets. If anti-Bolsheviks were successfully repelled then this, for Trotsky, was sufficient evidence that the repression was justified, for only a class dictatorship that held the (silent) sympathy of the majority could hold on to power.[10] It is this outlook that conditioned Trotsky's response to events like the Kronstadt rebellion of the spring of 1921. A distinguished historian of the Russian Revolution has argued that the Kronstadt programme reveals a Soviet Russia in the grips of a tight dictatorship, lacking in basic guarantees of civil rights. To this historian's conclusion that the Soviet government was 'a system which did not reflect the will of the people',[11] Trotsky would no doubt respond 'which people' and 'in whose interests'? For Trotsky, individuals did not have value as individuals, but for what class interest they bore. Thus, the Kronstadt rebellion had to be supressed because it objectively served the imperialist cause.[12] The Soviet government, in contrast, as a conscious class dictatorship, offered genuinely advanced workers the most meaningful type of political opportunities for participation and representation in class-based soviets.[13]

Third, Trotsky viewed revolution as a historical necessity. In turn, History had issued clear lessons on the relationship between democratically elected parliaments and the forward march of the revolution: parliaments had limited progressive potential that quickly turned reactionary. In a revolutionary situation, if a parliament was not swept aside in a timely manner, then the revolution would fail, evident for instance in the failure of the Paris Commune to overturn the National Assembly. Arguing for a similar link between parliaments and the emergence of counter-revolution across the former Russian Empire in the Russian Civil War, Trotsky stated that the class essence of the 'democratically elected' Constituent Assembly condemned it to extinction. The event which some historians see as the 'end of the Russian Revolution'[14] was for Trotsky merely an opening skirmish, in which a reactionary talking shop that reflected backwardness and confusion had to be suppressed by a superior soviet democracy that was actively creating its own majority.[15]

Fourth, employing his understanding of Marxism, Trotsky argued that the root cause of revolution was a contradiction between the need of productive forces to expand and the property relations that were restricting the possibilities for economic growth. The fundamental task of the revolution was therefore correct economic leadership. In the imperialist epoch this meant centralization of the economy and to this all other goals, including the democratic demand of national self-determination, were subservient. There is thus a connection in Trotsky's thought at this time between economic and political centralization or between the economic and political class dictatorship.¹⁶ He emphasized that a single economic plan had to be imposed by compulsion and the compulsion would be provided by the dictatorship of the proletariat, 'i.e., the most ruthless form of state, which embraces the life of the citizens authoritatively in every direction.'¹⁷

A final consideration that underpinned Trotsky's explicit espousal of class dictatorship over formal democracy in the early Soviet period was his perception of the role of the Bolshevik party. Independent candidates notwithstanding, pluralist elections in the modern era entail multi-party lists. For Trotsky, only the Bolshevik party expressed the interests of the advanced workers and of History and was thus the only legitimate party of the revolutionary epoch. The class dictatorship of the proletariat demanded a vote for a single, Bolshevik party. There could not be a revolution plus a plurality of parties seeking election. The Bolshevik party had earned for itself the right to a single-party dictatorship by the facts that it had organized a highly open and democratic revolution,¹⁸ and then successfully defended and led the revolution:

> The exclusive role of the Communist Party under the conditions of a victorious proletarian revolution is quite comprehensible. The question is of the dictatorship of a class. In the composition of that class there enter various elements, heterogeneous moods, different levels of development. Yet the dictatorship pre-supposes unity of will, unity of direction, unity of action. By what other path then can it be attained? The revolutionary supremacy of the proletariat pre-supposes within the proletariat itself the political supremacy of a party, with a clear programme of action and a faultless internal discipline [...] the last word belongs to the Central Committee of the party. This affords extreme economy of time and energy, and in the most difficult and complicated circumstances gives a guarantee for the necessary unity of action. Such a regime is possible only in the presence of the unquestioned authority of the party, and the faultlessness of its discipline. Happily for the revolution, our party does possess in equal measure both of these qualities.¹⁹

Democratic Concerns, 1923–9

Having established the arguments for the one-party dictatorship and the central role of the Communist party, as well as leading the Red Army to victory, from the autumn of 1923 Trotsky began to voice grave concerns about the health of the inner-party regime. There thereby began a debate that remained confined largely to internal party correspondence, party meetings and public articles, pamphlets and books, which raged until Trotsky's eventual expulsion from the USSR. It involved the emergence of various alliances, including with former enemies Zinoviev and Kamenev in the United Opposition (1926–7). At no point did Trotsky the oppositionist come close to winning a majority vote in the party.

Trotsky linked poor policy choices across a range of issues to increasing bureaucratization of the Communist party. This was characterized by the control of the party by a narrow circle at the top that impacted negatively on each area of the party's operations. Bureaucracy was, he maintained, the mindless and unthinking carrying out of duties defined by superiors. It led directly to the separation of the bureaucracy from the party that it stood above and ruled over and of the state apparatus from the people, whom it ruled without any care about ordinary citizens' needs and interests. Most crucially, the combined effect of this was to kill the living link between the party and the advanced workers that was the key alliance needed, for Trotsky, to guarantee the revolution's progressive development.

The chief institution responsible for the threat to the party, according to Trotsky, was its Secretariat. It was the Secretariat that systematically took over the party from above, appointing local party secretaries, for example, on the basis of their loyalty to the Secretariat rather than because of competency for the post. The outcome was mismanagement across the system, as all too often unthinking lackeys paid little heed to the problems that required sensible resolution in cooperation with knowledgeable people on the ground. Instead, officials without any sense of responsibility made ill-informed choices that were enforced from on high. The effect of bureaucratically made policy was a worsening economic picture that understandably disgruntled both ordinary party members and the general population. This discontent worked its way into factionalism in the party. Rather than accept its own responsibility, the Secretariat then pointed to such factionalism as a sin to be eradicated by force, in this way reinforcing the unhealthy party regime that was at the root of all problems. Indeed, the bureaucracy used the terminology and methods of the revolution as a mask behind which it moved against the revolution itself, for example using a dictatorship over the proletariat to undermine the advanced workers who were the driving force of a genuine dictatorship of the proletariat. The rule of the bureaucracy was a reactionary dictatorship to smother a progressive dictatorship.

There was for Trotsky abundant evidence of the dire state of the party under the rule of the bureaucracy. There was, for example, the effective exclusion of comrades in the party's highest organs, including in the Central Committee and the Politburo, from meaningful involvement in decision-making. Trotsky felt this with obvious force as an individual. He charged that changes in military personnel, for example, were taken because of 'factional considerations' behind his back, rather than through an open and honest selection process in which the chief concern would be appointing those comrades best qualified for the job. The result was a marked deterioration of the military's effectiveness alongside the loss of the wisdom and experience of an Old Bolshevik upon policy.

The closing of legitimate and necessary avenues for positive engagement not only was true for Trotsky as an individual but also applied, he argued, to the party as a whole. Trotsky compared the active, debating party of the civil war period to the moribund party of late 1923 onwards in which the party's base was being excluded from meaningful participation in economic and political policy formation. This situation was strangling the party's creativity and especially that of its youth sections.

The Fate of the Bolshevik Revolution

Trotsky's chief political aims of the 1920s were therefore two-fold: (1) to fight against 'bureaucracy' of the party and (2) to defend and restore to the party the spirit of Bolshevism of the period 1917–22. He thought that this could be achieved via several measures.

Above all, the leading group had to realize the dire consequences of its control. The least painful route would be for it to surrender its claim to represent Old Bolshevism while in fact destroying it. Trotsky was requesting of the majority in the Central Committee that it voluntarily stand down under the banner of a sincere willingness to improve innerparty life. Second, there had to be a democratization of the party, by which Trotsky did not mean the application of 'formal rules' such as the holding of elections on a regular basis and attention to turnout and participation rates. Trotsky dismissed a merger of parliamentary rules to the party as 'margarine democracy'. For Trotsky, party democracy was about ensuring that two essential features were in operation: (1) the leading role of the Old Bolsheviks and (2) the interaction of the Old Bolsheviks with the youthful party base.[20] This was not to be unrestrained democratization then, but one set within limits – just sufficient freedom to preserve a certain party spirit, a *zeitgeist*, that would protect the party against 'intransigency and degradation'.[21]

There were several weaknesses to Trotsky's analysis of party bureaucratization. First, there was no profound definition of what was meant by 'bureaucracy' and 'democratization'. On the latter, for example, there was no consideration of how to ensure freedom of expression outside of formal guarantees. Second, there was little attention paid to the forces that produce 'bureaucratization' or 'democratization'. Were these a product of underlying socio-economic trends or a consequence of the civil war, for instance? Third, there was no clear political strategy of how to battle against 'bureaucracy' and how to achieve 'party democracy'. What if the Secretariat, for example, was unwilling to cede power voluntarily? Finally, Trotsky did not see any tension or contradiction in his thought between the demand for democracy and the overriding emphasis on unity. Trotsky also ranted against the dangers of factionalism and of subverting the 'organizational principles of Bolshevism'. Welded to the Communist party and unwilling to break with it as the only instrument to move History forward, Trotsky as an oppositionist fought with two hands tied behind his back. There was next to no possibility of him overturning the party majority of the 1920s.

Democracy, Bolshevism and Stalinism, 1929–40

In the period from his exile from the USSR in 1929 to his death in 1940, Trotsky continued his lifelong political struggle for international socialism. He could print openly his numerous analyses of events in the USSR, but in conditions that were far from perfect. Not least, there were frequent deportations, house arrests and restrictions. This tended to confirm his less than complimentary view of the legal niceties of 'bourgeois democracy'.[22] The topics of democracy and dictatorship in the Russian Revolution were a recurring theme in his writings of the exile period, particularly in the context of defining the class nature of the USSR. If the rise of the bureaucracy signalled the defeat of Bolshevism–Leninism, of the connection between a healthy party and the worker vanguard, then what type of post-revolutionary politics was in operation? What links, if any, connected the post-1923 Soviet Union to the October Revolution?

Trotsky was a constant critic of political oppression and social inequality in the USSR. He had no doubt that the country was poorly governed, with negative consequences for economic growth and cultural advancement. The bureaucracy was a self-interested ruling clique that was defending its privileges to the hilt. To maintain its rule, it had to repress the advanced workers in the USSR and to engineer the defeat of international revolution. Socialism was absent from the Soviet Union not only because of its backwardness but also because of the current government's fear of socialism. That said the restoration of capitalism was equally threatening to the bureaucracy.

The Soviet Union was governed, according to Trotsky, by a transitional bureaucratic regime caught between socialism and capitalism. It drew its current strength from the property relations established by the October Revolution, that is a nationalized means of production. In no way was it a capitalist class, for it had no 'independent property roots'. It had no ownership of the means of production. It therefore depended upon the functioning of the socialized economy for its income and privileges. To the extent that the establishment of socialized property was the historically progressive victory of 1917, the USSR qualified as a type of proletarian dictatorship, in which the proletariat remained the ruling class. At the same time there were massive distortions and malignant growths in the dictatorship, all of which were related to the rule of the bureaucracy.

The sort of transitional society in the USSR described by Trotsky contained numerous paradoxes and contradictions. On the one hand, the workers were clearly distressed by the bureaucratic dictatorship. On the other, Trotsky argued that the continuing defence of socialized property by the state meant that the workers were also worried by the prospect of the overthrow of the Soviet state in its bureaucratic form for this would pave the way for capitalist restoration:

> The proletariat with clenched teeth bears ('tolerates') the bureaucracy and, in this sense, recognizes it as the bearer of the proletarian dictatorship. In a heart to heart conversation, no Soviet worker would be sparing of strong words addressed to the Stalinist bureaucracy. But not a single one of them would admit that the counterrevolution has already taken place. The proletariat is the spine of the Soviet state. But insofar as the function of governing is concentrated in the hands of an irresponsible bureaucracy, we have before us an obviously sick state [...] The further unhindered development of bureaucratism must lead inevitably to the cessation of economic and cultural growth, to a terribly social crisis and to the downward plunge of the entire society. But this would imply not only the collapse of the proletarian dictatorship but also the end of bureaucratic domination. In place of the workers' state would come not 'social bureaucratic' but capitalist relations.[23]

The Fate of the Bolshevik Revolution

In exile Trotsky wished to reveal the USSR's 'dual character' under Stalin, on one hand defending and the other hand undermining the proletarian dictatorship. Which side would emerge victorious would depend as ever, for Trotsky, on the inter-relation of class forces on the national and international stage. The duty of the true revolutionary, such as Trotsky, was evident.

Above all, there had to be a defence of genuine Bolshevism–Leninism. A strict line had to be drawn between Marxism and Stalinism, and between the Bolshevism of 1917 and the Communist party in the USSR. Trotsky argued that the status of any party was linked to the historical interests that it served. From this perspective, nothing could be further removed from Bolshevism–Leninism than Stalinism. The Bolshevik party led a successful revolution as a vanguard party in close connection with the most advanced sections of the working class, aspiring to start a world revolution. The Communist party under Stalin was a degenerated organization ruling over the proletariat in the boundary of one country. This was a not a natural development of a pristine Bolshevism, but arose out of concrete historical reality: the presence of backward elements (the peasantry, certain nationalities), a general heritage of oppression and misery, and the exhaustion of the advanced workers from the civil war and the failure of the revolution to spread beyond Russia. Bolshevism paid the utmost attention to the study of theory and the need to repel all variants of opportunism, whereas Stalinism was 'coarse, ignorant, and thoroughly empirical'. Bolshevism repressed parties, movements and individuals who stood in the way of historical progress. It did not shy away from putting down by force the Kronstadt revolt, for it realized that behind the call for 'democratization' lay capitulation to the restoration of capitalism. Stalinist violence, in contrast, aimed at the physical destruction of Bolshevism:

> The present purge draws between Bolshevism and Stalinism not simply a bloody line but a whole river of blood. The annihilation of the entire old generation of Bolsheviks, an important part of the middle generation, which participated in the civil war, and that part of the youth which took seriously the Bolshevik traditions, shows not only a political but a thoroughly physical incompatibility between Bolshevism and Stalinism.[24]

For the USSR to return to true Bolshevism, argued Trotsky, the advanced workers had to overthrow the bureaucracy. This would be a political, not a social revolution as the means of production were state-owned. The restoration of soviet democracy would, for Trotsky, entail the masses asserting their domination over the administration via the worker vanguard. This would occur not peacefully, but by force, including the application of measures of a 'police character' against the bureaucracy. Given that the essential condition of any revolution was, according to Trotsky, a healthy Bolshevik party, the likelihood of the advanced Soviet workers being able to found and build such a revolutionary organization under Stalinism was remote, the best efforts of the Left Opposition in the USSR notwithstanding. As he had argued since 1905, Trotsky saw the international revolution as coming to the aid of an isolated socialist regime. In the 1930s this meant the world revolution would turn transitional Stalinism into real socialism. But globally workers were in desperate need of Bolshevik leadership that had to be created anew. Founding the Fourth International was therefore Trotsky's solution to the interconnected problem of building socialist democracy, East and West:

> The first condition for successes upon the international arena is the liberation of the international proletarian vanguard from the demoralizing influence of Soviet Bonapartism, i.e., from the venal bureaucracy of the so-called Comintern. The struggle for the salvation of the USSR as a socialist state coincides completely with the struggle for the Fourth International.[25]

Stalin, dictatorship and the question of agency

The many analyses of Soviet politics, economy and society produced by Trotsky paid surprisingly little attention to Stalin. This was to change after Trotsky accepted a commission to write a biography of his nemesis. It is a fascinating study that became as much Trotsky's history of the Russian Communist party, a Trotsky *Short Course*, as a study of Stalin in the revolution and revolutionary movement. Indeed, the intention again and again is to show how Stalin had no influence or impact on the major events of Russian Social Democracy, from the early Georgian movement through to the revolutions of 1905, 1917 and even in Soviet history from 1917 to 1929. Nowhere and in nothing does Trotsky concede to Stalin an independence of thought or of initiative. On the contrary, Trotsky's Stalin is wary of revolutionary daring for this presumes a living connection with the real revolutionary force, the advanced workers. Stalin, always cut off from the revolutionary vanguard, was incapable of creative, strategic, Bolshevik leadership. Stalin made no contribution to Marxist theory that he was poorly versed in. Possessing no talent as a 'thinker, writer, or orator' Stalin was above all, for Trotsky, a committeeman *par excellence*: 'Stalin took possession of power [...] with the aid of an impersonal machine. And it was not he that created the machine, but the machine that created him.'[26]

For Trotsky, Stalin joined the revolutionary movement as a 'plebian democrat of the provincial type, armed with a rather primitive "Marxist" doctrine'. In the course of a revolutionary career that was to span several decades Stalin did not move beyond the limitations of his early self. In contrast to Trotsky's other political enemies of the time, such as Hitler and Mussolini, who could at least claim some personal impact upon their rise to power, Stalin remained a 'grey blur' right up to his accession as dictator of the USSR in 1929. In this sense Stalin was the most unhistorical historical figure one could imagine. According to Trotsky, the bureaucratic machine had to employ the state's propaganda and punitive resources to raise Stalin artificially to historical greatness. In reality, Stalin was nothing more than historical mutton dressed up in historical lamb's clothing:

Devoid of personal qualifications for directly influencing the masses, he clung with redoubled tenacity to the political machine. The axis of his universe was his Committee – the Tiflis, the Baku, the Caucasian, before it became the Central Committee. In time to come his blind loyalty to the Party machine was to develop with extraordinary force; the committeemen became the super-machine man, the Party's General Secretary, the very personification of bureaucracy and its peerless leader [....] [Stalin] put forward his quest for leader of the Party and then government openly in 1929, when for the first time, at the Congress, he delivered the main political report. He was forty-seven years old. During this report he was like a newcomer taking his examinations. He made crude errors which created whispers in the hall, but by this time the machine was irrevocably in his hands. The machine was commissioned to make the country aware of it.[27]

Lacking a programme, ideas and any connection to the Bolshevik revolutionary international heritage, Stalin's leadership was, for Trotsky, completely opportunistic. It was concerned above all with protecting the bureaucratic elite who had destroyed the Bolshevik Party and with concentrating as much power as possible in Stalin's hands. Trotsky presented this case with a usual literary brilliance: 'Stalin has always been what he remains to this day – a politician of the golden mean who does not hesitate to resort to the most extreme measures. Strategically he is an opportunist; tactically he is a "revolutionist". He is a kind of opportunist with a bomb'.[28]

This combination of extremism and opportunism was evident, according to Trotsky, in the key policies of the Stalin age, including the excessive industrialization, collectivization and the Terror. The 'left-turn' of the late 1920s, for example, was not a sudden conversion to the ideas of the Left and United Oppositions, for the way in which the policies were conceived, introduced and pursued revealed that Stalin had not the slightest comprehension of these programmes as originally put forward. It was rather the bureaucratic machine maintaining its grip on the USSR's surplus product by beating to a pulp the petty-bourgeois tendencies of the NEP at great cost to the country's ordinary workers and peasants. In order to complete its control over the USSR and masking its exploitative essence under the cover of Bolshevism, Stalin and the machine had physically to destroy the Bolshevik Old Guard. Even in mass murder, however, Stalin, according to Trotsky, proceeded not by an exact and well-thought out plan:

The elements of human degradation and self-abasement, of self-immolation, were gathered little by little. Pressure was increased – little by little. The unnatural mechanics of voluntary confessions grew quite naturally out of the pressures (in small inoffensive doses) of the totalitarian machine [...] the Moscow trials taken as a whole are astounding in their grandiose absurdity, as the delirium of a weak person armed with the full panoply of power [...] the trials are permeated with the spirit of totalitarian idiocy.[29]

One of the recurring questions for students of the early history of the USSR is, 'Given Trotsky's undoubted intellectual and revolutionary superiority over Stalin, how was it that Trotsky became the prophet unarmed and outcast?' It has been suggested that in the 1920s and beyond Trotsky fell victim of a youthful and prophetic prediction about the dangers of a Leninist party organization of intellectuals that substituted itself for the working class, in this way establishing a tyranny over the proletariat. The party would not itself be immune to the tendency for substitutionism:

> In the internal politics of the Party these methods [of thinking and deciding for others – IDT] lead [...] to the Party organisation 'substituting' itself for the Party, the Central Committee substituting itself for the Party organisation, and finally the dictator substituting himself for the Central Committee.[30]

Trotsky, who was not usually shy about claiming foresight for himself, dismissed the notion that the rise of the dictator Stalin was rooted in Bolshevik centralism or in a hierarchy of revolutionaries. In this context he described his work of 1904 as 'immature and erroneous in my criticism of Lenin'. Lenin as much as Trotsky, the mature Trotsky claimed, was aware of the dangers of 'committeemen' in the movement. Such 'committeemen' could not however come to prominence on their own efforts alone and certainly not out of any intellectual acumen. Political struggle was determined not by force of argument, for on this basis Trotsky would have emerged as Lenin's successor. The deciding factors were class relations and in particular the relationship between the revolutionary proletarian vanguard, the party and the internal and international situation.[31]

Looking back from the end of the 1930s, Trotsky claimed that in the 1920s he never stood a chance of winning power because the correlation of forces was against him. In fact he never engaged in a struggle that would have been futile. This may explain Trotsky's reluctance to give any sign that he was interested in power, such as the blank refusal to give the main political report during Lenin's last illness. Already by 1923, the mature Trotsky admits, the party had degenerated, swamped by 'the green and callow mass' of careerist bureaucrats. The working-class vanguard no longer had the revolutionary energy of 1917 and the civil war years. It was subdued, needing a breathing space and disillusioned by the defeats of the international revolution in Germany and elsewhere. The emergence of the counter-revolution therefore happened speedily over 1921–3. As Trotsky noted, 'Now everything occurs quickly, even degenerations.'[32]

It is remarkable that at the end of his life Trotsky saw that the Russian revolutionary traditions of Bolshevism evaporated so quickly, giving way to the rule of 'a kingdom of arrogant mediocrities' with Stalin as 'the most outstanding mediocrity of the Soviet bureaucracy'.[33] If a party of the Bolshevik mould could undergo such a rapid fall, then was there not some need of democratic guarantees, of the sort of multi-party socialist democracy demanded by the Kronstadt revolt? In this situation the concept of loyal opposition would have been central to the socialist project and Trotsky would not have been in the bind of claiming that he was warning a degenerated party about its degeneration, but being unable to step outside the party because 'one cannot be right against the Party'. To the problem of how to achieve the main goal of keeping the revolutionary spirit alive in a one-party system with a degenerated party that controls the means of communication and has at its disposal a police state, Trotsky could only answer to fight for a change in the correlation of forces. In this struggle revolutionary gains such as the October Revolution had always to be defended and the price of defeat in deaths and dictatorship accepted as part of History's unfolding:

> When pious moralists demand absolute "guarantees", that is utterly absurd. Such people want roses without thorns, revolutions without excesses, progress without the fear of reaction, and a leadership without any fear of degeneration. Unfortunately, there are no preventive means and no insurance against the inconsistencies of development.[34]

Conclusion

As a Marxist Trotsky believed that the achievement of communism was a historical good and a historical necessity. The underlying economic demands propelling humanity to this end were the need of the productive forces to reach their maximum expansion. If property relations stood in the way, then they would be burst asunder in revolutionary change. Yet this process was not inevitable. History required actors with the right tactical and organizational acumen to make the transition happen. In the course of the rise and fall of revolutionary potential, Trotsky implicitly and on occasion explicitly made a connection between the fate of individuals and movements and the broader historical conjuncture. When the revolutionary wave was at its peak, only the most honoured, respected and brilliant individuals could make a positive difference and lead a successful revolution. If the communist vanguard was replete with nonentities then a situation ripe for revolution would be lost. No Lenin, no October Revolution. Similarly, an individual revolutionary, no matter how shining their qualities, could not save a revolution in decline. This would bring forth the rule of the leader without qualities, Stalin. So, for Trotsky, the question of agency was mixed between historical forces and the role of individuals, between the economic base and the party vanguard. In the midst of this was the play of class forces on the national and international scale, with true Marxist acumen required to penetrate the genuine outlooks for the construction of communism.

Although communism was about the liberation of humans, in which each would attain the status of a Marx,[35] Trotsky was in no way bound by concepts of human rights and democracy in the transition. It was reasonable to shoot, to take hostages and to suppress freedom of expression if the path was being cleared of redundant historical groups.[36] The key focus, for Trotsky, was the health of the party vanguard and its relationship with advanced workers. If this turned faulty or corrupt, then the revolution was lost. Trotsky identified this as a pressing problem of the Russian Revolution around 1923. In retrospect he described his struggles of the period 1923–9 as a hopeless but necessary attempt to keep the revolutionary traditions of Bolshevism alive.

Ultimately, Trotsky had limited room for political manoeuvre as he remained tied to the one-party state and accepted that factionalism in the party was unacceptable. His recommendations for the restoration of a healthy party regime were vague and unconvincing. He could think of no formal guarantees to guard against degeneration, as he was no advocate of a formal anything. Once the revolution was lost, it was lost and one's revolutionary duty was to try and rebuild a communist movement and to fight again for another communist revolution.

Although some commentators have discerned in Trotsky a willingness to contemplate that the working class may not be humanity's saviour after all and that pluralism was necessary even in communist politics, Trotsky did not elaborate on this in any detail. One could not expect him to have done so, for it would have required a fundamental re-evaluation of the Russian Revolution as a mistake and of a refutation of the Leninism he spent his post-1929 period defending. Democracy and dictatorship undoubtedly coexisted in Trotsky's thought, but their interrelationship and the factors determining their rise and fall were poorly theorized. Ultimately, Trotsky believed that the international revolution would solve all contradictions.

CHAPTER 7
DISCIPLINE VERSUS DEMOCRACY: THE 1923 PARTY CONTROVERSY
James Harris

Through much of the 1920s, the Politburo was badly divided as party leaders disagreed about how best to build socialism out of the ruins of a war-torn economy. After Lenin was incapacitated by a series of strokes, the party had lost its unifying figure and the disagreements took on the nature of a succession struggle, a struggle from which Stalin ultimately emerged victorious. The story of the succession struggle has been told many times, such that its general contours are familiar to the point where the retelling seems almost pointless.[1] And yet it is the contention of this chapter that a re-examination of these events is absolutely necessary. The 'familiar' story dates back to the early Cold War, when reliable sources were thin on the ground. For a quarter of a century, we have had access to an exceptional wealth of archival files that promise new perspectives on the unfolding of the Bolshevik dictatorship. This chapter focuses on the first major episode of the succession struggle in 1923, when Trotsky took on the Politburo majority and was defeated at the 13th Party Conference in January 1924. It argues that this episode played a major role in the restriction of inner Party democracy and the emergence of a Party dictatorship under Stalin.

Despite his failure, Trotsky is generally presented as the hero of this episode, particularly insofar as he is credited with rallying healthy party forces against dangerous trends in the party regime. This familiar, old narrative asserts that Stalin was using his role as General Secretary to appoint cadres who would be personally loyal to him; that appointment of secretaries from above was replacing election by party organizations; that a gap was emerging between party bosses and the rank and file; that urgent reforms were needed to restore inner party democracy. There are, however, significant problems with this narrative. It ultimately derives from a version of events Trotsky himself composed, not in order to provide an objective account of the facts, but in an effort to discredit his rivals. The narrative tends to focus narrowly on matters of high politics in the Kremlin, when the central issue over which Trotsky and the Politburo majority were fighting was the direction of economic policy and where events outside Moscow were of critical importance. The narrative was so successful and durable because Trotsky was fighting the very figure that the West was fighting in the early Cold War: Stalin. But we now need to explore the archival record, filter out the polemics, re-examine the broader context of this first confrontation between Trotsky and the Politburo majority and consider how events outside Moscow influenced the struggle at the top. In short, this chapter will argue that in the context of the transition to the New Economic Policy (NEP), amidst economic crisis and administrative fragility and confusion, leading party officials at all levels of the apparatus wanted clear and unambiguous instructions from the centre. There was a perception that conflict at the top of the party hierarchy and running debate over the fundamental direction of policy at the top were unhelpful, indeed counter-productive of the basic imperative of establishing a stable economy and political order. Trotsky's persistent criticism of the party majority and demands for policy debate in this period were ultimately counter-productive of the longer-term development of party democracy. Divisions at the top were disruptive. They complicated what was already a difficult situation and thus the episode hardened a predisposition against policy debate more generally.

It is well known that Trotsky and Stalin did not get along,[2] probably for the same reasons Trotsky had difficult relations with much of the rest of the Politburo. It may not have helped that Trotsky was a well-educated child of wealthy landowners and Stalin was the self-taught child of a cobbler and a domestic servant. Although Stalin had been in the highest echelons of the Bolshevik Party for nearly five years before Trotsky defected from the Mensheviks, Trotsky had a well-established and very public reputation as one of Russia's leading social democratic revolutionaries when he came to work alongside Stalin. It is not surprising that Trotsky would see Stalin as a lesser figure and that Stalin would resent Trotsky as a johnnie-come-lately interloper. They clashed repeatedly during the civil war, for example, when Stalin criticized Trotsky's policies on military specialists and Trotsky complained about Stalin's incompetence on the southern front. Trotsky was clearly the dominant figure as the head of the Red Army during the civil war, but his decision to remain in that post once the war ended meant that he drifted somewhat from the political centre-stage. By contrast, the post-war context suited Stalin's strengths and he gained considerable power and authority as a consequence.

Victory in the civil war had put an end to the immediate existential threat to the revolution, but at the same time it brought into focus the enormity of the tasks that lay ahead. For the first three years of the revolution, the military had taken precedence over civilian authority, but by 1920 attention had shifted to the task of building an effective apparatus of government. It was an epic task. Much of the war had been fought in European Russia and much of the effective government administration was concentrated in the capital. Now the Bolsheviks had to govern 137 million people spread across the largest country in the world. They needed to rebuild and administer industry and infrastructure, to raise revenue, create jobs, rebuild and run the education system and hospitals, and provide basic municipal services in towns and cities. Of course they made use, where possible, of the officials who had populated the administration of the old order, but they were not interested merely in reproducing the old order. They wanted to create an entirely new kind of state, and for that, they needed to create new institutions and put their own people in charge of them.

This had been central to the logic of expanding the membership of the party from 1917. At the time of the February Revolution, the Bolshevik underground consisted of little more than around 20,000 members. By March of 1921, the figure had risen to almost three-quarters of a million,[3] but in the process the average educational level of members tumbled. Many of the 'Old Bolsheviks' were university-educated intellectuals. The overwhelming majority of the new recruits had an incomplete primary education *or less*. Very few had any administrative experience and their knowledge of Marxism–Leninism tended to be primitive at the very best. Complicating matters further still was the general confusion of government at the time of the revolution. The Bolsheviks were conscious that the chaos of 1917 – the perception that government was weak – had contributed to the downfall of the Provisional Government and they were determined not to share the same fate. As the Bolsheviks emerged from the civil war, they were deeply conscious that many of the new members they had taken on since 1917 were not suitable: incompetent, corrupt or self-serving. They felt they had no choice but to radically purge the party. Party membership was cut in half between 1921 and 1924. This smaller group was not going to have an easy time. In the early 1920s, the economy was near collapse. The countryside was descending into famine and there were fierce disagreements about how the state should evolve and how the economy should be rebuilt. As vast new territories were absorbed into Bolshevik control, the demand for capable officials grew, the work those officials were faced with became more complex and the task of ensuring that central directives were being implemented and that the basic functions of government were being carried out became more challenging.

This was Stalin's metier. He was appointed General Secretary of the party in March 1922. He bore responsibility for making sure that the system functioned effectively. The position of General Secretary, at least in its early years, is much misunderstood in the literature. It did not give Stalin the power to place his 'cronies' in positions of power. This was a job that nobody else was prepared to take because it was perceived to be nearly impossible. The General Secretary had to establish a system that tracked the skills and experience of hundreds of thousands of officials; that reported on the fulfilment of decisions; that identified weak and failing organizations and sorted their problems; that raised the qualifications of officials and distributed them to where they were most needed. To lend a little perspective on this, only the largest multinational companies have over 10,000 employees. Stalin had to organize 350,000 mostly poorly qualified, if not wholly unqualified (and largely semi-literate) 'staff', who together had to bring the world's largest country, with a population of almost 140 million, out of an appalling economic crisis amidst serious political divisions.[4] As we shall see, Stalin's Secretariat had its critics, but this was more than balanced by the respect Stalin gained for bringing a semblance of order to a chaotic system. But now we need to shift our attention to the economic crisis, the political divisions and the actions of Trotsky, Stalin and the rest of the Politburo.

The New Economic Policy, a retreat to elements of a market economy, underpinned the eventual recovery of the Soviet economy by the middle of the 1920s, but the transition to this new economic order was fraught with challenges and controversy. In 1920, industry was working at around 15 per cent of its pre-war levels. Work stoppages, strikes and angry meetings of workers were common responses to the inconsistent payment of wages, poor rations and terrible working conditions. Millions more were dying in epidemics of typhus, cholera and smallpox. Crime was rampant. This put a terrible pressure on local party and state organizations. The aphorism that 'all politics is local' applies here. The workers and peasants had a dim grasp of politics at the national level. They would not be contented with bland statements to the effect that the regime as a whole was ruling in their interests or promises of socialism at some still distant later time. They wanted food and jobs and a sense that order would be restored and living standards would rise in the very near term. Local officials were not confident they could deliver. It was not just because of the lack of skills and experience of officialdom or the frequent turnover of staff and conflicts among organs and departments over who was responsible for what. In the confusion and nervousness over the desperate situation, organizations were prone to angry debates about what had to be done. Disagreements in the centre were readily reproduced in the provinces. The views of the Workers' Opposition gained considerable currency in 1920-1. Debates raged and organizations were badly split. As a consequence, their practical work often ground to a halt. The situation was not improving. For many, the lesson that was taken from this episode, particularly in the provinces, was that party debates were counter-productive; that it was better to have a single agreed policy about which officialdom could be rallied, a clear chain of command and a flow of detailed instructions for turning things around. In short, local organizations up and down the country were prone to be hostile to the notion of democracy within the party.[5]

The impending end of the civil war offered a measure of hope for improvement in the national economy, but that meant that industry had to be converted from military to civilian production. Infrastructure, particularly the transportation system had to be substantially rebuilt. Trotsky convinced Lenin to mobilize soldiers in 'labour armies' to undertake this work. Through 1920, up to 5.5 million soldiers were put to work in the civilian economy where their labour could help set the economy on a path of stable growth. In his enthusiasm for the idea, Trotsky pushed for a militarization of labour more generally and harsh penalties for 'labour deserters', but that provoked a backlash in the party. As it became apparent that productivity of the labour armies was low and Red Army soldiers were desperate finally to be demobilized and allowed to return home, the idea was scrapped.[6] Time and again in the years that followed Trotsky would press policy initiatives against significant opposition in the party.

In the course of 1921, Lenin and many around him were coming to terms with the idea that the state did not have the resources or the skills to rebuild the economy on its own and that they would have to accept a partial restoration of capitalism. The benefits of this partial restoration of capitalism were not immediately apparent. Far from it. Famine raged across the countryside in 1921 and 1922. Trade between private producers in town and countryside grew very slowly.[7] As economic cost accounting was applied to large-scale industry, the least profitable state enterprises were shut and investment concentrated where it could be most effectively brought to bear. Unemployment grew. Costs had to be cut, productivity raised and the currency stabilized, and consequently many of those who had jobs found that their incomes continued to fall in real terms and wages were often paid irregularly. Labour unrest again reared its head.[8] It is not surprising that there was considerable disquiet about whether NEP was leading to capitalism rather than to socialism.

Lenin and the Politburo majority were not ready to give up yet. Given that agriculture generated the clear majority of the Russia's GDP, it remained clear to them that for some time yet, increasing peasant production was the best way – perhaps the only way – to generate the funds necessary to finance the development of large-scale, state industry. Meanwhile, they had to continue to close less efficient state enterprises, concentrate investment and equipment on the more productive ones and drive down production costs to generate profits and further investment, but that was exceptionally difficult because it exacerbated unemployment and labour unrest. The Politburo established a series of commissions to monitor the situation, take expert opinion and report on progress. Trotsky was given responsibility for the Commission on State Industry. When he presented his preliminary findings on 20 February 1923, it became clear that he was out of step with the rest of the Politburo. The consensus in the Politburo was that economic recovery would, for some time yet, continue to rely on small-scale private production and especially peasant production, but Trotsky was concerned that such an approach risked leading to capitalism rather than socialism. Trotsky proposed a radical series of measures that were contrary to the spirit of NEP, but which would accelerate the development of state industry and socialized (collective, as opposed to private) agriculture.[9]

After Trotsky's theses were discussed at the February Central Committee plenum, the Politburo demanded a series of revisions. It was not just that Trotsky's proposals stood to upset the logic and direction of the work of the rest of the Politburo. The majority was deeply conscious that disagreements about policy at the highest level tended to ripple out and repeat themselves in the provinces. The conflict with the Workers' Opposition in the previous summer had led to the complete paralysis of some organizations and neither the Politburo majority nor most Party secretaries wanted to see that happen. Another revision demanded by the Politburo majority concerned the relationship of Party organizations and economic organs. Trotsky had asserted in his theses that Party organizations were unduly interfering in the work of economic organs. He demanded that the removal and transfer of economic officials should be limited to cases of 'strict and unconditional necessity'. The majority and particularly Stalin were long aware of the fragility of local administration and the crucial importance of a coherent unified system for distributing cadres according to their skills to the party and state organizations where those skills were most needed. They were also concerned that Trotsky's proposals would also reignite *skloki* that had paralysed so many organizations in the previous couple of years.[10] The correction they demanded forcefully noted that 'it was the responsibility of party organisations [...] not only to determine where officials were most appropriately assigned, but also to take leadership of the work of economic organs.'[11]

After much negotiation across five separate sessions of the Politburo between February and April, a common text was agreed, but only just in advance of the 12th Party Congress. The March Central Committee Plenum discussed the issue and similarly demanded that Trotsky accept the corrections. This was not merely a matter of the delegates sniffing the wind and voting with Stalin or the dominant faction. Trotsky's theses and his defence of them were explicitly critical of the way regional party officials conducted their affairs and that group – constituting a majority of the Central Committee – did not take it well or approve of the implications of the restriction of their power that Trotsky was proposing.[12]

At the Congress itself, the Workers' Opposition and Workers' Truth factions were still present on the margins, in the form of widely circulated, unofficial, 'anonymous' policy platforms.[13] Some delegates expressed disquiet that many of their members had been removed from their posts in regional organizations and denied an official channel to express their views. Stanislav Kosior (Siberian biuro of the TsK) warned that it had become difficult to criticize shortcomings in the party without those criticisms being interpreted as factionalism,[14] but the majority took the view that party unity was needed to deal with the challenge of making NEP work. M. E. Uryvaev (The Supreme Council of the National Economy (VSNKh)) responded to Kosior saying that 'without party unity, we wouldn't have accomplished so much in the last year'. The comment won a round of applause and shouts of 'True! (*Pravil'no*)'.[15] The line of argument was echoed in other speeches, although there was no shortage of criticism of central policy. It was still clearly possible to have a frank discussion of policy while upholding the ban on factions instituted at the Tenth Congress.

In this febrile atmosphere, Trotsky delivered his report on state industry. As he took the stage, he was greeted prolonged and enthusiastic applause that reflected the strength of his authority in the party. At no stage in the course of his three-hour long speech did he refer to the tensions within the Politburo. Indeed Trotsky made a point, repeatedly, of noting the recovery of the economy would depend on the success of private production as the rest of the Politburo had insisted. But the broader thrust of the speech was that such a relationship of dependence was worrying and potentially a threat to the revolution. Most famously, he illustrated the continuing rise of industrial prices and fall in agricultural prices with a diagram that showed two intersecting lines in the shape of scissors. The cost of industrial production was rising despite substantial state subsidies and the income from the taxation of private peasant production was not looking like it would keep pace. The danger that the state might run out of money investing in slow-growing heavy industry while private production was growing in double digits came to be known as the Scissors Crisis. Trotsky chose not to lay out the alternative programme he had sketched in his disputed theses, but he left the audience in no doubt that solutions lay in encompassing central economic planning and the limitation of market forces.

None of this would have come as a surprise to the delegates who had been present at the March Central Committee plenum where Trotsky's proposals had been discussed and rejected. The discussion of Trotsky's speech at the Congress drew familiar criticism: Trotsky was being unduly pessimistic (Bogdanov); peasant production and private, artisanal manufacture were bound to recover more rapidly (Smilga); progress had been made cutting industrial costs and time was needed for further cuts to have their effect (Andreev); economic planning was already taking place on a sectoral level, but it was premature for encompassing plans (Rukhimovich). In his concluding speech, Trotsky gave no ground and lambasted his critics each in turn. He insisted that industrial prices remained too high and that at the current rate of subsidy, the state coffers would be emptied before heavy industry had recovered. Resolutions on the financing of state industry had to be passed on to a special commission elected by the Congress, where changes proposed by Trotsky were defeated by fourteen votes to eight.

Trotsky does not appear to have been discouraged by this setback. He may well have concluded that events would prove him right in the end, but it was not the only defeat he endured at the Congress. In his version of the disputed theses on state industry, he had also demanded that the power of the party to interfere in the work of the economic organs should be curtailed. Perhaps it should come as little surprise that a congress of *party* workers would not vote to limit their own powers. Clearly a solid majority felt that they, as party secretaries, should have the power to appoint and dismiss state officials and economic officials among them as the situation demanded. In their view that power was the best guarantee that party policy would be realized, that local power would be exercised coherently and that the forces of capitalism in the economy would be kept in check. As we shall see, of these two defeats Trotsky suffered at the Congress, the second was the more significant. In the spring and summer of 1923, there remained concerns about the effectiveness of NEP serious enough to warrant the considering a change in the direction of economic policy. The hundreds of senior party officials at the Congress wanted to see stable economic growth, rising employment and progress towards socialism and were not closed to a discussion of options, but they were not open to the limitation of their power. They had struggled and were still struggling to establish stable local government given chronic shortages of needed specialists and the general lack of administrative experience of the mass of barely literate party cadres.

There was no obvious improvement to the economy in the late spring and summer of 1923. In fact, industrial prices continued to rise and agricultural prices continued to fall. The 'scissors' continued to widen. This posed the obvious risk that come autumn, the terms of trade between town and countryside would be such that peasants would refuse to market the harvest. The party leadership remained committed to their strategy and accelerated it in important respects, though that was fraught with risks. Cutting industrial costs involved first and foremost closing the heavy industrial enterprises that were least efficient and the biggest drain on the state budget. That in turn exacerbated unemployment. The enterprises that remained open were put under terrible pressure to reduce the cost of production. The easiest way to do that was to reduce the wage bill and though enterprise directors had been instructed to find efficiencies elsewhere, many cut workers' wages or delayed wage payments, sometimes by months. Given the rapid rise of consumer prices, workers responded to the sharp fall in their living standards by going on strike. In all, 165,000 workers downed their tools in protest across 1923, with labour unrest peaking just as the all-important harvest was beginning.[16]

These were bleak times for the Politburo majority, but they held their nerve – more or less. They led a series of commissions to investigate and report on enterprises, industries and issues of particular importance to overcoming the current crisis.[17] This intensive work (from which Trotsky absented himself) served to reassure the majority that despite the labour unrest and the persistent widening of the gap between industrial and agricultural prices, their strategy would produce results in the end. The scissors could be closed and the recovery of heavy industry could be achieved without deepening state subsidies.

The leadership also began to take a much harsher line towards the Workers' Opposition and Workers' Truth group, which they accused of exacerbating the strike movement and directing the anger of workers against the current direction of policy. Some of their members had been referred to the Central Control Commission (TsKK) for censure after the publication of the 'anonymous' platforms at the 12th Congress.[18] By July, the Politburo asked *Pravda* 'and other organs of agitation and propaganda […] to conduct a systematic struggle' with these factions and 'deviations'.[19] By late August, as the strike movement was reaching its peak, the Politburo was inclined to take even harsher measures up to and including expulsion from the party. The decision was left to the Central Committee plenum in late September. When that larger body met, the assembled party secretaries did not hesitate to support the measures, including a requirement that party members report any factional activity to the political police (OGPU).[20] Although there were dissenting voices, the majority saw the factional activity as a hindrance to achievement of practical tasks. Trotsky himself fully supported the action. He was on record more than a year earlier that the OGPU should be brought in to end factional activity.[21]

Although Trotsky had no issues with the prosecution of the Worker's Opposition and other factions, he was angry that despite the further widening of the gap between agricultural and industrial prices, the proposals he had put before the 12th Congress in April were still not being considered. Through the summer and autumn there was a running battle between the State Planning Committee (Gosplan) and the Commissariat of Finance (Narkomfin) about how to close the 'scissors'. The Politburo Commission on the Scissors, led by Feliks Dzerzhinskii, intervened and began effectively to dictate economic policy from the party centre. This was bound to cause some upset among the disputing parties, particularly given that in October it was yet far from clear that Dzerzhinskii's Commission had the answers.[22] Trotsky could have attempted to take advantage of the anger at the Politburo's intervention, but rather than restate his views from April, in front of a group that had twice rejected his proposals in the last six months, Trotsky left the Plenum before it was finished[23] and wrote a long letter to the membership of the TsK and TsKK. In it, he pointed to the disaffection with the Politburo's economic policy and that the failure to express this disaffection was 'increasing the isolation of the TsK from the Party'. In other words, Trotsky, who had done little of the concrete work to deliver sustainable economic growth on the basis of NEP, was asserting that the party as a whole – and much of the TsK – was on his side and that it was the rest of the Politburo that was alone in defending the current strategy. In contrast to his speech at the 12th Congress in April where he made no direct reference to his disagreements with the rest of the Politburo, in the letter he asserted that their economic policy was a chaotic and wasteful mess, doomed to provoke an 'acute crisis'. He concluded by asserting that 'the Party would have the right to blame everyone who saw the danger, but did not openly name it.'[24] In essence, he was saying 'support me now or when the current policy finally fails, your party career will be in danger.' It was a bold, risky and characteristically arrogant political strategy.

The Politburo asked Trotsky not to circulate the letter until they had a chance to meet, but before that happened, they received reports of leaks to the Moscow organization and most probably beyond. Trotsky flatly and rather improbably[25] denied he was behind the leaks, but they had effectively forced the hand of the rest of the Politburo. Rumours of disagreements and of the suppression of criticism would be worse in the longer term than an open discussion which might be brought to a relatively rapid conclusion. The Presidium of the TsKK met on 13 October to discuss Trotsky's letter. The resolutions of that meeting expressed exasperation that the letter did not contain concrete proposals that could be the subject of a negotiation. Instead, the blunt attack on the current policy threatened to undermine ongoing efforts to close the scissors and set the economy on a stable footing. They understood from previous experience that a wider discussion would, at a minimum, distract attention from pressing economic issues, complicate the ongoing work of the Politburo commissions on the economic crisis and was likely to churn up conflicts and tensions in local organizations. The Presidium agreed to the circulation of the letter to members of the TsK and TsKK, while asking them not to draw the attention of the wider party to the differences of opinion until a special plenum of the TsK and TsKK could be convened to discuss the issues.[26]

Trotsky naturally anticipated that yet another meeting of these organs was likely to vote him down again, so he wrote a further, shorter 'declaration' and gathered forty-six signatures in support of it from inside and outside the TsK. That way, he made it harder for the Politburo to prevent it from circulating.[27] In contrast to Trotsky's letter from a week before which predominately addressed the 'mistakes' of the Politburo in economic policy, the declaration shifted focus to the 'inner-party regime'. The Politburo had become a 'factional dictatorship', according to the declaration. It made the case that the current leadership was able to impose its 'haphazard, poorly thought through and unsystematic' economic policies only by silencing its critics – by means of the suspension of the electoral principle in party organizations, the appointment from above exclusively of party secretaries loyal to the current misguided political line and the exclusion of the rank and file from the discussion of the issues of the day.[28]

The accusation was misleading in two important respects. First, although the Politburo was indeed imposing its economic policy, it was doing so by means of its commissions on wage policy, trade and the 'scissors', on which the leading officials of the disputing bodies, including NKFin, Gosplan and VSNKh, were represented and given the platform to express their differing view. Of course, the intervention of the Politburo flew in the face of Trotsky's proposal, rejected at the 12th Congress in April, that the party should stay out of the work of the economic organs. There may have been other ways to hammer out solutions to pressing economic problems, but these interventions of the Politburo in the circumstances of an acute economic crisis were not especially controversial in themselves. Second, the irregular application of the electoral principle in party organizations and the frequency of appointment of party secretaries were, as discussed above, a function of the persistent and severe shortage of cadres with needed administrative skills and of the propensity of internal disputes to paralyse organizations. The Secretariat shared the view with most party secretaries in the republics and provinces that an open discussion of the Declaration would not be helpful. 'Appointmentism' (*naznachenstvo*), to use the contemporary neologism, was not a tactic of dictatorial control. It did not guarantee Stalin or the policies of the Politburo majority support at party meetings. Party secretaries did not vote with the Politburo majority because they feared they would be replaced. Almost without exception they were Old Bolsheviks – experienced revolutionaries and not yes-men. There remained some disquiet about the internal party situation and about whether the majority could close the scissors and stabilize the economy. There were plenty of senior economic officials who thought the present economic policy might fail. Trotsky was trying to rally them to stand with him in opposition to the Politburo majority, but they were not convinced that the time was right to change course.

Trotsky failed again. Only this time, his tactics were getting him into trouble. The case was referred to the Presidium of the TsKK which expressed the concern that he was preparing to set up a faction in opposition to agreed party policy. Both Trotsky and the Politburo majority then circulated letters to the memberships of the TsK and TsKK. Trotsky's was fundamentally defensive. The Politburo went on the attack, drawing attention to the TsKK findings, accusing Trotsky of being ignorant of the state of internal party affairs and of creating divisions and fomenting opposition to the current political line in order to serve his personal political ambitions.[29] A joint plenum of the TsK and TsKK (25–27 October 1923) convened especially to discuss the matter. As Trotsky anticipated, the plenum did not go well for him. The resolutions, adopted by a vote of 102 for and 2 against, with 10 abstentions, referred to the Declaration of the 46 as 'disruptive' and an act of factionalism that 'threatened to create a crisis in the party' and as such a 'serious political error'.[30] They directed Trotsky to be more involved in the 'practical work of the Party and Soviet organs of which he is a member' or in other words to stop sniping from the sidelines and contribute concretely to the existing party line.

Support for the majority was being shored up by events on the ground. Labour protest in the form of strikes and demonstrations was on the wane as measures to stop the late payment of wages took effect. More significantly, in the course of October, the 'scissors' had finally begun to close as industrial prices began consistently to fall and agricultural prices to rise. The tide seemed to be turning, and that appeared to vindicate the economic policies of the majority at the same time that it made Trotsky's warning of impending catastrophe look less convincing. This was not a total defeat for Trotsky, though. The delegates had essentially rejected his critique of economic policy and called for the commissions on the 'scissors' and on wages to continue their work, but they were willing to acknowledge the validity of some elements of Trotsky's critique of the internal party situation.

The majority was conscious that the 13th Party Conference was due to be held in January 1924.[31] If they did not resolve their differences with Trotsky, the disagreements would filter down to local organizations and disrupt the practical work on which so much progress had recently been made. At the same time, they were aware that copies of the Platform of the 46 had continued to circulate, and with them, rumours of disagreements within the leadership.[32] A period of intense negotiation was complicated by a bout of malaria Trotsky had contracted while hunting outside Moscow in late October. The commission met at Trotsky's flat as he reclined, in discomfort, sweating profusely.

Throughout, Trotsky insisted that the electoral principle be enforced categorically and without exception. The majority remained concerned that appointments from above were still needed where party organizations lacked qualified cadres or where *skloki* (infighting) were bringing their work to a standstill. Trotsky accepted the ban on factions, but wanted the resolution to permit 'groups' sharing dissenting views to express them collectively. For the majority, this was tantamount to allowing the development of factions within the party. After all, what was the Platform of the 46? A collective expression of a dissenting view or an act of factionalism? In short, what they were debating in essence was whether Trotsky should be allowed to continue criticize the rest of the Politburo and openly gather support for his dissenting views.

The compromise resolution reached on 5 December and approved unanimously by the Politburo and Presidium of the TsKK, fudged the differences. It promised 'a real and systematic application of the process of workers' democracy' while at the same time upholding the ban on factions. This included 'the freedom to discuss [...] all the most important principles of party life, the freedom to debate these issues as well the opportunity to elect leading officials and biuros from top to bottom.' It did not include, however, the freedom to form factional groupings which are 'extremely dangerous to a ruling party, for they often threaten to divide or fracture the government or state machinery as a whole.' In essence, the resolution argued that 'constant and animated' discussion would prevent the emergence of the frustrations and disaffection that leads to the formation of factions. On the matter of election versus the appointment of officials from above, the resolution stated the election of all leading officials was the general rule and that officials should never be appointed against the will of the organization they would lead, but that in the context of NEP, appointment was sometimes necessary and the suitability of elected officials should be verified by higher organizations.[33] The majority thus felt they had a formulation with which they could present a united front to the upcoming Party Conference. They did not anticipate that Trotsky would also see the resolution as a victory for him and immediately use it as the basis for publicly returning to many of his long-standing criticisms of the majority. The resolution did not provide a foundation for unity, but rather a platform for Trotsky to draw attention once again to his disagreements with the leadership.

This became clear to the majority almost immediately. Not only was the Declaration of the 46 being circulated with renewed vigour, but Trotsky composed a letter, called 'The New Course', that his supporters circulated to the regional party organizations for discussion at the plenary meetings that took place in advance of the upcoming 13th Party Congress. In the letter, Trotsky argued that the 5 December resolution marked a recognition that the party 'centralism' had gone too far. The sort of top-down dictation and suppression of criticism that had been necessary during the civil war was giving way to a 'degeneration' (*pererozhdenie*) of the party's 'old guard' that was producing resentment, anger and the proliferation of opposition. He encouraged the party masses fearlessly to express their views and thus stop the degeneration by making the 'old guard' responsive to the will of the masses. The majority instantly grasped Trotsky's purpose. Trotsky's 'old guard' was a reference to the Central Committee – the group that had twice firmly rejected his criticisms of the current policies of the majority. Those policies had indeed provoked anger and resentment. They had increased unemployment, held back wage increases and defended the continuing necessity of capitalist trade between town and countryside. Although these unpopular measures were now setting the economy on a solid foundation for economic growth, Trotsky and his supporters were renewing their attack by circulating Declaration of the 46 and asserting that any attempt to suppress a broad discussion of the Declaration was a violation of the December 5 resolution.

The majority were horrified and appalled that all their efforts to find a compromise agreement were being used by Trotsky to intensify his attack on them. They had tried to work with him through the past year, not because they particularly valued what he could contribute to policy-making. That contribution had been minimal and fundamentally disruptive. They were conscious that he still had a reputation as one of the leading figures of the Party and the revolutionary movement. They could not easily have ignored him or removed him from the Politburo. But from this moment, they understood that it was impossible to work with Trotsky. In establishing with such clarity that he was determined to press his separate views despite repeated calls from the TsK and TsKK to desist and because his actions threatened to upset the progress the majority had made by inciting divisions in party organizations up and down the country, the majority decided to abandon any pretence of a willingness to work with him.[34]

They published 'The New Course' in *Pravda* on 11 December. They also allowed his supporters to publish articles in national newspapers, so as not to be vulnerable to the accusation that they were suppressing criticism, but they orchestrated a series of rebuttals in the same papers. The rebuttals noted that Trotsky's position had twice been rejected by the TsK and TsKK. Now, in encouraging the party masses ('*nizy*') to speak out against the 'old guard' Trotsky was effectively encouraging an attack on the TsK that could have potentially catastrophic consequences for Soviet power. This was an act of factionalism and the very reason why the ban on factions had to remain in place.[35] Both the supporters of Trotsky and of the majority then headed to the main regional party meetings that preceded the 13th Conference, so that they could defend their respective positions directly before the party membership.

Perhaps the greatest advantage the majority had was that the TsK, which represented the leaders of all the major regional party organizations, was most familiar with the conflict and overwhelmingly on their side. The majority could be reasonably confident that the leaders of these regional organizations would echo their criticisms of Trotsky in the regional press and thus draw lower-level organizations (e.g. *guberniia* and district organizations) as well as the rank and file towards resolutions censuring Trotsky. The local discussions appear to have been vigorous and relatively open. There were plenty of speeches sympathetic to Trotsky's position and agreeing that the party mass was being ignored. Plenty failed to see any threat to Soviet power presented by Trotsky's position. There were criticisms of Stalin and the majority and efforts to find a 'middle ground'.[36] A few organizations voted in support of Trotsky against the majority, but they were substantially outnumbered by those that supported the majority.

Such was the diversity of views and levels of engagement that summarizing the discussion is virtually impossible, but some general trends are reasonably clear. Much of the rank and file of the party, especially away from the major urban and industrial centres, tended to vote with their immediate superiors. In the early 1920s, the party press still did not reach many rural and semi-rural areas and many party members were still barely literate or even illiterate. From the districts up through the *gubernii* (provinces), particularly amongst those in positions of some responsibility and authority, there was a sense that divisions in the party interfered with the practical work they were undertaking. For example, the chairman of the Vinnistkii Okruzhkom was almost certainly projecting his views to some degree when he claimed that 'amongst the party mass there is no desire to engage in discussion when there is so much work to do'.[37] From bitter experience they knew that local squabbles (*skloki*) could paralyse organizations and it was not a stretch to see the current discussion as just such a personal conflict at the highest level. Many took a harder line than the Politburo majority, demonizing Trotsky's position in one way or another as anti-Leninist. Perhaps in part because one of their constituent organizations (Cheliabinsk) had sided with Trotsky, the resolutions of the 6 January Urals Obkom plenum of 6 January qualified Trotsky's 'persistent factional attacks' on the party apparatus as 'Menshevik opportunism [...] The plenum notes the responsibility of all delegates to all [local] party conferences to stop discussions on party construction that seek to overturn the Central Committee line [...] Continuing the discussion is a real threat to the unity of the Party and it must be stopped.'[38] Having one of your organizations at war with the rest just complicated work. I. M. Vareikis, head of the Kiev gubkom and member of the Ukrainian TsK, reported to Stalin as early as 16 December that though there had been significant support for Trotsky in the capital, the overall victory of the majority was 'certain'.[39] Not quite as certain as he let on, because in the subsequent days and weeks, he and his colleagues in the Ukrainian leadership sent letters to local party committees asserting the dominance of the majority and asking them to end the discussion, push for unity and prevent the emergence of further fractions.[40] Stalin and the Politburo majority did not need to threaten or cajole regional leaders into supporting them. They worked together for many months through the thick of the crisis and to its resolution. They shared the majority's irritation with Trotsky for his persistent criticism of the current line and his determination to incite a debate in the party and provoke a change of political course

At the 13th party conference, Trotsky's group was comfortably defeated. Aleksei Rykov opened the proceedings with an analysis of how the policies of the majority had overcome the scissors crisis and opened the prospect of stable economic growth. Supporters of Trotsky's line did not directly challenge that. They did not return to the tone of the Declaration of the 46 or suggest that the current line was 'incompetent' or 'dangerous' as they had done in the autumn, though they did make it clear that they still thought that there remained too much reliance on 'capitalist' trade between town and countryside and that 'socialist' state industry needed extra, planned state support. Molotov and Kamenev reminded them that they had predicted disaster and in fact everything was working out fine.[41] Much of Stalin's address on the issue of party democracy was devoted to Trotsky's 'mistakes': Trotsky and his group had developed a platform separate from that of the TsK and had fought against it by trying to pit the party membership against the TsK. He had formed a faction in violation of the decision of the 10th Party Congress and that must not be tolerated. All of Trotsky's words about democracy were, Stalin argued, just a 'tactical manoeuvre' to serve his factional ends.

He reiterated the general commitment of the majority to the further development of party democracy – in the form of the 5 December resolution of the TsK and TsKK – but he noted (rather vaguely) that some limits on democracy were needed because of the current conditions.[42] He illustrated this commitment and its limits with the example of the electoral principle within the party. Trotsky and his group had exaggerated the extent of 'appointmentism' (*naznachenstvo*) in the party, that is the practice of removing and replacing officials by superior party organizations. Stalin insisted that at least 90 per cent of leading party officials were elected by their organizations, but that it was still necessary to appoint officials from above in some circumstances.[43] Many of those who spoke after Stalin agreed that limits on democracy were needed for the time being because extending it prematurely could unduly complicate tasks of political leadership and economic administration.[44] More broadly, though, they agreed with Stalin that the attack of the 'opposition'[45] had been politically self-serving and needlessly damaging to the authority and unity of the party.

The resolutions of the Conference on party democracy essentially repeated those from the 5 December resolution. 'Workers' Democracy' meant 'the freedom for all party members openly to discuss all the most important issues of party life.' Leading party officials from the top to the bottom of the party hierarchy were to be regularly subject to election by the organizations they represented. Those officials were obliged regularly to report to the organizations they represented and were not to treat criticism of their leadership from within the organization as a manifestation of factionalism. But these came with two significant caveats: (1) that this did not grant to right to form factions, in the sense of organized groups 'directed against the party'; (2) 'in the context of NEP it is necessary to preserve certain limitations (on the electoral principle) especially in lower organisations, such as the confirmation of party secretaries by the party authorities immediately above it.' The resolutions were approved unanimously by the conference.

And yet this was not merely a return to the status quo from before Trotsky's 'New Course'. Few party leaders wanted to see a repeat of the events of the past month and the disruptive effects of Trotsky's persistent refusal to work with the majority – not Stalin, nor the other members of the majority, nor members of the TsK and TsKK, nor the regional leaders who still had a long way to go to calm their organizations and restore the normal flow of work. They wanted to be certain that Trotsky and his group would not be in a position to carry on as they had done after the 12th Congress, after two TsK and TsKK resolutions in the autumn and the December 5 resolution. In order to put a final end to this 'discussion', a further resolution was agreed[46] that explicitly condemned the actions of Trotsky and his group. The resolution characterized each major policy position of the 'opposition', including the criticism of the commitment to NEP and the criticism of the apparat, as a 'departure from Leninism' and 'petty bourgeois deviation'.

Furthermore, it characterized the actions of Trotsky's group as a 'flagrant violation of party discipline.'

The instructions that then followed these characterizations cut against the grain of the commitments made the previous resolution to encourage party democracy. The 'foundations of Leninism' were to be 'patiently explained' to organizations that had 'wavered' in the discussion, to new party members, to the major proletarian organizations and especially to party youth. Although the connection was not drawn explicitly, by implication it was the position of the majority that was uniquely Leninist and this educational work would explain the anti-Leninist nature of Trotsky's attack on it and perhaps any other possible attack on it. The main party newspaper *Pravda* was to 'systematically explain the foundations of Bolshevism and to conduct a campaign against all deviations from it.' Then, in a reference specifically directed at Trotsky's actions after 5 December, the resolution instructed that: 'The freedom of discussion within the party in no sense constitutes a freedom to disrupt party discipline. The Central Committee and all party centres in the localities should take immediate and severe measures for the preservation of iron Bolshevik discipline whenever attempts are made to undermine it.'[47]

The resolution illustrated the meaning of 'the violation of Party discipline' with a recapitulation of the actions of Trotsky's group in the past year. Trotsky had stood alone against the rest of the Politburo criticizing their policies and predicting disaster. He had contributed little to the day-to-day decision-making of the Politburo or to the work of the standing commissions that addressed aspects of the crisis. After the TsK and TsKK twice supported the majority against Trotsky, Trotsky turned fire on them, and called on the rank and file to protest. He leaked the Declaration of the 46 to lower organizations in order to evade the inevitable majority vote of the TsKK that disagreements should be resolved within the leadership. As the policies of the majority began to take hold, began to close the scissors and stabilize the economy, the majority sought one more time to compose a resolution to which Trotsky would agree. The majority thought they had obtained a united front with Trotsky in advance of the 13th Conference, but within two days of his signing a joint declaration, they learned that he had written to pre-Conference party meetings in the regions reiterating the main points of his attack on the majority and the 'apparat'. Stalin and the majority were incensed, but so were party secretaries the length and breadth of the country who had to deal with the fallout.

In the heat of the moment, at the end of the Conference, they may not have seen the extraordinary tensions between the two resolutions, but in time, the strictures of party discipline rendered the promise of extended party democracy almost meaningless. Within weeks, regional organizations were calling on the Secretariat to help them deal with the consequences of the 'discussion'. For example, in the Urals, reports to the obkom expressed concern that it had churned up hostility not only to party bosses, but also to factory administration and technical specialists, in a way that threatened to affect production. Support for Trotsky's group had fallen away in their stronghold of Cheliabinsk, Shadrinsk and the oblast' Komsomol, but the 'oppositionists' remained in charge, provoking a stand-off that brought the work of those organizations to a standstill. These organizations appealed to the Obkom, which in turn then appealed the

Secretariat to intervene and appoint new leading officials.[48] Fewer organizations wanted to have to deal with that again. When disagreements subsequently emerged within party organizations, each side would try to have the other removed for 'violations of party discipline'.[49] Party organizations regularly reported on their activities to meetings of the rank and file as the first resolution had dictated, but they tended not to solicit a frank exchange of views but rather they encouraged expressions of 'unity and cohesion in the ranks'.[50] Party education and policy 'discussion clubs' also appear to have been directed increasingly to the mobilization of support for the current political line. In the provinces, 'Party discipline' was trumping 'party democracy' and neither Stalin nor the majority acted with any vigour to reverse that trend.

Of course, one should not conclude from this that Trotsky was to blame for the decline of democracy in the party or the emergence of Stalin's dictatorship. That would be no more appropriate than to accept Trotsky's own version, presenting himself as the defender of the revolution from the 'conspiracy of the epigones' bent on building a dictatorship. This was not an episode that reflected well on either side. Although both Trotsky and the majority seemed to agree that more democracy was needed, neither side made much effort to clarify what they meant by it. Trotsky showed a relentless determination to force through a change in the political line, though he had done little to contribute to it, and despite clear evidence that his group was in the minority. This made his defence of party democracy, and the freedom to criticize policy, seem self-serving. At best, his 'democracy' was of a populist sort, trying to whip up popular resentments until the position of the majority became untenable. The majority, and Stalin chief among them, were hardly better. Stalin's chief responsibility as General Secretary was to ensure the political system worked and things got done. He was always more interested in result over process. For him, democracy was something to aspire to, like communism itself – something for the distant future – if it got in the way of getting things done, he wasn't interested. And in 1924, party discipline was more important than party democracy. Much worse was to follow.

PART IV
REPRESSION AND MODERATION

CHAPTER 8
DEMOCRACY AND VIOLENCE, 1917–37
J. Arch Getty

As the Introduction to this volume shows, Lenin was a trenchant critic of European parliamentary democracy. He denounced even the versions based on universal suffrage not because he was against voting but because even with widespread suffrage the propertied classes held on to real power behind the scenes. Instead, drawing on Marx's writings about the state always being the coercive tool of one class over others, he argued that real democracy could only be achieved through a dictatorship of the proletariat backed by the armed might of 'the people', meaning the Russian workers and peasants who had been historically disenfranchised. Lenin's conception of revolutionary democracy, which was shared by most other Bolsheviks, was inherently coercive and violent.

For a long time our historical literature followed the arguments of defeated Russian liberals and leftists that Lenin personally destroyed Russian democracy by imposing an unpopular dictatorship on the population from the top down. Since the 1970s, however, a growing scholarship has noted that Lenin's views were not inconsistent with class-conscious and even violent plebeian views at the bottom that he did not create or impose.

It is clear that in the two decades following 1917, democracy (however defined) was transformed into dictatorship. Again, for a long time we understood this development in personal terms. Following defeated oppositionist Trotsky (but notably not Nikolai Bukharin) we explained this as a calculated campaign by Stalin to build and cement his personal dictatorship. Either as Lenin's heir or usurper, depending on the author's politics, it was Stalin who single-handedly crushed popular democracy. As we wrestled with our exaggeration of Lenin's role, perhaps it is time to question Trotsky's version of Stalin's.

This chapter looks at this attenuation of the revolutionary democracy of 1917 through a different lens, one that does not focus exclusively on 'great man' conceptions of history. Lenin and the revolutionary masses of 1917 understood democracy as not only coercive, but locally based. Democracy and violence were two sides of the same local coin, and were at first in the hands of councils, or soviets, close to the ground. We shall argue that the transition from democracy to centralized dictatorship was related to the post-revolutionary government's need to monopolize violence by separating it from local-based revolutionary democracy. Such a centralization and devolution of democracy was common to many post-revolutionary regime consolidations in the twentieth century, whether or not a dictator was part of the picture. It was related to institutional change and predictable centralization more than to personal power-grabbing.

***

The Fate of the Bolshevik Revolution

The restive workers, peasants and soldiers who overthrew the Tsar in February 1917 called themselves the Democracy. Members of the 'Democracy' were society's have-nots and excluded the former elites. 'It included the working people and intellectuals who defended the interests of the common people [...] as embodying the will of the "entire democracy" or the revolutionary democracy that would triumph over all the dark forces of the country.' Democracy was understood 'not as equal rights for and power for all, but as politics in the interests of the poor.'[1]

The appearance of soviets in 1917, explicitly in opposition to elite society and the Provisional Government thought to speak for it, reflected this bifurcation. The 'Democracy' was embodied and practised in the smoke-filled mass meetings of various soviets, with workers and soldiers crowding the floor, hanging from the rafters, brandishing their rifles and 'voting' things up or down by mass shouting. It was not the technicalities of voting that mattered; it was the popular will of the downtrodden that had suddenly found voice.

Conceptions of 'democracy' and the threat from 'enemies' were inextricably linked. Russian plebeians had traditionally divided the world into 'Us' and 'Them'. 'Us', the Democracy, consisted of the working poor of country, town and army. This was the '*narod*', the People, which did not include the entire population. 'Them' included the rich, officers, exploiters, intellectuals and outsiders (especially to peasants.)

In the cauldron of 1917, this dualism became sharper when large numbers of angry and land-hungry peasant soldiers were armed. It was easy for them to imagine that the elite, bourgeois, treasonous 'they' were a threat to the Democracy. 'Popular talk of enemies resumed quite soon after the initial unifying euphoria of the February revolution [...] a dualistic vocabulary of enemies and traitors on the one side and friends, comrades, and brothers on the other.'[2] The enemy had to be stopped in order to save the Democracy. Lenin understood this and successfully positioned himself and his party to reflect and lead these impulses.

Mass violence I: The Civil War 1918–21

The Bolshevik Red Terror of the Russian Civil War is usually portrayed as having been centrally ordered and planned. Lenin's ideas and directives are said to be decisive: he launched the Red Terror of 1918 with a few memos; he and his associates always controlled it through a monolithic and obedient Cheka.[3] Yet much of that violence and terror percolated up from below and had not only a revolutionary but a democratic aspect.

Even though the February Revolution that overthrew the Tsar was a relatively peaceful affair compared to what came later, its aftermath saw a rash of lynchings and beatings of officers and landowners. The *narod* settled age-old scores in 'a spontaneous elemental discharge of hatred and vengeance against the privileged classes.' Another wave of elemental violence followed the October Revolution.[4] In both 1917 revolutions, central government control vanished. The collapse of the state 'coincided with the surge of founding violence mixed with wild vengefulness.'[5]

But it was the Civil War (1918–21) that saw a huge explosion of violence and terror. Some 3 to 5 million people died of war and famine in this breakdown of civilization and class vengeance was everywhere. As one peasant said,

> I stamped on my master Nikitinsky, trampled on him for an hour or maybe more [...] Shooting is letting him off, and too damned easy. With shooting you never get at the soul, to where it is in a fellow and how it shows itself. But I don't spare myself, and I've more than once trampled an enemy for over an hour. You see, I want him to get to know what life really is, what life is like down our way.[6]

On the White side, 'Commissars or Party members had stars, hammer and sickle, or "100%" (of the norm) cut or burned into their bodies. Older forms of execution were revived: quartering, stretching or cutting off of limbs and heads, drowning under the ice of frozen streams or lakes.'[7]

On the Red side, captured officers were special targets. Isaac Babel recounts several such episodes:

> 'Officers are dogs!' Trunov said [...] And Trunov picked out an officer's cap from the pile of rags and put it on an old man's head. 'It fits,' Trunov murmured, stepping up closer to him, 'it fits.' And he plunged his saber into the prisoner's gullet.

Other officers died because of their underwear. 'Golov quickly shot the prisoner in the back of the neck and jumped up to his feet [...] "Our mothers don't knit drawers like that for us," he told me slyly.'[8]

Before 1917 there had been little in Lenin's writings supporting terror.[9] But now he and his associates were not shy about supporting it to win the war. In September 1918, the Bolsheviks declared an official policy of 'Red Terror'. Aligning himself with the Trunovs, Golovs and the plebeian 'We' in general, Lenin now exhorted workers to 'rob the robbers' and to carry out 'street justice'.[10] In June 1918, Lenin wrote to G. Zinoviev who was party chief in Petrograd. 'We have heard that the workers of Piter want mass terror but you (not you personally) are holding them back. I protest decisively! We would compromise ourselves and counterrevolutionaries would think we are softies [*triapki*].'[11] Lenin sided with popular violence; he did not invent it.

Spontaneous violence was regarded as democratic because it was carried out by and defended the 'Democracy', the 'People'. Even the central Cheka (the 'All-Russian' Cheka, or VChK) was not in control. Local and regional Chekas were staffed and paid by the plebeian-dominated local and regional soviets.[12]

No government, revolutionary or not, could permanently tolerate uncontrolled, locally administered violence however useful it may be in specific situations. Even without a Lenin or a Stalin, any regime trying to pick up the pieces from a shattering revolution would sooner or later need to find ways to standardize and control violence. Such efforts inevitably meant taking control away from the grass roots, from the localities, from the Democracy. And despite a continuous string of orders and decrees, controlling it would take years.

Jurisdiction and centralization

According to its statute (*polozhenie*) of June 1918, the central Cheka was subordinated (*'pri'*) to the cabinet, the Council of People's Commissars (SNK). Yet it was district (*uezd*) and regional (*guberniia* or *oblast*) level soviets who chose members of Cheka commissions at their levels and determined their size.[13] Chekas were to 'fulfil the orders of soviets in investigations when necessary' and were to 'work in close contact with all regional Soviet organisations and give them any help and cooperation.' In cases of Cheka misconduct, the regional soviet or its executive committee (*ispolkom*) 'takes measures against them, up to arrest and sending them to court.'[14]

On the other hand, 'General leadership and direction of the work of the commissions belongs to the VChK,' which 'leads the work of all guberniia commissions and gives them direction' and whose orders could not be changed at lower levels. An 'Instruction' of December 1918 added that Cheka members were appointed by local soviet executive committees '*and* the VChK' [emphasis mine] which also now had the right to send representatives (*polnomochnye predstaviteli*, PP) with full voting rights to local Chekas.[15]

By the autumn of 1918, this ambiguity touched off a public conflict in the press between the central VChK and the network of mass soviets about who would control the Chekas. In some places, the conflict was more than a discussion. It had to do with who was empowered to impose the death penalty and with basic 'constitutional' questions about the revolution. In many places, local Cheka and soviet leaders arrested each other.[16]

Feliks Dzerzhinskii, head of the VChK, argued that Chekas at all levels 'are indisputably autonomous [of the soviets] regarding their work and must carry out implicitly all instructions issuing from the VChK, which is the highest organ to which they are subordinate.' Grigorii Petrovskii, Russian Commissar of Internal Affairs (NKVD), found VChK's reasoning unconstitutional and unilateral. Others argued that the soviets had to be supreme, arguing that the main slogan of the 1917 revolutions had been 'All Power to the Soviets' not 'All Power to the Cheka.' Not surprisingly, 118 of 147 soviet executive committees surveyed agreed: local Chekas should be departments of local soviets.[17]

Another draft statute for the Cheka in October 1918 complicated matters further by formally bringing the NKVD and the People's Commissariat of Justice (NKIu) into an already confused jurisdictional mess alongside the VChK and the Moscow Soviet. So local Chekas were appointed and paid by soviets, under the orders of the VChK and told to cooperate – whatever that might mean – with three other separate agencies. This 'did nothing to resolve the Vechenka's bitter struggle with the soviets for control of local Chekas.'[18]

As the Dzerzhinskii-Petrovskii argument showed, the outcome of the struggle related to democracy. Local soviets were still mass democratic institutions and the more power they lost, the less democratic the system became.

With the end of the civil war danger in 1921, various Bolsheviks, including L. B. Kamenev, argued for the abolition of the Cheka altogether. Others like Dzerzhinskii and Lenin thought that a political police was still necessary but with some legal controls. The compromise was the transformation of the Cheka into a GPU (State Political Administration) in 1922.

The transformation is usually characterized as simply a name change because the GPU retained the right to try and execute.[19] But a close reading of the documents shows that other issues were involved. Aside from some pious and increasingly vestigial language about GPUs being responsible to local control, the gist of the change was about taking things out of the hands of local soviets.

First, as we have seen, since 1918 local soviets had the right to investigate and arrest Cheka members and send them to court for 'misconduct or disorder'. Now, though, the new GPU took over the right to investigate its own chekists without reference to the soviets. As a gesture to legality – but not to the soviets – such cases of the GPU investigating itself were to be with the 'participation' of a procurator and with the obligation ('later') to inform the Justice Commissariat of the sentence imposed.[20]

Second, the GPU had the right to send its plenipotentiaries to the localities to 'unite, lead and coordinate' local GPUs.[21] Such central plenipotentiaries had appeared only intermittently in the localities. 'Political policing in the provinces generally involved sporadic visits by plenipotentiaries, along with military-style counterinsurgency operations.'[22] But the new GPU plenipotentiaries (PPs) were less and less itinerant circuit riders and would soon become resident in the provinces as permanent police bosses representing the Moscow centre.

The centralization trend continued in 1923. With the formation of the USSR, an all-union political police, the OGPU (United State Political Administration) was formed above the level of the republics. The OGPU preserved the powers the GPU had taken over from the old Cheka but again, more than a name change was involved. The OGPU represented a new layer of centralization of an already centralizing system, taking things another step away from local soviet control. Each union republic (Ukraine, Kazakhstan, etc.) retained its own national GPU but these were now to be 'supervised' by centrally appointed OGPU plenipotentiaries above all of them.

The OGPU also inherited from the Cheka and the GPU the right to try, sentence and execute persons involved in armed actions and banditry, which were still common after the civil war. With the formation of the OGPU, those extrajudicial rights were extended. An OGPU Special Conference (*Osoboe soveshchanie*) was formed with the right to exile 'socially dangerous elements' to up to three years in exile or concentration camp without judicial proceedings. Every union republic was to have its own OS, but each of them was to be chaired by a centrally appointed PP OGPU.[23]

Feliks Dzerzhinskii as leader of the Cheka-GPU-OGPU had jealously guarded its powers. With his death in 1926, local bodies jumped in and tried to take advantage of the situation to recoup some of their lost prerogatives by stealing personnel from the OGPU. The Central Committee had to call for 'decisively putting an end' to the 'many cases in which local party organisations without even seeking the permission of the OGPU have shifted police personnel to party and state work.'[24]

The final step in the centralization of political police functions and their final detachment from local or regional influence came in July 1934. The all-union OGPU and all the republican and regional GPUs were replaced by a single all-union NKVD.[25] All cases, including treason, counter-revolution and espionage, were to come before the regular courts or the Supreme Court.[26] Local democratic soviet control over violence was finished. Or so it seemed.

Arrests and centralization

Procedural questions about who could be arrested show another trajectory of centralization. In the civil war, the local Chekas could arrest whomever they wanted. If they arrested 'responsible' Soviet or party workers (which could be anyone with an impressive piece of paper), local Chekas 'must immediately, that is no later than 24 hours, inform the corresponding organisation where the person works,' that is after the fact.[27]

But Lenin-backed 'street justice' was still part of the culture. The locals continued to promiscuously arrest anyone they deemed to have anti-soviet views, including numerous technical specialists. The class instincts of local Chekas were not much constrained because two years later, Dzerzhinskii had to warn them about arresting too many specialists without giving any warning.[28] As late at 1928, ten years after the first moves to end local control of violence, '*demokratiia*' survived. The class enemy was still the class enemy. At the height of the centrally inspired campaign against disloyal specialists (The 'Shakhty Affair'), local detachments of the GPU had to be warned that while 'aggressively' pursuing the campaign against harmful counter-revolutionary elements, they must do so with 'maximum care, more than takes place at present,' arresting 'only the most malevolent counter-revolutionaries.'[29] As late as July 1931, the Politburo ordered (again) that no specialist could be arrested without prior permission of the relevant commissariat.[30] And again, such orders had a limited effect because a few months later, the Politburo had to complain about 'illegal arrests' of specialists.[31]

In most places, party presence was weak. Nationally, 67 per cent of the population lived in the countryside, but only 0.3 per cent of that population belonged to the party.[32] In 1925, nationally there was one OGPU agent for each 3,900 square miles, one for each 14,000 citizens.[33] A sea of unsupportive peasants included overtly hostile kulaks.[34] Valuable technical specialists were of dubious loyalty. Disgruntled remnants of White Army officers and soldiers, former members of anti-Bolshevik political parties and criminal gangs prowled the landscape. Armed bandits on horseback continued to plague the countryside well into the 1930s.[35] Kulaks had shotguns and ambushes of communists were not uncommon.[36]

In this environment, Moscow's exhortations to rule by drawing on social support and stepping up propaganda campaigns among a sullen if not hostile population must have seemed pointless to the locals. In order to get things done, violence seemed a reasonable tool of rule to the locals. Given this, it is hardly surprising that once collectivization began, 'Among local workers in both party and state administrative systems there were more than a few hotheads, internally disposed to command-repressive actions.'[37]

Mass violence II: Collectivization

As had been the case in the civil war, in the collectivization of agriculture that began in the late 1920s the Bolshevik leadership was prepared to countenance and approve mass terror from below if it furthered their policies. In both the civil war and collectivization, local violence was approved by a Bolshevik leadership that tried to control and direct it. In both cases, the perception was that the class enemy – counter-revolutionary elements in the countryside – threatened the regime. In both cases, there was a wartime atmosphere. In both cases, the regime's representatives thought they were fighting a new version of the 'us' versus 'them' of the civil war.

In both the civil war and collectivization, we are used to thinking in terms of Lenin and then Stalin centrally planning and directing violence. And although neither shrank from savage violence and killing, it would be a mistake to over-emphasize anyone's control. When forced grain collections began in 1927–8, 'completely independently [with the agreement of the corresponding party and state leaderships] local organs of the OGPU carried out arrests, confiscations of property and pronounced sentences of prison term or exile and so forth.'[38] Collectivization that followed in 1929 and 1930 saw a veritable civil war in the countryside, a cycle of official mass repressions and peasant resistance. It did not take long for regional party leaders to argue that resistance, including peasant attacks on officials, called for the use of lethal violence.

In May 1928, the Stalingrad party committee wrote to the TsK that 'the situation demands application of Article 107 [i.e., the death penalty] to kulaks engaged in food speculation. The article would be applied in very limited scale.' Stalin agreed.[39] In September 1929, the Politburo approved a similar request from the Lower Volga territory, to shoot up to fifty leaders of a purported insurrectionary organization. The Politburo's provisional approval noted, however, that with the exceptions of violent crimes against soviet and party officials, such actions were to be examined legally in the courts. The following month, in response to another telegram, the Politburo permitted the Lower Volga party organization to pronounce death sentences on five persons accused of 'terror'. But the Lower Volga communists were obliged to pass the information along to the Politburo for confirmation.[40]

Telegrams from the provinces asked for the right to conduct extra-judicial repression by troika. In October 1929, the Politburo agreed with the need for 'decisive and quick repressive measures, up to shooting, against kulaks organising terrorist attacks on soviet and party workers.'[41] However, the same Politburo directive insisted that 'conduct of corresponding measures, as a rule, is through judicial organs and in *specific* cases, when special speed is required, to punish through the GPU [...] with the agreement of the oblast party committee of the VKP(b) and in more *important* cases with the agreement of the Central Committee of the VKP(b).'[42] Six days later, the OGPU Collegium in Moscow issued an explanation of the Politburo directive, stipulating that troikas could apply sentences only after telegraphed approval of Moscow OGPU headquarters and adding a three-month limit on troika powers to repress.[43]

During collectivization, local party or police officials usually received permission to carry out death sentences. But Stalin insisted on the right to control repression and while he was willing to sanction mass shootings, his preference was to handle such things 'in judicial order.' In October 1934, L. M. Kaganovich sent a telegram to Stalin from Cheliabinsk: 'I would consider it possible to confer the right to confirm death sentences for one month to a troika [...] I ask you to communicate your decision.' Stalin replied, 'I don't understand what this is about. If you can, it is better to get by without a troika and confirm the sentences in the usual [judicial] procedure. Stalin.'[44]

Nevertheless, local police ran ahead of Moscow. Local OGPU administrations 'seized the initiative in this campaign.' By early November 1929 – that is nearly three months before Stalin officially launched the dekulakization campaign – the OGPU reported that it had arrested more than 28,300 individuals in support of grain procurement campaigns.[45] In January 1930, the central OGPU had to admit that it had lost control of its local representatives and of the process in general. Deputy OGPU chief Iagoda wrote to leading officials that 'We lead OGPU work throughout the Union, yet next door, right under our nose, we don't know what is going on.' After asking regional OGPU officials to report how many people had been arrested 'by all authorities,' he noted that nationwide arrests had hit 93,000 and ordered an end to mass arrests. Iagoda wrote that 'During this time, everybody "who felt like it" made arrests [...] Therefore it is necessary to point out in this order that arrests may be made only by persons who have the right to do so under the law.'[46]

Things had spun so far out of control that Stalin intervened publicly with his famous 'Dizzy with Success' article, in which he blamed locals for the 'excesses' of collectivization.[47] Although his article represented a cynical attempt to deflect responsibility for central policy, 'there is no doubt that the extensive "excesses" were at times as much the fault of traditional *proizvol* (arbitrary conduct) on the part of officialdom as a central policy poorly and ambiguously conceived.'[48]

In February 1930, OGPU plenipotentiaries were given the right to conduct the extrajudicial review of cases but only 'during the time of the campaign to liquidate the kulaks as a class.' The order stipulated, however, that such review must involve the participation of a procurator and the local soviet executive committee.[49] Such judicial supervision did not always take place, however, because the very next month a directive letter of the RSFSR Supreme Court complained that 'in a series of cases of counter-revolution, which demand verification of the essence of the case's facts and circumstances, judicial investigation did not in fact take place even when the final sentence was death.'[50]

As early as April 1924 the centre had taken steps to establish a monopoly on death sentences. A Politburo order (which had to be reaffirmed in March 1926 and often thereafter) decreed that local courts could not impose death sentences in political cases without the preliminary approval of the TsK.[51] In December 1929, a Politburo directive ordered courts to send copies of their sentences to a Politburo Commission which insisted on final review of the case.[52] In April 1931, the Politburo had to once again 'categorically confirm previous TsK decisions that death sentences for political cases must not be pronounced without the sanction of the TsK.'[53] Three months later, the Politburo had to repeat the order.

The TsK repeatedly paraphrased the original 1922 GPU charter, in which citizens arrested for political crimes could not be held without interrogation longer than two weeks or under detention for more than three months.[54] That the Politburo found it necessary to repeat this stricture is a sure sign that it was not being obeyed by the provincial leadership. In June 1932, the government issued an order 'On Revolutionary Legality' which criticized excesses. It also called for the prosecution of local officials responsible for illegal arrests.[55] Criticizing 'excesses' may have had some effect in this case. While in 1930–1, some 30,000 people had been shot, the number dropped to under 3,000 in 1932.[56]

On 9 February 1933, the Politburo complied with the request (*udovletvorit' pros'bu*) of the Belorussian Central Committee to give an OGPU troika the right to apply death sentences in cases of counter-revolutionary organizations, groups of kulaks and whiteguard elements.[57] In April, the Politburo similarly extended the right to examine cases on uprisings and counter-revolution (with application of death sentence) to troikas in Central Asia and Leningrad, the latter including S. M. Kirov.[58]

Stalin authorized severe repression against opponents of collectivization. But the documents show that it was regional officials who raised the question. As Stalin put it in May, 'demands for mass expulsions from the countryside and for the use of harsh forms of repression continue to come in from a number of regions.'[59] The right to shoot was something locals had to seek and was something Stalin sought to control and protect. Faced with the crisis of famine and crop failures, Stalin usually approved harsh punishment, but always with restrictions.

By mid-1933 the grain crisis seemed to be abating and as the Bolsheviks had done after the civil war, Stalin reigned in the power to execute. On 2 May 1933 he met with OGPU leaders and his notes from the meeting show that he was interested in limiting the number of people authorized to make arrests and to specify the dispositions of large numbers of those arrested.[60] Five days later, the Politburo *revoked* the rights of all troikas (except those in the Far East) to apply any death sentences.[61]

The following day, Stalin and Molotov circulated a decree ordering a halt to mass arrests in the regions. Stalin and Molotov stated that 'the moment has come [...] when we are no longer in need of mass repression.' Their circular complained that,

> Disorderly arrests on a massive scale are still being carried out by our officials in the countryside. Arrests are being made by chairmen of collective farms, members

of collective farm boards, by chairmen of village soviets, by secretaries of [party] cells and by district and territorial commissioners. Anyone who feels like arresting does so, including those who have no right whatsoever to make arrests. It is no wonder, therefore, that with such an orgy of arrests, the organs of the OGPU and especially the police have lost all sense of proportion. More often than not, they will arrest people for no reason at all.[62]

As with Stalin's 1930 'Dizzy with Success' article, there was more than a little scapegoating here. After all, Stalin had authorized mass violence in 1930 to carry out collectivization. But he had never authorized anyone but the OGPU to arrest people, nor had he nor OGPU chief Iagoda authorized the scale of the 'orgy of arrests'.

After the May 1933 decisions, the Politburo continued to approve local requests for the right to apply death sentences, but more rarely and always with restrictions. The approved targets now were almost always bandits and armed gangs. In July 1933, the Politburo approved a troika of the West Siberian OGPU to shoot bandits terrorizing the local population, but made the head of the territorial OGPU personally responsible. In August 1933, the Politburo decided to 'temporarily' permit (*razreshit'*) troikas in a few regions to apply death sentences to active bandits. (As we have seen, this right had been on the books since the formation of the GPU in 1922 but now had become subject to confirmation by Moscow.[63]) A year later, in September 1934, the Politburo approved a proposal to extend to Western Siberian first secretary Eikhe the right to approve death sentences for two months and then only at the initiative of Politburo member Molotov.[64]

In July 1934, the Politburo had found it necessary to repeat its strictures: all death sentences were subject to confirmation by the Political Commission of the Politburo.[65] This had hardly more effect than the previous warnings. In October 1935, Procurator of the USSR Roginskii protested the actions of a troika in the North Caucasus that had sentenced people to death for taking and receiving bribes under articles of the criminal code that envisioned five- to ten-year sentences. Before the sentences could be properly reviewed, the accused had been shot.[66]

In this period, local party leaders were more inclined to mass repression than Moscow. Stalin said then that mass operations were inefficient and alienated the loyal part of the population. He insisted on giving permission and *limity* – the opposite of quotas – in each individual case. This was the lineage of the 1937 mass operations of Order No. 447. It was about extrajudicial killing, and not everybody was on the same page.

What about Stalin?

Western historiography has curiously supported the same 'cult of personality' that characterized Stalinist propaganda. Everything is attributed to Stalin and there can be no other important actors or constraints on his omnipotence.[67]

It is a commonplace that Stalin controlled the political police and the judiciary in the 1920s. One authoritative study argues that in the 1920s 'Stalin, as general secretary, took quiet control early on of operational direction, information flow, and strategic leadership of the political police [...] Stalin's rise to power, and his dictatorship, cannot be understood apart from the history of the Soviet political police, and the development and power of the political police have not been understood apart from Stalin's rise to power.'[68]

In terms of both logic and documentary support, it is not easy to sustain such interpretations. It is difficult to associate Stalin's rise to power with his control over the political police. Before Ezhov's appointment in 1936, previous leaders of the political police were not Stalin's men. Dzerzhinskii's status was on a par with Stalin's and there is no evidence that Stalin controlled him. Nor is there any evidence that Dzerzhinskii 'helped Stalin in strengthening the authority and scope of practice of the police.'[69] In fact, the converse is much more likely. Menzhinskii, Dzerzhinskii's successor, had no obvious connection to Stalin and often blocked Stalin's suggestions.[70] Menzhinskii's successor Iagoda was also not Stalin's man. He supported Stalin's rightist opponents Bukharin and Rykov. Molotov claimed that Iagoda was appointed only because there was nobody else: 'We had to work with reptiles like that, but there were no others.'[71]

There is no doubt that Stalin personally authored the infamous August 1932 order calling for the death sentence to those stealing grain. There is no doubt that he ordered the use of lethal force in collectivization and in Order No. 447. There is no doubt that he signed orders to shoot some 40,000 members of the elite in 1937–8. And there is no doubt that in later years he ordered the execution of numerous military and party leaders.

But the story was different before the mid-1930s. Books and documentary collections about Stalin's power often have titles containing phrases like 'Stalin and the NKVD, 1922–xxx.' But it is impossible to find documents showing his interference in police matters before the late 1920s. Before then, Stalin's participation in political police activities was quite limited. As General Secretary, he received letters, proposals and arguments about the political police from Dzerzhinskii, Menzhinskii, Krylenko, Trotsky and others. It was his job to place these issues on the Politburo agenda. Therefore, his name appears on such documents emanating from others, but there is no evidence of his opinion on most of these. This is hardly equivalent to using or controlling the political police and historians' rhetoric aside, there is no evidence that Stalin used the GPU against his oppositionist opponents, as Bukharin and many local leaders wanted.

It was only in 1927 that he openly began to influence OGPU policies, *after* he had risen to power. In retaliation to the assassination of a Soviet envoy in Poland, he insisted on shooting hostages already in prison. The following year, he was a prime mover behind police persecution of technical specialists, taking the lead in the Shakhty Affair. It is therefore difficult to argue that control of the political police was instrumental to his rise to power. The support Stalin enjoyed by many elements in the party explains Stalin's rise to power quite apart from his later control of the political police.

The Fate of the Bolshevik Revolution

Mass violence III: The mass operations and centralized chaos

There is no space here for a detailed discussion of origins of the bloody 1937 mass operations in which three-quarters of a million people were summarily executed and many more disappeared into camps.[72] But the twenty-year centre/periphery history we have described already suggests an answer.

In the period leading up to Stalin's approval of NKVD order No. 447 launching the mass operations, local party and police leaders wanted to deal forcefully with a resurgence of anti-Soviet activity occasioned by kulaks returning from exile.

Stalin and Ezhov had been on record as opposing mass operations since 1933 and as recently as March 1937. In July 1937 Stalin changed his mind. He sent around a circular telegram specifying punishment for criminals and kulaks returning from exile. But local leaders suggested incorporating new categories of victims. Locals added 'those previously avoiding punishment', including people already in camps, former nobles, tsarist era gendarmes, priests and other religious 'sectarians', former participants in anti-soviet armed campaigns, members of former political parties (SRs, Mensheviks and others), bandits, Whites, criminals (including horse and cattle thieves and robbers) and other saboteurs of industry and agriculture. Local party leaders had complained about precisely these 'elements' back at the February 1937 TsK plenum.

Ezhov and Stalin reduced the execution numbers proposed by the fierce locals in half of the provinces by a total of nearly 20,000. When Stalin questioned one regional leader about the large number of enemies he was reporting, the reply was 'There are, in fact, many more Comrade Stalin. You cannot imagine how many there are!'[73]

Stalin had suggested grouping victims into a First Category (execution) and Second Category (exile to distant locations.) After meeting with local leaders, the Second Category became eight to ten years in camps or prisons instead of exile.

In the course of the 1937–8 mass operations, regional authorities routinely asked for increases in execution numbers and Stalin and Ezhov nearly always granted them.[74] 'The Politburo leadership aimed for a violent but "orderly" action, which would be oriented toward rules established from above. When some regions in the course of carrying out the operation asked the Politburo to raise their limits, the PB refused.'[75] Stalin and Ezhov subsequently approved local requests for increased limits for a total approved limit of 356,105 executions. In the event, however, locals shot 386,798 for a total of 30,700 unapproved killings.

The bloody mass operations of 1937–8 have been called a re-igniting of the civil war.[76] In a limited sense it recalled fighting the 1917 *Demokratiia*'s enemies. It was the third instance of a particular dynamic of repression in the two decades following the Russian Revolution in which central Bolshevik authorities unleashed whirlwinds of local, class-based bloodletting and settling of personal, political and class scores. The first was the civil war of 1918–21; the second was the enforcement of agricultural collectivization in 1928–33, which saw 'civil war' in the countryside.[77]

In each of these three pulsations of local violence, the targets were the same class enemies. In each of them, local police and party authorities were authorized to choose the quantity and identity of victims and to determine who would live and who would die. In each case, albeit to different degrees, the centre would permit or order mass violence for its own policy purposes and then scramble to clean up the mess and establish control.[78]

In these three crises, the central Bolshevik leadership imagined that it did not have the means to defend itself from real or imagined enemies without turning violence over to local authorities. Those local authorities were inclined to violence of their own which often displeased the centre which, while licensing local violence, tried to control it.

The 'peaceful' interludes between these three events saw restricted repression controlled by central authorities, combined with some kind of moderating legality. In this odd modulation, locals were three times given the power to decide whom and how many to kill, but increasingly only with the case by case permission of Moscow. The alternating peaceful and violent phases in these two decades had one thing in common: an increasing centralization of political policing.

This kind of centralization of punitive functions as well as the alternating dynamic of legality and repression is common in many revolutionary situations, even without a Stalin. The attenuation of local mass democracy by centralizing control of repression in Moscow was something *all* central Bolshevik leaders supported. That post-revolutionary process and Stalin's rise to power belong to different histories.

CHAPTER 9
STALINIST MODERATION AND THE TURN TO REPRESSION: UTOPIANISM AND REALPOLITIK IN THE MID-1930s
Olga Velikanova

A range of tendencies in Stalinist policies during 1933–6 historians see as moderating in political, economic, judicial and ideological developments, including trends towards more legality and nonlethal repression. This chapter discusses these moderating trends and suggests an evaluation of their place in the history of Stalinism between two peaks of state violence – collectivization (1928–32) and the Great Terror (1937–8). I argue that what looks like the moderation of policy stems from two different government contexts: sometimes it was an adjustment or ad hoc correction after 'excesses', at other times – on the level of metadiscourse – a relaxation motivated by the expectation of the advent of socialism in accordance with Lenin's plan.

There is no consensus on the nature of this period in the historiography. It is interpreted as an ideological reversal, a pragmatic retreat or plans for democratization.[1] As early as 1946 Nicholas Timasheff evaluated cultural and ideological changes in 1934–6 as a government retreat from socialist ideals (in silent recognition of their failure) towards traditional Russian cultural practices, encompassing the promotion of patriotism and traditional family life and a departure from the world revolution maxim. The purpose was to earn popular support, stabilize society and mobilize the population for the future war.[2] Recent studies do not see a refutation of socialism by the government during this period. David Hoffmann emphasizes Stalin's belief about the attainment of socialism, as the dictator understood it. Eugeny Dobrenko similarly highlights the purely representational character of socialism as a whole in context of an older Russian proclivity towards representationalism at the expense of realism.[3]

Questions remain: was moderation a preconceived plan? Why were moderate steps undertaken and why were they terminated? Why did obvious concessions overlap with continuing repressions? Let me start with the latter problem of inconsistency.

A pattern of duality can be seen in Stalinist politics in the mid-1930s when informal norms and practices often competed with formal legal structures and official claims. The political system was permeated by this duality: legal reform in 1934–6 coincided

---

This research received generous support from the University of North Texas Research grant and Scholar Fellowship at European University Institute, Florence, Italy (2014).

with the continuation of extralegal practices; freedom of conscience declared in all Soviet constitutions coexisted with religious persecution; the figurative power system of the soviets was paralleled by the actual power of the party; constitutional legal norms authorized by government bodies were degraded or modified by numerous (often secret) instructions and decrees issued by the NKVD and the party. The distance between official representations and their realization was huge. This duality produced zigzags that we observe in Soviet policies throughout the interwar period: (1) a tactical retreat from War Communism to the New Economic Policy (NEP) in 1921; (2) cancellation of NEP in 1928 and the resumption of a socialist programme; (3) Stalin's article 'Dizziness from Successes' in 1930; (4) the unexpected liberalism of the 1936 Constitution and then the turn to mass repression. Such consistency in inconsistency cannot be attributed solely to personal whims of leaders or to revolutionary chaos. The cause was fundamental and structural. Such radical changes of policy resulted from the incompatibility of the utopian ambitions of the Bolsheviks and Stalinists with the pressure of reality. The resulting strains were aggravated by voluntarism,[4] maladministration, dogmatism of the leadership and the breakneck speed of transformation. Moderate tendencies (and Stalinism as a whole) were so contradictory because policymakers were guided by the socialist ideal, yet at the same time had to cope with the 'imperfections' they saw on the ground – a backward population and economy, unmanageable local officials and a frightening international environment. To understand the contradictions of moderation in the mid-1930s we can analytically dissociate two causational factors: first, on the level of ideological metadiscourse, Stalinist expectations and visions of social harmonization with the advent of socialism and generational shift, and second, reactive, ad hoc adjustments after 'excesses'. While some moderation steps were programmatic, for instance, policies benefitting the youth, the promotion of young 'New People' and the introduction of the 1936 Constitution, other politics were situational and directed towards recovery after crises and the correction of mistakes and their consequences. In the discussion below, first I review generation politics, second, the ideological paradigm and then situational politics. In the conclusion, I reflect on why moderation turned to mass repression.

The first condition for moderation in the minds of Soviet leaders, closely connected to ideology, was the generational shift. In the mid-1930s the younger generation – 43 per cent of the population – did not know alternatives to the Soviet experience. Officialdom saw this generation as a new breed of man uncontaminated by the bourgeois past, educated in new values and as such a reservoir of loyalty. The leaders had come to believe that this generation could be trusted: as young parents and teachers – to raise children with socialist values (accordingly, the Family Legislation of 1936 enhanced the role of family[5]), as new technical cadres – to replace the old professionals and generally ready to be promoted to party, universities and managerial positions.[6] For Oleg Khlevniuk, Stalin 'install[ed] a new generation of functionaries blindly devoted to him.'[7] One foreign observer, Dr Rajchman, reported in 1936 on 'the preponderance of young people over old [...] and the increasing influence in social and political life of the young generation.'[8]

Several concessions, real and symbolic, made in favour of the youth were strategic. In March 1933, kulaks' children received voting rights. In December 1935, Stalin put age over class in his famous dictum, 'A son does not answer for his father.' This sounded like an invalidation of the previously incurable social origin label and inspired hope in the children of repressed or ostracized parents. The decree followed waiving social origin restrictions for admission to higher education institutions (only sporadically applied however). These concessions reflected the party leaders' belief that the new socialist environment played a primary role in a person's political development.

Another decisive force behind moderation in the mid-1930s was the Stalinist vision of attained socialism. The 1936 Constitution, with its election reform, universal suffrage and civil rights belonged to this metanarrative. It was a continuation and culmination of the grand socialist programme, elaborated by Lenin in *State and Revolution* and adjusted to realities of state-building in conditions of civil war; it was an organic evolution, rather than a change of political course, as Oleg Khlevniuk sees it,[9] or 'experimentation' as Yiannis Kokosalakis calls it in this volume.

The realization of socialism belonged to discursive accomplishments, described as 'the spectacle of socialism' by Dobrenko and as 'performativity' by Alexei Yurchak and Jeffrey Brooks.[10] The supremacy of representation in the construction of Soviet social reality was not entirely new. Since Peter the Great, Russia had 'pretended to be something it was not.'[11] With traditions of Potemkin villages and a historical pattern of simulating European civilization,[12] Stalin's socialism-building belonged to just such a 'catch-up discourse'.[13] However, it was not a pure and intentional deception, but rather a self-deception as Stalin sincerely believed in the power of will or word (with his logocentrism[14]) to realize the Marxist project: 'The role of so-called objective conditions has been reduced now to a minimum, while the role of the party has become crucial.'[15] Dealing with an uncountable population and immeasurable space, past state projects were able to impact only what they could reach – elites and costumes (like Peter I), façades (like Potemkin) and perhaps major cities.

Lenin's benchmarks in the building of socialism were constantly on the agenda. When Stalin launched a 'socialist offensive', he projected socialism as the result of the Five-Year Plan (1928-32). The 1936 Constitution finalized and celebrated this ideological programme.

In the mid-1930s, in public and confidential settings, Stalin, Viacheslav Molotov, Genrikh Iagoda and Avel Yenukidze repeatedly declared that the goals of the great socialist offensive had been largely achieved. They saw the victory of socialism in the economy and in changes to social and class structure. According to Marxism, changes in the base (relations of production) almost automatically shape the superstructure (ideas, values, religion, education, culture and policies). As soon as the economic base had been transformed through the Plan and collectivization, the builders of socialism focused on the superstructure. The 17th Party Conference in February 1932 formulated the political task for the Second Five-Year Plan (1933-7): to do away with 'capitalist elements' and class divisions in society and to mould all labourers into conscious and active citizens. This dictum was widely popularized. Throughout the summer of 1933, the idea was hammered into the minds of Leningrad workers in regular meetings after working hours that by the end of the Second Five-Year Plan a classless state would be established and all bourgeois classes eliminated.[16] In this context, the discourse of class, social origin and the disenfranchisement of former people waned in expectation of the advent of harmonious Soviet unity where boundaries between classes and nationalities would erode.

The first signals of class conciliation came in 1931 with Stalin's speech 'New conditions', which described the turn of old professionals from wrecking to socialism. Stalin's call to 'care about technical cadres' was an important step away from the harassment of professionals instigated by the Shakhty and Promparty show trials of 1928 and 1930.[17] In January 1933, the Central Committee Plenum declared that the economic basis of socialism had been built in the USSR as a result of the First Five-Year Plan. However, 'the consciousness of people is [still] behind their real conditions. The *kolkhozniks* are no longer individual farmers, they are collectivists, but their consciousness is still old and one of private property owners.'[18] Therefore, a struggle was necessary with the remnants of dying classes, who were exploiting the old consciousness in organizing sabotage, wrecking and theft. Five months later, however, Stalin recognized 'these three years of struggle led to a defeat of our class enemies in the countryside and to a final establishment of soviet socialist positions in the village.' Therefore, repressions in the countryside became unnecessary.[19]

The Soviet leadership was sincere in its optimistic evaluation of the transformation. We see this not only in discourse, in internal and top-secret communication, but also in pragmatic adjustments. On 25 May 1933, Yenukidze, Secretary of the Central Executive Committee of Soviets (TsIK), sent a working note to the Central Committee in which he celebrated a new consciousness among the *kolkhozniks* and accordingly proposed a more inclusive election law and changes to the constitution in favour of peasants:

> Due to the successful collectivisation of 65% of Soviet peasants and a significant organisational and economic strengthening of the collective farms, which turned members into a real and strong foundation of Soviet power, and considering the huge growth of the peasants' cultural level and increase of proletarian elements in the countryside (workers of state farms, Machine-Tractor Stations, mining industry, etc.), the TsIK decrees [...] introducing changes into the USSR constitution.[20]

Though not enacted at the time, Yenukidze's suggestion of moderate changes in election law later triggered a wider democratization. Direct, secret and universal elections – a core of the participatory direct democracy envisioned by Lenin in full-fledged socialism – were introduced by the 1936 Constitution, which ended the disfranchisement of former people, kulaks and priests.

The next step in the developing success story was the 17th Party Congress declaration in 1934 that 'socialism, the first phase of communism, has been realised in general' in the USSR. Stalin announced the 'elimination of the remnants of capitalist classes', the education of thousands of New People and evolution towards a classless society. Just a few purges of soviet and party bureaucrats were needed to achieve perfection.[21]

The practical step of this wishful imagery was Stalin's decision to proceed with inclusive election reform and changes to the constitution in January 1935, following Yenikidze's suggestion. The Seventh Congress of the Communist International that summer discussed the implications of the construction of socialism in the USSR in the context of world revolution. These public statements aimed to project the success and strength of Soviet power to its citizens and a foreign audience. Of course this was a public relations exercise, but internal communications convey how seriously the leadership took this maxim. Addressing the June 1935 Central Committee Plenum, Stalin said: 'The project of the constitution will be a kind of codex of the main achievements of workers and peasants, [...] for which people fought and which means the victory of socialism.'[22] In a personal letter to Molotov, he remarked: 'We should not mix the constitution with the party programme. It should contain what has already been achieved. While the programme is what we seek.'[23] David Hoffmann has stated: 'Privately as well as publicly Party leaders stressed the attainment of socialism and the "new order of classes" as the reason for a new constitution.'[24] Private exchanges suggest strongly that the 'victory of socialism' maxim expressed the Bolsheviks' fundamental beliefs, along with their overestimation of human agency in structuring history, dogmatism and proclivity for wishful thinking. The idea of building socialism worked as an engine in all policies, culminating in the liberal constitution and universal suffrage. But socialist policies, like collectivization for example, often generated unforeseen complications and crises that needed to be resolved – either by repressions or pragmatic adjustments.

Concessions in economic policy and repression were situational and inconsistent. They corrected the consequences of 'excesses' through forced, contingent or half-hearted measures (Khlevniuk has called it 'crisis pragmatism'). Such pragmatism is obvious when Stalin retreated from rationing in 1935 and wage equalizing in 1931 (both previously a norm in fundamentalist views of socialism and now called 'leftist'), as they were ineffective and the good harvest in 1933 permitted change. To motivate productivity, in 1934 the government shifted from distribution and barter in favour of commerce and a monetary economy.[25] The government allowed free trade in bread in 1935 but suspended it when it was inconvenient, for instance during the procurement campaign in autumn 1935, then in summer 1936. Moreover, it sanctioned 'purges of class-alien, speculative and theft-prone elements' in the procurement apparatus.[26] The introduction of a progressive piecework system in 1934 and the Stakhanovite movement in August 1935 were dedicated to increasing production. The latter gave rise to work norms derided on the shop floor as exploitation. Workers complained they could not perform hard physical work because they were underfed.[27] They felt their real wages begin to rise only in 1936 after bread prices were reduced.

1934–6 were 'the three good years' in the Soviet economy. The end of rationing in 1934 was presented as an achievement of socialism. Stalin's motto 'Life has become better; life has become more cheerful!' inflated by propaganda, was received sceptically by workers like Andrei Arzhilovskii in a Ural town. 'Just before 6 a.m. I went out and got in line for bread. My happy fellow countrymen were already standing there, getting used to socialism,' his diary stated on 4 December 1936.[28] Still, high prices and shortages annoyed an impoverished population.

After the overstrains of the First Five-Year Plan, the targets and pace of the second plan (1933-7) were reduced, mostly because of depleted resources. After a decade of neglect, moderate investments were directed to the production of consumer goods. In 1936 this grew from 18 per cent in 1935 to 27.2 per cent of all investment in industry. Growth in the clothes and footwear branches was 23.9 and 37.3 per cent, respectively.[29] The shortage of goods, however, was still acute and the population so worn out that people did not notice this growth: in 1937, a Muscovite L. Shtange complained in her diary about the lack of clothing and shoes in the city privileged in supply.[30] Another engineer visited forty Moscow stores searching for children's shoes and finally found a pair for 48 rubles - one-third of a monthly wage. He wrote to Molotov: 'You announced to the whole USSR that prices will be lowered [...] However, recently you raised the prices on textiles and shoes. It's too bad. Why do you make people angry? [...] Discontent grows. [...] This has continued for ten years. For how much longer?'[31] The government combated shortages, queuing and speculation by raising prices and turning to repression. In July 1936 the Politburo allocated more goods to four major cities, raising prices by 30 per cent and sanctioned a round of arrests of speculators: the NKVD extra-judicial *troiki* sentenced 4,003 persons and the courts 1,635.[32]

Repressive politics underwent the same pragmatic adjustments. Iagoda stressed in 1933 that triumphant socialism required new methods and directed the OGPU to shift from sweeping excisions to prophylactic politics, towards gathering information, undercover work and monitoring the larger population.[33] In 1933 prisons were discharged by half because of overcrowding and the lack of an agricultural workforce in famine-decimated Ukraine. But in 1932–5 the prison and camp population grew again 210.9 per cent rising to 1,251,501 persons.[34] In 1931 and 1934, decrees restored the civil rights of certain categories of exiled kulaks, but in 1935 when the five-year terms of 1 million special settlers came to an end, rehabilitation and liberation were partial and chaotic. Following the logic of the transformative nature of socialist labour, half a million collective farmers with smaller terms were rehabilitated and permitted to join *kolkhozy*,[35] but without permission to return to their homelands (practical considerations offered by the NKVD[36]). In February 1936 the exile of the children of the disenfranchised was abandoned (exemplifying generational politics).[37] But most 'kulaks' were still bound to their place of exile. Many subsequently fled. The year 1936 saw two waves of illegal migration: the returnees of the 1930 deportation and the flight from starving *kolkhozy*.[38]

In August 1935, 54,000 local officials accused of 'sabotaging' procurement were liberated. In 1936, 115,000 cases of people convicted under the brutal 1932 decree on the theft of socialist property were reviewed and a third freed.[39] Exiled specialists were allowed to work in their profession and their children to receive education.[40] The numbers of victims of repression in this period are contradictory, though a tendency towards nonlethal repression is obvious: the overall level of mass killing by the security agency declined from 20,201 in 1930 to only 1,118 in 1936. However, the number of persons sentenced by the OGPU/NKVD increased from 78,999 in 1934 to 274,670 in 1936.[41]

An important step towards a social truce was the April 1936 permission for Cossacks to serve in the Red Army. The Cossacks explained this by the need for soldiers in a future war. They said that the Soviet government began trusting the Cossacks after years of persecutions because 'no more Cossacks remained in the *stanitsy* (villages) - all [have been] exiled and convicted ... there are more new settlers (*inogorodnie*) now in the villages'.[42] This logic probably ruled throughout the government while they expected a harmonious body politic: enemies had been purged and replaced with a generation of New People. Another compromise was the new *Kolkhoz* Statute of February 1935 that permitted collective farmers to cultivate small private plots. This pragmatic concession, presented as a gift to the population, was silent recognition of the inability of the *kolkhoz* system to feed the country.

Another step interpreted by historians as moderation was the turn to more formal legality - an attempt to regulate and control the arbitrariness common in the collectivization process. Two models - of 'legality' and 'extralegality' - competed in the interwar period. Historically the suspension of legal procedure is at the core of politics that Giorgio Agamben called a 'state of exception' - when a government, in an emergency situation, usually war, views legality as too cumbersome and sluggish.[43] The Bolsheviks, who confronted the whole world with their socialist project, understood their position as one of permanent emergency which legitimized wartime practices, including the suspension of law in peacetime. Under Stalinism, extralegal violence, normally a provisional and exceptional measure, was institutionalized as a technique of government. The 1920s and 1930s saw a persistent pattern of cessation and reemergence of the extrajudicial power of the political police towards specific groups and offences.

On the one hand, the suspension of law accelerates and simplifies procedure, and on the other hand, it conflicts with the need of a ruler to control the state machinery. A clear legal framework adds legitimacy and stability to the system of power[44] as the adoption of the constitution projected. To reestablish manageability, the turn to legality included the organization of the USSR Procuracy in 1933 and legal reform during 1935-6. Repeatedly on 10 July 1931, 7 May 1933, 17 June 1935 and 13 February 1937, the Politburo attempted to monopolize control over the arrest of communists, professionals and all death sentences.[45] These repetitive Politburo reminders evidence poor implementation and chaos on the ground. It prompts historians to distinguish the leaders' intentions from the grass-roots practice. Official decrees and the Soviet constitution often present the history of intentions and representations, while their realization is a different story.

In 1934 the OGPU merged with the regular civil militia into the NKVD, which also incorporated the Gulag. This reorganization aimed to centralize control over violence[46] and make the institution appear more constitutional. After overuse of extralegal practices during collectivization and industrialization 'some kind of "constitutionality" was needed to regularize, to consolidate [...] to ensure a ruly and predictable working of the responsible institutions.'[47]

This turn from extralegality to 'legal formalism', however, was inconsistent as both modes had their merits in the eyes of organizers: simplification and speed in extralegality and more control and legitimacy in legality. Now Soviet leaders attempted to restore a state monopoly on violence, though they could not resist the temptation to resort to the speedy extralegal mode during crises. Institutional and personal rivalry also contributed to gyrations in policy, especially between the USSR Procuracy headed by Andrei Vyshinskii and the Commissariat of Justice led by Nikolai Krylenko.[48] Explaining these fluctuations, James Harris and Oleg Khlevniuk underline that Stalin had to consider the power balance within the party elite to secure his personal position against anticipated plots. Other triggers for oscillations were crises, such as famine and mass migration. The shift in sentencing towards legal norms, starting in July 1931, was interrupted by the rise in extralegality during the famine of 1932–3: *troikas* were introduced in Ukraine in November 1932, in Belorussia in February 1933, in West Siberia in March 1933 and in Leningrad in April 1933. Periodic mass police sweeps purged the cities of criminals, homeless children and the disenfranchised. Procuracy control, constitutionalized in 1936, was suspended during the Great Terror and restored in November 1938.

The low tide in state violence during 1933–6 did not mean the end of repression and mobilization as a mode of administration. The period saw growing numbers of arrested former party oppositionists,[49] party purges, repressions against wreckers, spies, 'social aliens' and citizens of German and Polish origin. The government also initiated new mass operations: the exile of 11,000 'former people' and 'oppositionists' from Leningrad in spring 1935; 'unreliable elements' from the borders[50] and 'socially harmful elements' from the major cities. As David Shearer has stated, the regime 'reduced the level of mass repression in rural areas [seen now sufficiently Sovietised – OV] only to intensify operations [...] in urban and other areas', where people fled from the regime's disruptive policies seeking jobs and food. Still, the picture of moderation in repression as a conscious and coherent policy is not convincing. Though mostly nonlethal, arrest, deportation and exile remained the well-used tools of the state administration. David Priestland justly summarized, 'There was, therefore, no "relaxation" of repression in the mid-1930s, as was once commonly argued. Rather, its nature changed.'[51] State repression during 1933–6 was less lethal and concentrated in urban areas.

Periodic 'cleansings' of strategically, militarily and politically important cities and other areas not only corrected results of excesses (migration, for example), but were probably seen by Stalinists as geographically expanding the map of socialism. By the mid-1930s the number of such 'regime' cities grew from three to thirty-seven and to seventy-five in 1940.[52] The Moscow reconstruction project and the building of a marble-clad metro in 1935 represented the city as an ideal socialist space – grandiose, clean of imperfections, inhabited by filtered citizens. A total of 400,000 people were deported from the largest cities in the 1933 passport campaign. Head of the NKVD, Genrikh Iagoda, reported that passportization had cleaned up the cities and made them 'models of socialism'.[53] There, in urban repression, socialist utopianism and realpolitik merged.

Adjustments continued during the Great Terror, thus making it difficult to define a timeframe of moderation if we take it as a conscious *course of policy*.[54] To stop the flight from *kolkhozy*, for instance, in 1937–8 the government provided food aid to starving villages, absolved *kolkhoz* debts and introduced some benefits to elderly and disabled *kolkhozniks*.[55] The campaigns towards 'the strengthening of socialist legality' and 'reconciliation with convicted socially aliens' (as promised by the constitution) continued. On 23 October 1937, the Politburo ordered a Procurator inspection of criminal cases of rural officials and then of collective farmers charged with minor crimes. It revised the cases of 1,176,000 persons: closed 107,000 cases, rehabilitated 480,000 people and liberated 23,000. Decrees from November 1937 and January 1938 denounced the dismissal of relatives of convicts from their jobs and education institutions. A number of purged communists were readmitted to the party.[56] Of course, the apocalyptic scale of simultaneous repressions and mass killings prevents interpreting these measures as part of moderation politics. Episodes of adjustment in 1937–8 go against the magnification of similar steps in 1933–6 as political reform. What is summarily interpreted as moderation was not monolithic policy. It originated from diverse motives and pursued various tasks: long-term ideological and short-term practical considerations. It also lacks characteristics of distinct policy per se – coherence, recorded design and purpose.

Ambiguity about the *raison d'être* of the discussed adjustments raises the question of when and why this relatively peaceful period ended. While the long-term causes of the turn to mass repression in summer 1937 are well discussed, the timing and specific triggers are understudied in literature. Why did discourse about friendly classes end and the 1937 February–March Plenum open a new round of attacks with a shift from targeting the party-state elite and oppositionists towards the general population, the so-called 'anti-Soviet elements'?

On the turn to mass repression in 1937, Stephen Kotkin recently speculated: 'There was no "dynamic" forcing him [Stalin] to do so, no "factional" fighting, no heightened threat abroad. The terror was not spiralling out of his control. He just decided, himself, to approve quota-driven eradication of entire categories of people in a *planned* indiscriminate terror.' Khlevniuk has pointed to signals of a shift in repression from elite to mass purges at the beginning of 1937.[57] Sheila Fitzpatrick also detected that something changed in the period from December 1936 to February 1937: 'There had been a genuine impulse toward democratisation at an earlier point, but this impulse had disappeared almost completely by [...] the February–March plenum.'[58]

Harris, and many others, explains the timing of the mass repressions through the regime's lingering insecurity about popular support in case of war,[59] heightened in 1937 by the return of deportees. However, this alone, he acknowledges, could not explain the shift in the parameters of repression.[60] Moreover, kulak-deportees had already started to return in 1935–6 and it was only the discussion of the constitution that massively revealed not only their failed reeducation, but embitterment. Peter Whitewood views the background of the military purges in May–June 1937 as the catalyst of mass repressions in July.[61] He speculates that Stalin's fear of an infiltration of foreign agents in the Red Army sparked similar concerns about 'unreliable elements' in the wider population. However, mass operations against commoners started earlier. On 27 March 1937 the NKVD Circular 23 ordered to prevent by all means church people from penetrating into the lower soviet apparatus and on 8 June it ordered the liquidation of church people and sectarians. Arch Getty more convincingly explains this escalation as 'pre-election fever', 'precipitated by the unexpected dangers posed by the new constitution' and election law.[62]

Getty points to a change in Stalin's thinking in 1937: 'For a long time Stalin minimized the threat [of anti-Soviet elements] in the countryside [...] By July 1937, though, he had become convinced of the danger, changed his mind, and personally triggered the mass terror.'[63] Analysis of 'Journals of registration of outgoing documents' shows the change in character of Stalin's resolutions already in mid-1936 – from slack and irresolute towards energetic and punitive. Khlevniuk sees heightened incoherence, awkwardness and confusion in Stalin's resolutions in 1937, accompanied by 'explosions of fury'.[64] Yet what made Stalin change his mind?

Several developments in winter 1936–7 could have influenced Stalin's reversal in views on society and politics. Besides Stalin's protracted conflict with regional party-state clans[65] and the inflammatory role of new NKVD head Nikolai Ezhov, his conceptualization of, first, popular commentaries on the constitution and, second, the results of the 1937 census deserves serious consideration. Together with international developments – the insurgence of opposition in Spain and the November 1936 German-Japanese Anti-Comintern pact that heightened Stalin's fears – popular discussion of the constitution can provide the missing piece in the puzzle for why relative moderation ended and mass repressions began.

The unexpectedly liberal constitution was a major part of moderation while, as I showed, the authors anticipated that socialist transformations would inevitably reeducate the people. Granting democratic liberties and voting rights to the former 'enemies' in 1936 grew from the Marxist maxim that new socialist relations of production, combined with appropriate 'cleansings' of society, education and propaganda would shape a new consciousness and a new Soviet unity of 'friendly classes' and nationalities. Stalinists envisioned New People in the Stakhanovites[66] – confident that 'the socialist personality had come into being'. After the old intelligentsia emigrated or were deported, purged and/or disciplined in the Cultural Revolution, a new generation of intelligentsia was cultivated. Stalin now ordered the end to attacks on the intelligentsia in 1931. Literacy was declared universal and vodka consumption declined. Collective labour at special settlements, *kolkhozy* and construction sites, like the Belomor Canal, reshaped even criminals and kulaks into useful socialist citizens.[67] Writers engineered new Soviet souls. A writer, A. M. Gorky, upon returning to the USSR from emigration in 1932 was amazed at how far the masses had changed and their new political consciousness. According to newspapers, the Soviet new personality – hardworking, educated, and devoted to socialism and the collective rather than individual good – had become a reality, though not yet a mass phenomenon. How seriously the government took these projected transformations is seen in its practical steps towards new society: the enfranchisement of 'former people' in the constitution, suggested contested elections and the shift in OGPU methods, the expansion of welfare and even food aid to the converted peasantry in the hungry years of 1936–7 (contrasting with treatment of peasants as saboteurs in the 1932 famine).

However, popular discussion of the constitution dashed these high hopes. It brought unexpected disillusionment to its organizers. The democratic character of the constitution and the shift in official discourse encouraged citizens to voice an entire spectrum of opinions that exposed societal disagreement. The clamour for civil rights and support – real and orchestrated – for the innovations of the constitution contrasted with mass discontent, disapproval of new liberties, warnings about numerous enemies and demands for continuing segregation of 'former people'. The public complained about scarcity, over-taxation, bureaucratic arbitrariness and the breaking of religious freedoms. Threats of uprisings in case of war, condemnations of *kolkhozy* and distrust in the constitution were recorded in discussion materials as 'anti-Soviet moods'.[68]

The expansion of the franchise (10.8 per cent of all recorded comments) met extremely articulate opposition. Arguing with Stalin's programmic thesis that all classes had become socialist and friendly, many commentators warned about resilient anti-Soviet attitudes in the population: 'Former merchants, kulaks, and other exploiters have not yet transformed themselves and forgotten their former wealth. During elections they can propagate their views and attract unstable, hesitant citizens. Former people should be restricted in their rights.'[69] One V. Kulygin, from Kirov *krai*, disapproved of granting civil rights to exiled kulaks: 'Many, especially the elders, resist personal transformation and remain hostile to Soviet rule.'[70] The Red Army soldier Kalganov rejected the franchise of priests because in the future war they may betray the socialist fatherland. Numerous were fears among the public that old enemies – especially former kulaks and detested priests – could use new constitutional liberties and suffrage to obstruct the construction of socialism.[71] Stalin heard these warnings. It is exactly these two groups who became the first targets of operations against commoners in 1937.

The arguments and motivations of these critics, the representativeness and accuracy of the discussion materials are deliberated elsewhere,[72] but here more important is how Soviet leaders, Stalin, first of all, read these commentaries submitted by various state organs. Such warnings about enemies in the grassroots undoubtedly attracted the attention of the chronically suspicious dictator much more than praises for the constitution. We know that the people's forewarnings were on Stalin's mind from his speech at the Eighth Congress of Soviets in December 1936. Sticking to his wishful vision, he rejected the idea that former White Guards, kulaks and priests, if allowed to vote, would present a threat to Soviet rule. He added ominously that even if these enemies were elected, people held responsible would be those who had conducted their propaganda poorly.[73] Surely, this threat was taken seriously by functionaries.

Let us imagine how Stalin could internalize citizens', officials' and *chekists'* warnings provided to him by the NKVD and TsIK, who collected popular comments on the constitution. He regularly received admonitions about enemies from the NKVD.[74] He knew that *chekists* had a tendency to overemphasize dangers,[75] but the same warnings came now from party and soviet officials nervous about the contested secret elections. On top of that, popular comments recorded by the TsIK about omnipresent enemies confirmed the alarming reports. These gradually sunk in and raised his feeling of insecurity.

The discussion campaign revealed to Stalin that society had failed to sufficiently Sovietize. The voices in the discussion, despite orchestration, were not unanimous in their approvals and conformity as expected. Mikhail Prishvin, a writer, thought the discussion became a kind of test for Sovietness after which freedom would be allowed. '[The government] […] expects real hosannas [praise] […] from the people, and then, after they [the government] are confident of the genuineness of the hosannas, [they will] say: […] speak, write whatever you want freely.'[76] To the leaders' disappointment, society did not fit into an ideological template. It had not *yet* lived in the prescribed way, but remained religious, divided, unmanageable and parochial: a roadblock to socialism.

In launching the constitution, the ideological motives (the accomplishment of socialism) intertwined with political and managerial goals of improving the effectiveness of government through a new election law – to use democratic procedures to motivate, revitalize or outvote sluggish, corrupt and unreliable officials and purge enemies on all levels.[77] Afraid of being dismissed in democratic elections, the cadres time and again obstructed implementation of the constitution. In Stalin's logic, both anti-Soviet elements in a population encouraged by new freedoms *and* reluctant officials needed a final purge ('once and for all') for a successful socialist transformation. This logic can explain the timing of the political shift from relative relaxation in 1933–6 to the Great Terror. Getty focuses mostly on the sabotage of constitutional liberties by the regional elites, but popular hostility itself reported by them and internalized by Stalin made the dictator expand repressions from the elite and bureaucrats to the ordinary masses – believers, kulaks and anti-Soviet elements. As a result, in 1937–8, 767,000 of 1,344,923 people were convicted in operations against anti-Soviet elements.[78]

Finally, the discouraging results of the January 1937 census received on 25 January and 14 March confirmed the General Secretary's misapprehension about the condition of society, for example, no universal literacy and the high degree of religiosity of the population – 57 per cent of the USSR's population, and 70 per cent in Smolensk oblast. Probably the incongruity between the actual progress in society and the leadership's projections, as revealed in the discussion commentaries received in October–November, led the government to classify the census data in advance. In December 1936 a directive to census workers demanded: '*Not one figure* from the census can be published.' As the task of the census was to quantify social changes of the last decade, including the 'elimination of the hostile classes,'[79] the census and the discussion of the constitution shared a common purpose – to monitor society.[80] Both campaigns revealed a society altered, with 'fixed structures and social barriers dissolved,' but 'far from being as homogeneous as the leadership may have imagined.'[81]

How could Stalin conceptualize the social situation as revealed in 1936 and at the beginning of 1937 with a mind as suspicious as his? The social conciliation declared in the constitution was premature; enemies were still numerous and active, and society was against conciliation. The fight had not ended, a *final* purge necessary. At the February–March Plenum, Stalin proclaimed: 'We need to end the opportunistic complacency

Utopianism and Realpolitik in the Mid-1930s

(*blagodushie*) and philistine carelessness' and he returned to rhetoric about 'exasperation of the remnants of the broken exploiting classes'.[82]

Before the plenum, on 15 February, Stalin received a secret note with inventories of 'anti-Soviet elements' which included eighteen categories: 'former people', kulaks, former members of socialist parties, more than 1.5 million expelled members of the Communist party and around 100,000 'alien' and 'socially harmful' people.[83] Stalin carefully underlined the figures in the note. Stephen Kotkin has noted: 'Suddenly the number of punitive enemies were colossal and they were everywhere.'[84] Society's reactions to the constitution had destroyed Stalin's 'complacency'. Such a trajectory in Stalin's thinking seems plausible, supported by his rhetorical switch at the plenum, the cancellation of contested elections in October 1937 and post-Terror rhetoric such as the reintroduction of the social unity thesis.[85] When utopia (harmonious society) showed its discord with reality (warnings about hidden enemies and resistance of party bosses), Stalin retreated to mass purges. The first, second and third in the list of targets were former kulaks-returnees as defined by the Order 00447 from July 1937 opening the mass operation.[86]

The events of the Spanish Civil War in August–October 1936 may have also contributed to Stalin's reevaluation of Soviet society and the growth of his insecurity. The term 'fifth column' originated in Spain to define the wartime internal opposition's insurgency and was eagerly adopted by official Soviet discourse because it corresponded to Stalinists' intrinsic fear of traitors inside the besieged fortress of the USSR. With the Spanish insurgency in mind, reports of hostile domestic elements could sound especially frightening in the context of constant Stalinists' fears of war triggered in December by the Anti-Comintern Pact. Thus, during winter 1936–7 Stalin reevaluated conditions in society and decided to expand repressions and purges to the wider population. The constitution *became* a sham.

'Peaceful' periods like NEP and the mid-1930s turned out to be far away from a social truce. Both periods saw popular dissatisfaction, extralegality and mass operations.[87] The moderate adjustments described above and the 1936 constitution motivated historians to interpret them as liberalization of *policy* enabled by economic stabilization and international and political factors: as part of a plan for restoring social stability inside, and projecting a positive image of the USSR abroad. However, the idea of a designed breathing space for an overstrained population seems alien to a system built on permanent mobilization and an emergency model. Endless mobilization campaigns in the mid-1930s (the passport campaign, the abortion law and the constitutional discussions) and the absence of 'normalization' after the Second World War cast doubt on the motive of giving respite to the populace. Interpretation of Stalin's moderation as planned democratic and participatory *reforms* also seems an overstatement here.[88] Relaxation was *implied* by default, a self-emergent product of the completion of Lenin's plan to build socialism. The victory of socialism announced at the 17th Party Congress *implied* that excessive pressure was now unnecessary. Stalin articulated this logic: 'As a result of our success in the countryside [the defeat of class enemies] the time has come when we are no longer in need of mass repression.'[89] Government expectations (not plans) of relaxation (not reform) belonged to a master narrative of socialism's victory through the five-year plan and the elimination of 'enemies'. Moderation evolved on two levels – utopian and realpolitik. As Stalinists manoeuvred between paradigmal expectations of a triumphant socialism and realpolitik on the ground, they failed to pursue a coherent policy.

PART V
NATIONAL TENSIONS AND INTERNATIONAL THREATS

CHAPTER 10
DEBATING THE EARLY SOVIET NATIONALITIES POLICY: THE CASE OF SOVIET UKRAINE
Olena Palko

The February Revolution marked the starting point of a complicated process of social, political and economic transformation within the Russian Empire. Nationalist movements emerged on the peripheries demanding sovereignty and the Provisional Government attempted to accommodate these disperse demands for autonomy and independence. Nonetheless, it was the October Revolution and the Soviet regime that irreversibly changed the administrative and cultural map of the former autocratic and centralized empire. The Bolshevik Party's seizure of power in 1917 allowed its leaders to act on their promises for national self-determination, an important concept developed by Lenin during heated debates during wartime. The First World War gave Lenin an opportunity to champion a much coveted proletarian revolution on the ruins of the Romanov Empire, provided he would find a way to reconcile with the nationalist elites who had hoped to use the war as a catalyst for nation-building. In such a way, the success of the Bolshevik proletarian dictatorship became inevitably linked to national liberation, and the national question – albeit regarded as a remnant of the bourgeois states – entered the Bolshevik agenda for the decades to follow.

The Bolsheviks' view on the national question evolved overtime and the tactics of the party were defined by the immediate political, economic and social context as well as their short-term and long-term objectives. The Bolsheviks promised to liberate the workers and give real power to the working class. Nonetheless, in the immediate post-revolutionary period the conditions were not yet ripe for a true proletarian dictatorship. Instead, the threats of the civil war and foreign intervention forced the Bolshevik leadership to focus on how to secure their political power over the vast area inherited from the previous autocratic regime. The civil war required quick solutions to the almost total political and social alienation in which the Bolshevik Party found itself. Instead, their victory raised anew the question of how to modernize the country. An utterly egregious civil war experience made it clear that the sovietization campaign would not succeed without mass indigenous participation.

The author would like to thank the initiative 'Ukrainian Research in Switzerland' (URIS) for providing financial support and especially Prof. Dr. Frithjof Benjamin Schenk and the Department of History at the University of Basel, as well as the editors of this volume, for their comments on various drafts of this chapter.

Overall, the Bolsheviks wished to turn proletarians into the ruling class, whereby the party would be its true vanguard. And they needed to engage workers to participate in politics. There were difficulties, however. First, those workers were illiterate and needed to learn literacy along with the Marxist doctrine. Second, there was a century-long legacy of distrust of central institutions. The use and the promotion of national languages could provide a remedy to both. Learning to read Marx and Lenin in their mother tongues would ease the process of political socialization, while transferring party work into local languages and engaging the locals into the party-state apparatus would make it look 'near and dear' to the people, as Stalin later explained.

The fulfilment of those tasks could not be immediate, however. They were to be achieved through the new nationalities policy of *korenizatsiia* (literally, indigenization), launched in 1923 Union-wide. *Korenizatsiia* was designed to exploit the national factor in the political modernization of diverse peoples of the Soviet Union and to propagate universal Soviet values in a variety of national languages. Its ultimate goal was to 'usher the *entire* population through the Marxist timeline of historical development'[1] and to achieve socialism. The new central government encouraged the formation of various heterogeneous communities with distinctive national identities. The Soviet Union would thus come to be defined as 'the world's first Affirmative Action Empire' or 'the world's first state to institutionalize ethno-territorial federalism.'[2] However, by the end of the 1920s, this promotion of ethnic differences came into conflict with a more pressing objective of Soviet modernization.

Soviet Ukraine represents one of the most fruitful cases in examining the objectives and limitations of the Bolshevik approach to the national question. The republic, with its economic and social potential, would be crucial to the success of the wider revolution. Nevertheless, unlike most newly created Soviet republics, Ukraine had a relatively well-developed national movement and a history of independence, albeit short-lived. Consequently, here the Bolsheviks had perhaps the most arduous experience of the civil war and it took three campaigns for the Red Army to win over the republic. In addition, Ukraine's contiguous western border made the republic an ideological battlefield and an outpost of Soviet foreign policy. This struggle later manifested over party divisions on the implementation of *korenizatsiia*, to an extent unheard of in any other Soviet Republic.

This chapter conceptualizes the Bolshevik approach to the national question in the Soviet border regions by examining how local challenges forced the central party leadership to adjust its universal objectives. In the case of Soviet Ukraine however, this process of elaborating and implementing the nationalities policy was not linear. The civil war and the *korenizatsiia* policy caused Bolshevik theory and practice to diverge over issues of centralization and perceived security problems.

Self-determination versus party centralization: The Bolsheviks and the civil war

During the pre-war years, Lenin was greatly engaged in polemics with other European socialists over the national question, perceiving its solution as being closely linked to an anticipated European war. Lenin expected that such a conflict would lead to a defeat of the great empires, especially the tsarist monarchy, this 'most reactionary and barbarous of governments,' and thus contribute to the socialist cause of proletarian emancipation.[3] According to him, the immediate support to national struggles within the empire's borders would help the proletarian revolution in the long-term. This prompted him to introduce popular slogans of national self-determination into the Bolsheviks' programme and proclaim the national question an inherent part of the international revolutionary movement. As explained in April 1916, the task of the proletariat could not be achieved 'unless it champions the right of nations to self-determination.'[4]

Indeed, Lenin's approach was reflective of the wartime zeitgeist: nationalist movements were on the rise worldwide and national elites kindled patriotic feelings and national pride among their fellow countrymen. Such movements also thrived in the former Russian Empire. Nonetheless, the Provisional Government, while condemning the restrictive tsarist regime, declaring the equality of all citizens and ensuring cultural autonomy, failed to respond to the demands of regional separatists. The final decision on the national question was postponed until the convocation of a Constituent Assembly, the elections to which were scheduled for late-November 1917. Such a moderate response corresponded to the horizon of expectations of the political leaders in Ukraine, however. The first legal act-declarations of *Tsentral'na Rada* (Central Council), the national legislative authority established in Kyiv on 4 March 1917, proclaimed Ukraine's autonomy and reassured its non-separation from Russia 'in order that we and all her peoples might jointly strive toward the development and welfare of all Russia and toward the unity of her democratic forces.'[5]

The October Revolution, however, changed this mainstream autonomous orientation. Local elites, often with foreign help, quickly reacted to the events in the former imperial capital and started making provisions for independence. Those actions did not contradict the announced Bolshevik position on the national question: 'The Declaration of Rights of the People of Russia', issued shortly after the Bolsheviks had taken power in Petrograd, guaranteed equality and sovereignty for all peoples within the former Russian Empire, ranging from self-determination to complete independence. The declaration had an explosive effect on the former Romanov Empire. By 1920, Poland, Finland and the Baltic states were fully independent while national movements had emerged in the Caucasus and Central Asian provinces, leading to the formation of separate republics in Azerbaijan, Armenia and Georgia. In Ukraine, where neither the socialist-oriented Ukrainian People's Republic nor the German-controlled conservative Ukrainian State was able to consolidate their power, the demands for self-determination were voiced by left radicals. Members of both the Bolshevik and non-Bolshevik communist parties articulated plans of a sovereign Soviet Ukraine and its own self-standing communist party.

However, the threat of complete disintegration of the former empire and subsequent loss of control over the region forced the Bolsheviks to reconsider the speed with which their general democratic principles could be implemented. The balance between self-determination and party organization needed to be found. Hence, the experience of the civil war in the borderlands became the first instance when Bolshevik theory and practice diverged. Indeed, in his early writings, Lenin expressed great tolerance to local separatism and nationalism. Nonetheless, this affirmation was always subordinate to the ultimate goals of the proletarian revolution. On 28 January 1918, in his speech during the Third All-Russian Congress of Soviets, Stalin, then Commissar for Nationalities, made it clear that self-determination was 'a means of attaining socialism' and as such should be limited only to the toilers of each nation.[6] Yet the proletariat, following Lenin's teaching, was ideologically immature and relied on its vanguard, the Communist Party. With proper guidance, the proletariat – the only bearer of the right to self-determination – would never secede from the world's first proletarian state. As Stalin explained, 'now that Russia is a Socialist Republic and the champion of the great ideal of freeing the oppressed classes all over the world, there is no longer any reason for separating from Great Russia'.[7]

Moreover, Lenin regarded self-determination as an exception, rather than a general rule. Between the two policies of self-determination and party organization, the latter clearly prevailed: 'democratic centralism' remained the main guiding principle in state and party organization. As stated in the resolution of the 1919 Congress of the Russian Communist Party of Bolsheviks (RKP(b)), a separate status granted to the Soviet republics did not mean that the party would also be reorganized as a federation of independent communist parties. Instead, the central committees of the Communist Parties in these republics were recognized as regional committees of the RKP(b) and as such were entirely subordinated to its leadership.[8]

Not surprisingly, this discrepancy between Bolshevik theory and practice was quickly exploited by those regional party and non-party leaders who continuously opposed centralization. The first attempt to uncover Bolshevik hypocrisy in the national question came from within the party. In his pamphlets 'Jesuits' policy' (1915) and 'Russian social democracy and the national question' (1917), Lev Iurkevych, a former Ukrainian social-democrat, who after 1905 joined a section of the Russian Social Democratic Workers' Party (RSDRP(b)) in Ukraine, accused the Russian Marxists of chauvinism, despotism and national enslavement.[9] In 1919, this critique was picked up by the Ukrainian Bolsheviks Vasyl' Shakhrai, the Commissar for Military Affairs in the first Ukrainian Soviet government, and Serhii Mazlakh. In their brochure 'Concerning the Moment: What Is Happening in and to Ukraine', the two Ukrainian Bolsheviks accused their Russian fellows of chauvinism, hence justifying Ukraine's claims for independence.[10] Overall, early critiques of the Russian Bolsheviks concerned the discordance between a separate status of Soviet Ukraine and the inferior position of its Bolshevik Party.

The pamphlet was published during the heated debates between those demanding the autonomous status of Ukraine's Bolshevik party and those promoting a centralized party organization. The idea to merge different regional organizations of the RSDRP(b), which were mainly situated in the industrial Donbas area, into a separate Bolshevik Party was linked to the German occupation of Ukraine, under whose support the conservative government of Pavlo Skoropads'kyi was established in late April 1918. A Bolshevik leader in Ukraine, Georgii (Iurii) Piatakov argued that an autonomous party would have more control over and understanding of the situation in the region since the Russian Bolsheviks were simply too far away to respond on time. Instead, the leader of the Katerynoslav group Emanuil Kviring spoke of the greatest importance of Ukraine's industrial areas for the future of the Russian Revolution, which could be weakened if the autonomy of Ukraine's Bolshevik Party and Ukraine be adopted.

Nonetheless, the escalation of the civil war forced the Russian Bolsheviks to finally define their stand on Ukraine. Bound by the Treaty of Brest-Litovsk, the party could not declare war against Germany, an ally of nationalist governments in Ukraine. The creation of a Ukrainian Socialist Soviet Republic in March 1918 thus enabled the Bolsheviks, through the Ukrainian Soviet government, to enter into open war with the German occupation forces. Ukraine's independence was compromised by the status of its Bolshevik Party, however. Despite the decision of the Taganrog conference (19–20 April 1918) on the independent status of the Communist Party of Bolsheviks of Ukraine (KP(b)U), the first party congress, held in Moscow in July the following year, voted for its integration with the RKP(b). The KP(b)U retained an autonomous status with its Central Committee (TsK) acknowledging the authority of the TsK RKP(b); Stalin entered the Ukrainian TsK as the liaison with the RKP(b).[11]

While the Russian and Ukrainian Bolsheviks were looking for options on how to reconcile their promises, other left-wing parties and movements went ahead in defending the unconditional sovereignty of a Soviet Ukraine. Admittedly, during civil war the Bolsheviks did not have the rhetorical monopoly on preaching the ideas of proletarian emancipation and a socialist future, being obliged to compete with a number of native communist parties, the biggest of which was the Ukrainian Communist Party of *Borot'bysty* (derived from the party newspaper *Borot'ba*, Ukrainian for 'struggle'). Stephen Velychenko maintains that these parties emerged in reaction to the moderate socialism of the Ukrainian nationalist government and chauvinistic Russian Bolshevik rule, which initially disregarded the national sentiment of the population.[12] Their members believed that communism and nationalism were compatible, hence the revolution in Ukraine could be both social and national. They advocated for an independent soviet Ukraine, an equal partner in the future union of soviet republics.

During the civil war, the national communist parties underwent major transformations, gradually evolving towards an acceptance of the Soviet regime. Nonetheless, Ukraine's independence remained their primary goal.[13] They opposed the Bolshevik-led Soviet Ukraine, since it united 'all sorts of Russian nationalist elements from the Black Hundreds to the revolutionary intelligentsia in Ukraine […] joining forces with the Bolsheviks to help reconstruct a "united and indivisible Russia".'[14] The Bolsheviks themselves were considered as proponents of Russian imperialism[15] and 'a hypocritical party which continually violates its own principles'.[16] Overall, their chauvinism was regarded as detrimental to the entire communist endeavour in Ukraine.[17] Instead they envisaged a union of all communist parties in Soviet Ukraine into a separate body, which would become an equal member of the Communist International.[18]

Nonetheless, in May 1919, in the face of General Anton Denikin's advancing army, the Borot'bysty expressed their readiness to cooperate with the Bolsheviks and to share government responsibilities. The Bolsheviks, however, were wary of their fellow revolutionaries. On the one hand, they were desperately looking for political allies in the civil war, more so since the Ukrainian communists could offer a link with the resentful Ukrainian peasantry and intelligentsia. On the other hand, the Bolsheviks did not trust these parties. Lenin considered the Borot'bysty as 'a party, which aims to split the military forces and supports banditism; it is violating the basic principles of communism and thereby plays directly into the hands of the Whites and of international imperialism.' Whilst encouraging the merger, the Ukrainian Bolsheviks were instructed to collect information on 'the non-proletarian and most disloyal nature' of the Borot'bysty activity.[19]

In fact, in their early days, the Russian Bolsheviks hardly had any unified view on Ukraine. Their treatment of national affairs depended mostly on the immediate challenges which they faced on the ground. This lack of comprehensive policy perhaps explains why the Bolsheviks, while seeking alliances with local leftist movements, continuously persisted in their anti-Ukrainian attitude and violently reacted against any nationalist sentiments within or without the party. This discrepancy soon drove back the occasional support the party had managed to gather. It became clear that if the Bolsheviks wanted to establish control in the region, they needed to reconsider their attitude towards Ukraine. In short, the Bolsheviks needed to offer a feasible alternative to 'bourgeois nationalism' of the Ukrainian governments and national communists by embracing their separatist discourse.

A turn in the national policy was marked by the TsK RKP(b)'s resolution 'On Soviet Rule in Ukraine' in late 1919. In the resolution, adopted after the victory over Denikin's White army, it was assured that the RKP(b) was committed to 'removing all barriers to the free development of the Ukrainian language and culture.' The Bolsheviks in Ukraine were instructed to treat the existing nationalist tendencies 'with utmost patience and tact, countering them with a word of comradely explanation of the identity of interests of the toiling masses of Ukraine and Russia.' Ukrainian was declared 'a weapon of communist education of the toiling people' and a tool in establishing 'the closest contact between Soviet institutions and the native peasant population of the country.'[20] The Bolsheviks, also seemingly, conceded to the debates on Ukraine's independence. In his letter 'To the toiling masses of Ukraine after the defeat of Denikin,' Lenin reassured that it was 'self-evident and generally recognized that only the Ukrainian workers and peasants themselves can and will decide whether Ukraine shall amalgamate with Russia or whether she shall remain a separate and independent republic, and, in the latter case, what federal ties shall be established between that republic and Russia.'[21]

National communists were also invited to join the government of Khrystian Rakovskiy (in place until July 1923), where they occupied posts in education, justice and communication. In addition, a merger of the national communist parties was initiated. In March 1920, some 4,000 former Borot'bysty members were admitted to the KP(b)U on a case-by-case basis.[22] In total, by mid-1920, around 30 per cent of the KP(b)U's 11,087 full members and 2,439 candidate members had previously belonged to other political parties.[23] This unification of the leading communist movements initially proved to be mutually beneficial: the Bolsheviks were able to eliminate important political rivals while the Borot'bysty gained access to important leadership positions, further promoting Ukraine's autonomy and cultural development from within the party ranks. For instance, the former Borot'bysty Vasyl' Ellan-Blakytnyi and Oleksandr Shums'kyi joined the TsK KP(b)U, the latter also acquired a seat in the Politburo. Since May 1919, Ukraine's Commissariat for Education (Narkomos) was headed by the Borot'bysty – Hnat Mykhailychenko, Mykhailo Panchenko, Shums'kyi and Hryhorii Hryn'ko.[24] In such a way, former Borot'bysty not only gained control over the republic's cultural and intellectual life, but also started to play a decisive role in implementing the nationalities policy. It was under the Narkomos' chief authorities that the main orders for the future policy of *korenizatsiia* were issued.

Ethnic diversity versus assimilation: *Korenizatsiia* in the context of Soviet Ukraine

As discussed above, to win the civil war and reunite the former imperial territories, the Bolsheviks were forced to make concessions to nationalist sentiments and form alliances with non-Russian political elites. Nevertheless, these tactical agreements would not suffice if the Bolsheviks wished to consolidate their power and establish political and social systems that would last. More importantly, the Bolsheviks needed to change the way the party was perceived in Ukraine. Instead of an image of a Moscow-led occupying military force, it needed to become an embodiment of revolutionary and national liberationist ideals of the local population. This change in approach reflected a more general moderation of nationalities policy within the Soviet Union. By the end of the civil war, it had become obvious that the national question in the peripheries could not be ignored, even more so with the threat posed by independent Poland, under Józef Piłsudski, to the recently acquired western Soviet borderlands. The possibility of losing Ukraine became especially apparent after the united Ukrainian-Polish Army drove the Bolsheviks out of Kyiv in May 1920.

Amidst the Soviet–Polish War, Stalin highlighted the urgent need to reassess the position of the Soviet government on the national question and redefine the centre-periphery relationship. In October 1920, he observed that the very success of the Russian Revolution depended heavily on gaining trust of the peripheries: 'central Russia, that hearth of the world revolution, cannot hold out long without the assistance of the border regions, which abound in raw materials, fuel and foodstuffs. The border regions of Russia in their turn would be inevitably doomed to imperialist bondage without the political, military and organizational support of more developed central Russia.'[25] According to Lev Kamenev, another Bolshevik leader, the civil war had taught the party a valuable strategic lesson: 'the unity between the centre and the periphery is necessary for the survival of both the centre and the periphery. The communist society in Moscow cannot be built without establishing a fair relationship with those peoples living around the Donets [coal] basin, or around Baku oil, or Siberian bread, or steppe pastures.'[26]

The Fate of the Bolshevik Revolution

This new approach to the national question was approved by the 1921 Party Congress. Far-reaching political, social and economic modernization of the former imperial lands was seen as a remedy to the alienation of the peripheries, their distrust towards the centre and attempts by local nationalists to solicit foreign intervention. Apart from state-encouraged modernization and economic equalization, the shift in the national question was conditioned by the urgent need to engage local populations into politics, turn them into genuine supporters of the Soviet experiment. Native languages were seen as means of spreading new Soviet values among outlying populations who would, consequently, contribute willingly to building socialism throughout the former Romanov Empire.[27] To achieve this, party activists needed to 'preach against [slogans of national culture] in all languages, "adapting" themselves to all local and national requirements.'[28] The Party Congress, therefore, called for a comprehensive national programme, establishing local administration, promoting national languages and cultures and recruiting indigenous elites into the party rank and files.

The success of this task relied on active participation of indigenous populations and the creation of new Soviet elites. As highlighted by Stalin, in order to make Soviet power 'near and dear to the masses of the border regions of Russia,' it was necessary to integrate 'all the best local people' into the Soviet administration, since 'the masses should see that the Soviet power and its organs are the products of their own efforts, the embodiment of their aspirations.'[29] However, 'the best local people' were not, as yet, members of the Bolshevik Party. Thus, in the immediate aftermath of the civil war, the party looked to establish a consensus with those 'intellectual forces of local origin,' who did not necessarily agree with Bolshevik ideology.

In addition to encouraged merger of different political forces, the party also found a compromise with the pre-revolutionary intelligentsia, incentivizing cooperation with numerous educated specialists and engineers, whose skills and technical knowledge were urgently needed during post-war reconstruction. Moreover, the party sought reconciliation with recent political émigrés. Numerous Sovietophiles and *zminovihivtsi* (Rus. *smenovekhovtsy*), who showed readiness to reconcile with the former enemy and participate in building the Soviet state, received official amnesty and were invited to return to Soviet Ukraine. Lastly, the early 1920s proved to be the heyday of the so-called *poputnyky* (Rus. *poputchiki*) or fellow travellers. The term was first used by Leon Trotsky to refer to artists who presented a kind of transitional art, 'organically connected with the Revolution, but which [was] not at the same time the art of the Revolution.'[30]

Engaging the old intelligentsia, however, could offer only a temporary solution to the lack of loyal Soviet cadres. Indeed, they enjoyed a rather privileged position in the Soviet society and played an important role during the transitionary period of the early 1920s. However, those fellow travellers who had offered their tacit support to the party in power could hardly disseminate Soviet values and inspire the masses to join the process of constructing socialism. Moreover, hardly any of them could become trustworthy representatives of Bolshevik ideology in the long run. While endorsing national differences, the party's central leadership was ultimately seeking to create a homogeneous Soviet identity based on a shared set of values which could only be internalized through mass mobilization and participation.

Bohdan Krawchenko argues that Ukrainization of the KP(b)U had a demographic character: modernization brought more rural Ukrainians to the cities, where they joined the working class and subsequently the party ranks.[31] Nonetheless, the Ukrainization of the party ranks was spontaneous. Engaging indigenous, yet loyal cadres soon became a key priority, as defined by party congresses in 1921 and 1923. In the following years, party membership skyrocketed. The 1927 party census already attested that 69.7 per cent of party members and 99.5 per cent of candidate-members had joined in or after 1922.[32] Overall, party indigenization achieved incredible results. Within a couple of years, the number of Ukrainian bureaucrats increased from 35 per cent in 1923 to 50 per cent in 1925 and 54 per cent in 1926. The percentage of ethnic Ukrainians in party organs also grew from 23.6 per cent in 1922 to 47.0 per cent in 1927 and 53.0 per cent in 1930, while by 1926 the number of Ukrainians in the government amounted 56.5 per cent.[33]

While party entrenchment was an accepted objective, the question of proletarian Ukrainization was one of the most difficult to agree upon. Historically, Ukraine's cities were often Russian outposts, reflecting the century-long tradition of tsarist assimilation and Russification. In 1897, for example, native Ukrainian-speakers constituted less than a third of the urban population.[34] Increasing rural-to-urban migration during the 1920s changed this dynamic. As a result, by the middle of the decade, the republic's industrial working class already consisted of three more or less equal groups: Ukrainians, whose national self-identification was the same as their native language; non-Ukrainians (especially of Russian and Jewish origin); and Russified Ukrainians, who identified themselves as Ukrainians but whose native language was Russian.[35] As a consequence, despite a common understanding of how important the working class was for comprehensive Ukrainization, the party was wary of defining these ethnically diverse proletarians as its immediate target since it could make the process appear non-voluntary.

The question of whether the Russian-speaking industrial working class should be considered as a target of Ukrainization entered the Bolshevik agenda in earnest after the appointment of Lazar Kaganovich as First Secretary of the KP(b)U in March 1925. In June 1926, a TsK KP(b)U Plenum called for reinforcing comprehensive Ukrainization, encompassing the industrial proletariat, higher education, all-Union institutions and the government bureaucracy.[36] Despite the many objectives, it was proletarian Ukrainization that sparked heated debates over the scope of this policy and exposed fundamental differences between central-oriented and Ukraine-minded factions in the KP(b)U. These debates once again exposed the limits of Bolshevik particularism, when the realities on the ground forced the party centre to reconsider their broader commitments on the national question.

In regard to Russian-speaking Ukrainians, the main challenge was whether to consider them as Russians or Ukrainians. In the first instance, they were to be exempt from the Ukrainization campaign; in the second, become its main targets. For Shums'kyi, now the Commissar for Education, however, the working masses were not Russians, but Russified Ukrainians who simply needed to reinternalize native Ukrainian culture and language. Addressing the slow pace of the policy in Ukraine at the 1925 KP(b)U plenum, Shums'kyi pointed at those in charge, especially Kaganovich, who due to his ethnic origin and close ties to the centre (Kaganovitch was a Ukraine-born Jew and Stalin's protégé) had little interest in the policy's success.[37] Hence, Shums'kyi suggested replacing Kaganovich with Vlas Chubar, Mykola Skrypnyk or another Ukrainian who would ensure proper implementation of Ukrainization.[38]

Stalin indirectly responded to Shums'kyi's criticisms in a letter to Kaganovich dated from 26 April 1926.[39] According to Stalin, the Commissar for Education had misinterpreted the very concept of Ukrainization, conflating Ukrainization of the party and other apparatuses (a declared objective of the policy) with that of the republic's proletariat. Ukrainization of the working class was supposed to be a natural and gradual process, whereas Shums'kyi was seeking to impose it 'from above'. Forcing the Russian-speaking working masses to renounce their Russian language and culture, according to the Soviet leader, 'contradicted the principle of the free development of nationalities [...] and [was] equal to national oppression.' Stalin predicted that Ukrainization from above could provoke 'an outbreak of anti-Ukrainian chauvinism among the non-Ukrainian proletariat' as well as 'the alienation of Ukrainian culture from the All-Soviet culture [...], the Russian culture and its greatest achievement, Leninism, altogether.'[40]

Following Stalin's letter, Shums'kyi was soon demoted and replaced by Skrypnyk, who was seen to comply with the centralist view on *korenizatsiia*. Indeed, Skrypnyk maintained Stalin's view on natural Ukrainization of the republican working class, believing that 're-identification' could be achieved by combining demographic Ukrainization with the necessary promotion of Ukrainian culture. Instead of enforced Ukrainization 'from above', Skrypnyk developed a strategy to encourage workers to identify themselves with Ukrainian culture and language. Since the use of the Ukrainian language was obligatory only for government employees, the linguistic Ukrainization of the workforce could only be achieved by creating a total Ukrainian urban environment: a favourable setting in which the working masses would either convert or became inclined towards the Ukrainian language and a new proletarian culture.[41]

This was to be accomplished by, firstly, increasing the prestige of the Ukrainian language and culture, and, secondly, bringing Ukrainian culture directly to the proletarians. Cultural work was therefore regarded as the main vehicle for drawing workers into the Ukrainian milieu. This included evening language and country studies courses, public lectures in Ukrainian, distribution of books and periodicals, organizing reading circles, concerts, theatre performances and film screenings. As a result of the combined efforts of Soviet modernizers and Ukraine's cultural managers, by 1934 three-and-a-half times as many workers identified themselves as Ukrainians than in 1926 and the percentage of the working class who identified as Ukrainian increased from 51.7 in 1926 to 59.2 in 1934.[42] Nevertheless, Ukrainization did not make Ukrainian the everyday language of the urban populace. Despite concerted government efforts, Russian continued to dominate economic, industrial, political and academic spheres, whereas Ukrainian was confined to education, propaganda work and cultural initiatives.[43] Instead of becoming mono-lingual, urban centres were transformed into enclaves of bilingualism where workers and state functionaries remained dominated by Russian culture. These overall moderate results raise the question of why the party centre attempted ardently to restrict proletarian Ukrainization and in what way it had become a matter of utmost political importance.

Indeed, in the Soviet hierarchy the working class mattered most with Bolshevik doctrine being entirely built around the necessity of working-class mobilization. The declared objective of industrialization required a far bigger influx of workers, meaning that the party needed to continue reaching out to the peasantry, the source of the future workforce. Social and ethnic heterogeneity of the working class meant that there could never be a single ideological line on which the party could base its propaganda. Moreover, local factional struggles created a situation where multiple interest groups attempted to present themselves as the 'vanguard of the working class,' which, according to Lenin, could not formulate any independent ideology of their own. Since class political consciousness could only be brought to the workers from without,[44] the party's central leadership needed to react quickly against any non-authorized attempts to control the process of workers' mobilization. The factional struggle within the KP(b)U and the hostile international climate of 1926–1927 had therefore made Ukraine's Russian-speaking industrial working class the bastion of the Russian Revolution.

Within the KP(b)U, Shums'kyi came to represent the Ukrainian faction, which consisted mainly of former members of national communist parties. Shum'skyi was one of their most prominent members, who made a successful career in the Soviet government and as a Commissar for Education oversaw the entire cultural and educational process in Soviet Ukraine. The success of Ukrainization reaffirmed Ukraine-minded communists that their vision of a Soviet Ukraine was indeed possible. James Mace somewhat optimistically suggested that 'Skrypnyk temporarily achieved what Ukrainian communists had advocated since Mazlakh and Shakhrai, recognition that Ukraine was a country in its own right, ruled by a regime which was clearly Ukrainian in its policies and goals.'[45] The reinforcement of Ukrainian separatism in the mid-1920s proved that the Bolshevik efforts to convert their former opponents into loyal followers through compromise had failed. Instead, the growing share of ethnic Ukrainian members and their preferential position within the party created a new Ukrainian Soviet elite, who started demanding more political, economic and cultural autonomy for their republic.

The inner-party struggle was not the only threat to the success of *korenizatsiia*, as envisaged by the central leadership. Since the early debates on its implementation, there were regular concerns that the policy would unleash and reinforce nationalist forces on the ground. Party directives demanded high results in implementing Ukrainization but provided little to assist reaching set targets. For instance, despite the official declaration of its completion on 1 January 1926, comprehensive linguistic Ukrainization among governmental employees was never met.[46] Whereas governmental employees were usually passive in complying with Ukrainization requirements, the Ukrainian language and culture were aggressively promoted at the local level by the non-party intelligentsia.

This led to 'spontaneous' Ukrainization, as nationalist elements started taking advantage of the benign climate in the republic. While Shums'kyi blamed the party's failure 'to capture, direct, and compensate non-party efforts appropriately,' the central leadership blamed 'anti-Soviet elements', who had decided to capitalize on Ukrainization's success.[47]

As noted by Kaganovich, Ukrainization led to two parallel processes: 'the process of our growth, the growth of the Soviet culture and society; and the process of the growth of hostile forces, which attempt to master this process'[48]; the former was to be accelerated, the latter – combatted. The danger of those nationalists who, like the former Borot'byst Shums'kyi, 'changed their tactics but not their ideology,' was outlined in a top-secret GPU report '*Ob Ukrainskom Separatizme*' (On Ukrainian Separatism), issued on 4 September 1926. According to the GPU, Ukrainization had been exploited by all those nationalists who, having given up their hopes for overthrowing Soviet power, accepted it as an unavoidable fact. However, they started using the new weapon of 'cultural work' to 'place supporters of the national idea in all important parts of the state organism.'[49] To regain control over the implementation of Ukrainization, the party needed to undermine public faith in this policy and the pre-revolutionary elites.[50]

One of the biggest show trials of the late 1920s, concerning the alleged conspiratorial organization Union for the Liberation of Ukraine (*Spilka Vyzvolennia Ukrainy*, SVU), created an excellent opportunity to tackle both the old intelligentsia and eager local 'Ukrainizers'. The SVU trial had serious repercussions and signalled a process of accelerated monopolization of the artistic and cultural spheres in Soviet Ukraine. Firstly, it led to the elimination of the Ukrainian Academy of Sciences' autonomous status, thereafter subjugating it to the party agenda. Secondly, the trial brought to an end the lenient attitude towards *zminovikhivtsi* and fellow travellers, many of whom were direct targets of prosecution. Thirdly, it weakened the local initiative for Ukrainization, since some 30,000 people, including many Ukrainian educators and schoolteachers, were arrested in connection to the SVU.[51]

There was yet another element to the Shums'kyi affair. Before occupying the post in the Narkomos, Shums'kyi had been the Ukraine's representative in Poland and a liaison to the Communist Party of Western Ukraine (KPZU). The KPZU, seen as a mechanism to influence the alignment of political forces in Poland, was financially and ideologically supported by Moscow. Nonetheless, the Ukrainian question was one of the most significant in the KPZU programme and its members aimed to unite all Ukrainians, including those under Polish and other Western governments, within the borders of Soviet Ukraine. KPZU representatives ardently embraced Shums'kyi's vision of a comprehensive Ukrainization and later expressed great concern over his demotion in 1926. To make matters worse, the defection of the KPZU leadership occurred at the height of the war scare of 1926–7, when Soviet leaders were anticipating an attack from an alleged anti-Soviet coalition, with Poland at its forefront. Unsurprisingly, Shums'kyi's Polish-backed calls for wider political autonomy quickly came to be perceived as anti-Soviet. In 1926, foreign considerations took over practical necessities, and *korenizatsiia*, originally designed to foster a positive image of the Soviet authorities internationally, was recalibrated along national security lines.

Lastly, by the end of the 1920s, the objectives of *korenizatsiia* began to directly conflict with other core Bolshevik policies. Rapid industrialization led to a major clash between central and regional elites, who sought to maximize regional control over the allocation of investment resources and demanded more authority in economic administration.[52] The Soviet Union, despite its federalization, acted as one economic entity with decentralization perceived as a threat to the wider modernization project. It was clear that successful industrialization required constant centralized planning and control over regional performance. This was administrated by a single Central Planning Committee, or *Gosplan*, established in 1921, whose authority widened significantly by the decade's end. Such economic dependency contradicted the view of the regional elites, for whom 'nationality, resources, and local political power [became] officially linked.'[53] Hence, by the end of the twenties, *korenizatsiia*'s economic aspects came to the fore, demanding economic decentralization of the Soviet Union to correspond to its federal system of government.

The debates on the amount of regional control over the national economy were especially heated in Ukraine, since the republic was seen as the key in delivering production targets. The demands came from both within the KP(b)U leadership and the non-party elites and ranged from the need to reconsider industrial locations to transforming Ukraine into a single economic unit. At the 1927 Party Congress, Kaganovich advocated expanding planned targets and increasing capital investment in the republic.[54] The KP(b)U leader aimed to reinforce Ukraine's former industrial dominance and continuously defended local interests at the central level. The economic side of Ukrainization, however, was formulated by two economists, Hryn'ko and Mykhailo Volobuev. From 1924 to 1926 Hryn'ko, a former Borot'byst, had overseen the Ukrainian *Gosplan* before taking the post of deputy head of the all-Union *Gosplan*. Volobuev chaired the *Narkomos*' programme of adult education and literacy.[55]

The plan for rapid industrialization reignited the debate on regionalization, according to which the republic was seen as a number of administrative districts with different economic functions. According to Hryn'ko and Volobuev, this had undermined Ukraine's potential as a single national economic unit. Moreover, it contradicted the objectives of Ukrainization, which meant to establish the link between the industrial working class and the peasantry.[56] In Volobuev's words, Ukraine became a 'European-type colony', economically and financially exploited by Russia.[57] Not only was its national economy over-reliant on raw materials and natural resources, but one third of Ukraine's taxes were being utilized outside of the republic. Instead, he advocated rational allocation of resources and financial autarky, which could help Ukraine develop a more balanced economic base and better contribute to the economic growth of the Soviet Union as a whole. Needless to say, Volobuev's position on the national economy, articulated in 1928 on the pages of the party journal *Bil'shovyk Ukrainy*, was quickly compared to the opinions expressed by Shums'kyi. Both were accused of promoting national deviationist position, labelled respectively '*volobuevshchyna*' and '*shums'kism*' and were subsequently deposed and relocated.

The Fate of the Bolshevik Revolution

Bolshevik ideology had originated in a complete and total rejection of the oppressive tsarist regime. Its implementation was intended to bring peace, distribute land and give bread to the people exhausted by the First World War, and overcome the political and social chaos into which the Russian Empire had descended by 1917. Most importantly, the Bolsheviks promised to liberate the peoples of Russia from national, social and political restraints. To achieve all this, they needed to defeat numerous enemies of the revolution first. The Bolshevik takeover in Petrograd was swift yet this could not guarantee control over Russia's peripheries. Neither could military supremacy ensure immediate victory over political and ideological opponents, as the experiences of the civil war had shown.

The Bolsheviks needed to secure popular support which would allow them to realize their liberationist vision. Significantly, the success of these long-term goals depended on the party vanguard's ability to establish the dictatorship of the proletariat in the country, which had neither the industrial capacity nor a well-developed working class. Popular mobilization was the answer to all Bolshevik concerns with the party quickly coming to understand the potential of the national factor for inciting mass mobilization. National languages and national elites were thus necessary to engage the working class and reach out to the peasantry, who even a decade after the revolution remained hostile to those in power.

Soviet Ukraine became key for the success of their political projects; yet its internal contradictions posed a genuine threat to the Bolshevik dictatorship. Various nationalist forces fought continuously with the Bolsheviks in trying to preserve their control over territory and its resources. Moreover, during the Soviet–Polish War, the competing interests of the two governments converged in Ukraine. Nevertheless, the fiercest opposition to the central vision unexpectedly came from within the Ukrainian Bolshevik Party itself. The success of *korenizatsiia* in Soviet Ukraine created an illusion that local political elites had the power to decide on republic matters, and to discuss and even challenge the political line set in Moscow. Yet Bolshevik modernization under Stalin required uniformity and compliance with the centre, including readiness to surrender the levers of control to the central party leadership.

By the end of the 1920s, it became obvious that Bolshevik ethnic particularism had created more problems in Ukraine than it was intended to resolve. As a result of Soviet modernization campaigns, more people had gained access to higher education and promotion opportunities, whereas *korenizatsiia* gave preferential status to those fluent in local languages and created ethnic Ukrainian elites who owed their status and positions to the Soviet regime. These new nationalized elites began challenging the central leadership, attempting to gain control over the power structure and decision-making. More importantly, regional leaders started questioning the internationalist (Russian) nature of the industrial proletariat – the political base of Bolshevik ideology – and demanded a say in the industrialization campaign. The alternative views of the Ukrainian communists ran counter to those brought down from Moscow. As a result, they were quickly labelled as political enemies standing in the way of Soviet progress.

Two Five-Year plans sufficed for the Soviet Union to catch up with, and even surpass many of its European neighbours. Moreover, Soviet industrial achievements coincided with major strides in social modernization. In 1939, the party leadership proudly declared the success of 'the greatest phenomenon in the history of humankind,' claiming to have overcome social-class boundaries through attained literacy levels, access to professional education and guaranteed gender equality.[58] As soon as 'backwardness' became a word of the past, and the party membership reflected the national composition of the republics, there was no further need to encourage national differences. Although *korenizatsiia* was never suspended officially, its course was significantly redefined by the urgent need to address the growing influence of the nationalized regional Soviet elites, while further encouraging industrialization. Unsurprisingly, responses to both challenges coincided. With calls for greater economic efficiency beginning to supplant ethnic interests, nation-based persecutions could be easily justified. The intensity of terror in the late 1930s reflected the strength of the national 'deviations' in the party during the 1920s. In turn, the national Soviet elites became strongest in those areas where the Bolsheviks had taken longer to consolidate power during the civil war and where more drastic concessions to the speed and scope of the Bolshevik 'cultural revolution' needed to be made, encapsulated in the example of Soviet Ukraine.

CHAPTER 11
THE INTERNATIONAL SITUATION: FEAR OF INVASION AND GROWING AUTHORITARIANISM
Peter Whitewood

For Vladimir Lenin and the Bolsheviks, the primary function of their revolution in 1917 was to spark further uprisings in the more advanced countries of Western Europe. This would bring forth worldwide revolution and usher in world communism. For them, this was the only role that a revolution in a struggling empire with a large peasant majority, an underdeveloped working-class and backwards-industrial base, could possibly play. In fact the revolution would not survive without spreading further afield. As a result, when European revolution failed to ignite, the Bolsheviks faced a serious security dilemma: Russia was surrounded by countries with governments hostile to communism. Civil war that erupted in 1918 only underlined the precarious position of the Soviet government. Western capitalist powers – Britain, France and the United States – all gave financial and material support to the Bolsheviks' enemies, first in an effort to keep the eastern front open against Germany and then in an effort to snuff out the Soviet government. As far as Lenin was concerned, this was evidence of capitalist encirclement.

Bolshevik victory in the civil war did not provide a sense of security. Even though the immediate danger to the revolution had been overcome, the Bolsheviks would never forget the assistance given to their enemies by capitalist powers. Moreover, the Bolsheviks were convinced that the capitalist world would never reconcile to their revolutionary state and would continue to seek its destruction. All of this heightened the dangers posed by the outside world and there were serious consequences. Historians have recently given more attention to Bolshevik leaders' misperceptions of foreign threats and how this explains their use of political violence.[1] Yet less attention has been given to how Bolshevik perceptions of the international situation shaped the dictatorship itself in the 1920s.[2] This chapter will show how a perpetual fear of foreign intervention encouraged Bolshevik leaders to retreat from the democratic impulses of 1917 and from the workers democracy promised at the outset of the revolution. The Bolshevik Party was instead pushed further towards authoritarian practices, accelerating the consolidation of a one-party vanguard-led state that placed growing limits on intraparty discussion. Perceived security concerns shared across the Soviet elite were a powerful force in the weakening of democratic practices in the 1920s.

In examining how the Bolsheviks understood the outside world and the impact this had on democratic practices, this chapter will concentrate on the perceived threat of war between Poland and the Soviet Union. This was the most common foreign policy preoccupation for the Bolsheviks in the 1920s. Indeed, having experienced stunning defeat against the Poles at the Battle of Warsaw in August 1920 – a clash that brought the Soviet–Polish War to a close – the Bolsheviks fully expected renewed war against Poland, supported by powerful capitalist states, in the years after.

Fears of renewed war, 1921–3

After narrowly avoiding defeat by the White Armies and interventionist foreign powers at the height of the civil war, the Bolsheviks found themselves in more secure circumstances in the early 1920s. Appraising the outside world in February 1921, Lenin proclaimed that the 'greatest danger point' to the revolution had passed. He saw major conflict in the near future as a risky undertaking for capitalist powers facing economic crises and rising revolutionary movements at home. Yet Lenin warned against complacency: the external threat had not been eliminated.[3] Open war against the capitalist world was unavoidable and until then, the revolution – isolated in the world – would be forced to exist under conditions of capitalist encirclement.

It was in this context that the Bolsheviks judged newly reconstituted Poland as the most dangerous international threat to the revolution. The Soviet–Polish War officially ended when the Treaty of Riga was signed on 18 March 1921, but this was nothing more than an uneasy compromise (with the majority of treaty conditions ultimately going unfulfilled).[4] For this reason, failure to usher in peaceful relations in 1921 has been described as the starting point of a cold war between the two countries.[5] Indeed, formal peace did little to ease Bolshevik concerns that the Entente would once again push Poland into war when the time was right. Lenin made precisely this point prior to the signing of the treaty in early 1921. Even though he saw war as a risky undertaking for the revolution's enemies, Lenin proclaimed that foreign capitalists were 'spending millions and millions to organise another invasion in spring.' Yet without the assistance of a pliable state bordering Soviet territory, he argued, these efforts would come to nothing. It was Poland (and Romania) – sold to the capitalists 'lock, stock, and barrel' and vulnerable to manipulation – who might 'rush headlong into the craziest adventures.'[6] For Lenin, despite the formal end of hostilities against Poland, the international situation remained precarious.

Lenin was not alone in this reading of the outside world. The Soviet political police estimated that a new military attack might come in spring or summer 1921 and pointed to extensive activity of Polish intelligence agents in Ukraine.[7] Similarly, Bolshevik negotiators at the peace talks with Poland in 1921 could not discount a rapid resumption of hostilities. Soviet representative Adolf Ioffe, for instance, suggested to People's Commissar for Finance, Nikolai Krestinskii, that the Bolsheviks accept the Polish government's demands for gold as deliveries could be staggered over two or three years, staving off another invasion during this time.[8] There were some moderate voices in the early 1920s. The People's Commissariat of Foreign Affairs tended to report a more benign picture of the foreign threat in 1921. People's Commissar Georgii Chicherin, for instance, received a stream of diplomatic reports describing consensus within the Polish government for quickly achieving a peace treaty, yet these equally stressed continuing international hostility towards Soviet Russia and concerted efforts spearheaded by the French to create a union of anti-Soviet border-states.[9]

It is clear that the Bolsheviks did not rule out another military clash against Poland after the Treaty of Riga and this soon shaped strategies for new international alliances. In October 1921, Maksim Litvinov, Deputy People's Commissar for Foreign Affairs, recommended that the Bolsheviks arrange a defensive alliance with Germany because Poland was likely to remain a '"sword of Damocles" hanging over our heads.' (The Soviet foreign ministry would later warn of imminent war against Poland and Romania in early 1922.)[10] Commissar for War, Leon Trotsky, in an order from the Revolutionary Military Council from November 1921, took aim at a shadowy military clique in Poland headed by Józef Piłsudski pushing for renewed war and stressed that the Red Army needed to be prepared for the worst.[11] Yet as we have seen, Poland was regarded as the instrument of war; the Bolsheviks continued to see the British and French governments as the crucial backers.

As had been true in the previous war against Poland, the Bolsheviks identified Ukraine as a weak spot in their defences and as a potential bridgehead in a future clash with the west. Consequently the western front, in comparison to other civil war fronts, was converted to peacetime military district status only in April 1924.[12] Mikhail Tukhachevskii, famed commander of the 1920 Battle of Warsaw, returned to oversee the western front between January 1922 and March 1924. Moreover, banditry in Ukraine, coordinated by separatist leaders such as Symon Petliura (and given covert support by Polish intelligence), was at times interpreted by the Soviet political police as directed by Poland in advance of a military assault.[13] The activity of bandits in the borderlands was a common source of complaint in Soviet notes to the Polish government and tied to the potential resumption of hostilities.[14]

Fears about imminent war were eased – or at least downplayed – by senior Bolsheviks at the Eleventh Party Congress held between March and April 1922. The congress recognized that Poland (and Romania) had represented direct threats in autumn 1921 but that peace had been ensured because of military preparations and effective diplomacy.[15] Nevertheless, further intelligence about a military attack quickly filtered through to the leadership. Sergei Kamenev, commander in chief of the Red Army, reported to Iosif Stalin at the end of April that recent intelligence indicated that Poland and Romania were considering launching military action in late spring or early summer. According to Kamenev, a military meeting in Romania had been attended not only by the Polish military attaché but also by representatives of the French government, Petliura and the White General Petr Wrangel.[16] This news was followed up two weeks later with a report from the political police's foreign department describing 'serious discussions' in Latvia about a possible conflict between Poland and Russia.[17] Soviet intelligence reported over the coming months on French–Polish–Romania military cooperation, the movement of Polish troops to the borders of Ukraine and the possibility of a new attack if conditions were right to spark the internal collapse of the Bolshevik state.[18] The French government was rightly presented in these materials as striving to create a unified Polish and Romanian military force for potential action in Russia and to be held in reserve against Germany. Soviet intelligence agents also accurately assessed Poland's inability to wage war independently. This was only possible with the assistance of powerful countries to bankroll a new conflict. For the party leadership, however, none of this made war any less inevitable in the future.[19] By the end of 1922, rumours about war continued to circle when Mikhail Frunze, commander of the Ukrainian military district, received a report on 'lively' discussions in Polish military circles about war in the east and the supposed efforts by Petliura's bands to encourage Polish intervention.[20] In early 1923, Soviet intelligence agents in Ukraine were tasked with obtaining Polish, Latvian and Estonian mobilization plans.[21]

Fears about a new war were significantly heightened when international crisis erupted in Western Europe in 1923 after French and Belgian troops occupied the Ruhr industrial region in January following the failure of the German government to meet its reparations payments. Hyperinflation soon hit the Germany economy sparking a strike wave across German cities that culminated in the failed Hamburg insurrection in October. The Politburo threw its support behind the German Communist Party in the summer, envisaging another revolution. But with revolutionary optimism came fears of new war. For some Bolsheviks, a conflict with Poland was now more likely than ever. Until the collapse of the German uprising became clear in the autumn, the prospect of Polish military intervention to quash the insurrection was taken seriously (the Bolsheviks believed that the Polish government would never permit their country to be surrounded on both sides by revolutionary states). There was now serious talk in Bolshevik circles of using the Red Army to protect the nascent German revolution as the crisis matured.[22] Trotsky in particular was determined to go to war if necessary, writing to Karl Radek at the outset of the crisis that the Bolsheviks could not stand aside if Poland attacked Germany.[23] Grigorii Zinoviev, the most prominent supporter of the German communists, like Trotsky, wanted more resources committed to the army.[24] At the Twelfth Party Congress in April 1923, Zinoviev proclaimed that the occupation of the Ruhr meant that war had in fact already arrived; it was merely war by other means.[25]

For this reason, during the course of 1923 Soviet military and GPU intelligence agents kept a close eye on potentially threatening troop movements and mobilizations. They reported that the French general staff believed that war with Germany would evolve into war against Russia and that military union with Poland was an essential part of French strategy towards Germany.[26] Soviet intelligence tracked the movements of French marshal Ferdinand Foch and his efforts to forge a military alliance between France, Poland and other border states in the event of war with Russia.[27] Alarmingly, Soviet intelligence from March noted that a majority within the Polish general staff now believed that another war should be launched against Russia to overthrow Soviet power and guarantee the Polish eastern border. Other reports noted the build-up of Polish military supplies in border regions and on the right bank of the Vistula.[28] GPU operatives on the ground in Ukraine recorded that Polish representatives were discussing war and the possibility of Polish troops being sent to Kiev.[29] Soviet intelligence reported on the adaption of Polish railways to match those in Eastern Ukraine.[30] The Red Army began to war-game possible conflicts, accepting that the international situation in Western and Central Europe made armed conflict between the Soviet Union and Poland, Romania and White organizations, inevitable.[31]

That the Bolsheviks took the threat of war seriously in 1923 can also be seen in the secret military preparations undertaken during the crisis. The Red Army in general terms was in no condition to fight in a major conflict, something that had been laid bare in a report on Soviet defences in May 1923. This judged the Red Army as clearly lagging behind the Polish Army and called for its urgent strengthening.[32] Other weaknesses in Soviet defences had also been highlighted during the year. Head of the GPU, Feliks Dzerzhinskii, described problems in Soviet transport infrastructure and the inability to efficiently move troops. He concluded that Poland would be able to carry out a successful short strike towards Kiev.[33] Concrete plans for war were thus put into motion, particularly as the crisis in Germany reached a peak.[34] On 18 September 1923, the Politburo ordered a strengthening of Red Army units on the western front, in the Ukrainian military district and in air defence.[35] The following day, the Revolutionary Military Council ordered an increase in the number of political officers on the western front.[36] In October, student communists were called up as political officers on the western front and demobilized Red Army men returned to the ranks.[37] In November, Soviet industry officials in Ukraine began to secretly prepare for the evacuation of enterprises, factories and workers in the border region in case war suddenly erupted.[38] Rumours of war were now widespread.[39] The Ukrainian GPU recorded lively conversations about forthcoming war among Poles.[40] Polish intelligence agents likewise reported that Kiev was alive with signs of preparation for new conflict.[41]

Despite growing anxiety about a clash with Poland and the raft of military preparations, war never materialized. The Hamburg uprising fizzled out almost as soon as it began, bringing the wider crisis to an end. However, what matters is how the Bolshevik leaders had misperceived the threat of war in 1923. There were undoubtedly certain circles in Poland – particularly within the military and intelligence services – pushing for war in 1923. However, the centre-right National Democrats dominated Polish politics during that year. Their priority was closer economic relations with Russia, not launching another invasion. The National Democrats disagreed entirely with the aggressive approach championed by Piłsudski and his supporters. In fact, Piłsudski had resigned as chief of the general staff in May and his allies were subsequently ousted from government. The years 1923 to 1925 saw Polish policy towards Russia more firmly reoriented towards seeking trade agreements. Notably, the Polish government recognized the formation of Soviet Union in December 1923.[42] In short, voices clamouring for war near the Polish government were weakened at the very moment that the Bolsheviks took the threat of war most seriously. The 1923 war scare reveals how precariously the Bolsheviks viewed their position in the world and the degree to which they misperceived the nature of foreign threats.

The Fate of the Bolshevik Revolution

Capitalist encirclement and dictatorship

The international crisis of 1923 coincided with rising political opposition inside the Bolshevik Party. At the height of the crisis in October, Trotsky and the Left Opposition launched a scathing attack on the party majority, criticizing it – and Stalin in particular – of presiding over the bureaucratization of party life, the creation of a secretarial hierarchy and for placing limits on internal discussion and intraparty criticism. The response from the party majority to this challenge was shaped by a number of priorities, but it is clear that perceived threats of invasion and capitalist encirclement, unbroken since the end of the civil war, played important roles in the shutting down of Trotsky and his supporters. Lenin had already established this as a precedent. In early 1921, when tensions were running high about the resumption of hostilities against Poland, Lenin and the party majority faced criticism from minority political groups, the Workers' Opposition and Democratic Centralists. Both criticized weak democratic practices, the growing bureaucracy and inadequate worker representation in senior party bodies.[43] At the time Lenin responded that these problems could not be immediately remedied for a number of reasons, not least because workers lacked adequate experience of government, but also because the threatening international situation made dictatorship necessary. In an article published in *Pravda* in January 1921, Lenin argued:

> The Entente capitalists will surely try to take advantage of our Party's malaise [political disputes] to mount another invasion [...] We need have no fear of this because we shall all unite as one man, without being afraid to admit the malaise, but recognising that it demands from all of us a greater discipline, tenacity and firmness at every post.[44]

In his opening speech to the Tenth Party Congress two months later – which approved the ban on factions in the party – Lenin proclaimed that past discussions and disputes had been an 'amazing luxury' for a party shouldering such responsibilities and 'surrounded by mighty and powerful enemies uniting the whole capitalist world.' Lenin again argued that foreign powers were taking advantage of internal party disputes, with foreign presses spreading rumours of communist weaknesses.[45] None of this is to say that the Bolsheviks' perception of international relations was the sole cause of the ban of factions. Yet it is clear that for Lenin at least, at a time when the country faced powerful enemies from within and without, the party needed to be more united than ever before.

Lenin reiterated the necessity of dictatorship with similar justifications at the Third Congress of the Communist International held between June and July 1921: 'This dictatorship is essential as long as classes exist, as long as the bourgeoisie, overthrown in one country, intensifies tenfold its attacks on socialism on an international scale.' Describing dictatorship as a 'state of intense war', Lenin argued that resistance from the working classes around the world was the only restraining force on the international bourgeoisie, though war could 'never be ruled out'.[46] In this context, free political organization could not be permitted. As Lenin explained to the oppositionist Gavriil

Miasnikov in a letter from August 1921, this would simply give another weapon to the world bourgeoisie.⁴⁷

Similar criticisms were aired at the Eleventh Party Congress in the following year. Here, senior Bolsheviks again cast calls for stronger democratic practices as impermissible in a dangerous international environment. Criticizing Aleksandr Shliapnikov, leader of the Workers' Opposition, Lenin argued against free political organization and emphasized the threat of war as the primary danger:

> I have indicated the three conditions under which it will be possible for us to hold on: first, that there shall be no intervention; second, that the financial crisis shall not be too severe; and third, that we shall make no political mistakes [...] Of course, even today the bourgeoisie may attempt another armed intervention, but they will find it much more difficult than before; it is much more difficult today than it was yesterday. To ensure ourselves the opportunity to learn we must make no political mistakes. We must waste no time playing with the unity of the Party, as Comrade Shlyapnikov is doing.⁴⁸

Trotsky was likewise critical of opposition in the party at the congress and claimed that hostile states were turning this to their advantage: 'It is not an accident that the radio station of the Polish government sent extracts from comrade Miasnikov's pamphlet out to the whole world.' Trotsky also remarked that the writings of Aleksandra Kollontai, a figure closely associated with the Workers' Opposition, were being quoted abroad.⁴⁹ The congress ultimately deemed the activity of the Workers' Opposition impermissible for several reasons: the continuing difficult economic circumstances, the presence of 'capitalist elements' in Russia, the spread of famine and the threat of invasion.⁵⁰

Similarly, in the year of Ruhr crisis and at the Twelfth Party Congress in April 1923, Lev Kamenev discussed the international position of the revolution and the question of party unity in his opening comments. He argued that enemies surrounded Soviet Russia on all sides and that unity in the party was necessary, adding that the Bolsheviks were in the position of the 'most shelled post' in the world proletarian revolution.⁵¹ Stalin framed his case for party unity in a way that he would repeat in later years. Arguing that the party had become too large to allow broad open discussion, he made a comparison to circumstances before the revolution. For Stalin, the Bolsheviks were in the same position as they had been in 1912 when surrounded by opponents; the difference now was that their 'enemies' were on an international scale. Moreover, Stalin claimed that there was no reason to doubt that preparatory work for a blockade or intervention was not taking place. For this reason, open discussion in the party could not be permitted, especially when this discussion concerned the most important questions: war and peace. Attacking the suggestion of allowing more liberal discussion in the party, Stalin added: 'We can't talk about questions of war or peace on the streets [...] we need to remember that in an environment when we are surrounded by enemies, a sudden blow, or unexpected manoeuvre, decides everything.'⁵²

Consequently, when Trotsky and the Left Opposition moved to challenge the party majority more concertedly in October 1923, the threatening international situation was again emphasized as another reason why this was unacceptable. Most clearly, the resolution from the Joint Plenum of the Central Committee and Central Control Commission at the end of October 1923, which roundly condemned Trotsky and his supporters on the basis of their programme and behaviour, noted that 'we have already entered a period that can be called direct combat' and made reference to current events in Germany and the possibility of war against Poland. In this moment, the resolution stated, 'factional discussion' was prohibited.[53] Sticking to his past views, Trotsky agreed that factionalism in the party was dangerous when war threatened (though by this time he had moderated his opinion on the immediate threat from Poland and insisted that relations had improved between the two countries). Important for Trotsky, however, was that his criticism of the majority should not be characterized as factionalism. Nevertheless, Trotsky had put himself in a difficult position by continuing to accept the premise that factionalism was dangerous when war threatened.

At the end of 1923 the party majority temporarily conceded to party-wide discussions on workers' democracy, but 'factionalism' was still ruled out.[54] At the same time the ever-present threats of war and capitalist encirclement continued to raise questions about whether more robust party democracy and intraparty criticism were permissible. At the Thirteenth Party Conference in January 1924, Stalin made his views on the impossibility of party democracy in the context of possible war particularly clear:

> I have already said that there is another group of conditions, of an external nature, and in the absence of these democracy in the Party is impossible. I have in mind certain international conditions that would more or less ensure peace and peaceful development, without which democracy in the Party is inconceivable. In other words, if we are attacked and have to defend the country with arms in hand, there can be no question of democracy, for it will have to be suspended [...] What Trotsky offers is deeply mistaken; it runs counter to Bolshevik organisational principles and would lead to the inevitable disintegration of the party, to its softening, turning it from a single party into a federation of groups. In conditions of capitalist encirclement, we need not only a united, not only a skillful, but a party of real steel, capable of withstanding the onslaught of the enemies of the proletariat, capable of leading the workers to the final battle.[55]

That Lenin, Stalin, other senior Bolsheviks in the party majority, but also leading oppositionists like Trotsky, argued that political freedom was potentially dangerous when Soviet Russia existed under capitalist encirclement is not to argue that this was the sole consideration for the maintenance of a one-party dictatorship. However, as we have seen, the Bolsheviks saw the outside world in more dangerous terms than warranted and this understanding of international affairs in turn shaped attitudes towards whether democratic practices were permissible. From the Bolsheviks' point of view, a unified and disciplined party dictatorship remained critical for survival in a hostile international environment. It certainly ruled out the formation of factions and other political groupings, the central accusation levelled against Trotsky and his supporters. And while Trotsky outright rejected this characterization, his endorsements of the nature of foreign threats and the principle of unity in the party when war threatened boxed him into a corner. These same concerns emerged again in the late 1920s when another war scare erupted and the opposition once more found themselves with little room for manoeuvre.

The Piłsudski coup and the war scare

In the mid-to-late 1920s, Soviet leaders were again preoccupied by the threat of war and ordinary people were just as concerned. In 1927 a war scare erupted across the Soviet Union, sparking outbreaks of hoarding and panic buying. The war scare in 1927 has sometimes been presented in the literature as manufactured by the Soviet leadership and designed as a tool to put pressure on the political opposition.[56] However, as we have seen, there is little to suggest that fears of war emanated solely from above or were designed instrumentally. Soviet intelligence reports from the ground level about a new conflict were unremitting in the early 1920s. Moreover, it was not just the party elite, but Commissariats of Defense and Foreign affairs, military intelligence and the political police, which discussed the likelihood of war in the near future. There was a shared understanding about the Soviet Union's precarious position in the world and one shaped by a long-held and ideologically informed understanding of international affairs. As we will see, key members of the opposition continued to be some, if not the most ardent, supporters of this worldview.

The roots of the 1927 war scare can be found in the still tense relations between the Soviet Union and Poland. The country was the subject of increasing anxiety among Soviet leaders in 1926 and, in March, the Polish Commission of the Politburo ordered more attention given to Polish affairs.[57] Rumours of Piłsudski's return to power had started to circle, particularly following the fall of Aleksander Skrzyński's government in May. As far as the Bolsheviks were concerned, this would greatly escalate the danger of war. The leadership also believed that Piłsudski's return would shift the balance of geopolitical power and push Poland more closely towards Britain's orbit.[58] OGPU leaders, Genrikh Iagoda and Artur Artuzov, stressed the danger shortly after Piłsudski's return to power in mid-May and pointed to examples of recent aggressive British behaviour towards the Soviet Union, particularly in terms of trade restrictions and supposedly large-scale intelligence operations. The assumption was that Piłsudski's return to power was through British design. Notably, Iagoda and Artuzov described Piłsudski as the 'guard dog' of the British in Eastern Europe and argued that he would try once more to forge a Polish federation with Ukraine and Belorussia. In response, the OGPU was to strengthen counter-measures against espionage and to keep a close eye on Polish affairs.[59]

Piłsudski's coup d'état in May was anticipated, but it made the threat of war more pressing for the Soviet leadership.[60] Piłsudski had already invaded once before during the Soviet–Polish War and had pushed interventionist stances while sat on the sidelines of Polish politics. After the May coup, preventing Polish aggression assumed a greater priority. The People's Commissariat of Foreign Affairs recommended that Poland be isolated from its neighbours to prevent the formation of an anti-Soviet coalition.[61] Red Army leaders, who had lobbied for higher levels of investment since 1924 on the grounds that Soviet defences could not withstand invasion from a coalition of states led by Poland, sounded the alarm again in summer 1926. The Soviet Defence Commission subsequently agreed to take 'urgent measures for strengthening the defense potential of the USSR'.[62] Tukhachevskii was once again sent to the western front (this time to Minsk) and Aleksandr Egorov to Kharkov.[63] Some regarded the situation as highly dangerous. Before his death in July, Dzerzhinskii vehemently argued that Piłsudski would now try to seize Belorussia and Ukraine, a warning he relayed personally to Stalin.[64] On the ground in Ukraine, GPU agents reported on the renewed hope among separatists that Soviet defeat at the hands of Poland would bring about their independence.[65]

Not all were as alarmist as Dzerzhinskii, but even more measured appraisals of Soviet–Polish relations emphasized the dangerous environment after Piłsudski's return to power. People's Commissar for Foreign Affairs, Chicherin, was gloomy about the recent turn of events, writing to the OGPU head that Poland was trying to conclude agreements with the Baltic states, forcing the threat from Poland to be taken seriously.[66] Soviet military intelligence forecast growing Polish militarism – and with it the threat of war – but its agents believed that the Soviet Union was safe from attack until at least spring 1927.[67] The situation was bad, but it was not yet a crisis. Military intelligence rightly estimated that Poland required external assistance to build its military strength. Ultimately, however, should Poland be ready and pressured into war by Britain, it would represent a serious adversary.[68]

As to how Stalin judged the threat of war in the late 1920s, in public he sided with the view of military intelligence rather than with the alarmist Dzerzhinskii. In his speech to the Fifteenth Party Conference in November 1926, Stalin proclaimed that whether capitalist states were in a position to attack was still to be seen, but regardless, the Soviet Union remained in a position of encirclement. This was not a moment of respite and war could not be ruled out.[69] It is possible that Stalin downplayed the threat for the benefit of the conference. Indeed, a few months later in February 1927, Maksim Litvinov suggested to Stalin that there was no reliable information that Britain was pushing Poland towards war. Stalin raked him over the coals and spoke about the existence of an international conspiracy against the Soviet Union and the inevitability of war.[70] Stalin's close allies were evidently in agreement. In mid-1927, Lazar Kaganovich accused Piłsudski of waging a war against Moscow to seize Ukraine and claimed that Polish fascism was backed by 'foreign imperialism'.[71]

Stalin's appraisal of the nature of the Polish threat is also revealed in his reaction to the murder of Petr Voikov, the Soviet plenipotentiary in Poland, by a White monarchist in June 1927. In a telegram sent to Viacheslav Molotov immediately after Voikov's death, and relying on his gut instincts, Stalin wrote that he 'felt the hand of England' behind Voikov's murder and suggested that the British government wanted to provoke war between Poland and the Soviet Union, repeating 'Sarajevo'.[72] The allusion to the assassination of Franz Ferdinand is suggestive of the danger that Stalin saw in Piłsudski's Poland under British influence. The British government had already severed diplomatic relations with the Soviet Union one month before, following raids on the Soviet trade delegation and All-Russian Co-operative Society in London that the British authorities believed were fronts for Soviet intelligence.[73]

Yet despite seeing a British conspiracy to wage war, Stalin still did not judge this as imminent in 1926 or 1927. Writing in *Pravda* in July 1927, Stalin accused the British government of preparing war against the Soviet Union but argued that this had been forestalled for two reasons: the peaceful policies carried out by the Soviet Union and the reluctance of countries such as Poland to 'serve as dumb tools of the [British] Conservatives to the detriment of their own interests'. Even so, Stalin claimed that capitalist powers would not stop in trying to provoke war and the immediate task facing the Soviet Union was to improve its economic power and military strength.[74]

Renewed pressure on the opposition

Heightened concerns about war against Piłsudski's Poland and its capitalist backers placed more pressure on the political opposition at the height of its activity. Concerns about war continued to circumscribe open party discussion as had been true in previous years and created new concerns about the opposition undermining state defence. Dzerzhinskii saw internal disputes in the party as dangerous with Piłsudski back in power. In July 1926, he claimed that Piłsudski would detect weakness in the Soviet state because of the activity of the opposition.[75] While Stalin was not as adamant as Dzerzhinskii about the imminence of war, he conveyed similar messages regarding the continuing dangers posed by factionalism. At the Seventh Enlarged Plenum of the Executive Committee of the Communist International (ECCI) in December 1926, he argued that a 'united party armed with iron discipline' was essential when imperialism was such a strong force in the world. In this context, attempts to undermine party unity or create a new party had to be 'rooted out'. In May 1927, again at a plenum of the ECCI, Stalin referred to a 'united front from Chamberlain to Trotsky'.[76] Stalin followed this up in a *Pravda* article from July 1927 containing another scathing attack on the opposition:

> What, after all this, should be said of our luckless opposition in connection with its latest attacks on our Party in face of the threat of a new war? What should be said of the fact that it, this opposition, has found the war threat an appropriate occasion to intensify its attacks on the Party? What is there creditable in the fact that, instead of rallying around the Party in face of the threat from without, it considers it appropriate to make use of the U.S.S.R.'s difficulties for new attacks on the Party? Can it be that the opposition is against the victory of the U.S.S.R. in the coming battles with imperialism, against increasing the defensive capacity of the Soviet Union, against strengthening our rear?[77]

One month later, in another speech, Stalin explicitly connected the internal and external threats to the Soviet Union:

> Comrades, we are faced by two dangers: the danger of war, which has become the threat of war; and the danger of the degeneration of some of the links of our Party. In setting out to prepare for defence we must create iron discipline in our Party. Without such discipline defence is impossible. We must strengthen Party discipline, we must curb all those who are disorganising our Party.[78]

Other senior Bolsheviks shared this view and likewise argued that the opposition was undermining Soviet defence and even threatened to stab the country in the back during war.[79]

Trotsky denied this volley of accusations and argued on the contrary that the opposition was the only group capable of steering the country through tense international times. Other members of the opposition lower down the chain took the same view and saw their programme as necessary for successful navigation of the international environment, especially curbing the influence of kulaks, as not doing so risked creating an internal front during war.[80] As part of his defence, Trotsky provocatively made reference to Georges Clémenceau who had remained in opposition to the French government during the First World War until there was opportunity to take the leadership. After a backlash, Trotsky clarified his position in September 1927, arguing that his comments had been distorted and rejected the accusation that the opposition threatened to take power 'after the Clémenceau manner'. Yet at the same time, he again accepted the need for unity when war threatened: 'The dictatorship of the proletariat in a country which is surrounded by capitalist states does not allow either the existence of two parties or the factional splitting of a unified party.' For Trotsky, the problem remained the party elite's circumscribing of open discussion and its unaccountability. For him, the threat of war had no bearing on this: 'It is a lie that the danger or even war itself excludes the self-action of the party, which discusses and decides all questions and which directs and checks all its organs from top to bottom.'[81]

In making this case, Trotsky faced exactly the same problem as in 1923. He continued to agree that the Soviet Union would be endangered if the party split into factions and that unity was required in the face of war with the capitalist world. On the latter danger, Trotsky was unequivocal in 1927, writing to the Central Committee in June that the threat of intervention was 'unquestionable'.[82] Moreover, in the Platform of the United Opposition, produced in 1927, he argued:

> Another task of equal importance is to consolidate the ranks of our party, to put an end to the open speculation of the imperialist bourgeoisie and the leaders of Social Democracy on a split [...] All the organs of the international bourgeoisie and the Social Democrats are now showing a quite unusual interest in our inner-party disputes. They are openly encouraging and spurring on the present majority of the Central Committee to exclude the Opposition from the leading organs of the

party, and if possible from the party [...] Moreover, we can buy ourselves off from a war, if that is possible – and conquer in the war, if we have to fight – only if we preserve complete unity; if we disappoint the hopes of the imperialists for a split or an amputation. Such a thing would benefit only the capitalists.[83]

For Trotsky, party unity would be damaged and the Soviet Union endangered if the opposition was expelled. The party majority saw the exact opposite. Indeed, Trotsky's conception of party unity meant 'above all maximum active participation by the entire mass of the party.'[84] The majority saw this as unacceptable considering the international threats facing the Soviet Union. Even to allow more open discussion was regarded as potentially dangerous. The nature of political participation was thus the crux of the dispute and positions were irreconcilable. However, there was one crucial point of agreement. Trotsky fatally undermined his position by accepting the need for unity when war was on the horizon. In fact the danger posed by the outside world had not been seriously disputed since 1917. The controversy was in how the party should respond and what exactly constituted 'unity'. And there was no chance that the party leadership would liberalize democratic practices when it judged the threat of war as acute. Critically, Trotsky did nothing to dispel this worldview. The conclusion therefore should not be that the party majority used the war threat instrumentally to crush internal critics. That Stalin wanted Trotsky out of the way was no secret, but as we have seen, the party, the opposition (and wider population in 1927) were convinced that it would not be long until the Soviet Union was at war. This was a long-standing conviction within Bolshevik circles that stemmed from their understanding of the international circumstances of the revolution. As far as the Bolsheviks were concerned, reams of intelligence, the evidence of hostile action by foreign governments and war scares in the 1920s supported this worldview. If anything, Trotsky's firm endorsement of future war only further cemented an authoritarian response to the challenges posed by the outside world and with it the maintenance of a one-party vanguard dictatorship with diminishing democratic standards.

Following Trotsky's expulsion from the Soviet Union, the international situation worsened in a very real sense in the 1930s. The response from the Soviet leadership was the further sharpening of the dictatorship and an increasing use of political violence. All the while, Trotsky remained a thorn in the regime's side from exile. His continuing opposition from abroad in turn became integral to the conspiracy theories that underpinned the Great Terror, themselves inseparable from the threat of war.

PART VI
CULTURE AND SOCIETY: EXPERIMENTATION AND CONTROL

CHAPTER 12
BOLSHEVIK REVOLUTION AND THE ENLIGHTENMENT OF THE PEOPLE
Sheila Fitzpatrick

'Were we, Communist propagandists, ever really concerned with anything other than the enlightenment of the people?' Anatolii Lunacharskii, first Soviet People's Commissar of Enlightenment, asked rhetorically in 1919.[1] It seemed axiomatic to Lunacharskii, a deeply humanist Bolshevik intellectual, that a basic point of socialist revolution – perhaps even *the* basic point – was to give the oppressed masses access to the education and culture denied them under capitalism and thus make their lives more meaningful. To be sure, many of his party colleagues probably saw things differently, particularly at the height of the civil war, when armed struggle, consolidation of power and revenge against the class enemies were the tasks of the day. Yet there were some Old Bolshevik intellectuals who agreed with Lunacharskii about the centrality of enlightenment as a revolutionary mission. One of them was Lenin's wife Nadezhda Konstantinovna Krupskaia, an education specialist, who after the October Revolution became Lunacharskii's deputy at the People's Commissariat of Enlightenment, known by the acronym Narkompros.[2] For Krupskaia, popular education was a central revolutionary aim and the role of party and government in education was not benevolent tutelage from above but rather the encouragement of popular 'self-activity' (*samodeiatel'nost'*) from below in grassroots soviet-type organizations.

Krupskaia always spoke and wrote as if Lenin had the same understanding of the task of popular enlightenment as she did and gave it the same high priority. Her view of Lenin, though part of the orthodoxy of Soviet historians and education specialists in the post-Stalin period, is one that fewer Western or post-Soviet Russian scholars have taken seriously for many years. The Western historiography generally offers a cynical interpretation of Lenin, with lust for power, readiness for terror, hostility to popular spontaneity and indifference to the welfare of the people his salient characteristics. For Leonard Schapiro, the October Revolution was 'the story of how a group of determined men seized power for themselves in Russia in 1917, and kept others from sharing it.'[3] To Richard Pipes, Lenin was a 'cynical and aggressive' politician with a 'policeman's mentality' and a 'mass murderer' to boot.[4] In the summation of a recent non-academic biographer, 'having achieved power illegitimately, Lenin's only real concern for the rest of his life was keeping it.'[5]

In an exception to this near consensus, Lars Lih has argued that the pre-revolutionary Lenin should be seen as something like a revivalist missionary who perceives, with excitement, a latent popular awakening to religion that it is his task to cultivate and guide.⁶ Education was a part of this process, but not one to which Lih pays particular attention; he indexes it only under 'Education as metaphor'.⁷ In my view, however, Lenin's concern for education was not just metaphorical. As leader of the Soviet government after the October Revolution, he paid very practical and concrete attention to education and during his last illness it became one of his central concerns.

Krupskaia is a central figure in this context, both as someone close to Lenin and, after his death, as an interpreter of his legacy; and my discussion will treat her not simply as a spouse with educational interests but as one of the 'significant others' in his intellectual and political world.⁸ Krupskaia was passionate about popular education and the need for grassroots participation. In a 1919 polemic with critics, she wrote:

> We were not afraid to organise a revolution; we are not afraid of the popular masses; we are not afraid that they will elect the wrong people to the Soviets, bring in the priests. We want the people to direct the country and be their own masters [...] We are always thinking in old terms, that if we do not spare ourselves and work day and night in the people's cause, that is enough. But it is not enough. Our job is to help the people *in fact* to take their fate into their own hands.⁹

Lenin supported Krupskaia in this particular controversy, but can we imagine him writing these words? The answer given by van Ree in this volume would be an unqualified 'no', and, on the basis of Lenin's early- and middle-period writings alone, I would be inclined to agree with him. But people, including great historical figures like Lenin, are complicated: what they write does not necessarily encompass the full range of what they think or feel, and what they think and feel often contain unresolved contradictions. This is a volume devoted to understanding what, if anything, the 'democratic' aspects of Lenin amounted to. As the editors point out in their Introduction, 'democracy' meant something different to Lenin, and to radicals of his generation and milieu, than it does to us. Among the things it could mean was grassroots participation in a society's political and cultural life. In the following pages, I will explore the questions of whether the enlightenment of the people really mattered to Lenin and whether, if so, he conceived of it as something instilled by the revolutionary party from above or generated through popular participation from below.

Although much of Krupskaia's day-to-day activity in the years of pre-revolutionary emigration was work in the party Secretariat, keeping up conspiratorial contacts with Bolsheviks inside Russia under Lenin's direction, she had cut her revolutionary teeth working in an evening Sunday school for adult workers in the industrial suburbs of Petersburg back in the 1890s.¹⁰ She always felt that was her natural sphere of work, telling a party colleague back in 1904 that this was where she wanted to work come the revolution.¹¹ In emigration, she developed a strong interest in progressive pedagogical theory, contributing to the main Russian liberal journal on the topic. She wrote a monograph, *Public Education and Democracy*, summarizing the development of the progressive educational movement in Europe and America, with particular focus on workers' schools and the part of labour in schooling, which finally appeared in print in

Russia in 1917.[12] An admirer of John Dewey's 'activity' methods, as well as the German educationalist Georg Kerschensteiner's ideas about the 'labour school', Krupskaia was a strong advocate of comprehensive schools from which rote learning, punishment and indoctrination of 'bourgeois' patriotism and religion had been banished.

Lenin's father was an inspector of schools and he himself had done some teaching of workers as well in the 1890s – it was a basic part of the formation of social-democratic revolutionary intellectuals of his generation – but the experience of teaching workers made less impact on him than it did on Krupskaia.[13] At his first meeting with Krupskaia, at a conspiratorial gathering of Marxist revolutionary intellectuals, he made his contempt clear when someone suggested supporting the work of the (legal, liberal) Illiteracy Committee: in Krupskaia's account,

> He laughed, and there was something harsh and dry in his laugh (I never heard him laugh that way again). 'Well, if anyone wants to save the country by working in the Illiteracy Committee,' he said, 'we're not stopping him.'[14]

While Krupskaia may not have heard that 'harsh, dry' laugh again, others probably did: the Lenin with whom she shared her life from the first fifteen years or so of their marriage was sternly focused on the organization of a conspiratorial party of professional revolutionaries and was pleased to be regarded as 'tough' in the community of émigré social democrats. No doubt, as Lih argues, Lenin's sense of the urgency of this task was derived from his perception of a spontaneous upsurge of working-class revolutionary sentiment which must be channelled into action, but it is hard to find much concrete evidence of non-instrumental interest on his part in grassroots activity. Even the remarkable blossoming of soviets in the capitals and then throughout Russia in the 1905 revolution left him relatively cold: as a late-returning émigré who soon went back into emigration, Lenin's first-hand contact with the soviets was brief and unsatisfactory and his contemporary writings show little sign of the exhilaration felt by those revolutionary leaders like Trotsky who were more closely involved.[15]

In the years between 1905 and 1910, education and popular enlightenment were enough of a theme in Lenin's writings to provide Soviet compilers with almost 300 pages of text, but these were incidental paragraphs from works on other topics, not free-standing texts.[16] His main involvement in education-related issues at this period came in connection with his conflicts with a political rival, the Marxist intellectual Alexander Bogdanov, whose advocacy of the development of 'proletarian culture' as an instrument of revolutionary transformation he rejected in favour of a more down-to-earth insistence on the need for popular education (which implied, at least in the first instance, mastering 'bourgeois culture') to give workers the skills they needed for revolution and participation in post-revolutionary government.

In the last years before the war (1910–14), however, education, along with nationality questions, moved into a central place in Lenin's writing. The policy of the tsarist education ministry, educational and school reform, Jewish schools, national minorities in schools, rural teachers and university students were among his wide-ranging topics,[17] and in 1913 he drafted a speech criticizing the failure of the tsarist Education Ministry to address urgent problems of cultural backwardness and lack of popular access to education to be delivered in the Duma by a Bolshevik deputy.[18]

The shift of Lenin's interest to education clearly reflected Krupskaia's involvement in writing on pedagogical theory and educational policy at the same period, despite the current strains in their marriage (it was the period of Lenin's affair with Inessa Armand). It may be, as the memoirist Valentinov suggests, that Lenin was somewhat sceptical about some tenets of Krupskaia's progressive educational faith, notably with respect to punishment,[19] but he certainly did his best to get her monograph on the subject published; and just weeks before the February Revolution of 1917, he spun the idea of a project (which Krupskaia later characterized as 'fantastic') for the two of them collaborating on compiling a *Pedagogical Dictionary* as a money-making proposition.[20] In her memoirs of Lenin, Krupskaia characterized this period of Lenin's work as his 'preparatory course in socialist construction,' by which she evidently meant that the party-political concerns that so often preoccupied him were on the backburner and he was looking ahead to the kind of big problems that would have to be tackled after the revolution.[21]

Lenin and Krupskaia arrived back in Russia in April 1917, travelling together on the sealed train from Switzerland. But their reactions on return were very different. Lenin threw himself into party organization, challenging the dual power and Provisional Government and, from the summer, focusing on a Bolshevik seizure of power. Krupskaia, by contrast, gave up the work in the party Secretariat she had done for many years in emigration and went to work on education in the Vyborg district soviet of Petersburg. The opportunity created by the February Revolution to interact (legally) with workers at the grassroots gave her great satisfaction and she showed no sign of sharing Lenin's feeling of urgency that the revolution be pushed forward to the next stage.[22] Indeed, they seem to have been as separate, mentally and even physically, in the months between April and October 1917 as they had ever been since their marriage back in the 1890s.

Even in their years working together in emigration, Krupskaia, though a devoted wife and practical assistant, seems to have had a somewhat different approach to politics than Lenin. She was always more interested in contact with the grassroots than he was, less preoccupied with factional polemics and ideological hair-splitting and sometimes sceptical of Lenin's enthusiasms about particular revolutionary tactics, especially if they were likely to produce violence.[23] On their arrival at the Finland Station in April 1917, Krupskaia was reportedly aghast at the uncompromising radicalism and intransigence of Lenin's speech.[24] In June, she failed to share Lenin's enthusiasm for militant street demonstrations, saying 'It won't be peaceful, so perhaps it should not take place.'[25] In October, she was not privy to Lenin's plans for seizure of power, arrived late at Smolny (coming in from Vyborg with some fellow workers from the soviet) on the crucial day and later could not remember for sure if she and Lenin had had any direct contact there – 'a spectator of the Bolshevik revolution,' as her biographer puts it, 'and not one with a very choice seat at that.'[26]

Lenin had called for 'all power to the soviets' in April; and in *State and Revolution*, written in August–September, he systematically surveyed Marx's writing on the Paris Commune of 1870 and other topics for clues about what a post-revolutionary government might look like. It would not be a parliamentary representative system, since the experience of the Commune had shown that the revolutionary working class 'cannot simply lay hold of the ready-made state machinery and wield it for its own purposes.'[27] Instead, at the apex of the system would be a 'working, not a parliamentary body, executive and legislative at the same time' – in other words, something like the Paris Commune as described by Marx, which Lenin increasingly equated with the soviets that had sprung up in Russia in 1905 and 1917.[28] Because of the happy 'interruption' of the October Revolution, Lenin never had time to complete the final chapter, which would have dealt with 'The Experiences of the Russian Revolutions of 1905 and 1917,'[29] and thus never got round to any serious theorizing of the soviets. The Bolshevik seizure of power at the end of October, though a party action, was done in the name of the soviets, during a national soviet congress, and it might reasonably have been expected that the new governing body would have been the standing executive committee elected by the congress.[30] Instead, with no prefiguring in any of Lenin's previous writings or any serious advance discussion within the party or its leadership, it turned out that the revolutionary government was to be a totally new body, the Council of People's Commissars (Sovnarkom), which was in effect a cabinet of ministers nominated by the Bolshevik Party Central Committee and headed by Lenin.[31]

Setting up this new Sovnarkom-led government and making it work efficiently were to be Lenin's dominant and constant preoccupation for the next few years.[32] This was a radical and thorough-going change of practical orientation for him – from conspiratorial party-centred revolutionary leader to government leader – which brought with it all kinds of intellectual readjustments. In his 'Immediate tasks of the Soviet government,' written in March–April 1918, the top priority was to 'organize the administration of Russia,' which meant the establishment of 'strict nation-wide accounting and control of production and of the distribution of goods,' completing the nationalization of banks, imposing a monopoly of foreign trade and collecting taxes as well as continued struggle against the bourgeoisie.[33] In comparison with the urgency of these tasks – as well as the still more urgent military and international ones that quickly presented themselves – grassroots soviet democracy was understandably on the back burner, a little less present with every iteration by Lenin of the new regime's challenges.[34] The dictatorial powers essential to the new regime must be somehow combined with the grassroots democracy, no doubt, but that was not today's most urgent problem. As the Bolsheviks learned to run the country, the masses should continue to hold meetings, not as part of the new administrative structure but as a cultural and educational practice conducive to their psychological welfare.[35] Meanwhile – a new theme, emerging for the first time in the spring – the Soviet government needed to seek the help of 'bourgeois' technical specialists who knew how to run things.[36]

While local soviets withered as grassroots participatory institutions, they were incorporated into the new governmental structure as local executive branches of Sovnarkom and the central People's Commissariats (ministries), with full-time officials and specialized departments. The process of Soviet 'bureaucratization' was universally deplored, insofar as anyone was paying attention during the desperate years of the civil war, but it was hard to see a practical alternative.[37] There was, however, one People's Commissariat that put up a valiant though unsuccessful fight against the trend: Narkompros which initially resisted the creation of soviet education departments staffed by appointed personnel, which it regarded as 'bureaucratic' and tried to set up elected 'educational soviets (*sovety narodnogo obrazovaniia*)' as an executive instrument in their place. One of the strongest advocates of educational soviets was the deputy commissar, Nadezhda Krupskaia.[38]

Narkompros quickly developed an ambitious and idealistic plan for broad-ranging educational reform, including a network of adult educational institutions would be created to teach literacy, inculcate socialist values and give the population the cultural basis for political participation. Krupskaia's main administrative responsibility in Narkompros was adult education, often called *politprosvet* (political enlightenment).

Krupskaia saw educational soviets as a key instrument to 'organize the self-activity of the masses in education,'[39] meaning to establish schools and adult education on the basis of popular participation. The educational soviets were to be elected in the same manner and by the same constituency that elected the general soviets, but with the addition of elected representatives of teachers and pupils from senior grades. Once it became clear that Narkompros was going to have to accept education departments with appointed staff, in line with the general administrative set-up of specialized departments jointly subordinate to local soviets and central government ministries, their function vis-à-vis the departments was defined as 'controlling and advisory (*kontrol'no-soveshchatel'nye*)'.[40]

Although the education departments never caught on in practice, they were mandated in June 1918 by Sovnarkom (under Lenin's chairmanship)[41] and written into the 1919 party programme (whose education section was drafted by Lenin),[42] which before recommended them as a means of 'inducing all the working population to participate activity in the spread of enlightenment.'[43] Lenin singled them out for praise as an example of grassroots participatory democracy in one of his major political statements in the spring of 1918[44]; and according to Krupskaia, he said of the informal workers' councils that her Vyborg education department had set up before October (her model for the educational soviets) that this was exactly the way the future government apparatus should function, backed up by 'commissions of male and female workers who are at the heart of things, in touch with everyday life, work conditions and what at any given moment most concerns the masses.'[45] For Krupskaia, educational soviets were the 'hobbyhorse' that she persisted in advocating for many years, part of her long-standing campaign to encourage grassroots participation.[46]

Lenin's support of the idea of educational soviets was not an anomaly but part of a consistent pattern of his support for Narkompros's educational reforms in the early Soviet years. He supported the Commissariat consistently on budgetary issues involving education in Sovnarkom,[47] drafted a number of decrees and instructions on education for Sovnarkom and the Politburo, spoke repeatedly at educational conferences and wrote dozens of letters to party and government leaders and local officials trying to get educational initiatives implemented, valuable specialists and threatened Narkompros workers protected, and bottlenecks opened.[48] Throughout these years, Narkompros was involved in running battles with other institutions about educational reform, focusing particularly on its preference for general versus professional education, its dislike of class discrimination in schools and protection of 'bourgeois' teachers and professors. On these issues it almost invariably had Lenin's support.[49] When the Commissariat ran into trouble with the economic commissariats (eager for an increase in the supply of skilled labour), the Komsomol (keen on aggressive measures of class discrimination against the bourgeoisie) or the party Central Committee, Lenin was the man Narkompros relied on for help.[50]

This was the more notable in that Lenin was the only member of the top Bolshevik leadership who was a reliable patron and protector of Narkompros. Trotsky, once he had stopped running the army, was analytically interested in the question of post-revolutionary cultural transformation, but that did not translate into any particular practical interest in education (he rejected outright Lenin's suggestion in 1922 that he take over the overall direction of education as Lenin's deputy at Sovnarkom).[51] Bukharin was at this point a cultural leftist, who thought Lunacharskii too tolerant of 'bourgeois' influences.[52] Although (or because) his wife headed the Leningrad education department, Zinoviev tended to be critical of the Narkompros leadership in Moscow.[53] As for Stalin, education and the arts were not his bailiwick and he stayed out of debates on such matters at this period.

The controversies in which Narkompros was involved came closest to being central issues for the party in the winter of 1920–1, when the would-be autonomous proletarian cultural organization Proletkult, along with its Narkompros patron Lunacharskii, was firmly slapped down by the party Central Committee. Lenin, suspecting the influence of his old opponent Alexander Bogdanov on Proletkult, was a prime mover in this, but in the backlash against Narkompros – which involved calls for reorganization and replacement of Lunacharskii as commissar – he played the role of mediator, enabling Lunacharskii to keep his job.[54] At the same time, he actively supported Krupskaia, who at this point was heading Narkompros's extramural administration, in her fights with the army and the Central Committee over how much overt politicization of adult education was appropriate and whether the 'command' methods of instruction favoured in the army during the civil war were acceptable in a civilian context.

Rejecting criticism that Soviet *politprosvet* had always been too inclined towards general education, Krupskaia later wrote trenchantly:

> On the contrary, the danger of was always on the side of agitation. Even reading, the teaching of reading, was distorted into agitational chatter (*agitboltovnia*). This was a terrible nuisance in the work.
>
> At first they used to link the work closely with the independence of the masses and with propaganda. The Party gave this line, especially Vladimir Ilyich, who placed enormous emphasis on the independence of the masses and dreamt of the broad development of libraries, of bringing the whole population to study, to reading aloud. The business began to develop on a big scale, but the civil war forced us to pay more attention to agitation, particularly artistic agitation. When the

Civil War came to an end, an enormous number of military workers poured into *politprosvet*, bringing all the methods of the front into its work. The independence of the population, all forms of deepening the work, were brought to nothing[55]

Lenin seems to have shared these views. After Krupskaia's Narkompros administration for extramural (*vneshkol'noe*) education was renamed Glavpolitprosvet in 1920, he expressed his distaste for the term *politprosvet* on the grounds that 'the task of Narkompros is to help people to learn and to teach others,' not to indoctrinate or make political agitation. Elsewhere, he defined the purpose of Soviet *politprosvet* as 'training the masses in organizational and economic skills' (*not* publicizing the party platform or polemicizing with political opponents).[56] Trying to make propaganda for communism in the villages was worse than a waste of time, he wrote in 1923: 'as long as our countryside lacks the material basis for communism, (such propaganda) will be, I should say, harmful, in fact, I should say, fatal.'[57]

This position, part of a broad-ranging dissatisfaction with the way Soviet power was working in the last years of his life, when he was largely sidelined by illness, was characteristic of the 'late Lenin' discovered by Western historians after the appearance of his full collected works in the 1960s.[58] Focusing on the late Lenin, with his critique of bureaucratism and oligarchy in Soviet rule, offered an alternative to the Schapiro/Pipes version of Lenin. It appealed to some Soviet historians too, in a de-Stalinizing context, although their focus was largely on Lenin's insistence on the need for a 'cultural revolution' to overcome Russia's historic backwardness.[59]

Lenin was straightforward in admitting that there had been a change in his priorities.

We have to admit that there has been a radical modification in our whole outlook on socialism. The radical modification is this; formerly we placed, and had to place, the main emphasis on the political struggle, on revolution, on winning political power, etc. Now the emphasis is changing and shifting to peaceful, organisational, 'cultural' work [...] to education.[60]

Once that the proletariat had taken power, 'enlightening' the people (Lenin placed the word in inverted commas) was the only thing remaining to be done – 'but to achieve this "only," there must be a veritable revolution – the entire people must go through a period of cultural development.' This would mean at least two decades work of hard, non-glamorous work, but 'without universal literacy, without a proper degree of efficiency, without training the population sufficiently to acquire the habit of book reading and without the material basis for this [...] – without this we shall not achieve our object [of socialism].'[61]

While Lenin described this as a 'radical modification', this did not imply any apology for previous priorities. 'What was wrong with focusing first on the political challenge of taking power and then, when that had been accomplished, on the cultural tasks of popular enlightenment?', he asked, after reading Sukhanov's critical account of the October Revolution.[62] In any case, as far as education was concerned, there was substantial continuity as far as Lenin's personal involvement, if not government policy as a whole, was concerned. Jottings on education that he published from his sickbed in January 1923,[63] arguing for more funding for Narkompros and its educational tasks, with literacy teaching the highest priority, could have been written any time in the past five years – absent his suggestion that current economic circumstance allowed an increase in teachers' rations and the starkness of his conclusion that the necessary increase in funding for Narkompros would have to come out of the pockets of other branches of government.

The need to fight 'bureaucratism' was another leitmotif of Lenin's late writings, with particular emphasis on establishing mechanisms of workers' control on the one hand and overcoming 'Communist conceit' that prevented officials making good use of 'bourgeois' experts, on the other.[64] What was *not* part of the late Lenin's prescription was any attempt to revitalize the soviets. By general consensus, local soviets as vehicles for grassroots democracy were virtually dead by the early 1920s[65] and the introduction of NEP brought no attempt to revive them. True, Lenin wrote a Bolshevik comrade, G. Miasnikov, who had complained about limitation of freedom of the press and other abuses advising him to stop kvetching about such 'bourgeois intelligentsia' concerns and throw himself into the 'slow difficult arduous spadework' of making things work at the local level. 'Reviving the Soviets' was another of Miasnikov's concerns and Lenin encouraged him to raise the issue.[66] But Lenin himself took no such initiative, and no policy of soviet revitalization was launched during his lifetime.[67]

It may be no accident that, in the period of Lenin's late writings, he and Krupskaia were closer – politically and intellectually, as well as physically – than at any time since their return to Russia in 1917. After his massive stroke in May 1922, she was both his carer and 'his unofficial political assistant [...] a role she had given up in April 1917.'[68] In the latter capacity, she clashed bitterly with Stalin, Lenin taking her side in a sequence of events that led to the famous postscript in his 'Letter to the Congress' (otherwise known as his 'Testament') accusing Stalin of being 'too rude' and thus not the right kind of person to be the party's General Secretary.[69] Mutual suspicion and dislike persisted between Stalin and Krupskaia, who in the succession struggle after Lenin's death would join Zinoviev's Opposition to Stalin.[70]

One of the things that most infuriated and threatened Stalin was Krupskaia's belief that she was the best interpreter of Lenin's thought and wishes. She made this point with regard to education through tireless iteration in speeches and writings of the high priority Lenin gave this sector, especially the extension of basic schooling and the elimination of illiteracy; his insistence on the need for higher budgetary allocations; his support for general rather than specialized professional training and his criticism of enlightenment efforts in the village that were too crudely agitational.

The same points were made repeatedly in the closing section of Krupskaia's memoirs of Lenin, mainly written in the 1930s and under considerable political pressure, in which an anodyne and dry account of political events, seemingly written by a committee, is punctuated by paragraphs where Krupskaia is clearly trying to get across her own understanding of Lenin. This included the claim that initiative and the 'independence of the population' were as dear to Lenin as they were to her. In their conversations, she wrote, he always pressed her to tell him more, from her practical experience in education, about the various forms of grassroots initiative. In Krupskaia's recounting, this was not only about education but, more broadly, about the forms of democratic Soviet rule.

> Because Vladimir Ilyich thought that I understood how to draw the masses into the business of state administration, he particularly liked to talk to me on these themes. He had some strong things to say about the 'rotten' bureaucratism that had wormed its way into everything.

So convinced was he of her expertise, that he 'unexpectedly' got her appointed to a Sovnarkom commission on one-man-management (*edinonachalie*), charging her

> to watch out that one-man-management in no way weakens ties with the masses – it has to be combined with an ability to work with the masses. Ilyich was trying to use the experience of each to build a state of a new type. The task before Soviet power, at the head of which Ilyich now stood, was to build a type of state apparatus yet unknown in the world, depending on the broadest masses of the toilers, rebuilding the whole social fabric and all human relationships along new socialist lines.[71]

Krupskaia saw Lenin through the lens of her own beliefs and sense of priorities, which focused strongly on popular education and work at the grassroots. Her version of Lenin foregrounded aspects of his thought and practice that were most congenial to her and tended to gloss over other aspects,[72] and I think it unlikely that he would ever have been as dismissive as she was about the danger that the masses, if given a completely free hand to 'take their fate into their own hands,' might 'elect the wrong sort of people.'[73] Still, it is hard to dismiss Krupskaia's version of Lenin entirely. Not only did she know the man, perhaps better than anyone else, but the external record, when closely examined, confirms much of what she claimed about him. The degree of Lenin's expressed concern about popular education and work at the grassroots varied over time: before 1910, he was impatient when such concerns looked to him like bourgeois philanthropy or populist sentimentalism, hence a distraction from the revolutionary movement; between 1910 and 1917, no doubt in response to both disappointment of revolutionary hopes and Krupskaia's current theoretical work, he paid much more attention to education; as leader of the Soviet government after the Bolshevik Revolution, he insisted on the priority of education and gave consistent support to Narkompros on educational questions; and in his last illness, with Krupskaia at his side, a grassroots 'cultural revolution' as well as the dangers of 'bureaucratism' in the Soviet administration was uppermost in his mind. In light of this, it seems reasonable to treat such concerns as a persistent (if waning and waxing) aspect of his view of revolution and its purposes.

These findings are, of course, relevant to any discussion about the democratic potential of the Bolshevik Revolution, as well as to the interpretation of Lenin's political thought.

If Krupskaia was even only partially right about where Lenin stood on participatory democracy, that requires some amendment of the currently received view of him, making it hard to sustain a view that he was nothing but a cynical power-grabber with no scruples and few if any ideals. Grassroots democracy may have been more or less irrelevant to Lenin at the height of the revolution, but it was not irrelevant once the dust settled and Lenin again had time to think about what a socialist administration would actually mean. To be sure, he was never as interested in the soviets and their democratic participatory potential as Krupskaia was; and one may well find his arguments wanting and his practical proposals inadequate. It appears, nevertheless, that grassroots participatory democracy was indeed a part, if often a secondary one, of his vision of socialist revolution.

CHAPTER 13
WALKING THE RAZOR'S EDGE: THE ORIGINS OF SOVIET CENSORSHIP
Polly Corrigan

In 1923, Pavel Lebedev-Polianskii gave a speech about the work of the newly formed Soviet censorship organization, of which he was the head. The Main Administration for Literary and Publishing Affairs (known in Russian as Glavlit for short) had been set up in 1922. Looking back on the first year of their work, Lebedev-Polianskii noted that Glavlit was often reproached for its work, but that it had to prohibit anything that would 'hinder the building of Party and Soviet' while at the same time avoid 'violating the cultural interests of the country.' He complained that '[t]he work of Glavlit is exceptionally difficult. You have to walk a razor's edge all the time.'[1]

Censorship in the 1920s was indeed a balancing act. Once characterized as an inevitable feature of a totalitarian regime[2] or as a phenomenon that was in some way unique to the Bolsheviks,[3] the phenomenon of censorship in the early Soviet era was more complex both in intention and function. New interpretations of state power have led to new ways of conceptualizing censorship, not as one act of top-down prohibition, but as a more diffuse activity. While many scholars still take the view that Soviet censorship fits the top-down definition, the evidence demonstrates that censorship in the Soviet 1920s shares aspects of this more heterogeneous censorship found in other nations and other historical periods.

The vast majority of the citizens of the new Soviet Union were illiterate; serfdom had been abolished less than half a century before. The Bolsheviks saw literacy as a tool with which to begin to create a society in which every worker could participate and contribute their share. Beyond that, the Soviet leadership dreamt of using literature as a way to reach out to the masses – to educate and inspire them, just as they in turn had been set on the path of Marxist revolution by the reading they had done, while in exile and in prison.[4]

Stalin himself was a great reader, who would advise his sons to rely on the lessons of the Russian classics during the Second World War: 'You will need to make decisions. But if you read a lot, then in your memory you will already have the answers how to conduct yourself and what to do. Literature will tell you.'[5] Although the Bolsheviks were inspired and nourished by books, reading had also taught them that writers often use their talent to criticize those in power and that readers are devious and find ways of reading what is forbidden. How to harness this power, yet avoid the corrupting influence of the written word? This question would prove far more complex than the simple choice between culture and Soviet power suggested in Lebedev-Polianskii's 'razor's edge' metaphor. It was less a case of a walk along one razor and more of a dance around several, in which the steps kept changing and the music would stop and start suddenly.

Lenin was highly critical of the tsarist system of censorship and had explicitly not wanted a system of censorship – at least, not one that resembled the pre-revolutionary system. In an essay on literature written before the revolution, Lenin made clear his disgust with the censorship of the imperial age: 'An accursed period of Aesopian language, literary bondage, slavish speech, and ideological serfdom!'[6] In the same essay, Lenin made clear that he believed in freedom of the press. However, the key to understanding Lenin's conception of a free press turns on his definition of the word 'freedom': 'We want to establish, and we shall establish, a free press, free not simply from the police, but also from capital, from careerism, and [...] free from bourgeois-anarchist individualism.'[7] Ever aware of the lessons of the French Revolution, around the same time as this essay was written Lenin had noted in his diary the inconsistent attitudes of the Paris Communards towards the French press, which he believed had contributed to the defeat of the Commune.[8]

This apparent contradiction, between the condemnation of Russian imperial censorship and the need for a new censorship that would serve the interests of the proletariat, is central to understanding the early years of Bolshevik censorship, which wove together elements of classic censorship – the forbidding of the written word to silence enemies – with educational elements of 'speech regulation' in a combination that reflected the extraordinary dynamism and upheaval of the years of revolution.

The new censorship found practical expression in the very first months after the revolution, when the decision was taken to close down newspapers that were perceived as anti-revolutionary. In a session of the All-Russian Central Executive Committee of Soviets of Workers', Soldiers' and Peasants' Deputies in November 1917 Boris Kamkov, a left-wing Socialist Revolutionary, framed the ban in terms of a classic model of censorship – the closing down of free speech. He argued that the ban was morally comparable to pre-revolutionary censorship:

> When Bolshevik newspapers were closed down [under previous regimes] we expressed our indignation along with our Bolshevik comrades. No one has yet called for the overthrow of the existing regime, yet press freedom is being infringed without due cause. We are [morally] obliged to rescind these repressive measures, which bring shame on the Russian revolution.[9]

On the contrary, Lenin explained, the very existence of those newspapers was itself a constraint on meaningful freedom of speech, because the main aim of those newspapers was not to print the 'truth' but to underpin the agenda of the capitalist bourgeoisie. Lenin declared: 'We must get away from the notion that a press dependent on capital can be free. This is an important question of principle.'[10]

The distinction made by Lenin was subtle. While the character of this censorship is the same as the censorship he fought against – taking the form of the closing of newspapers – the objective is different, as it was argued in terms of class struggle. The aim was to serve the proletariat and not to simply silence the enemies of the regime. Even though Lenin decried the 'literary bondage' of the pre-revolutionary years, he had nevertheless sketched out a rough plan for a system of censorship long before the revolution. He visualized a system of total control of publishing by and for the proletariat in which Soviet citizens themselves would: 'keep an eye on all this work, supervise it in its entirety, and, from beginning to end, without any exception, infuse into it the lifestream of the living proletarian cause.'[11]

To oversee every published item – 'without any exception' – sounds simple. In fact, it was a tall order, complicated by the need to build such an organization, to recruit and train the necessary staff, before they even began to set the parameters of what could and could not be published. Through the early 1920s, this began to change. With the creation of the main Soviet censorship organization, known as Glavlit, the boundaries of Soviet censorship slowly became clearer, often through debate. The system was just about workable, but it was by no means 'total' nor was it always entirely successful.

In the first decade of Soviet power, censorship was a response to a number of interlocking factors, chief of which was the programme of mass literacy organized by the new Soviet state. Here another balancing act began: between illiteracy, backwardness and innocence on the one hand – and progress, wisdom and cynicism on the other. As the Bolsheviks perceived it, the aim of the Soviet programme of mass literacy was not thought control as an end in itself, but engagement with a new and more complicated political process than the Soviet population had faced before. It was not about simply silencing enemies, as a more 'classic' reading of censorship might suggest.

A policy of state censorship as a response to mass literacy is not unique to the Bolsheviks; it has been a common response to the questions that a literate population throws up in many countries over the centuries. What was different about the Soviet experience was the particular way that they combined elements of both education and political security. The balance between these two aspects – another razor's edge – coupled with their fierce belief in the importance of literature and the written word would ultimately overpower their attempts to manage what Soviet citizens were reading. The central role of literature in inspiring many Bolsheviks meant that the question of censorship was one that they all wanted a say in and would intervene personally on throughout the 1920s.

Censorship and Soviet censorship

Lebedev-Polianskii conceived of the work of Glavlit in terms of a relatively simple dichotomy: censorship as the prohibition of written material that would obstruct the building of a successful Soviet state, without damaging its cultural integrity. Weighing the fate of the Soviet state against cultural progress was an equation that would never add up, because Lebedev-Polianskii had bypassed Lenin's own thoughts on censorship, especially the conceptual division between the use of (pre-revolutionary) censorship as a tool of bourgeois conservatism and the idea of (post-revolutionary) censorship as an anti-bourgeois weapon. This distinction is important, as censorship had a very specific meaning in the early Soviet period, different from the one used by scholars 100 years later. A glance at more recent developments in the thinking on censorship, as well as some useful historical examples, provides a useful backdrop against which to analyse what was implicit in the Bolshevik approach to censorship.

Speech regulation?

The recent literature on censorship in the USSR has witnessed a flourishing of understanding of the nuances of censorship. While Arlen Blium described it as an act of 'systematic, single-minded and universal control', Samantha Sherry called for a definition free of this 'top-down' approach, instead describing it as 'a system of control which can range from explicit orders to the implicit actions of the author him/herself, all of which result from the overarching state ideology [...] regard[ing] censorship as a continuum, from explicit censorship to implicit censorship.'[12]

Where censorship was once understood to signify the actions of an institution, usually a national government, to prohibit the speech of an enemy, this view has evolved into a quite different conception of censorship, which interprets it as a more ubiquitous process that is present at various different levels of a society thus making it: 'unavoidable, irrespective of the given socio-political context' and therefore no more likely to be found in one ideological context than another.[13] This revision in the analysis of censorship helps us to directly address the specifics of censorship in the early Soviet years. In particular, it speaks to the issue of the challenges and opportunities for the state of a newly literate society.

Rather than viewing censorship as one homogenous activity, this new thinking presents different sub-categories of censorship, including the concept of 'speech regulation', which relates to censorship with an educational or social goal. Although rarely applied to the Soviet context, in these early years, we find plenty of examples of speech regulation. These efforts at control were non-traditional in their motives: they did not arise from a desire simply to repress dissenting voices, but from the goal of promoting a specific set of social values. They were also non-traditional in their practices. Soviet leaders engaged with a lively and diverse literary world and explored ways to encourage writers to take on Soviet values. They also turned the censor's pencil on themselves. These actions were examples not of classic censorship, but of speech regulation. They found that they had to regulate certain areas of speech in order to uphold their ideological principles, not because of a rigid dogmatism, but because they believed it was impossible to deliver the liberation of the proletariat without these constraints on some areas of speech.

Historical parallels

In the early modern period in Europe, higher levels of literacy triggered concern among those in the state and church about what newly educated readers might be tempted to read. Catholics feared uncontrolled reading would lead to the spread of Protestantism and the learned feared the rise in 'superficial' reading matter, with members of the clergy even going as far as to warn against the 'negative effects' of too much reading.[14] Different ways of reading signalled different ways of thinking, new channels for the spread of ideas and this was a threat to the stability and identity of the nation. Those in power had felt that they had no choice but to institute the first widespread censorship laws.[15]

Yet this development has not been interpreted as a move towards authoritarianism on the part of early modern states but a necessary phase of their development. Annabel Patterson argues that censorship played an important role in the formation of new and emergent nations, because nations in the process of defining or searching for their own identity often regard that identity as bound up in the literature of the day. Thus, censorship naturally becomes a tool to shape the nation. As Patterson explains, the early modern period in European history was a time when 'all the major powers were themselves emergent nations, engaged in a struggle for self-definition as well as for physical territory, and when, in consequence, freedom of expression not only was not taken for granted, but was a major subject of political [...] concern.'[16] At this stage of development, freedom of expression was a threat to a new nation, because all aspects of social, economic and political development were still in flux and could so easily become destabilized.

In the UK, the passing of the Obscene Publications Act of 1857 was driven by an upswing in literacy, combined with a new urban populace – an ideal market for cheap books.[17] Classic censorship persisted well into the early twentieth century: as James Joyce traipsed around Europe trying to get his masterpiece *Ulysses* published, copies of his book were not only banned in the United States and Europe, they were burned or confiscated by those governments and those who tried to sell them were put in prison.[18]

Despite the recent lively debate about what constitutes censorship, scholars still identify the Soviet example of censorship as the 'classic' or regulatory model, rather than as a censorship of a more ambiguous variety. Discussing various examples of 'social and discursive exclusion', Beate Muller asserts that it is only the example of the writer in a totalitarian state whose book is denied publication by the cultural authorities that meets 'the requirements of the term censorship.'[19] Again, in Patterson's analysis, the Soviet era is identified as a time of 'greater repressiveness', which was cemented by 'the codification of communist esthetics.'[20]

Censorship in principle

In December 1919, the Council of People's Commissars issued a decree entitled, 'On the Eradication of Illiteracy among the Population of the RSFSR,' which announced the intention to terminate illiteracy in all Soviet citizens between eight and fifty years of age – with the specific intention of making possible 'conscious participation in the political life of the country.'[21] Documents from the province of Vologda provide us with some insight into how local authorities attempted to take on this enormous task. Before any actual teaching could begin, the authorities needed to identify who was to be taught and appoint staff for the organizations that would run the programme. In February of 1920, Vologda's Provincial Department of Public Education held a 'Literacy Week' during which instructors would be sent out to find out how many of their local citizens were illiterate. Towards the end of 1920, 32,296 local citizens in Vologda had been identified as illiterate and 430 'liquidation schools' (from *likvidatsiia negramotnosti* meaning 'liquidation [elimination] of illiteracy') had been set up, in which 8,500 adults between the age of twenty-five and forty were enrolled. By the end of December, just forty adults had graduated as fully-fledged readers from three schools.[22] The instructors and members of the Extraordinary Commission for the Elimination of Illiteracy had a mountain to climb if they were to meet the target of teaching the remaining 32,256 adults to read.

At a national level, the Commissariat of Enlightenment (the Soviet ministry of education and the arts), headed by Anatolii Lunacharskii, held responsibility for the programme of mass literacy. At this point censorship was a vital part of education policy, as it was crucial to keep firm control over what and how the Soviet population was learning and what they were reading as part of this process. It is highly significant that the education ministry played a role in Soviet censorship, as this points to an educational basis for the desire to censor that, as already noted, is one of the ways of identifying speech regulation as opposed to than classic censorship.

In January 1920 the State Publishing House, which existed under the direction of the Commissariat of Enlightenment, was given a formal censoring role. After this date, nothing could be printed without State Publishing House permission. During these years, Nadezhda Krupskaia was at the forefront of similar policies of speech regulation, including removing 'obsolescent' literature from libraries.[23] The aim of these arrangements was to help Soviet citizens make proper choices about what to read, so that in turn they would make good choices about how to help to build the Soviet state.

However, as time passed, elements more resembling classic censorship were consolidated. In the summer of 1922, Glavlit (*Glavnoe upravlenie po delam literaturii i izdatelstv* or the Main Administration for Literature and Printing Affairs) was formed by the Council of People's Commissars to take control over all aspects of censorship. This was by no means the end of the involvement of Lunacharskii's Commissariat, which continued to oversee Glavlit and even had the power to appoint the head of the organization. But in the structure of Glavlit's leadership, there was another important clue as to how the Bolsheviks conceptualized censorship. The Soviet political police – at that point known as the GPU – were given a hand in the running of Glavlit, including a say in the appointment of the organization's two assistant heads.

This combination of education (speech regulation) and security (classic censorship) is central to understanding Glavlit and how it functioned, as they illustrate the dual nature of the process of Soviet censorship. The Soviet censor is often perceived only as a one-dimensional creature, intent on silencing dissenting authors, but in actual fact the work of the Soviet censor was just as complex and multi-dimensional as in other nations and during other periods of history.

The Origins of Soviet Censorship

This inbuilt divide between the representatives of Soviet education and security at the head of Glavlit can be seen in the formulated aims of the organization: 'to prevent publication and distribution of works which (1) contained propaganda against the Soviet regime, (2) divulged military secrets, (3) stirred up public opinion through false information, (4) aroused nationalistic and religious fanaticism, or (5) were pornographic.'[24]

These aims encompass elements of both classic censorship, such as the preservation of military secrets and speech regulation, such as the ban on pornography. They mirror the aims of the early modern Europeans by trying to prevent the publication of work that either diminish the state in the eyes of the reader through propaganda or false information or would stand in the way of the creation of the state as they had conceived it, in this case by preventing religious or nationalist fervour.

While a traditional definition of totalitarian censorship might focus on the banning of texts by certain authors, the vision of censorship outlined in the aims of Glavlit is more complex than this. By and large, the aims bring the focus of censorship to the protection of the reader. In this, they follow the rubric set out by Lebedev-Polianskii, by simply trying to prohibit anything that would turn Soviet citizens against their own state. Although censorship was also a method of muzzling those who might criticize the Soviet regime, this was not its initial impulse – or at least, not its only impulse. The aim was also to decontaminate the world of the written word, newly opened up for the great majority of Soviet citizens, from anything that might detract from their ability to take part in the political life of their new homeland. As Stephen Kotkin notes in his examination of the cultural life of the inhabitants of Magnitogorsk: 'Soviet censorship [...] was not merely an act of suppression; its chief goal was to inculcate values.'[25]

Here again, in Kotkin's formulation, we see those two aspects of censorship – the need to suppress and the need to educate. When formulated in this way, the two aims of the censor seem almost polar opposites; one is negative, a removal or a denial and the other positive, reinforcing and even uplifting. The tension between these two aspects of censorship made its practical application a complex process.

Putting censorship into practice

Censorship, as it was practiced on a day-to-day basis, was a somewhat patchy process, undertaken by censors with various backgrounds and levels of education. At first, it was not understood as a permanent policy but a pragmatic necessity, as Lunacharskii's regretful comments confirm: 'What else is there to do?' he wrote, 'A time of transition is a time of transition.'[26] Intervention from the political police was a regular feature of Soviet censorship in the 1920s. Members of the Politburo, including Stalin himself, were closely involved with censorship during the 1920s and their approach was improvised and fluid.

In the years of the civil war, classic censorship flourished, dominated by a security agenda. In 1918, legislation defining the boundaries of military censorship was produced,[27] and in 1919 minutes of a Politburo meeting titled 'On the Censorship of

Materials on the Theme of Foreign Policy,' expressed concerns that military information in the press may be picked up by foreign powers.[28] Documents from meetings of the Politburo and Central Committee in 1919 suggest that security was one of the main aims of censorship, with fears raised about the possibility of foreign policy secrets being given away in the Petrograd press.[29] In these documents there is explicit reference to the concept of 'censorship' with discussion of 'censoring newspapers' to prevent reports of a military nature from being read by the Bolsheviks' enemies.

Despite the immediate demands of the war, censorship of civilian reading matter was also the subject of much debate by the Soviet leadership. Lunacharskii seemed to be unable to even make up his own mind, writing that 'Genuine art [...] cannot sing in a cage' while admitting that censorship must not be feared, even in the case of literary fiction: 'for its banner, its elegant exterior, might hide a poison for the still naive and benighted spirit of the great masses.'[30] But when Lunacharskii tried to defend the freedoms of Soviet writers, Lebedev-Polianskii reprimanded him, arguing that the very same writers had 'a manifestly preposterous character with a significant share of deliberate lies.'[31]

Gradually this debate began to evolve towards a model of censorship that could be defined as speech regulation. Trotsky, who had written extensively on literature and revolution, found himself at the centre of much of the debate. In 1921, he sent a top-secret memo to the Politburo, demanding their views on the 'absolutely unacceptable' verse by Demian Bednyi that had been published in that day's copy of *Pravda*. Trotsky suggested that the language had a coded meaning and while he held back from suggesting any kind of prohibition, he proposed warning the editors of *Pravda* to look out for 'these kind of tricks'.[32]

In another letter written in 1922, Trotsky's discussion of censorship again had an educational bent. He expressed his worry about the effect that 'bourgeois, individualistic literature' could have on the Soviet youth and called for closer attention to the world of poetry, as well as the need for literature that actually represented the Bolshevik outlook: 'We need to pay more attention to questions of literary criticism and poetry, *not only in the sense of censorship*, but also in the sense of publishing. It is necessary to produce more and more of those works of art that are imbued with our spirit [emphasis added].'[33] The distinction between the act of censorship and the encouragement of 'Bolshevik' writing suggests that Trotsky himself is dividing the act of censorship up into different categories – the first being 'actual' censorship and the second paying of careful attention to how to create literature in tune with Bolshevik aims. While Trotsky himself may not use this terminology, it is clear that this second category of censorship might be defined as speech regulation, its basis firmly in the educational domain.

By 1924, Trotsky found that his own writings were at the centre of a row over censorship. The minutes to a meeting of the Politburo in November record that the Politburo 'considers it necessary to inform the Central Committee [...] that the absence of Trotsky's book "The Year 1917" in bookshops creates rumours about the prohibition of the Central Committee of this book.'[34]

The switch in Trotsky's role was a sign of the volatility of the political situation. This was not just a question of Trotsky's standing in the party. Stalin's effort to silence the voices of political rivals is often cited as evidence of his totalitarian determination to eliminate his enemies. However, one instance of censorship in the mid-1920s indicates that even Stalin was more concerned with speech regulation for educational purposes than he was with the silencing of his adversaries. On 2 March 1927, Stalin took the extraordinary step of writing to the editors of three major newspapers, including *Pravda*, explaining why they must censor the speech he himself had made on the previous day:

> I am very sorry that I had to delay the printing of the speech yesterday. But you must understand that I was guided only by the interests of the cause. I spoke quite frankly at the meeting. I did it because there were no stenographers at the meeting, and knew that my speech would not be recorded. I wanted at least once, at one large meeting, to say everything frankly about one of the most important questions of our international policy [...] it is impossible to print it in this form if we want to avoid possible misunderstandings and, perhaps, even complications in the external world.[35]

It is clear that in this instance, censorship was not used as a tool of the powerful against the weak, but as a tool of speech regulation. It seems that events were moving at such a pace during this decade that Stalin had decided that sometimes even his own truth about the situation was just too much for the reading public.

A Politburo document from 1923 confirmed that education was an important element of censorship: 'our censorship should have a pedagogical slant.'[36] This aim is repeated in an article written by the leadership of Glavlit around 1924, albeit with a more political edge, in which the organization was described as: 'an instrument for counteracting the corrupting influence of bourgeois ideology.' The article went on to outline the two paths of their censorship policy: the 'administrative and censorial pursuit' of writers, as well as the exertion of 'skilful ideological pressure' on writers.[37]

While these examples of censorship demonstrate an educational approach, much of the work of Glavlit did proceed in a more traditional fashion – with censors reading and banning books. From the days following the revolution, libraries were emptied of ideologically 'undesirable' books. Krupskaia recorded as early as mid-1918 that the number of such volumes in many regions of the USSR was 'greatly reduced'.[38] In 1925 alone, the Glavlit Leningrad province office banned a total of 448 books for political and ideological reasons. The majority of these, some 255, were those published by private publishing houses that were still in existence. Far fewer books published by co-operative publishers were banned, only eight in fact.[39]

The stories of writers who suffered arrest or worse during this period are well-known. In 1921 the poet Nikolai Gumilev, husband of Anna Akhmatova, was accused of taking part in an anti-communist plot and executed by the Cheka. Akhmatova herself found that her poetry was increasingly contrasted with that of the 'Maiakovskii faction' and between 1925 and 1940 she was unable to get any of her poetry published in the USSR. Osip Mandelstam was another poet whose misfortune at the hands of the Soviet authorities is well-known thanks to the memoir of his wife Nadezhda.

The Fate of the Bolshevik Revolution

For Mikhail Bulgakov, author of *The Master and Margarita*, the 1920s were a turbulent time. His satirical short story *The Fatal Eggs* had been returned to him by his editor, with 'about twenty passages underlined which I would have to change because of the censors.'[40] In the same year he experimented with journalism, commenting ambiguously as he did so: 'My story "Bohemia" appeared in the first edition of *Krasnaia Niva* today. It's my first venture into the specifically Soviet petty journalistic sewer. I reread the piece today and I like it very much.'[41]

In 1926, Bulgakov's flat was searched by agents of the OGPU and his diaries and one manuscript (*The Heart of a Dog*) were confiscated. In his statement to the OGPU, Bulgakov spoke with disarming openness (or calculated remorse) about the story he had written: 'I think that this story turned out to be much darker and angrier than I had envisaged while writing it, and I can understand why it has been banned.'[42]

Nevertheless, despite these well-known cases of repression of writers, by the late 1920s Lebedev-Polianskii was not happy with the work of Glavlit. In the spring of 1927, in a missive to the Orgburo, he summarized their first five years. He struck a somewhat pessimistic note, writing that the original aims of Glavlit, as outlined in 1922, had not really been followed for various reasons including what he describes as 'political reasons' and that the detail had been worked out as time went along. He looked back on the joint work of the party and the organs of censorship and reflected on the problems of censorship and particularly on the problems of adapting private publishers 'to the desired state' and preventing them from 'pursuing profit.'[43]

Censorship and the political police

Lebedev-Polianskii's disappointment at the failure of Glavlit to work in the way he had hoped illustrates just how complex and difficult the work of the censor is. Perhaps because of this complexity, Glavlit was never quite the only organ of censorship in the USSR. The process of regulating culture was such a massive and evolving matter that from the start other state institutions were involved, notably the political police, known in those years as the Cheka or the GPU/OGPU, who took an increasingly dominant role in the process through the early 1920s.

The Cheka provided assistance in the process of censorship in a surprising variety of ways. In the words of one Russian historian, every member of the political police, 'from a [...] militiaman and a district warden to the head of the NKVD' all pitched in to help with matters of censorship when needed.[44]

The Cheka was represented in the Glavlit leadership. Its officials spent a great amount of time compiling reports about the thoughts and deeds of the Soviet intelligentsia throughout the 1920s. But it went further than that. During the first years of Glavlit's existence, the Cheka was also involved in the actual work of censorship too, as is made plain in a report titled 'Report of Petrogublit 1923–24'. Local offices of Glavlit were known as 'gublit' (a shortened version of *gubernskii otdel literatury i izdatel'stv* or provincial office of literature and publishing houses). The report states that:

The Origins of Soviet Censorship

The GPU, and in particular the Politcontrol GPU [the office of political control], is the organ with which Gublit most of all and most often has to deal with and keep closest contact, Politcontrol carries out the final control of the publications to which Gublit has had preliminary authorization; it also acts against all infringers of the laws and rules on censorship.[45]

A letter from a librarian working at Gosizdat addressed to Lenin, written in January 1922, made clear that in terms of censorship of foreign literature, the Cheka still had the upper hand over Gosizdat, despite the latter holding official responsibility for the matter. The letter informs Lenin that Gosizdat does not have a regular or up-to-date supply of 'whiteguard' literature (which Lenin had requested). After making a couple of suggestions as to how he could organize a supply of such material – including via Kamenev who apparently received such reading matter occasionally via visitors from abroad – the librarian opted for the most likely: 'I think that through the Cheka it will be faster and more regular.'[46] Perhaps as a result of this letter, a resolution of the Politburo in May 1922 proposed by Feliks Dzerzhinskii asked Politburo members to become part of the apparatus of censorship themselves, requesting that they 'give 2–3 hours a week to view a number of non-Communist publications.' Once they had completed their reading, they were instructed to send written feedback for the rest of the Politburo.[47]

The presence of the Cheka in the activities of censorship demonstrates the element of classic censorship in the character of Soviet censorship. The role of a police force as a regulator of speech is clearly a characteristic of a traditional type of censorship. However, even the involvement of the Cheka in the process is a little ambiguous, because of perceptions of the role that the Cheka played in Soviet society. From its inception in 1917, it was supposed to be a completely different and novel type of state police, a total break with the imperial Okhrana. The Cheka – and specifically Dzerzhinskii, the organization's first head – was seen to be imbued with a 'moral purity'. Dzerzhinskii himself was often portrayed as the bringer of light and even repression itself was recast as a positive process which had 'life-affirming' qualities and was ultimately 'the expression of the will of the proletariat and the peasantry.'[48]

It is easy to see how this quasi-religious role of the Cheka speaks to the educational mission of the Soviet censor, thus blurring somewhat the distinction between these two categories of censorship. This in turn seems to open up the possibility of a new definition: a fusion of both classic censorship in which the means of censorship is the political police and a censorship in which the aims are educational and therefore fall under the heading of speech regulation. Perhaps this is a censorship that is unique to these early years of the Soviet Union.

The linguistics of censorship

When the Bolsheviks talked about 'censorship', they often managed to avoid using that precise word, instead using euphemistic language, even when it was clear that the intention was to control what people read. Trotsky, Lunacharskii, Stalin, Kamenev and several others regularly wrote memos and messages to one another and to various writers and printers on censorship. When they did refer to 'censorship', it was usually not related to censorship of literary material, but to matters of the printed word as it related to foreign policy and the security of the nation. For example, when Stalin telephoned the editors of various newspapers, including *Pravda*, to ask them to cease publishing the exchange rate of the ruble, he spoke of a 'ban'.[49]

In her analysis of forbidden books in the Soviet era, Varustina notes that in Russian there are two adjectives to denote the word 'forbidden', both with subtly different meanings. Understanding these differences helps to illuminate the Bolshevik approach to censorship. The first term is '*zapretnye*' and the second is '*zapreshchennye*'. While they both have the same root ('*zapret*', meaning 'prohibition' or 'ban') and can both be translated as 'forbidden' in English, Varustina argues that Russians understand them to have slightly different layers of meaning. While '*zapreshchennye*' is a more everyday variety of impermissibility and is more often found in combination phrases to describe physical objects such as 'forbidden goods' or 'forbidden films', '*zapretnye*' has a stronger linguistic resonance to it and is found in the phrase 'forbidden fruit'. She argues that this gives it an added meaning, which can be expressed as something like: 'desired, but forbidden'.[50]

An examination of the regularity of the use of these two terms in government documents during the 1920s demonstrates that the Bolsheviks leant towards using the word that was less loaded with meaning. The term '*zapretnye*' is hardly used at all, in any government document. By comparison, the term '*zapreshchennye*' appears multiple times, including in several documents concerning matters of censorship.[51]

For example, writing after Lenin's death in 1924, Lebedev-Polianskii explains that one copy of every image commissioned for Lenin's memorial will be sent to Glavlit and adds: 'This will enable us to create an archive of permitted and forbidden drawings.'[52] The word he uses here to denote 'forbidden' is '*zapreshchennye*'.

The subtle distinction between these two words illustrates that even in the language used about censorship there is a diversity that reflects the deep and complex nature of what it means to attempt to regulate the literature of a nation. The more regular use of '*zapreshchennye*' in the official discourse on censorship suggests a type of ban that is more pragmatic, improvised; a ban that speaks of speech regulation rather than classic censorship. It was not so much a question of 'thought control' or of a moral judgment about the nature of the text in question, as the use of the word '*zapretnye*' might indicate. Instead, the more frequent use of the word '*zapreshchennye*' might speak of a more immediate response to a text that was recognized as contingent and necessary, given the extreme nature of the work that the Bolsheviks were trying to do, of which they were all well aware.

Conclusion

For centuries, monarchs and governments have acted to control what their citizens were reading. This impulse was often justified as a way of protecting those citizens, although more commonly it was a way to defend national identity and security. In the case of the Bolshevik revolution and the subsequent years, a similar struggle took place. However, in this period there were some notable features that set censorship apart from both historical and contemporary comparisons. First, the project of mass literacy in the new Soviet Union was initiated by the Bolsheviks themselves and with the deliberate aim of engaging Soviet citizens in the political process. Secondly and allied with the first point was Lenin's own comprehensive rejection of the idea of pre-revolutionary censorship and his complete willingness to use censorship in a post-revolutionary setting. Both the programme of literacy and the use of censorship followed a very particular political programme, in a very particular political context. As a result, the way that early Soviet censorship functioned was a unique synthesis of different strands of what we now understand as censorship. It exhibited features of classic censorship – implementation assisted by the political police, the banning of texts. However, there was also a clear element of educational censorship – or what is now known as speech regulation – within early Soviet censorship, working to uphold the values of the new Soviet state and act against texts that might violate those values. This can be seen clearly in the aims of Glavlit and in the practical interpretation of those aims throughout the 1920s.

The quotidian reality of Soviet censorship underscores the many different ways in which the Bolsheviks talked and thought about the process. What is clear is that to them, it was certainly not just another tool with which to fight their enemies. The language they used to discuss and write about the process demonstrates a plurality of approaches to the problem of what citizens should be allowed to read. The manner in which Stalin even went so far as to censor himself is again redolent of a censorship of social values, rather than the work of a tyrant.

Lastly, there hangs a question mark over what the involvement of the political police in the process of censorship signifies. To most, this would be the cast-iron evidence that Soviet censorship was totalitarian in its nature – after all, the involvement of the state police is a classic measure of an authoritarian system of censorship. However, in these early years of censorship, it is possible to argue that even this was more complex than this. At this stage, the Bolsheviks conceived of the role of the political police as a force that would enact the will of the proletariat. In this role, as defenders of Bolshevik values, it could be argued that the role of the political police contained an element of speech regulation. Knowing as we do how the relationship between political police and the proletariat would develop throughout the 1920s and into the terror of the 1930s, this seems implausible to say the least. Nevertheless, there is evidence to suggest that in the early 1920s, although the means was the use of a political police force – and thus 'totalitarian' in nature – the aims were educational and therefore not what we might expect of a traditional style of censorship. In this, as in so many other aspects, Soviet censorship was very far from Lebedev-Polianskii's formulation of a choice between the two sides of the razor's edge. In the heat of the revolution, for perhaps the first and last time, censorship became a complicated fusion of different approaches, discussed in different ways, but all finding their roots in the specific context of the years of revolution, the Bolshevik programme of mass literacy and Lenin's conception of a revolutionary censorship that would serve the proletariat. The state could not become what the Bolsheviks wanted without the citizens learning to read and also being kept away from what might damage the future of the Soviet state – they were one and the same aim.

The contradictions inherent in Lenin's plan to establish freedom of the press through proletarian control of all printed matter – to use censorship as a means to freedom – were further complicated by the practical difficulties of creating and running an institution fit to carry out this complex role. A policy that may have been perceived as a temporary solution hardened into something permanent. As the 1920s gave way to the 1930s, the situation began to change in very visible ways. The Soviet state continued to build a network of institutions around the arts, beginning with the creation of the Union of Writers, followed quickly by the Committee on Artistic Affairs. Although neither of these organizations had an explicit censorship role, both worked to control and regulate the works of their members in particular ways and the development of the idea of socialist realist writing fed into this regulation as well. Yet what is interesting is that these new institutions, coupled with Glavlit and the OGPU, could never deliver a satisfactory process of censorship, a process in which all new publications conformed to ideological standards. Whether or not Soviet censorship was 'totalitarian' in its aims, Glavlit were severely criticized by the Politburo well into the 1930s for their 'totally unsatisfactory' work.[53]

Although censorship in the Soviet Union began as an ideological necessity for the Bolsheviks, backed by simple, self-evident principles, the reality was that it was never an easy thing to administer. The growth of Glavlit and other organizations certainly streamlined the process somewhat, but the questions that were raised in the debate over censorship in the 1920s – how to manage the sheer volume of literary output in a country as huge as the Soviet Union, what could and could not be said, where the line is between censorship and ensuring the literary identity of the nation – had not been fully answered by the end of the 1920s and would continue to be debated through the 1930s.

CHAPTER 14
REVOLUTIONARY PARTICIPATION, YOUTHFUL CIVIC-MINDEDNESS
Andy Willimott

In the wake of the October Revolution, young enthusiasts were encouraged to view themselves as an avant-garde, as cadre – as revolutionary society. The keenest youths formed a core component of the nascent political bodies and social organizations (*obshchestvennye organizatsii*) of the new revolutionary state. They joined the Communist Youth League (Komsomol), as well as contributing to cultural campaigns against illiteracy, religion and drunkenness. Impatiently, they pressed. Empowered by visions of the new socialist society, they sought to participate in revolutionary construction.

The great contradiction of the October Revolution, laid bare in Lenin's *State & Revolution* (1918), is that it promised to facilitate the re-appropriation of state powers and institutions by the proletariat, while, at the same time, an alternative statist vision sought to manage social initiatives and guard against the 'whole of society'.[1] In other words, the new Soviet republic came into being as an emancipatory and restrictive idea. Change was to come through participation and coercion. In *State & Revolution*, Lenin discerned the shoots of a future socialist order among the soldiers' committees, workers' militia and the various deputy soviets. Looking for the self-organized masses and ground-level association that Marx and Engels said would form the basis for the 'Dictatorship of the Proletariat,' Lenin saw the beginnings of a new ruling class ready to assume the initiative and establish themselves as the forerunners of socialism. Building on the legacy of the Paris Commune of 1871 – touted as the first example of socialist initiative and proletarian order – Lenin envisioned a new 'commune-state'. Yet, as Lewis Siegelbaum has noted, Lenin and the Bolsheviks also inherited from the Russian revolutionary intelligentsia an ambivalent attitude towards social initiative; they sought to release the participatory potential of the masses, while, at the same time, harbouring an inbuilt distrust of spontaneity, social ignorance and short-term impulses.[2] This contradiction fundamentally shaped the manner of revolutionary participation across the opening decade of the new Soviet state. Social initiative and activism were to be nurtured but not allowed free rein – an unwieldy proposition.

Among proletarian social forces, youth were seen as primary heralds of the new society. In bodies such as the Komsomol, formally founded in 1918, with the approval and active support of the Bolshevik Party, young people were promised the space thought necessary to fulfil this revolutionary destiny. As leading Bolsheviks envisioned it, the next generation – those unspoiled by the customs of the past – were to be the ones to see communism through.

Practically speaking, the Komsomol sought to achieve these goals by sponsoring and promoting local meetings, study circles, *subbotniki* (voluntary weekend work), as well as numerous mass campaigns through which new cultural norms and values could be disseminated. All this was conducted under the auspices of centralized control and evolving party-state mechanisms. And, by 1918, those that had pushed for the proletarian youth movement to remain outside the derestriction of the Bolshevik/Communist party soon found themselves operating outside a developing sphere of acceptable autonomy. But much of the Komsomol's work relied on local initiative and popular engagement with implementation drives. By the early 1920s, mass campaigns involving mass active participation formed a central part of the Komsomol's cultural mission. Komsomol members and aspiring members often found themselves in dialogue with the ideological imperatives of their day – with the actions and beliefs of those on the ground feeding back into the leadership's concerns, helping to shape the manner by which revolutionary imperatives unfolded. In some cases, with party control varying from region to region, and with little guidance from the Komsomol leadership, local initiative became a driving force.

Likewise, beyond institutionalized bodies such as the Komsomol, youths found themselves engaged in a wide variety of other social organizations, from 'mass organizations' aligned to party-state missions, including the League of Militant Godless, the 'Down with Illiteracy!' society and the paramilitary civil defence league OSOAVIAKhIM, to smaller cultural-enlightenment societies, mutual aid groups and sports associations.[3] By the mid-1920s, the OSOAVIAKhIM had acquired 2.6 million registered members, while many of the small associations scattered across the Soviet Union remained limited to a few hundred or a few thousand members.[4] At the same time, less formal, more irregular associations sprang up, including a number of amateur radio clubs composed of young enthusiasts keen to embrace new technology and spread the message of socialism.[5]

Many of the young people involved in these activities would have understood all of this as part of the evolving concept of Soviet *obshchestvennost'* – a Soviet 'civic-mindedness'. Devotion to 'social work' (*obshchestvennaia rabota*) and nascent 'social organisations' (*obshchestvennye organizatsii*) became a sign of revolutionary commitment – a means of displaying your vanguardism. Notoriously tricky to translate and to capture the contextual nuance of its meaning, it has been suggested that *obshchestvennost'* denotes a variation of civil society as understood in the West, a public sphere, a form of professional association, a public identity or an imagined civic community engaged in constructing a collective vision of society.[6] In this sense, it represents something missing from our traditional image of the Soviet system: a missing node, network or construct between state and society, between ideological imperative and Lenin's 'whole of society'.

In his book *Historical Materialism*, Nikolai Bukharin argued that having spent their early years fighting to establish a new state, it was now time to refocus their efforts on Soviet *obshchestvennost'*. Distinguishing between state (*gosudar*) and the people (*narod*), here *obshchestvennost'* was understood as the network of voluntary organizations in which proletarian democracy would flourish. This was the enlightened social initiative from which a 'commune-state' would be formed.⁷ Writing in the mid-1920s, Bukharin went on to state that 'small grass-root cells' would form 'Soviet public opinion' (*sovetskoe obshchestvennoe mnenie*) and aid cultural transformation.⁸ Bukharin tried to practise what he preached. He became a self-appointed advocate of the *rabsel'kor* (worker-village correspondent) movement, encouraging readers to write in to Soviet newspapers and periodicals on matters close to home. His experience as editor of *Pravda* persuaded him of the virtues of amateur-letter writing as a means of developing an authentic proletarian public opinion. Bukharin never saw this as a means of fostering political pluralism, explains Zenji Asaoka, but he did expend a great deal of energy protecting *rabsel'kor*.⁹

During the First Five-Year Plan, Bukharin maintained a belief in the merits of Soviet *obshchestvennost'*. Speaking at the Eighth Congress of the Komsomol, in May 1928, Bukharin called on the league's membership to arrange themselves in small voluntary units to carry out unofficial inspections of shops, stores, factories, institutions, markets and even commissariats. He presented this to the Komsomol as a way to 'dig out the bureaucratic adversary' – understood as the traditional, pre-revolutionary state-based forms of governance (*gosudarstvennost'*) that stood in the way of the commune-state.¹⁰ He insisted that voluntary association remained key to the wider revolutionary project. The populist character fostered at the beginning of the Plan built on such readings. Nevertheless, as Stalin's star ascended, as a siege mentality took root and as early enthusiasm for spontaneity in the industrial sector gave way to concerns about stability, the scales rocked back roundly towards *gosudarstvennost'*.

That interface between state and society – the tension between participation and party control – is the point of intrigue for this chapter. Imposing conditions of limited democracy during the civil war, the Bolsheviks nevertheless clung to idealized visions of Soviet society and sought to make room for autonomous action – for the earliest shoots of the commune-state. *Obshchestvennost'* offered a bridge to the commune-state, entering Soviet parlance as a discursive formulation that suggested and stimulated an active and newly emboldened portion of society.¹¹ In this regard, the Komsomol and its broader membership became purveyors of an emergent Soviet *obshchestvennost'*. The cultural activities overseen by the Komsomol, as well as their explicit or implicit support of various mass organizations formed part of a wider ambition to integrate a fragmented population into an ideologically coherent Soviet society. From an idealistic standpoint, mass organizations and volunteer activities were seen as the germs of revolutionary society – the popular think-tanks from which untapped collective potential could be harnessed. From a practical standpoint, such developments were seen as a means of gaining mass support and providing the new state with legitimacy. Either way, for active participants the end goal was the construction of revolution society. This has been referred to as a complex communications network between something akin to nascent revolutionary interest groups and political authority – making all participants part of the state and the Bolshevik project.¹² As we will see, youth participants were embroiled in the development of *obshchestvennost'* not just as a series of human groups, but as a public identity tied to the Bolshevik project.¹³ They formed part of its tentative structural formulation, while also giving it meaning and connecting it with wider revolutionary discourses.

As the editors of this volume note in the introduction, mass politics and an expanding vision of participatory politics at the beginning of the twentieth century were part of a series of pan-European trends that helped shape the contours of the Soviet experiment. The emergent Soviet state was both a product and a reaction to the political forms and discourses stimulated by broader European discussions on democracy. Soviet *obshchestvennost'* became a means of drawing the ideologically conscious into revolutionary state management – a radical answer to modern political concerns. In the Soviet context, however, it is worth stressing that *obshchestvennost'* was not an inherently *liberal* force, in keeping with established notions of liberalism. After all, as van Ree highlights elsewhere in this volume, Lenin rejected European liberal democracy and parliamentary representation in favour of a 'radical-democratic' vision that promised to involve the people, notably the proletariat, in the administrative apparatuses of state. A precedent had been taken from Marx's assessment of the Paris Commune as a 'working' rather than a 'parliamentary' body. The focus was on drawing the labouring masses into the management of state, not holding the party-state accountable to the opinions of the 'whole of society.' This was in itself an exclusionary idea, with democracy being built around one segment of the population – the segment that held the most promise for a more harmonious future. It was taken for granted that this would lead to a fuller and richer democracy than otherwise possible. The end goal was a participatory self-administered state with all citizens, as Lenin put it, forming 'one nationwide … "syndicate."'[14] Van Ree labels this 'a technocratic conception with politics collapsing into administration.' In this sense, the role of the participant was to assist the party and party policy, not to challenge it. Soviet *obshchestvennost'* was wholly compatible with the logic of Lenin's 'radical-democratic' vision. Those that engaged in *obshchestvennost'* presented as conscious, trusted persons involving themselves in the management of the state and the fulfilment of revolutionary goals. Social organizations such as the League of Militant Godless and the 'Down with Illiteracy!' society saw themselves laying the way for fuller participation, raising the cultural level of the masses to facilitate a broadening involvement in 'radical democracy'. Under this formula, revolutionary participation and party discipline were not incompatible. And, under Stalin, participation became evermore firmly tied to party unity and discipline.

Soviet-Civil society?

First coined in the late eighteenth century, the term *obshchestvennost'* gained new meaning from the 1840s, with sections of the intelligentsia embracing it as a descriptor for social or public engagement. It gradually became associated with progressive society and their attempts to advance change.[15] Sections of autocratic Russia – with its unwieldy empire and rigid absolutist structures – were gradually beginning to respond to post-1789 discourses on the nation-state, civic government and popular sovereignty. States could no longer present themselves simply as the territories and peoples of a sovereign; they had to represent and give voice to their societies.[16] After 1917, as Michael David-Fox observes in a perceptive review of recent work in this area, the term *obshchestvennost'* increasingly came to denote non-governmental association 'in the sense of being *de jure* yet not *de facto* independent of the party-state.'[17] *Obshchestvennost'* was associated with the leading voices and opinion of an emergent Soviet society.

Revolutionary participation built on this developing conceptual construct. But, until recently, little attention has been paid to it. Pointing to late tsarist discussions on *obshchestvennost'*, some researchers have challenged the assumption that Russia had no experience of civil society or civic agency. Tsarist Russia, Joseph Bradley argues, has been 'commonly regarded as an example of a failed civil society.' But, he underlines, in the late eighteenth and nineteenth centuries Russia did develop 'a public sphere and an associational life based on the model of the European enlightenment.'[18] As Adele Lindenmeyr's work demonstrates, during the era of the Great Reforms, in the 1860s, Russia's intelligentsia were at the forefront of an extraordinary growth in voluntary and charitably associations. The state was compelled to develop new policies towards 'associational public activity.'[19] Responding to the abolition of serfdom, urbanization and accelerated economic development, public activity became integrated into central debates about reform. By the turn of the century, some 10,000 voluntary and charitable associations had been formed. Representatives of the late tsarist state nurtured associational activities, particularly in the areas of public health and education. This was, as Bradley comments, a time of 'unprecedented state-sanctioned public discussion of government policy, local conditions, and projects for national renewal.'[20]

Yet, while studies on Russia's nascent civil society have helped to expel the myth of Russian exceptionalism, they have not fully explained contemporary readings of *obshchestvennost'* in late imperial Russia or the adoption of the term after 1917.[21] *Obshchestvennost'* carried connotations of civil society and civic agency, but it also held a particular resonance within the Russian cultural context.[22] Vadim Volkov warns that civil society (*grazhdanskoe obshchestvo*) is a normative model – applied retrospectively – that has distracted scholars from the traditional usage of political language, cultural contexts and cross-cultural translations.[23]

The associated construct of 'public sphere' offers a less problematic, perhaps a less iterative, way of conceptualizing *obshchestvennost'*. In her research on the social organizations and non-governmental associations of the 1920s, I. N. Il'ina even referred to the existence of what she called the *obshchestvennaia sfera* (civic/public sphere).[24] Vadim Volkov and A. S. Tumanova, pioneers in the reassessment of the conceptual history of *obshchestvennost'*, respectively associate the term with 'socially active groups' and a 'part of society that thinks with categories of public welfare and progress.'[25] They each highlight the essential quality of public-ness or civic-mindedness embedded within *obshchestvennost'*. Indeed, as Ilya V. Gerasimov reiterates, the idea of public-spiritedness and public paternalism was inbuilt into the self-perception of Russia's intelligentsia.[26] The cultural status of the intelligentsia and their commitment to a vision of public-paternalist duty thus helped to elevate the concept of *obshchestvennost'*, particularly across the nineteenth century.

Also, a component aspect of civil society, the emergence of autonomous professional bodies, can be discerned within *obshchestvennost'*. Alongside charitable and voluntary associations of various sorts, numerous learned and professional institutions were established in late imperial Russia. As in the West, active professionals felt encouraged to proffer modern solutions to modern problems. The latest in science and the human sciences was discussed and disseminated. Psychiatrists, psychologists and criminologists, as Daniel Beer has shown, grappled with the effects of urbanization and industrial modernization.[27] The modern professional was on the rise. Connectedly, it is no coincidence that the era of the 'thick journal' – the nineteenth-century vessel of political, cultural, literary and scientific enlightenment – coincided with the ascendency of *obshchestvennost'*.

But, David-Fox astutely cautions, while the 'public sphere' and 'professionalization' do not necessarily clash with the culturally specific phenomenon of Russian *obshchestvennost'*, they are 'not necessarily tailored' to it. The dichotomous notion of public/private spheres emerged out of Jürgen Habermas's now much-recounted post-war observations of Germany, before being applied to much of Europe and the Anglophone world.[28] Many have commented on how this model fails to account for differences in the Russian/Soviet experience, which drew on a heritage of collectivism over individualism, lacked a strong discourse of individual rights and came to distinguish between different levels of private and/or personal affairs.[29] Equally, it has been pointed out, 'remarkable degrees of professional achievement were attained in Russia without the [same] formal attributes of autonomy from the state' as in the West.[30]

Yasuhiro Matsui argues that while in Europe civil society was initially wrapped up with the notion of bourgeois society – originating, as Hegel and Marx observed, against the backdrop of a burgeoning free economic activity that checked the state's ability to practise arbitrary governance – the Russian term, *obshchestvennost'*, conversely, 'had been coined and circulated mainly as a concept indicative of an "imagined collective agent" for transforming an autocratic regime over the course of the nineteenth century.'[31] This was just as, if not more likely to take the form of a participatory or coterminous relationship between agent and state – as opposed to adversarial. Assessing the meaning of *obshchestvennost'* in a post-1917 setting, Karl Loewenstein explains how the literary figures of the Khrushchev period still imaged themselves as part of this broader collective agency or 'imagined community'. They believed they were charged with leading and directing Soviet society. *Obshchestvennost'*, as an identity, grew in significance under Khrushchev. Championed as 'engineers of the human soul' by Stalin, writers had long believed they had privileged access to knowledge inside Soviet society. And, given the opportunity, many writers vied to be 'opinion leaders' in Khrushchev's era of reform. Some openly identified as *obshchestvenniki*. They did not see themselves as 'lone freedom fighters,' Loewenstein explains, 'but as members of a community trying to re-establish its internal cohesion.' They did not seek individual freedom, but collective autonomy and the chance to provide new direction for Soviet society.[32]

Here a reinvigorated *obshchestvennost'* gives insight on the dynamics of *the Thaw*, while also drawing our attention to preserved and cultural-specific notions of public engagement in the Soviet Union. The Soviet leadership did not accept independent organizations questioning their decision-making, but at various points and to varying degrees, they did support, co-opt and promote *obshchestvennost'*. The party understood that socialist revolution had to be accompanied by the formation of socialist public opinion – an interest in the development of socialist ideology and Soviet revolutionary imperatives. And certain groups felt compelled to perform the role of opinion leaders – even initiating what Oleg Kharkhordin has called 'loyal critique of the regime's dysfunctions.'[33] This was the case with what one member of the Writer's Union called the 'writers' community' (*pisatel'skaia obshchestvennost'*) during *the Thaw*.[34] And, as Il'ina has shown, it was also the case some thirty years earlier, with several pre-revolutionary scientific, cultural and social aid associations surviving beyond 1917; with Proletkul't, the Esperanto society and numerous 'enlightenment' organizations forming between 1917 and 1920; and with the founding of many 'mass organizations' during the 1920s.[35] Cooperatives, youth organizations, cultural-enlightenment societies and sports associations also fostered a sense of *obshchestvennost'* within a budding Soviet citizenry.[36]

A growing number of scholars agree, it is 'plausible to argue that a new kind of public involvement became an integral part of the soviet order.' This presents a noteworthy development in our understanding of how Soviet citizens conceived of the Soviet state.[37] 'For many', expounds David-Fox on the significance of this research,

> participation in it may have become an empty ritual, like voting in a single-candidate election, but even so the new Soviet *obshchestvennost'* could have preserved certain forms and values developed earlier. For others – and this could well be the topic of future research – Soviet public engagement may have meant something more significant.

Ultimately, the evolving notion of *obshchestvennost'* evades easy categorization. But both before and after 1917 it was, as Volkov describes, a 'discursive referent' associated with the carriers of public opinion or an 'imaged collective agent.'[38] With certain types of public activism and popular mobilization promoted and even demanded after 1917, Soviet *obshchestvennost'* extended a culturally specific construct into a new polity.[39] In turn, many young idealists embraced this construct as a means of developing and performing a public identity tied to the Bolshevik project.

Speaking *obshchestvennost'*

Picking up on Il'ina's work, Matthias Neumann notes that an *obshchestvennaia nomenklatura* formed among the Komsomol and at the centre of a 'mounting web of new social organizations.'[40] Across the 1920s, it became standard-fare for party and Komsomol representatives to be layered into social organizations and local projects.

The Fate of the Bolshevik Revolution

From a party perspective, this was seen as an essential way to ensure a level of control and influence over revolutionary affairs. But, Neumann explains, this *obshchestvennaia nomenklatura* was never just a sterilized list of approved appointments. As Komsomols were encouraged to join new social and mass organizations in their droves, they became a driving force in the creation of an *obshchestvennaia nomenklatura*.[41] Writing in the leading youth journal *Iunyi kommunist*, in 1926, a young Komsomol member named N. Zhukov proudly proclaimed that he and some fellow activists were successfully establishing a *Soviet obshchestvennost'* in the countryside. Together they sought to permeate all committees at the village and *volost'* level, believing their guidance and tutelage to be of great value. They readily assumed party functions, even advocating further such roles for the Komsomol. Zhukov reported that they played a key role in establishing local commissions and sections within the village soviet. He also announced that they had grown the membership of the local peasant committees in the *uezd* and established Peasant Committees for Mutual Aid.[42] Here the expansion of key socio-political organizations, such as Mutual Aid, was tied to the ground-level initiative and enthusiasm of people like Zhukov.

In 1926, Komsomol activists accounted for 6.2 per cent of the members of *volost'* soviets.[43] Local Komsomols often acquired administrative positions in the local party-state apparatus – putting themselves up for election and even organizing elections to village soviets. The Komsomol, Neumann posits, was in its own right a form of social organization, but as a representative of Soviet power it assumed party and state functions, too. As Neumann explains, the 'subordination of the Komsomol to the party enabled the latter, at least in theory, to exert its influence through different channels down to the local Komsomol organization.' Yet the reality on the ground often looked distinctly different. Weak relations between Komsomol cells and the party organization, particularly in rural areas, created space for a self-motivated *obshchestvennost'*.[44]

Young enthusiasts, such S. A. Balezin, found themselves establishing Komsomol cells in small villages where there was no formal party representation. In 1920, in Pavlovsk, near Perm, Balezin assembled a twenty-strong cell of Komsomols and youths aspiring Komsomol membership who he led on political-enlightenment campaigns and anti-religion marches in the surrounding region.[45] By 1921, having impressed the Komsomol district committee, he moved to Ufa, to partake in larger cultural-enlightenment campaigns and social organization work. Still only nineteen, in 1923, Balezin joined the Red Army as part of a regional propaganda attachment, before entering higher education. His initiative earned him more opportunities. Upwardly mobile in the post-revolutionary context, figures such as Balezin formed a part of the emergent Soviet *obshchestvennost'* and *obshchestvennaia nomenklatura*. His loud commitment to 'social work' (*obshchestvennia rabota*) became a hallmark of his identity and informed his outlook on revolutionary life. And, crucially, in certain locations, his practical pursuit of 'social work' played a very real role in maintaining and advancing the Bolshevik revolutionary project. He was ultimately accountable to the central Komsomol-party apparatus, but, along the way, very often it was Balezin who fostered the promotion of revolutionary principles.[46]

Revolutionary Participation

The popular understanding of 'social work' (*obshchestvennaia rabota*) among Komsomol and Soviet youth can be discerned in the youth press. When *Komsomol'skaia pravda* held a political drawings competition, in 1926, one of the entrants depicted the 'social work' expected of a young activist. Entitled the 'universal plug', the activist at the centre of this drawing is depicted with water up to his neck. He faces the seemingly hopeless task of stemming the flow of 'social work' that is slowly engulfing and overwhelming him. Represented as water, 'social work' leaks out of small holes in a revolutionary wall. The holes are labelled 'society', 'cooperation', 'political club', 'chess [club]', 'radio [club]', 'editorial board', 'committee' and 'report'. These represent the values and duties associated with a good activist/*obshchestvennik*, as well as the various societies and bodies that he is expected to be part of. It can be assumed that he is charged with promoting a collectivist society, fostering cooperation between various bodies, managing and partaking in numerous clubs and activities, forming part of local and amateur editorial boards, as well as sending communiqué on the latest local developments. In the picture the young activist has the fingers of his oversized hands jammed into the holes, but 'social work' continues to flow through, threatening to consume him. The revolutionary project seems reliant on the voluntary efforts of this activist, his exaggerated, superhuman hands fully stretched and contorted in a manner that cannot be sustained for long.[47]

Sent from a Moscow-based Komsomol cell, and deemed worthy of printing within the pages of *Komsomol'skaia pravda*, this satirized illustration demonstrates that 'social work' had become an intrinsic and accepted feature of activist life. As a 'loyal critique', mocking yet celebrating the revolution's reliance on the young activist, it can be seen to reveal the developing parameters of Soviet *obshchestvennost'*. The individual who sent in this depiction offers a criticism of activist life at the ground level – perhaps setting a challenge to the leadership of the Komsomol and party – while also tying himself to a public identity or 'imagined collective' clearly thought worthy of adoration. Similar representations can be found on the pages of numerous youth publications at this time.

In the same year, *Komsomol'skaia pravda* ran stories that stated it was the duty of such activists and *obshchestvenniki* to tackle the growing issue of 'drunkenness' and 'hooliganism' – mounting war on anti-revolutionary values and cultural habits. The heroism of the civil war fighter, it was suggested, was now needed in the battle against socials ills and old habits.[48] Here Soviet *obshchestvennost'* was presented as an 'imagined collective' that incorporated the revolutionary lexicon of heroism and other exemplary revolutionary traits.

Around this time, some were encouraging more 'social work' among the student population. In a short article entitled 'Academism and *Obshchestvennost'*,' published in the student journal *Krasnyi Student*, a certain E. Petrov urgently expressed his belief that it was crucial more be done to 'link students' academic work with their public [duties].' Petrov feared that not enough was being done in this area. A lack of engagement clearly would not do. These institutes were the pinnacle of education and training; those who attended Soviet institutes of higher education were meant to be the best and the brightest – future leaders. But, Petrov argued, students were forced to choose between academic achievement and public-spiritedness. It should be the 'main objective of all educational institutes,' Petrov insisted, 'to properly organise all areas of human life.' The 'slogan of the day,' he continued, should be 'no single student can avoid social work.' 'Student organisations, clubs, debating circles, wall-newspapers' – all were required alongside the 'good public workers' (*khoroshikh obshchestvennykh rabotnikov*) who were going to lead them. The student population (*studenchestvo*) were expected to lead *obshchestvennost'* within their institutes and support local revolutionary projects wherever possible. Petrov wanted Soviet institutes and the local party-Komsomol apparatus to do more to integrate and facilitate this work.[49]

Upon entering the Social Education Institute, Petrograd, Balezin formed a similar opinion. He noted with concern the divide between 'social work' and academic curriculum. He felt that the local Komsomol cell was perpetuating this divide by treating 'social work' merely as an activity undertaken by students, not integrating it into student life. He even noticed that some Komsomol representatives were dismissive of academic study – creating a barrier between the most studious learners and meaningful revolutionary participation.[50] But, crucially, Balezin found expression for his vision of good practice within another revolutionary concept – one that allowed him to fulfil his ambition of combining institute life and 'social work'. Among the many new ideas discussed and embraced by the first wave of Soviet students, the urban commune proved the most alluring for Balezin. Here groups of young activists united in requisitioned apartments or student dormitory rooms and agreed to live by a new socialist code. They pooled money and resources as an example of equality; they discussed and undertook activities as a group as an example of collectivism; and they embraced domestic and cultural revolution as an example of socialist civilizational advance. Already an established entity within the institutes of higher education by the beginning of the 1920s, Balezin saw communes of between three and ten students coming together to share all their possessions, putting their stipends into a 'common pot' (*obshchii kotel*). He saw them eat, drink, work and undertake leisure activities together. He saw young men and women live side-by-side, promoting equality between the sexes. This was a carefully considered and thoroughly modern socialist approach to life – a display of intent. For Balezin and others like him, the urban commune became a vessel through which to pursue 'social work' and a wider commitment to the Revolution.

Balezin's first foray into commune life came in 1923, when he helped to bring together a group of six students who were willing to live collectively, embark on 'social work' and help each other in their studies. Among other things, noting a lack of course materials, this group reproduced their lecture notes, turning them into an ad hoc textbook for their fellow students. Their 'social work' drew on their collective strength to make up for a shortfall in state resources. In the autumn of 1924, in the wake of a raging storm that flooded much of Leningrad, Balezin and the commune formed one of the many relief teams that volunteered to perform salvage missions in the city. This event helped to cement the group's resolve. Following the flood, the commune expanded in number and looked to progress their revolutionary mission still further. They held debates and events in their domestic quarters; they worked with the Komsomol cell to produce propaganda posters for their institute; and they even established a public canteen (*stolovaia*) to encourage the practice of communal dining.⁵¹ The commune simultaneously nurtured a sense of internal and external duty to the Bolshevik revolutionary project. Inside the urban commune members tried to live an exemplary socialist lifestyle – they sought to turn themselves into ideal socialists and to provide a replicable model for the future society. Outside the urban commune members vied to partake in what were considered 'cultural-enlightenment' activities – working as a collective and/or assisting local Komsomsol campaigns to hasten the advance of socialism in their immediate surroundings.

Other communes forming around this time spoke of aiding their fellow proletarian students and workers, helping the Komsomol to organize local meetings and campaigns and producing 'wall-newspapers' (*sten-gazety*) or information for bulletin-boards in their institutes.⁵² Some consciously drew on the example of the pre-revolutionary student *kruzhki* or debating circles, where the latest musings of the intelligentsia and various liberal or radical publications were discussed and debated at length. Establishing their own *kruzhki*, early Soviet students looked to replicate the social influence of these formations for their own time.⁵³

Fully committed to living an exemplary socialist life and undertaking 'social work' as part of a collective group, some commune activists openly identified as *obshchestvenniki*.⁵⁴ Acting as a support to, in some cases pressing, the local Komsomol became a key component of this self-definition, especially after 1928, as the communes became embroiled in the mounting industrialization drive. Increasingly, commune activists saw it as their duty to partake in collective group work or brigade work in the factories. They undertook to demonstrate good working practices, but they also tried to extend their *kruzhki*, debates and cultural campaigns onto the shop floor.⁵⁵ This did not escape the attention of prominent Bolshevik revolutionary and wife of Lenin, Nadezhda Krupskaia, who had been keeping a keen eye on the urban communes since she first learned of these activist formations in 1921. Recognizing their commitment to production targets, rationalization and the idea of *samokritika* (self-criticism) – when the party encouraged the rank and file to call out bad practice from within the system – Krupskaia referred to these youths as 'public-worker activists' (*rabotnik-obshchestvennik* and *rabotnitsa-obshchestvennitsa*) and championed their further development.⁵⁶

Extending on Krupskaia's contemporaneous observations and viewing these urban communes as carriers of a developing discourse on Soviet *obshchestvennost'*, it is possible to delineate some of the values that were starting to define this emergent concept – or, at the very least, the young activists' understanding of the values that defined it. Looking at the issues that galvanized and inspired these revolutionary formations, in other words, it is possible to add lived texture to Soviet *obshchestvennost'*. The most glaring feature of urban commune life, its communalism, was consciously and vociferously pursued as a means of overturning the traditional nuclear family – rejecting it as the basic unit of society.⁵⁷ In their founding agreements (*ustavy*), many communes declared hostility towards their own families and the values upon which they were formed. Some even regulated or banned contact with birth families for fear that sentimentality would detract from their collective goal of establishing the new basic unit of society.⁵⁸ While no two communes were exactly alike, they did, in varying ways, and to varying degrees, promote comradeliness as the new social bond and the concentrated *kollektiv* as the new organizational unit of currency.

Similarly, many communes embraced the emancipation of women from the drudgery of traditional domesticity – this was part of 'the women's question,' as the literature of the day put it. Practices remained diverse, some groups were more committed than others, contradictions and cultural hangovers continued to abound, but idiosyncratically the communes strived towards a vision of society that put women on an equal footing with men.[59]

Another central feature of commune life was the restless pursuit of rationalization – founded on the belief that it was possible to develop a 'scientific approach' to life and work. This manifested itself in myriad ways. But, at its core, it developed from a fundamental rejection of the accidental manner of life that activists believed had been jettisoned in 1917. Communes set out their codes of living, subjecting themselves to internal review. Life was measured and monitored against statistics, with, for instance, communes comparing their level of cleanliness to the national averages printed in the press. Many appropriated Taylorist practices in the form of strict timetables regulating every part of the day, including communal mealtimes, study, labour, 'social work', reading, leisure activities and bedtime.[60] As waves of rural workers entered the industrial sector across the opening years of the First Five-Year Plan, the communes only became more determined to press for rationalization – more convinced than ever of the necessity to confront old inertias and the poor practices of the 'backward strata'.[61]

Not unlike their civic-minded counterparts in the West, the young, self-proclaimed *obshchestvenniki* were in dialogue with the latest press publications and political developments of the day. 'Periodicals are taken in everywhere,' observed the German travel Klaus Mehnert. What is more, he continued,

> Every level space in the Moscow bookshops is piled up with pamphlets dealing with burning questions. [...] There are little booklets consisting of eight printed pages and costing from two kopeks [...] I came across a hundred pamphlets concerning the Komsomol alone; fresh from the press they flooded the whole Union.[62]

Periodicals and pamphlets were the new, modern source of information. They were targeted, direct, specialized, current and ever-updating. As Mehnert reported, they provided 'a definite attitude to topical questions.' And they were 'ravenously devoured' by young dynamos like Balezin and company. Immersed in these fast-paced, up-to-date publications, such activists sought to bridge the gap between thought and action.[63] This modern form of publication was designed to foster socially active engagement. And it did. Marx famously said, 'The philosophers have only interpreted the world, in various ways; the point, however, is to change it.' In a similar vein, Soviet periodicals and pamphlets were for doers and go-getters, not contemplators.

Devouring publications, even setting aside money from their shared earnings for subscriptions, commune activists and self-proclaimed *obshchestvenniki* pieced together a value-laden vision of the world they wished to create, extending key ideological imperatives and models into practice. In this way, they embraced and gave meaning to an emergent Soviet *obshchestvennost'*, building and perpetuating the concept.

Managed *obshchestvennost'*

Across the 1920s, Soviet *obshchestvennost'* also developed concomitantly with growing concern over the return of old habits under the New Economic Policy (NEP) and a cultural revolution that targeted any such signs of ideological retreat. The return of market forces with the implementation of NEP, in 1921, created a cultural 'other' in the form of the NEPman and the reemergence of old pastimes, such as fine dining and luxury consumerism.[64] As Anne E. Gorsuch argues, NEP came to symbolize 'the older generation's lack of courage and conviction.'[65] That NEP threatened a retreat seemed reason enough to stimulate an activist reassertion of revolutionary values. This was the context in which urban commune activists and *obshchestvenniki* were tempered. Youth, generational conflict and *obshchestvennost'* incited. Juxtaposing the cultural surplus of NEP, Komsomol periodicals rallied around the 'new way of life' (*novyi byt*), 'new life' (*novaia zhizn'*) and the 'new person' (*novyi chelovek*) – continually reproducing a picture of life in the future commune-state.

The likes of Zhukov, Balezin and Petrov – those engaged in Soviet *obshchestvennost'* and rejecting revolutionary retreat – helped to form a constituency for 'Stalin's Revolution'. After all, the curtailment of NEP, in 1928, beckoned forth just the sort of uncompromising revolutionary assault that they had been calling for. It was just this sort of enthusiasm, energy and vision that Bukharin tried to rally at the Eighth Congress of the Komsomol, in May 1928, when he called on youths to form 'light cavalry' and take the initiative in the working culture of industry.

But, at the same time, that original contradictory and ambivalent Bolshevik attitude towards spontaneity was playing out here. Towards the end of the 1920s, the party was becoming increasingly concerned to ensure that the Komsomol and those active within its structures did not function as a rival political organization or an ungovernable source of influence. At the behest of the party, the Komsomol leadership developed a greater interest in the social and cultural initiatives of its various branches and cells. The leadership talked of learning from these initiatives, but they also sought to bring them under control and ensure they operated in alignment with party-state priorities.[66] Under these conditions, the *obshchestvennaia nomenklatura* increasingly became a means of aligning Komsomol activities and initiatives with the party-line. The Komsomol leadership assumed more control of the social initiative and public engagement undertaken in its name.[67] The leadership still desired voluntarism, as Gorsuch put it, but they were also 'afraid of it, torn between their need for youthful initiative and their desire to maintain control over the actions of youth and their revolutionary imaginings.'[68]

From 1928, at the outset of the Great Break, the Central Committee started to narrow the parameters of Soviet *obshchestvennost'*. Fewer official social organizations were sanctioned, and controls were tightened. Larger professional organizations, as well as local societies, suffered suspicion after the Shakhty and Promparty trials of 1928 and 1930. The NKVD issued new rules for the re-registration of social organizations in 1929.[69]

What was happening here? In forming a constituency for 'Stalin's Revolution' and the rejection of NEP, young *obshchestvenniki* like Zhukov, Balezin and Petrov also embraced a return to civil war aesthetics. They embraced the language of 'brigade' and 'light cavalry'. Paradoxically, they invoked the spirit of a time when *gosudarstvennost'* took clear priority over *obshchestvennost'*. The ensuing hyper vigilance of Stalinism put a check on the vitality of social initiative and its initiators. As Asaoka views it, at this time '*obshchestvennost'* was primarily invoked for national interest without regard to its original goal of promoting social maturation.'[70] The Stalinist leadership appeared less assured in the ability of social initiatives to shepherd in the commune-state. Centralization, bureaucratization, mass mobilization and recruitment, and the drive for conformity and ideological purity reduced the scope and diversity of revolutionary participation. The existing *obshchestvennost'-gosudarstvennost'* equilibrium tipped decisively towards the latter for the foreseeable future.

That is not to say that Soviet *obshchestvennost'* simply disappeared. As Neumann argues, it continued on as a tightly controlled component of a 'managed Stalinist civil society.'[71] Social organizations such as the International Organization to Aid Revolutions (MOPR), the League of the Militant Godless and OSOAVIAKhIM continued to operate until the end of the 1940s. Most famously, it was in the 1930s that the 'housewife-activists' (*obshchestvennitsy*) worked to establish more public canteens, childcare facilities and laundries. They promoted the advance of revolution and Soviet society through 'cultural and daily-living work' (*kul'turno-bytovaia rabota*).[72] Consciously or not, they picked up the same baton that the urban communes and many other activist groupings had been carrying across the 1920s. Creating 'self-managed canteens' (*samodeiatel'naia stolovaia*), in particular, was a cause championed by both the communes and *obshchestvennitsy*. Alongside the continued existence of house-leasing cooperative partnerships (ZhAKTy) – a body of residential alliances involved in the self-management of their domestic spaces and activities – the Stalinist leadership still welcomed such social initiatives on the 'cultural and daily-living' front. This was an '*obshchestvennost'*, Matsui explains, 'based on cooperativeness' and 'residents' communality'. An *obshchestvennost'* permitted to develop in a lower priority area, yes, but also an *obshchestvennost'* of 'cultural and daily-living work' that became embroiled within the mechanisms of the Stalinist state.[73] Some housewife-activists found themselves appointed as cultural supervisors of upper organs in the Sub-*raion* Unions of Housing Cooperation. This was a section of socialist 'civic agency' still in partnership with the authorities.[74]

That unwieldy proposition present at the inception of Soviet governance – developing social initiative and statist control – continued to inform the idea of Soviet governmentality, even as the scales dipped further in the direction of *gosudarstvennost'*. Even as the number of non-governmental, non-bureaucratic human groups diminished under Stalin, the discursive notion of *obshchestvennost'* survived. This was a Soviet *obshchestvennost'* first expressed and embraced as a means of revolutionary participation during the open decade of the new Soviet state. This was an *obshchvestvennaia rabota* through which future Soviet citizens would identify. A parents' *obshchestvennost'* built around improving school education emerged in the mid-1930s; a very cautious discussion of *obshchestvennost'* and medical autonomy in cases of abortion arose out of the wartime period; and, after Stalin's death, *obshchestvennost'* was again promoted and widely discussed.[75] The promise of self-governance and the commune-state once again came to the fore under Khrushchev. And it surely informed the policies of Gorbachev – the Hamlet of the Soviet state's attempts to foster a partnership with socialist 'civic agency'.

As a tentative discursive notion Soviet *obshchestvennost'* never disappeared, yet never overcame *gosudarstvennost'* either. It went through residual and emergent spells. It offered a means of conceptualizing revolutionary participation and a connection to the idealized commune-state. But, at the same time, that great contradiction at the heart of Soviet governmentality – the desire to nurture participation, but not let it get in the way – framed and curtailed the contours of *obshchestvennost'*. During the Great Break, this contradiction was particularly sharply felt. The Stalinist leadership needed activists to break resistance to revolutionary tempos, but they were especially conscious of maintaining order. From this perspective, attempts to bring *obshchestvennost'* under stricter control were not just a case of quietly forgetting about ideology and being wholly pragmatic or manipulative; they were about balancing and sustaining participation with the competing desire for increased statist management. The 'power-corrupts,' 'evil-personality,' 'dictatorial-dogma' arguments of the totalitarian canon have long been abandoned as a satisfactory way of explaining the change that occurred after 1917 or 1928. Accepting that Stalin spoke the same in private as he did in public, serious studies no longer present Soviet ideology as a counterfeit or a foil for dastardly master planners. As David-Fox notes, 'civil participation may have to be considered a feature of totalitarian dictatorship as well as a backbone of middle-class democracy.'[76] The balance between participation and compulsory state measures – striking the desired level of control while incorporating social initiative – was an evolving and contradictory feature of the Soviet experiment.

CHAPTER 15
LIBERATION AND AUTHORITARIANISM IN THE EARLY SOVIET CAMPAIGN TO 'STRUGGLE WITH PROSTITUTION'

Siobhán Hearne

On 31 May 1930, the Commission for the Improvement of Women's Life and Labour (*Komissiia po Uluchsheniiu Truda i Byta Zhenshchin*, KUTB hereafter) met to discuss the progress, or lack thereof, of the Soviet government's campaign to 'struggle with prostitution' (*bor'ba s prostitutsiei*), which was launched in 1918. Soviet politicians largely defined prostitution as an unwanted vestige of the bourgeois past, so the core aim of the campaign was the complete eradication of commercial sex. Prostitution was regarded exclusively as a heterosexual act, so attempts to eliminate the sale of sex ignored the well-established male sex trade and professed to focus on achieving women's economic, social and political equality.[1] However, during the meeting, it became clear that members of the commission held conflicting opinions about the main causes of female prostitution, as indicated by the following quotations from the transcript:

> The girl who sells herself for silk stockings must be subject to the strictest public condemnation.[2]
>
> –*Nikolai Semashko, Central Executive Committee.*

> Since 1929, women have been dismissed from their jobs, refused assistance at the labour exchange, and not accepted for work anywhere. These women then go straight to the street.[3]
>
> –*Borob'eva, Central Union of Housing Cooperatives.*

Some administrators regarded prostitution as an economic problem and a product of unemployment and poverty. For these commentators, the solution was simple: provide education, training and alternative employment. In contrast, other activists rejected the idea that all prostitutes were blameless victims of the capitalist pre-revolutionary regime and sought to restrict women's ability to work as prostitutes. These contrasting approaches to solving the 'problem' of prostitution ran alongside one another from the outset of the campaign. The divergence between the two perspectives dictated the course of the struggle, which was marked by the simultaneous introduction of liberal and illiberal administrative measures. This chapter explores the various forms of administrative persuasion, coercion and propaganda deployed by the early Soviet state to eliminate what it perceived to be an obsolete social practice. The chapter is structured around two key objectives of the struggle: ending female unemployment and removing stigma.

The early Soviet government's campaign to eradicate prostitution formed a flashpoint within a wider ideological battle to remake society. Before 1917, the old tsarist government legally tolerated prostitution, regarding it as an unpleasant, but necessary, outlet for male sexual desire. Under the system of legal toleration, brothels were licensed by the state and women who sold sex had to register with the police, attend regular medical examinations, and abide by a whole host of rules governing their visibility and behaviour.[4] Under the old regime, only philanthropic groups composed of Russia's educated elite provided assistance for women wanting to leave prostitution.[5] The Russian imperial state regarded prostitution as a 'necessary evil', whereas the Bolsheviks generally subscribed to Marxist classifications of commercial sex as an inevitable result of the social and economic conditions of capitalism.[6] Prominent Bolsheviks alleged that the introduction of socialism would alleviate these conditions, and insisted that assistance for women was to be provided by the state, rather than by 'bourgeois philanthropists'.[7] Therefore, the struggle with prostitution was tied up in discussions amongst experts regarding what exactly constituted productive labour and how far the state could legitimately intervene into the lives of its citizens.

Debates regarding the best methods to wage the struggle with prostitution were a complex set of negotiations regarding which remnants of the old society were redeemable and irredeemable.[8] Legislation introduced in the 1920s identified those who profited from the labour of female prostitutes as incompatible with the new socialist society. Selling sex was not a crime nor legally tolerated from 1917 onwards, yet brothel keeping and pimping were criminalized in 1922, carrying a minimum sentence of three years' imprisonment.[9] Buying sex was not a criminal offence, but the Soviet government used the press and health propaganda to strongly discourage men from visiting prostitutes. *Pravda* occasionally published the names and workplaces of male clients found during brothel raids.[10] Health posters warned men that their brief forays into commercial sex could have long-lasting and detrimental consequences for their wives and families if they contracted a venereal infection.[11] In contrast to the pre-revolutionary period, women who sold sex were not the only group held responsible for the transmission of venereal diseases. In 1926, any individual who knowingly infected, or intended to infect, another person with a venereal disease could face imprisonment for up to three years.[12]

Attempts to shift the blame for prostitution onto the shoulders of brothel keepers, pimps and clients, rather than women who worked as prostitutes, did not reconcile the contradictory nature of early Soviet approaches to female emancipation, which were categorized by a chasm between state ambitions and realities. On the one hand, the Soviet government articulated a desire to transform gender relations and improve women's social and economic position through wage labour, yet did not adequately challenge the dominance of women in unskilled industries and the additional household labour that was largely performed by women.[13] In campaigns of sanitary enlightenment, the Soviet government clung to pre-revolutionary negative stereotypes of women who sold sex and depicted them as the source of all venereal infections.[14] In discussions regarding prostitution, the Soviet government divided prostitutes into two types: those who sold sex to escape poverty and a small minority of so-called 'professionals'. Official discourse categorized the latter category as 'malicious' (*zlostnyi*) or 'hardened' (*zakorenelyi*) lost causes, and they made effective villains in health propaganda. Because of these two categories, recommendations for how to wage the struggle swung between liberal and illiberal measures: liberating women from poverty and unemployment on the one hand and restricting the ability of women to make a living solely from prostitution on the other. As the 1920s progressed, the 'two types' theory became crystallized in official imagination, which lay the groundwork for the increased repression of prostitutes as antisocial elements in the 1930s.

The fight against female unemployment and poverty

Official explanations for why women became prostitutes privileged narratives of poverty and desperation. It is highly likely that many women engaged in prostitution throughout the 1920s, especially given the social and economic upheaval of the revolutionary year of 1917, as well as the periods of War Communism (1918–21) and the New Economic Policy (1921–8). The introduction of rationing and the requisitioning of food and agricultural supplies under War Communism pushed more and more women and girls into desperate economic situations.[15] Official statistics reported a rise in prostitution in the early 1920s, as the number of prostitutes known to the authorities in Petrograd climbed from 17,000 in 1920 to 32,000 by the end of 1922.[16] Severe famine in the years 1921–2 also caused increased prostitution.[17] In 1921, the Cheliabinsk Department for Political Education (*Gubpolitprosvet*) issued a poster addressing how the famine opened up opportunities for sexual exploitation. The poster acknowledged that the disaster caused 'thousands of women to struggle for existence' and condemned the 'spiders who were happy to exploit a woman's need for a slice of bread'.[18] In addition, unemployment soared following the civil war, as employers fired thousands of workers, a large percentage of whom were women and replaced them with demobilized soldiers.[19] By July 1923, an estimated 41.4 per cent of women in Petrograd were unemployed.[20] The dominance of women in unskilled industries and the widespread preference for training male apprentices meant that women's wages were consistently lower than men's throughout the 1920s.[21] Even during the mass industrialization of the First Five-Year Plan, almost 55 per cent of those registered as unemployed were women.[22]

In March 1919, the People's Commissariat of Social Welfare issued a circular with an extensive plan for the struggle with prostitution. Certain measures focused on liberating women from economic instability and homelessness through the organization of dedicated dormitories, increasing the minimum wage and generally improving living conditions.[23] However, illiberal measures also featured in the circular. The commissariat praised the closure of offices for hiring domestic servants, restaurants with private rooms and private craft workshops, where apparently 'under the guise of apprenticeships, young women are prepared to be sacrificed for their love'.[24] Given the dominance of women in domestic service and workshops before 1917, these closures would have limited women's access to paid employment and arguably encouraged some to turn to prostitution.[25] To build on this supposed success, the commissariat recommended prohibiting young women from working in teahouses, restaurants and taverns, and even toyed with the idea of sending unemployed teenagers to work in the countryside's cornfields. Finally, the commissariat called for the immediate establishment of an agricultural colony and a workhouse (*dom trudoliubiia*) for 'hardened prostitutes'.[26] Even though Soviet politicians marketed the struggle as a process of female emancipation, there were ideological flaws from the outset. The People's Commissariat of Social Welfare classified working-class women as weak-willed and easily seduced into prostitution, echoing the assumptions of philanthropic organizations in the pre-revolutionary period.[27] Under the banner of protection, the authorities endeavoured to limit women's employment options only to labour defined as appropriate by the state. Women who refused to comply were to be forced into closed institutions and labour colonies.

Assumptions about female moral weakness encouraged activists to seek out and 'rescue' potential or current prostitutes. In 1929, the Leningrad Committee for the Struggle with Prostitution called for the establishment of a 'special cadre of inspectors' to patrol the labour exchange and identify women believed to be 'standing on the verge of prostitution'.[28] The inspectors would also look for potential prostitutes among the women brought to police stations across Leningrad and at the Institute for the Protection of Maternity and Infancy (*MatMlad*) in Vyborg. These women would be offered material assistance, cultural education and if illiterate, directed to their nearest literacy (*Likbez*) centre. The committee regarded this measure as the best method for preventing women from entering prostitution as it eradicated two key pull-factors: poverty and illiteracy. This financial assistance, education and emotional support of the committee would have certainly benefited some women in need. However, the vague category of 'standing on the verge of prostitution' could have been used to legitimize the committee's interference into the lives of any woman who they perceived to be vulnerable. In the capital, the wider public were encouraged to help wage the struggle by policing urban space. In 1931, the Moscow *Oblast'* Committee for the Struggle with Prostitution sent out an 'inspection brigade' (*obsledovaniia brigada*) to patrol the streets looking for women working as prostitutes.[29] Groups of volunteers inspected lodging houses, tenements and public lavatories both day and night to ensure that all areas of urban space were 'under public control'.[30] The monitoring of leisure spaces was also recommended in the name of the struggle. In 1918, the enforced closure of cafes at 7 pm and the organization of regular hotel raids featured among recommendations for how best to eradicate prostitution in Petrograd.[31] From the mid-1920s onwards, mixed-gender bathhouses were closed in Moscow after these establishments were outed as hotbeds of commercial sex in the popular press.[32] These illiberal administrative measures would have imposed limitations on the working locations and activities of women working in commercial sex, pushing them further underground and opening them up to police harassment.

Women were required to self-refer to receive assistance at one of the Soviet Union's labour dispensaries (*trud profilaktoriia*), which were established in Moscow and other major cities from 1924. These centres offered women infected with venereal diseases (in most cases, prostitutes) lodgings, work training, paid employment, free medical treatment and education. The key aim of the dispensaries was to reform prostitutes into skilled, conscious and productive workers who were strongly committed to the construction of socialism. As the flagship project of the struggle, Soviet doctors and politicians were keen to showcase the dispensaries' apparent overwhelming success in reforming prostitutes. In 1927, *Pravda* announced that 500 women had been 'returned to a working life' in Moscow within a period of two years.[33] Foreign visitors to the Soviet Union also wrote glowing accounts, such as Russian-born academic Fannina Halle and American relief worker Anna Haines.[34] For foreign doctors visiting the capital in summer 1935, trips to the Moscow labour dispensary were on the programme, alongside excursions to Lenin's mausoleum, Gorky Park and the metro.[35]

To receive assistance in the labour dispensary, women had to conform to an ideal of the redeemable woman. Residents were required to fill out forms with 100 questions about their childhood, tastes and interests, temperament and sex life periodically during their stay at an institution.[36] The ideal redeemable woman was typified in a 1927 *Pravda* article, which detailed how a 'sick, shaky woman', unemployed, homeless, infected with a venereal disease and with a desire to give up prostitution, was accepted into a Moscow labour dispensary.[37] Unemployed domestic workers (*domrabotnitsy*) were also perfect candidates for this role.[38] When dismissed by their employer, domestic workers simultaneously lost their source of income and living space, despite legislative attempts to guarantee them time to find alternative housing.[39] At a KUTB meeting on 31 May 1930, Konova, the representative from Moscow's Krasnaia Presnia district, used the image of the domestic worker as the antithesis of the professional prostitute. She recounted her meeting with one of these women:

> She said, "Yes, I am a domestic worker. The people who I lived with threw me out. I have a child. I have nothing left to do". When we offered her a place at the dispensary, she readily agreed. When I asked her if she knew of other women (prostitutes) she was ashamed. She said that she only started doing it recently and did not know anybody.[40]

Whether real or fictional, this woman fit the ideal of the redeemable prostitute. She had turned to commercial sex only in a period of desperation, she was ashamed of working as a prostitute, and mostly importantly, she was grateful for the opportunity to change. Unlike other 'hardened' prostitutes, a stint at the labour dispensary and a good douse of propaganda would surely reform her into a conscious Soviet citizen.

The Soviet government was keen to showcase success stories from the dispensaries to demonstrate the superiority of socialist methods of re-education through labour. On 31 October 1931, the first conference for former residents of labour dispensaries was held in Moscow. Accounts of these conferences boasted how women who had previously worked as prostitutes were now even university students, shock workers, Komsomol members and elected representatives of district soviets.[41] Delegates spent most of their time expressing their gratitude to the Soviet government and congratulating their fellow comrades for their complete transformation. However, some limitations managed to unsettle this glowing narrative of liberation. The head doctor of a Moscow labour dispensary, Dr Danishevskii, described the behaviour of the majority of discharged residents as 'less than satisfactory' and 'undisciplined', with some even turning to drink.[42] In the year of the first conference, 42 per cent of women admitted to Moscow dispensaries dropped out.[43] Even Halle, a fervent supporter of both the Soviet government and the labour dispensary, included a heated exchange between former residents and Dr Danishevskii in her account of the conference. One delegate complained that due to housing shortages, she had been sharing a room with seven other women for the past two years, even though she was a shock worker and candidate for party membership.[44] Despite the interruption of many other women in agreement, the discussion was promptly shut down.

The issues of resources and funding further limited the success of the labour dispensaries. In 1930, the People's Commissar for Health, Nikolai Semashko, described Moscow's network of labour dispensaries as 'underdeveloped', as the ten centres across the city and region could accommodate a mere 584 women, whereas there were at least 757 prostitutes known to the authorities.[45] The situation was further strained outside the capital, where sometimes women had to travel hundreds of kilometres to reach their nearest dispensary.[46] The Soviet government did not provide sufficient financial support to every local government. In 1925, three-quarters of all dispensaries across the Soviet Union were financially dependent on the Central Commissariat, which often could not deliver the necessary funds.[47] In Sevastopol', the city Soviet relied on donations from employees of the political departments of the Black Sea fleet and the Crimean ASSR in order to open a dispensary.[48] Even in the second city of Leningrad, when a labour dispensary finally opened in 1928, it was funded by ticketed lectures, concerts and donations from the public.[49] The Department of Social Security closed the Leningrad dispensary after just five years on the basis that women could just travel to the dispensary in Moscow.[50] The dispensaries' funding deficit even made it onto the pages of *Pravda*. In November 1935, an article celebrating the re-education of 'former prostitutes, thieves and gangsters' into new Soviet citizens at Moscow dispensaries ended with a desperate plea for increased funding: 'since (dispensary residents) express a genuine desire to change their way of life, it is criminal to push them back onto the streets'.[51]

The realities of widespread female unemployment, poverty and economic instability certainly coloured the official classification of prostitution as predominantly an economic problem. The majority of those directing the struggle believed that prostitution was an exchange that women were pushed into only in the complete absence of choice, rather than an occupation selected from a series of options. Some commentators found it inconceivable that certain women continued to work as prostitutes even following offers of alternative employment and the opportunity to participate in the construction of the socialist state. This inability, or unwillingness, to comprehend that women's entry into prostitution also resulted from a complex interplay between gender hierarchies, economic circumstances and individual choice meant that frustrated officials reached for moral explanations regarding irredeemable 'malicious' prostitutes when the struggle achieved only limited success. The campaign's fixation on economic vulnerability of women served to reinforce stereotypes about female weakness and helplessness, which resulted in the introduction of more illiberal administrative measures.

Anti-stigmatization

Throughout the 1920s and 1930s, the Soviet government advocated ending the stigma associated with working as a prostitute. Prostitutes were victims of social and economic circumstances beyond their control and could not be criminalized nor discriminated against for their actions. Former prostitutes should not be ashamed of their pasts and instead should celebrate the transformation gifted to them by the Soviet state. Despite discourses of liberation, the struggle was built upon the idea that there were two distinct types of prostitute: those who were willing to be re-educated and those who were not. In 1925, an *Izvestiia* article reported that there were 3,000 women of the latter category across the Soviet Union.[52] Discourses of liberation and authoritarianism ran alongside each other, as officials attempted to reconcile the necessity of ending discrimination against women who sold sex with the equally urgent need to deal with the 'irredeemable' (*nespravimaia*) prostitute. As historians Nataliia Lebina and Mikhail Shkarovskii have shown, from the beginning of the Second Five-Year Plan, the Leningrad authorities deported more and more 'hardened' prostitutes to the Svirsk labour colony while simultaneously providing women who sold sex with paid employment, charitable donations and assistance in obtaining documentation.[53] The inherent tension of simultaneously advocating welfare and repression meant that anti-stigmatization campaigns were destined to be unsuccessful.

The struggle campaign occurred against a backdrop of debate regarding what constituted socially beneficial and productive labour. According to Marxist ideology, waged labour was a component of female emancipation as it facilitated the development of class-consciousness.[54] Despite involving the exchange of services for payment, the Soviet state did not regard prostitution as labour and certainly did not consider prostitutes to be workers. Vladimir Lenin sneered at prostitutes' attempts to unionise in Weimar Germany, ridiculing the German Communist Party's role in their organization as 'painting every prostitute as a sweet Madonna'.[55] Alexandra Kollontai was equally outraged by the idea that prostitution could constitute productive labour, as she criticized the professional prostitute for 'reduc[ing] the reserves of energy and the number of working hands' building the new socialist state.[56] Despite the struggle being marketed as a 'struggle with prostitution, not prostitutes', the image of the irredeemable prostitute-as-parasite contaminated anti-stigmatization debates.

Right at the beginning of the struggle in Petrograd, the regional committee prohibited certain words and practices in order to treat prostitutes with dignity and break with pre-revolutionary practices.[57] At a 1918 committee meeting, the old terminology for a brothel, a 'house of toleration' (*dom terpimosti*), was banned, as was the condemnation (*oblichenie*) of women engaging in prostitution.[58] While the committee generally agreed with these proposals, others were up for debate. Certain committee members suggested when prostitutes were arrested for other misdemeanours, only female administrative investigators should lead their interrogations. Professor F. A. Val'ter, a venereologist who had practised during the pre-revolutionary period, enthusiastically agreed with this proposal and even recommended that the measure be extended to all arrested women 'in the interests of their honour and dignity'.[59] Val'ter cynically, and heteronormatively, added that female investigators would apparently prevent detainees from 'engaging in debauchery' in order to ensure a favourable outcome in their case.[60] Other committee members dismissed the proposal from the outset. The representative from the People's Commissariat of Justice's remarks was laden with moral judgment as he insisted that 'women engaged in indecent occupations' needed to be treated differently from 'women in general', as the latter category did not experience the same prejudice that 'prostitutes bring upon themselves'.

Even though official policy rejected the moral condemnation of prostitutes, those in positions of relative authority continued to emphasize the apparent moral distance between themselves and women in the commercial sex industry. This fixation on morality led to the dismissal of social factors or individual choice as drivers for women's entry into prostitution, as well as the further stigmatization of prostitutes. The memoir of Anna Bek, a physician who worked in both the late imperial and early Soviet periods, illustrates how state discourses regarding economic exploitation and personal prejudices often became intertwined. In Chita in 1918, a group of prostitutes invited Bek to a meeting to protest against the Bolshevik's recent closure of brothels. Bek recalled her contributions to the discussion:

> Taking the floor, I expressed my negative attitude toward their shameful life. I informed them that the government would not chase them out onto the street but rather was opening a dormitory with different kinds of workshops where they would be taught to live by honest labour.[61]

The explicit moral judgements within Bek's statement constitute a rejection of the official classification of prostitution as an economic problem. This tension between official ideas and personal prejudices was apparent in Petrograd's regional committee. In January 1919, when the committee had been up and running for less than a year, the Petrograd Commissariat of Labour withdrew their representative on the basis that they did not believe that prostitution was in fact a 'socio-economic problem'.[62] Committee members questioned whether there was a 'special category' of women, 'for whom prostitution was the consequence of degeneracy and a painful need because of psychological disorder,' a late nineteenth-century criminological theory that Alexandra Kollontai dismissed as 'bourgeois'.[63] Despite this, the chairperson of the Petrograd committee took this suggestion seriously and recommended the organization of a special diagnostic institute.

Prejudice against women working in the commercial sex industry also found expression in the early Soviet courtroom. The criminalization of brothel keepers and pimps failed to shift responsibility for prostitution fully onto the shoulders of facilitators and profiteers. Even though prostitution was not a criminal offence in the early Soviet Union, some women who sold sex were still treated as criminals.[64] For example, in August 1920, a Moscow court detained Praskov'ia Baranova, a woman from Tula province, simply 'for prostitution'.[65] In August 1921, another woman was tried in court for both engaging in prostitution and infecting a Red Army soldier with a venereal disease, despite the fact that the latter offense was not criminalized until 1926.[66] The woman was sentenced to compulsory hospital treatment and warned that she would be imprisoned for five years in a labour camp if she did not 'return to an honest life'. In 1921, the People's Commissariat of Justice was forced to overturn the convictions of several women charged with engaging in prostitution.[67] The People's Commissariat of Health issued another circular in 1923 to remind local authorities that any oppressive measures against prostitutes, such as raids and compulsory examinations, were categorically forbidden.[68] Despite this, in 1925 Soviet jurist Mikhail Strogovich claimed that investigators and prosecutors continued to arrest prostitutes under the guise of other offenses, such as noise disruption and gambling.[69] In Petrograd in the early 1920s, the city police treated the solicitation of men as cases of hooliganism.[70] Worse still, certain local authorities clung to pre-revolutionary practices throughout the decade. The police in Altai region continued to register prostitutes onto police lists and force them to attend medical examinations until 1924.[71] In Blagoveshchensk in Amur province, these practices continued until 1930.[72]

Throughout the 1920s and 1930s, the stigmatization of prostitutes continued. In 1926, the Leningrad Committee for the Struggle with Prostitution commended the work of outpatient clinics and venereal dispensaries, where in theory prostitutes could receive free, or at least affordable, treatment for their illnesses.[73] However, the committee stressed the need to ensure that clinics did not deny women medical assistance after learning of their occupation, which suggests that women's access to medicine could be dependent on their engagement in 'respectable', rather than stigmatized, employment. The committee also called on trade unions to prevent employers from dismissing women for being infected with a venereal disease, as they did not 'pose a threat to their fellow worker' while receiving treatment. Instead, they argued that dismissal from work actually pushed women into prostitution by removing their source of income.

At a 1929 meeting, the Leningrad Committee recognized that their campaign to end the stigmatization of prostitutes and bring them back to productive labour had fallen flat. To combat this, they endeavoured to seek out all 'prostituted women' and offer them a place on a social patronage scheme.[74] The key aim of the scheme was to provide prostitutes with financial support and education to enable their gradual transition back to work in a field deemed useful by the Soviet state. Only 'seasoned comrades' and 'female activists' were allowed to be mentors, as they were more likely to treat patrons with respect. Mentors were 'categorically forbidden from using the word prostitute' and employers were advised to avoid revealing the woman's former profession.[75] In order to re-enter the 'productive' labour force, the former prostitute was required to conceal her past. At the 1931 conference for former residents of labour dispensaries, delegates addressed this issue in detail. One female Komsomol member who claimed to be unashamed of her former occupation dominated the debate, yet other remarks indicated the contrary. One woman commented that it was 'disagreeable' to draw their fellow workers' attention to their pasts and another stated that women entering the labour force from the dispensaries had to 'do more than others […] to prove [their] worth'.[76] One delegate's husband claimed that it was obvious that 'people did not behave properly to the women in the factories', but urged women to expose those who reinforced stigma.[77] Despite attempts to facilitate a smooth transition between prostitution and 'productive' labour, former prostitutes were still discriminated against.

Some local authorities encouraged the use of threats to stop women selling sex, especially following the criminalization of venereal disease transmission in 1926. In this year, the Leningrad Committee issued the following instructions to regional administrators: 'warn the prostitute that if she infects another person, she will be prosecuted, and this applies to any type of venereal disease'.[78] Reliable statistics for the number of prosecutions of individuals for transmitting venereal infections do not exist, but it is reasonable to assume that many were prostitutes, given the inseparability of prostitution and venereal disease in official imagination.[79] A 1927 article in *Pravda* alleged that prostitutes were responsible for over 50 per cent of all venereal diseases in Moscow.[80] The Leningrad Committee claimed that prostitutes were the source of 40 per cent of all venereal infections across the city in 1926.[81] Even in 1932–3, when nearly half of all infected men in Leningrad claimed to have caught their infection from a 'casual encounter' (compared with 14 per cent from paid sex), the Leningrad authorities concluded that the men must just be lying about the source of their illness.[82] The perceived link between prostitution and venereal diseases contributed to the vilification of prostitutes as malicious transmitters of infection. Throughout the 1920s, sanitary enlightenment posters depicted women who sold sex as diseased, dangerous and decadent NEPwomen.[83] In 1928, the Sevastopol' district committee recommended the periodic staging of show trials for 'maliciously diseased' prostitutes in order to prevent others from engaging in commercial sex.[84] Even those firmly committed to improving the lives of economically vulnerable women replicated this discourse. In April 1930, Baranova, the head of the KUTB, wrote to a labour dispensary in Ivano-Voznesensk to request the admission of a woman in need. The KUTB fought consistently at a local and national level to include women in industrialization and to bring women's issues to the forefront of state policy until its elimination in 1932.[85] Baranova's letter to the dispensary stated that the woman was not only involved in prostitution, but also 'deliberately and maliciously infected her fellow citizens'.[86] Baranova's vilification of the woman in question suggests that she regarded prostitution as a tool used to subvert the Soviet state, rather than an economic necessity.

The campaign to eradicate prostitution constantly reiterated the connections between commercial sex and disease, which served to further stigmatize women who worked as prostitutes. In February 1925, *Rabochnaia Gazeta* published a letter from a certain 'Prostitute Tanya', who wrote 'on behalf of many' to accuse the Soviet government of pushing prostitutes further into poverty. Public condemnation of her profession had caused her earnings to dwindle and housing shortages meant that rent prices were extortionate. The newspaper published a reply to Tanya written by Semashko, in which he claimed that her grievances were evidence 'that the plan adopted was right' as it meant that the eradication of prostitution was underway.[87] He claimed that, as prostitution was the chief source of venereal diseases and 'the heaviest of national calamities', Tanya's own economic concerns had to come second to the interests of the wider community.[88] Despite the struggle apparently being with prostitution rather than prostitutes, the women who worked in the commercial sex industry suffered financially.

As the struggle progressed, recommendations for the introduction of illiberal administrative measures became much more explicit. Since the beginning of the campaign, labour colonies for 'hardened' prostitutes had openly existed and various city police departments routinely arrested women believed to be selling sex, as noted earlier in the chapter. In Rostov-on-Don, the police kept lists of the 'most malicious' prostitutes and regularly subjected them to administrative measures.[89] In April 1931, the Moscow *Oblast'* Committee for the Struggle with Prostitution stated that they would comply with the executive committee's decision from 1928 regarding the establishment of forced labour institutions for those who 'resisted labour re-education'.[90] Similar measures of forced re-education were in place for vagrants and 'professional beggars' from the late 1920s.[91] By May 1931, the Moscow Health Department vowed to open a closed labour dispensary for prostitutes infected with venereal diseases who refused to work. Some regional prosecutors believed that these measures did not go far enough and called for the introduction of a new article in the criminal code to sanction forced labour for professional prostitutes.[92] A representative of the Moscow Soviet called to change the campaign slogan of the struggle to 'work, and if you do not want to, we will force you'.[93]

In January 1931, the Moscow *Oblast'* Committee for the Struggle with Prostitution conducted a survey of prostitutes in Moscow and the surrounding region. Compared with a 1928 survey, the number of prostitutes working on the streets had apparently decreased six times over, although certain members of the committee blamed this on the severe frost at the time of the investigation.[94] The committee fundamentally disagreed on how to interpret the results of the survey and could not decide on a unified plan to move the struggle forward. Some members wanted to direct attention towards the well-dressed NEPwomen who sat drinking in cafes and the *Mossel'prom* canteen, apparently charging 40 roubles per encounter.[95] Others advocated harsh repressive measures against prostitutes' male customers. Many attacked the sexual double standard that penalized just women for prostitution, calling for the government to enforce the obligation to pay alimony more stringently and advocating the training of women in the male-dominated industries of carpentry and stonemasonry.[96] Nevertheless, Semashko, the chairperson of the committee, focused on the NEPwoman stereotype. He expressed the urgent need to deal with the 'dolled-up women who do not want to work', by 'removing their seal-skin coats and sending them to Solovki'.[97] While various local police forces had deported prostitutes from the outset of the struggle, the recommendation of such policy from Semashko, a member of the Central Executive Committee, signified the greater acceptance of repressive measures.

Throughout the 1930s, calls for the repression of prostitutes increased in tandem with official appeals to intensify the class struggle and rid society of groups deemed to be dangerous. In 1932, the decree 'On the Establishments of a Unified Passport System in the USSR and the Obligatory Registration of Passports' gave local authorities the power to 'cleanse' urban centres of criminal and antisocial elements and sentence them to stints at corrective labour camps. This legislation codified the category of 'socially harmful element' as a distinctly punishable social identity, defined as a person either with criminal convictions, ties to the criminal world, or a person with no definite place of work.[98] 'Hardened' prostitutes would have certainly fit this category.[99] Women suspected to be prostitutes with 'no defined place of employment or residence' were accosted by the police and sentenced to harsh punishments as socially dangerous elements.[100] In 1934, the Leningrad Komsomol produced a memorandum on the struggle with prostitution in the city, in which they discussed the danger posed by the 'two types' of prostitute. The biggest threat to the success of the struggle was no longer posed by 'professional' prostitutes (as apparently 90–100 per cent of them were known to the police), but by women who sold sex casually and sporadically.[101] The Komsomol presented the latter group as an internal enemy that needed to be eradicated, as these women 'regarded themselves as fully legitimate people' and were in possession of trade-union cards and passports. As the decade progressed, the number of individuals calling to end the stigmatization of prostitutes dwindled, as their voices were drowned out by the pervasive repression of the Stalinist state.

Conclusion

The early Soviet campaign to struggle with female prostitution oscillated between liberal and illiberal administrative measures. The destigmatization of women who sold sex and their integration into wider society was the official party line, yet bureaucrats at both central and regional level often ignored this recommendation and even reverted to pre-revolutionary policing practices. Even from the outset of the campaign, Lenin and Kollontai condemned women who made their living solely from selling sex as shirkers who were incompatible with socialism. The Soviet government put measures in place to assist women who wanted to stop engaging in commercial sex, but women had to confirm to the stereotype of the 'redeemable woman' in order to receive support. Furthermore, the Soviet government's inability or unwillingness to provide adequate financial support for the struggle meant that the campaign was heavily dependent on volunteers and charitable donations to both locate women in need and open labour dispensaries.

The Soviet government's failure to eradicate prostitution was rooted in fundamental ideological flaws that were evident from the very outset of the struggle, namely Soviet officialdom's reluctance to think beyond purely economic incentives when explaining women's engagement in commercial sex. The idea that providing alternative employment was enough to prevent women working as prostitutes ignored other crucial pull factors, such as personal choice, gender hierarchies and the unavailability of equally lucrative employment for women. The stubborn focus on economic factors increased the stigmatization of women who worked as prostitutes and crystallized the theory that some prostitutes were deliberately subversive and irredeemable. As the 1920s drew to a close, the opposing stereotypes of the needy woman who sold sex to avoid starvation and the decadent and diseased prostitute were irreparably crystallized in both official and popular imagination and calls for the repression of the latter category of woman grew ever more insistent.

CHAPTER 16
SOVIET CANTEENS IN PRE-WAR USSR, 1917–41: PROMISES OF EMANCIPATION AND EVERYDAY VIOLENCE

François-Xavier Nérard

In the foreground of a poster designed by Maria Feliksovna Bri-Bein in 1931, a group of three people, a man and two women, are looking to a series of saucepans. The central woman is tasting the soup (or whatever it is, the drawing is almost abstract) from one of them. The background is divided into two parts. On the left, a worker is cooking soup in a huge, modern, soup pot. On the right, behind a window, we can see a refectory, huge, luminous, with diners seated at different tables. The slogan 'Woman worker! Fight for a clean canteen and a healthy food' is written on the upper (in black capital letters) and bottom (in red) parts of the poster. Everything seems evident and peaceful in this drawing.

Yet, like many Soviet pictures, this one is misleading.[1] At the time when the poster was published, 'clean' canteens were more than often shabby places. Because of massive shortages, the 'healthy' food was dull and tasteless. Cabbage soup, of a poor quality, was the ineluctable menu offered to the consumers.[2] Even more delusory is the irenic atmosphere of the poster. The everyday experience of customers and workers (administrators, cooks or waiters) was radically different. Canteens were rather places of conflicts and violence.

For most of the period we are dealing with, this violence was symbolic. This was a routine one, a day-to-day brutality: cooks and directors were often attacked in the press, in party meetings for the poor quality of food, for stealing products, for not working properly. *Stolovye* were also a place where customers were subjected to rudeness of the personnel, emptiness of the plates or low quality of the food and its total absence of taste. Frustrated customers turned their anger against workers or sometimes, even if it was very rare, to the authorities. One day, a customer, as a Harvard Project respondent told us, spoke to one of the portraits of Stalin hung on the walls of the *stolovaya* and 'told' him: 'you should eat this soup!' He was eventually arrested by the NKVD after his words were reported.[3] The repression of 1937–8 made this violence physical. People, as elsewhere in the country, were arrested and, sometimes, shot. Tensions heightened by years of conflicts fuelled this process. Even if they were not always the direct causes of repression, they made it credible.

This chapter tries to explain the violence generated by the functioning of the system. How did a project aimed to create a *novy byt* and a new person, liberating women from the 'slavery of the kitchen', promoting collective way of eating, give birth to violence between individuals and to institutional repression? Unlike some other works in this volume, this is a history, almost written without the names of Stalin, Trotsky, Lenin or Zinoviev, but nevertheless a Soviet, all too Soviet history. The ruthless Stalinist Soviet Union is often studied through the prism of political violence, concentration camps or the personality of the Great leader. This chapter argues that social history can also bring some very relevant answers to the very political question of the meaning of Soviet power and its everyday practices of violence. The rise of violence in the Soviet system is of course linked to the 'persistence of the "transitional" dictatorship' the editors of this book stressed in the introduction. Our point is to show that these political roots of violence echoed with social and institutional processes that were partly autonomous. It will show how an apparently a-political field, food consumption and distribution, can be a good vantage point to understand how the system developed and produced violence and difficult conditions of life.

Canteens and fortresses

Twice in Soviet history, out of nothing, millions of canteens were open all over the country in a very short period of time: during the civil war from 1918 onwards[4] and then during the years of industrialization beginning at the end of the 1920s. Both times, Bolshevik leadership was driven by necessity.

Canteens had to be constructed as fast as possible, because urban and working populations had to be fed. There was no time to think: hunger and economic needs left no other choice other than to go forward by every possible means. In 1918, Petrograd and Moscow were on the verge of famine. Canteens were an answer for allocating the always rarer food resources. Ten years later, they were meant to feed the new workers on the main projects of the First Five-Year Plan and, once again, to deal with the scarcity of food.

The disappearance of food was indeed rapid and impressive after Stalin's Great Break in 1929. Food production and food distribution in the country were totally disorganized. In 1934, livestock was 55 per cent lower than in 1928 and cereal production 15 per cent lower. In 1932–3, when some parts of the USSR were struck by a devastating famine, the rest of the country was hungry.[5] In the cities, Soviet authorities declared war on private trade for food and manufactured goods: market squares were closed and street vendors chased away. Even if it proved unsuccessful, the main consequence of this policy was the rise of prices, making the private market a very expensive, if vital, source of supply. Queues, in front of shops most often empty, were the rule to get some food in the cities. This total disorganization occurred in a rapidly transforming country: the urban population doubled between 1926 and 1939, so did the number of workers in the factories. Feeding the builders of socialism was therefore an absolute necessity. But the task proved to be Herculean.

Penury was the rule. Industrialization needed all the means that the country had to offer. What factory director was actually ready to divert precious resources to build a canteen? Where were the construction materials to be found? Where could hundreds of thousands of tons of food be found in a hungry country? The size and the ambition of the project added more insurmountable difficulties. Thousands of qualified cooks were needed, but they did not exist. Nor did the buildings supposed to host these canteens. In reality, authorities had to cope with a situation they hardly controlled, or even understood. Canteens were not common in the industrial world. The experience to build on was grim.

But this story made of necessity and material difficulties was nowhere to be heard. Instead, the authorities put forward a voluntarist narrative. The rising of the collective catering system was part of a structured ideological project, coinciding perfectly with the Bolshevik world view: collective food was supposed to be healthy and rational, central for the development of industrial production, a key element in the construction of a new world. Canteens were therefore thought as a place of modernity, of rationalization and hygiene, in one word a place of *kulturnost*. Canteens were meant to contribute to the education and formation of Soviet citizens, and they were part of a kind of civilizing process. They were to be clean, well-equipped and should serve tasty and healthy food. This was why the authorities decided to develop a huge web of canteens, to take care of the people. Politically justified, this project was to be carefully and rapidly implemented.

The Bolshevik voluntarist stance left little room to doubt and to patience. Collective catering was undoubtedly one of the fortresses that the Bolsheviks were meant to storm.[6] Once decided, canteens had almost immediately to become real. This was not a promise for the future, but a reality to happen right away. To convey this feeling, Bolshevik public discourse used a mix of quantitative and qualitative methods. Elements of this representation were openly available to the Soviet population through newspaper articles, public speeches, banners hung in public spaces, images, propaganda posters and photographs. Most texts were written in the present tense, even if they referred to a reality that did not exist yet. In Nizhnii Novgorod, a banner on the entrance of the newly opened factory-kitchen, a place designed to mass-produce food to be distributed in the nearby factories,[7] proclaimed: 'The Factory-Kitchen *cheapens*[8] the cost of the meals, *improves* the quality of the food and *creates* normal work conditions for production'.[9] In the dining halls, alongside with the portraits of Lenin and Stalin, other slogans read 'Collective dining *frees* the women workers from the chain of kitchen slavery and *ensures* the possibility of a new *byt*, a new way of life' or 'A rational diet *is* imperative for the health and the success of the working masses.'

Everything was done to prove this. Statistics were central: they were used to show the tangible reality of collective catering. Papers and reports at all levels were full of figures: millions of Soviet people were fed in thousands of new refectories. For example, canteens at the Gorky automobile plant produced 147,000 'dishes'[10] a day in 1932 when almost 15 million dishes were served every day in the whole country.[11] A resolution by the

Central Committee itself in August 1931, meant to become one of the main normative texts on the topics, actually begins with this quantitative approach:

> The Central committee notes that, during the revolutionary period the collective catering system considerably developed: 5 million industrial workers eat in collective canteens, 3.8 million more working-people in the cities, 3 million hot breakfasts are served in the schools, the web of canteens reached 13,400 units, a noticeable number of factory-kitchen and mechanised canteens have been built, in capital construction more than 200 million roubles have been spent for the last three years.[12]

To make this blooming even more 'real', photographers and designers were also mobilized. Brilliant photographers as Aleksandr Rodchenko in Moscow or Leonid Surin in the Urals[13] were recruited. They shot the best of these new canteens to embody the reality of the Soviet proclaimed project. Their photographs were published in important papers such as *Pravda* or in special brochures. They showed perfect dining halls, filled with clean and well-dressed guests. In photographs shot by Maksim Dmitriev,[14] during the inauguration of the factory-kitchen of Nizhnii Novgorod, some of the eaters even wear a tie. Several house plants can be seen on the tables, particularly in the foreground. There are also carafes on almost all the tables, knives, salt and pepper pots, maybe a pot for horseradish. Workers and guests are eating their already-bitten bread using forks.

This narrative aimed to convey a feeling of an irresistible movement forward, of a controlled plan. The fortresses were stormed and conquered. Words and pictures were however not powerful enough to mask the dire situation of Soviet canteens. All sources agree: official reports, secret documents, letters from Soviet people to the authorities or even brief articles in the press. The reality was a lack of food, poor hygiene, poor quality, queues and monotony of the plates. At the climax of this penury in 1931–2, it was not uncommon for the workers to find small pieces of broken glass, rats or cockroaches in their soup. Hundreds of files in the archives corroborate such a description throughout the period.[15] Testimony by Moscow inspector Zemliachka in 1931 at Sormovo plant in Nizhnii Novgorod is a perfect example among many others: 'Then we saw in the pots where tea is prepared pieces of potatoes, of pasta and so on. Moreover, the water is not boiled because the boiler has not been repaired.'[16] This was the first form of symbolic violence produced by the Soviet collective catering system: customers were forced to eat inedible food and confronted by a lack of interest from the servers.

The authorities could have justified this gap between the promises and the reality in many different ways. They could have explained, as they partly did in 1918–19, that this was a temporary phenomenon, that the immense effort of industrialization entailed short-lasting inconveniences. This was not their choice. A kind of leitmotif can be found in the Soviet press about the illegitimacy of 'objective reasons' as an excuse for not correcting problems.[17] A caricature published in *Stalinets,* the local newspaper from the Uralmash factory in Sverdlovsk, one of the main sites of the First Five-Year Plan, illustrates this point fairly well.[18] On the front page of the 26 October 1932 issue, the secretary of the party cell of the catering organization, the *narpit*, was represented as a lonely man spitting and surrounded by a sea of spittle. The play on words was clear for the readers: he was accused of not giving a damn about the problems of the plant's canteens (the Russian expression *naplevat'*, meaning 'not give a damn' was made on the verb *plevat'*, 'to spit'). The cartoon was actually mocking the justifications he gave to the situation and suggesting that he was only hiding behind 'objective reasons' or 'lack of workforce'.

These attacks made it impossible to explain difficulties with objective and rational reasons. They narrowed the range of possible interpretations of the problems noticed by every canteen customer. They prevented the management of the collective catering from verbalizing the real mechanisms at the origin of the dysfunction. This had huge consequences.

Scandals, resilience and violence

In the absence of possible *technical* explanations, authorities had to choose other ways of dealing with the problem of poor food quality and production and to answer this crucial question: why did the promised healthy and efficient canteens fail to materialize?

The first approach they had was to *openly* denounce the situation. The authorities staged outrage in front of the dire reality of canteens all over the country. All the problems were aired: speeches were given, party bosses or functionaries organized meetings where cooks and heads of canteens were summoned and regularly told off for the poor quality of their work. Pages of the newspapers were full of angry articles describing the dysfunction of the canteens. A portrait of the inefficient collective catering system was not very difficult to draw: lack of food, lack of hygiene or rudeness was exposed in almost every issue of, at least, local and regional newspapers. This surprisingly open discourse had, however, one characteristic that aligned with the idea that the party and the government were always right. Problems were never treated in a systematic way: they all find their origins in local situations and personal responsibility and errors. There were, of course, changes over time, but this overall characteristic is pretty much constant from 1918 onwards.

With objective reasons rejected, individual responsibility was emphasized. Chance was even considered as a dubious explanation. When a rat was found in the workers' soup in Krasnoe Sormovo plant in October 1931, the regional party committee was not fully convinced by the conclusions of the inquiry (the rat jumped by itself into the pot) and tried nevertheless to find a human culprit.[19]

Whether the authorities really believed in wrecking or if this was merely scapegoating is hard to tell. At this point, what matters is the use by the officials of *public* scandal and *public* denunciation. Problems were not hidden. On the contrary, they were stated and described. In most democratic societies, scandal is provoked by journalists or activists, whistle-blowers who expose wrongdoings or unmask lawbreakers. This often challenges the authorities and may cause a government to fall. In Soviet society, on the contrary, it was the authorities themselves who were making the scandal public. This proved to be very violent for ordinary people as for managers who risked being exposed in the pages of the press or during purges or party meetings and often caused more problems than it solved.

Scandals were often revealed during campaigns where the press played a crucial role. This strategy of public denunciation also assumed a form of mobilization. For weeks, newspapers focused on the same question, publishing articles over and over again on the same topic. Regional authorities, local industrial managers, heads of canteens and simple Soviet readers were all part of a system that raised tension and expectations. For a short period of three months, in 1931, the regional newspaper *Uralskii rabochii*, the Worker of the Urals, organized three 'raids' on the canteens of Sverdlovsk, during which journalists and volunteers carried out inspections of the canteens and their work. These inspections were the place of symbolic and recurrent violence, an intrusion of outsiders in the way the canteens were working and repeatedly pointing out errors and problems. Reports, almost always critical, and then meetings to discuss these reports made this process long enough. The cooks of Sverdlovsk even officially protested against these recurrent inspections accusing them of making their work impossible.[20]

K. Garasko was the head of the organization responsible for all the canteens of the Uralmash district in Sverdlovsk between June 1933 and July 1934. During this period, he was regularly attacked in the pages of the local paper. In June 1934, ten out of twenty-six issues dealt, in a way or another, with collective catering and often criticized Garasko explicitly. Day after day, short or long articles accused him of working poorly or of embezzling food for his private consumption. He was finally fired on 5 July. His fate is unknown,[21] but one can imagine how violent this kind of campaign might have been for him.

The treatment of Garasko was part of a general phenomenon: when Aleksei Burov, the second party secretary for the Gorki region, brought together the cooks of the region for a meeting, his words were clear, half-joking ('I am a secretary of the regional committee, in charge of the workers' food supply and, I must confess the truth, I know very few names of good cooks [when I know a lot of bad ones]'.[22]), and more than half-threatening: if cooks were to accept rotten food, they'll 'be sent to severe isolation regime camps'.[23]

But this public use of scandal is only one layer of the violence in Soviet society. It also generated other brutal moments. Recurrent attacks can be traced in their hundreds at all levels of the system, producing an atmosphere of violence, but also a kind of desensitization, a familiarization to the violence. People got used to it, finding ways of dealing with it, of protecting themselves and their friends. This, in turn, led to the unleashing of an even greater violence. Words in the papers being replaced by public purges and dismissals. Dismissals then replaced by trials and arrests, and prison sentences or shootings.

In January 1933, the paper *Kolkoznyi put* published a series of articles on the social origins of the people working at the factory-kitchen of Sverdlovsk. A lot of *outsiders* in Soviet society could be found there: dekulakised persons, a former mill owner, a horse owner and so on. When party members of the factory-kitchen met to discuss these articles, it appears that everybody knew about these outsiders. They had been consciously recruited and somehow protected at a time when everybody was searching for former kulaks. No solidarity, however, existed once the reality was revealed. These people were fired and the managers of the factory blamed.[24] It is, as if, when facing symbolic and real violence, society provided shelters for outsiders. Eventually, these were attacked and exposed, but they often managed to form again somewhere else, subsequently prompting more violence. Authorities were therefore forever trying to solve 'once and for all', to use the sadly well-known expression for the operational order 00447, what could not be solved at all.

There are a plethora of examples of desensitization to the scandal. During the second half of the 1930s, the so-called books of complaints were supposed to be found in all administrations, shops or places opened to the public (even if it was far from always the case[25]). There, citizens were able to write their remarks on the poor quality of services or products. Directors had to reply, but in reality, they paid very little attention to these grievances: their answers were in general superficial and careless. In February 1936, to workers complaining because of a fly found in the soup, a director answered: 'the fly was not contagious!'[26] Workers from the evening shift in a factory complained that they were 'hungry as by the evening nothing is left at the buffet,' and were told by the director 'I gave instructions, but they were not obeyed!' Later, in 1937, when a customer revealed that he found two cockroaches on his sandwich, the director suggested to 'apply the highest measurement of social protection to the cockroaches.' An irony that sounded very strange in the period when these measures were applied to hundreds of Soviet citizens.[27]

When Rosalinda Zemliatcha, a well-known official from Moscow checked the Sormovo plant in Nizhnii Novgorod, one could have expected that this woman called by the poet Dem'ian Bednyi 'the terror for bureaucrats and the pen pushers'[28] would have been feared. It was far from the case. When she summoned a local trade-union head to a show trial, she received an answer that he did not have the time as he had to take part in a presidium meeting of the local trade-union committee!:

> I told him that we could have the presidium meeting and with all its members we could go and listen to what the workers have to say about the food provisioning. To this, he answered that he cannot postpone this meeting, as the meeting agenda has been planned a long time ago.[29]

No real sanctions (and mostly blame) were decided by the local authorities after her inspection, leaving no hope for a real improvement.

This brings us back to the neglecting of 'objective reasons'. Holding individuals responsible did not solve the problems that kept arising over and over again. Nothing really changed because nothing could change as the only explanation put forward was sabotage. This was further reinforced as the collective catering system was not a priority in the practice of many responsible people. This obvious lack of interest from the authorities in collective catering is important to highlight and was different from other more sensitive fields. One of the secretaries of Gorkii obkom, for instance, used the expression *melochi obshchepita*, the 'little things' of collective catering.[30] Factory directors were not interested in diverting their money to these places, as fulfilling their production plan was a higher priority. Even simple Soviet people did not want to eat in these canteens when they had the choice. Militants, cooperative workers or more generally persons in charge of the *obshchepit* therefore had to do whatever they could to attract customers and money or face failure by closing refectories, often only a few months after they were opened.

The impossible improvement of an ever-failing system was a major dimension of the Soviet collective catering experiment. This undoubtedly provoked a sense of powerlessness and of despair that could prove to be very frightening. Violence was, from time to time, a way, the only way, to get out of this dead end. This was particularly the case during the so-called Great terror.

Liquidation of the consequences of sabotage

During 1937 and going into late 1938, a whirlwind of violence swept through the country. The point here is not to write this story. However, repression affected the collective catering system as it did many other professional sectors.

All over the country, arrests and tension were raised after the February–March Plenum of the Central Committee. On 13 June 1937, a meeting held in Moscow was devoted to the 'fight against sabotage in the collective catering system.'[31] Participants were people in charge of canteens from all over the country. The recent arrest of Ian Olski, the head of the sector gave a special meaning to these exchanges.[32] The verbatim record of the meeting shows how tense the situation was for the workers of the system when the accusation of sabotage could be addressed to any of them at any time. Criticism was mainly directed upwards to the head of the system, even to Anastas Mikoian himself, who was accused of not being sufficiently present by one of the participants.[33] The meeting showed how explanations for the situation confused people. The directors of canteens and cooks tried to focus on their working conditions and referred to material problems. Yet at the same time, they used the violent vocabulary about spies and enemies, although most of the time these words were directed to already 'unmasked' people. One of the participants, in despair, complained that 'we are not a commercial system, not a productive system, we are none of a system. We are without any system, without any law.'[34] But one of his colleagues, Israel Gitis, the Moscow head of the restaurant, cafés and canteens administration refused these structural explanations and criticized his colleagues:

> Bear in mind, comrades, about every case of foreign objects [found in the food], I'll tell you as a way of criticism and self-criticism, that the majority of workers still don't understand that every occurrence [can be explained] at 99% by the [action of the] enemy.[35]

The same ambiguity can be found in Nizhnii Novgorod (called Gorkii since 1932). There, also, arrests had not stopped since the summer of 1937. The collective catering system was no exception. The head of the canteen trust, Piotr Adamovich Tarasevich, had been arrested on 17 December.[36] Aleksei Burov, second secretary of the party regional committee, a close collaborator of the former First Secretary Eduard Pramnek,[37] had also been arrested with all the top leaders of the province in June 1938. He had been in charge of questions linked with food, rationing and distribution since the beginning of the 1930s. Tarasevich's deputy Shokhin was also dismissed in July, although not arrested.[38] These were the most well-known among many others.

As elsewhere in Soviet Union, the official explanation of the repression was linked to spying and sabotage. During the sixth regional party conference, at the beginning of July 1938, Iulii Kaganovich, the new first secretary of the obkom declared, 'in our province and in our provincial party organisation operated during the last few years an underground right-trotskyist, sabotage, spying, terrorist and subversive organisation headed by Pramnek, Pakhomov, Stoliar, Pogrebinskii, Burov and Zashibaev and others.'[39] The charges filed against the former officials were not known precisely. Incriminating articles from the penal code were vague enough to allow a large spectrum of interpretation.

Most of these people working in the *obshchepit* system were however not arrested and shot because of their professional activities. Tarasevich was arrested because of his Polish nationality and because of his 'links' with Olskii, the central head of the *obshchepit* and a former chekist. In his personal file, his professional activities were almost not mentioned at all. Rather he was accused, like many victims of the Terror, of spying for Poland.[40] Burov fell because he was part of the Pramnek team. But this information remained largely unknown to the population, who could only see what was happening and had to make sense of these arrests.

People, who knew the arrested in their professional environment, tried therefore to find traces of their sabotage. Explicit links between professional activities and terror were made especially during the so-called campaign on 'liquidation of the consequences of sabotage'. In the Gorkii region, a special meeting concerning the collective catering system was organized in the capital city on 11 August 1938, bringing together seventy-one people.[41] This was meant to rationalize and give a sense of what had happened during the last year. The official line was clear: all that was wrong may be explained by the clear and conscious action of enemies from inside. These enemies have been unmasked, but now we have to think about the way to deal with this.

As in Moscow, the Gorkii meeting revealed the difficulties experienced by the participants in interpreting what had happened in recent months. The top bosses stuck to the sabotage narrative. Individuals were to be unmasked. These were the first words of Prokoviev, Tarasevich's successor:

> These tasks, above all, consist in the necessary and extremely rapid liquidation of the consequences of the sabotage and addressing the question of the definitive uprooting of the enemies of the people. We need to purge the Soviet apparatus of enemies and their afterbirth, to give more importance to verified employees of our

organisation, to the Bolshevik education of the specialists and to the liquidation of the so many shocking things that exist in the system of trade and of collective catering.[42]

Even though he criticized these words (as 'too insipid'[43]), Sukhanov, a gorkom representative, followed the same logic during his interventions that looked for the 'hand of the enemy' behind all the problems.

Some participants, however, tried to criticize this approach. This was particularly the case of a certain Fedosseev from the Kaganovitch district:

> Here, we need to act, we need to look at what's happening and not only to accuse people, saying that they don't want to work, we need to look at what is making their work difficult. There was Malyshev, the food provisioning was bad. Now there is no more Malyshev, but the provisioning is bad again. The provisioning sector is poorly working.[44]

Before, at the beginning of the meeting, as Prokoviev was trying to explain that problems were not linked to a deficit of food products but to the incompetence of managers, somebody in the room shouted, 'tell us please where there is cheese, sausages and tomatoes!'[45]

But this was a dangerous route. Bolshevik leaders refused to think in terms of the shortcomings of the system. It would have been too risky and staggering. Reading the verbatim report of this meeting, one has the feeling that some participants approached the limits of the thinkable and some ideas could not be said or even thought. The concluding speech of Sukhanov not only closed the meeting but set the limits. That interpretation had to be political was the message he developed in harsh terms.

After three days of discussion, Sukhanov stated:

> Staff, this is the first and the main thing we need to deal with in order to really liquidate the consequences of sabotage. Purge the staff, study them, form them. How is the situation in your trust? We know, and some of the participants have correctly said that Tarasevich did not work alone. Nobody here will ever believe us if we say that this obscene enemy worked alone in the trust. [...] This means that he left behind profound roots, that went deep down and are very well masked. [...] Why don't you unmask them? Because we, comrades, don't master enough the art of unmasking. You should know that to catch an enemy is not a simple affair, a trivial affair.[46]

Saying this, Sukhanov opened once more the field to personal attacks, to denunciations, to violence. But no real discussion on the way the collective catering system had to work was possible.

The years 1937 and 1938 were years of great violence for the Soviet people and among them for those working in the numerous canteens all over the Soviet Union. They were denounced in the pages of local and national newspapers. Some of them were brought to justice, condemned, sent to camps or even shot. Others were caught in the jaws of the special operations of the NKVD. They had to take part in numerous meetings and forced to take part in the violence, naming people guilty or supposedly guilty of the countless problems canteens had to cope with.

Violence, though of a different kind, had been an everyday feature for these people's lives since the launching of the construction of thousands of canteens all over the country. Canteens lacked everything: premises, qualified staff and most of all food. The urgency in which they were built and the overall shortages in the country led to canteens that were never able to fulfil the promises vaunted in the official discourse of clean, hygienic, healthy and efficient places. This unavoidable failure led to the first violence. Customers were forced to eat inedible dishes in dark and dirty halls. Servants were not able to justify the unjustifiable and protected themselves by rudeness and symbolic violence. Some thought of only themselves and began to steal. Managers lied and tried with all the flexibility in the law to do what they could to feed the workers. In doing so, they were often on the other side of Soviet legality and likely to be persecuted. This sword of Damocles was also an everyday form of violence.

The authorities made it even more unbearable. No reflection was ever possible on the reasons for these problems. The impossibility can be explained most simply by the fact that no direct criticism of the government was possible. Moreover, the voluntarism of the Bolsheviks could not be hemmed in by 'objective reasons'. Through their commitment, staff and customers had to make things happen, to storm the fortresses.

This absence of thinking about real causes made it impossible to solve problems that therefore were always there. The only way was to hold individuals responsible for the dysfunctions. This, also, led to the need to unmask people. The explosive cocktail for 1937 was ready.

NOTES

Introduction

1 Carl Friedrich and Zbigniew Brzezinski, *Totalitarian Dictatorship and Autocracy* (Cambridge, MA, 1956); Merle Fainsod, *How Russia Is Ruled* (Cambridge, MA, 1954); Leonard Schapiro, *The Origin of the Communist Autocracy: Political Opposition in the Soviet State, First Phase, 1917–1922* (London, 1955); Leonard Schapiro, *Origin of the Communist Autocracy* and idem, *The Communist Party of the Soviet Union*, 2nd ed. (New York, 1960); Robert V. Daniels, *The Conscience of the Revolution* (Cambridge, MA, 1960), pp. 11–12, 111; Adam Ulam, *Lenin and the Bolsheviks: The Intellectual and Political History of the Triumph of Communism in Russia* (London, 1965); Richard Pipes, *The Formation of the Soviet Union, Communism and Nationalism, 1917–23* (Cambridge, MA, 1954); idem, *The Russian Revolution* (London, 1990); idem, *Russia under the Bolshevik Regime* (London, 1994); idem, *The Three Whys of the Russian Revolution* (Toronto, 1995); and Merle Fainsod, revised edition., *How Russia Is Ruled* (London and Cambridge, MA, 1963).

2 Robert C. Tucker, *Stalin as Revolutionary, 1879–1929: A Study in History and Personality* (New York, 1973); Stephen Cohen, *Bukharin and the Bolshevik Revolution: A Political Biography 1888–1938* (New York, 1973).

3 Daniels, *The Conscience of the Revolution*; Cohen, *Bukharin and the Bolshevik Revolution*.

4 Alexander Rabinowitch, *Prelude to Revolution* and *The Bolsheviks Come to Power* (New York, 1976); S. A. Smith, *Red Petrograd: Revolution in the Factories* (Cambridge, 1983).

5 Moshe Lewin, *The Making of the Soviet System: Essays in the Social History of Interwar Russia* (New York, 1985); Sheila Fitzpatrick, 'The civil war as a formative experience', in Abbott Gleason, Peter Kenez and Richard Stites (eds), *Bolshevik Culture: Experiment and Order in the Russian Revolution* (Bloomington, 1985), pp. 57–76; Robert Service, *The Bolshevik Party in Revolution: A Study in Organizational Change, 1917–1923* (London, 1979); T. H. Rigby, *Lenin's Government: Sovnarkom, 1917–22* (Cambridge, 1979).

6 Yanni Kotsonis and David L. Hoffman, *Russian Modernity: Politics, Knowledge, Practices* (New York, 1999); Stephen Kotkin, *Magnetic Mountain: Stalinism as Civilization* (Berkeley, 1997); Kotkin, 'Modern times: The Soviet Union and the interwar conjuncture', *Kritika: Explorations in Russian and Eurasian History*, 2/1 (2001), pp. 111–64; Michael David-Fox, *Crossing Borders: Modernity, Ideology, and Culture in Russia and the Soviet Union* (Pittsburgh, PA, 2015).

7 Gustave Le Bon's 1896 work: *The Crowd: A Study of the Popular Mind* (Dunwoody, 1968); Oswald Spengler, *The Decline of the West* (Allen and Unwin, 1918); Jose Ortega y Gasset, *The Revolt of the Masses* (W.W. Norton, 1932).

8 Martin Pugh, *The Making of Modern British Politics 1867–1939* (Blackwell, 1982), pp. 5–6.

9 On resistance to the extension of the suffrage, see, for example, Janet L. Polasky, 'A revolution for socialist reforms: The Belgian general strike for universal suffrage', *Journal of Contemporary History* 27/3 (1992), pp. 449–66; Sven Beckert, 'Democracy and its discontents: Contesting suffrage tights in Gilded Age New York', *Past and Present* 174 (2002), pp. 116–57; R. Szpoluk, 'Masaryk's idea of democracy', *The Slavonic and East European*

Review 41/96 (1962), pp. 31–49; Jesús Millán and María Cruz Romeo, 'Was the liberal revolution important to modern Spain? Political cultures and citizenship in Spanish history', *Social History* 29/3 (2004), pp. 284–300.

10 David H. Close, 'The collapse of resistance to democracy: Conservatives, adult suffrage, and second chamber reform, 1911–1928', *The Historical Journal* 20/4 (1977), p. 112.

11 V. I. Lenin, 'State and revolution', in James E. Connor (ed.), *Lenin on Politics and Revolution* (New York, 1968), pp. 191–2.

12 Ibid., p. 209.

13 Ibid., p. 192.

14 Ibid., p. 211.

15 Ibid., p. 207. Lenin is quoting Marx: 'The Commune was formed of the municipal councillors, chosen by universal suffrage in the various wards of Paris, responsible and revocable at any time. The majority of its members were naturally working men, or acknowledged representatives of the working class.'

16 Ibid., p. 209. Towards the end of the pamphlet he asserted that all of society 'will take part in the administration of the state.' If these ideas are connected, it would create an absurd situation in which all of working population would be subject to election.

17 Ibid., p. 197.

18 Ibid., p. 198.

19 Thomas F. Remington, *Building Socialism in Bolshevik Russia: Ideology and Industrial Organisation, 1917–1921* (Pittsburgh, 1984), chs. 2–3.

20 Wendy Z. Goldman, *Women, the State and Revolution: Soviet Family Policy and Social Life, 1917–1936* (Cambridge, 1993).

21 Lynne Mally, *Culture of the Future: The Proletkult Movement in Revolutionary Russia* (Berkeley, 1990).

22 Peter H. Solomon Jr., 'Soviet penal policy, 1917–1934: A reinterpretation', *Slavic Review* 39/2 (1980), pp. 195–217.

23 Daniels, *The Conscience of the Revolution*, ch. 4; Remington, *Building Socialism in Bolshevik Russia*, pp. 115–16.

24 V. I. Lenin, 'Can the Bolsheviks retain state power?' in V. I. Lenin (ed.), *Selected Works* (London, 1969), p. 381.

25 V. I. Lenin, 'Better fewer, but better', in Lenin, *Selected Works*, pp. 700–1.

26 Sheila Fitzpatrick, *Education and Social Mobility in the Soviet Union 1921–1934* (Cambridge, 1979); Michael David-Fox, *Revolution of the Mind: Higher Learning among the Bolsheviks, 1918–1929* (Ithaca, 1997).

27 *Trinadtsataia Konferentsiia Rossiiskoi Kommunisticheskoi Partii (Bolshevikov)* (Moscow, 1924), pp. 93, 100–1.

28 Ibid.

Chapter 1

1 I will use the New Style calendar throughout.

2 V. I. Lenin, 'Gosudarstvo i revoliutsiia', *Polnoe sobranie sochinenii*, vol. 33 (Moscow, 1962), p. 19; also p. 81 (from now on: *PSS*).

3 Ibid., p. 116.

Notes

4   Ibid., p. 100.
5   Neil Harding, *Lenin's Political Thought*, vol. 2, *Theory and Practice in the Socialist Revolution* (London, Basingstoke, 1981), chs. 5, 6.
6   Kevin Anderson, *Lenin, Hegel, and Western Marxism: A Critical Study* (Urbana, Chicago, 1995), pp. 155–6.
7   Christopher Read, *Lenin: A Revolutionary Life* (London, New York, 2005), ch. 5. Quotation p. 171.
8   Ibid., p. 171.
9   James Ryan, *Lenin's Terror: The Ideological Origins of Early Soviet State Violence* (London, New York, 2012), pp. 74–6.
10 Christopher Hill, *Lenin and the Russian Revolution* (London, 1947), pp. 107–8.
11 Alain Besançon, *The Intellectual Origins of Leninism* (Oxford, 1981), p. 262.
12 See, for example, Harding, *Lenin's Political Thought*, pp. 98–102; James D. White, *Lenin: The Practice and Theory of Revolution* (Basingstoke, New York, 2001), p. 135; Read, *Lenin*, p. 169. See also Vincent Barnett, *The Revolutionary Russian Economy, 1890–1940: Ideas, Debates and Alternatives* (London, New York, 2004), pp. 54–5.
13 Lars T. Lih, *Lenin* (London, 2001), pp. 136–7.
14 See A.J. Polan, *Lenin and the End of Politics* (London, 1984), especially chs. 2, 3. Quotation p. 94. For another critique of the illiberal character of Lenin's proposals in *State and Revolution*, see Robert Service, *Lenin: A Biography* (London, Basingstoke, Oxford, 2000), pp. 293–8.
15 Tamás Krausz, *Reconstructing Lenin: An Intellectual Biography* (New York, 2015), pp. 190–6.
16 Ibid., pp. 196, 198, 201–2.
17 Ibid., pp. 199, 202.
18 Ibid., pp. 178–80, 198.
19 Nikolai Bukharin, 'Toward a theory of the imperialist state'. Available at https://www.marxists.org/archive/bukharin/works/1915/state.htm (accessed 24 August 2017).
20 See Sidney Heitman (ed.), *Nikolai Bukharin: A Bibliography* (Stanford, 1969), p. 29; Stephen F. Cohen, *Bukharin and the Bolshevik Revolution: A Political Biography, 1888–1938* (London, 1974), p. 39.
21 Nikolai Bukharin, 'Der imperialistische Raubstaat'. Available at https://libcom.org/library/der-imperialistische-raubstaat-nikolai-bukharin (accessed 24 August 2017). For Lenin's notes in this version of Bukharin's text: *PSS*, vol. 33, pp. 331–8.
22 'Internatsional molodezhi (Zametki)', *PSS*, vol. 30, pp. 227–8.
23 'Manifest der Kommunistischen Partei' (Marx/Engels, 1848), Karl Marx and Friedrich Engels, *Werke*, vol. 4 (Berlin, 1977), p. 481 (from now on: *MEW*).
24 'Der achtzehnte Brumaire des Louis Bonaparte', *MEW*, vol. 8, pp. 196–7.
25 'Der Bürgerkrieg in Frankreich' (1871), *MEW*, vol. 17, pp. 336–43.
26 See, for example, 'Herrn Eugen Dührings Umwälzung der Wissenschaft' (1877–8/Engels), *MEW*, vol. 20, pp. 261–2; 'Der Ursprung der Familie, des Privateigentums und des Staats' (1884/Engels), vol. 21, pp. 165–7.
27 *MEW*, vol. 4, p. 482.
28 'Von der Autorität', *MEW*, vol. 17, p. 308.

29 'Herrn', *MEW*, vol. 20, p. 262.
30 Karl Kautsky, *Das Erfurter Programm: In seinem grundsätzlichen Teil erläutert* (Bonn-Bad Godesberg, 1974), pp. 124–5, 212–17.
31 Karl Kautsky, 'Die neue Taktik. IV: Die Eroberung der Staatsmacht (Schluss)', *Die Neue Zeit*, vol. 30/2./46 (1912), pp. 725, 727, 732. See also Karl Kautsky, *Die Soziale Revolution*, vol. 2, *Am Tage nach der sozialen Revolution* (Berlin, 1902), p. 16.
32 See 'Marksizm o gosudarstve', *PSS*, vol. 33, pp. 123–307, for example p. 172.
33 Lenin to Kollontai, 17 February 1917: *PSS*, vol. 49, p. 388; Lenin to Armand, 19 February: ibid., p. 390. For Lenin on Kautsky and Pannekoek: 'Pis'ma iz daleka', third letter (24 March): *PSS*, vol. 31, p. 39; 'O zadachakh RSDRP v russkoi revoliutsii' (written 29 or 30 March), vol. 31, p. 76. For the Lenin-Bukharin debate on the state, see also Harding, *Lenin's Political Thought*, pp. 94–8, 102–9, 114–17; Anderson, *Lenin*, pp. 152–3; White, *Lenin*, p. 142.
34 *MEW*, vol. 20, pp. 259–60.
35 'Zur Kritik des sozialdemokratischen Programmentwurfs 1891', *MEW*, vol. 22, pp. 231–2.
36 'Die Bauernfrage' (1894), *MEW*, vol. 22, p. 504.
37 Rudolf Hilferding, *Das Finanzkapital* (Frankfurt M., 1973), pp. 503–7.
38 See, for example, Paul Lensch, *Die deutsche Sozialdemokratie und der Weltkrieg* (Berlin, 1915), pp. 54–64.
39 See M. E. Falkus, *The Industrialisation of Russia 1700–1914* (London, Basingstoke, 1972), pp. 68–9, 77–8 (quotation p. 77); Barnett, *Revolutionary Russian Economy*, pp. 27–9, 35; Alexander Polunov, *Russia in the Nineteenth Century: Autocracy, Reform, and Social Change, 1814–1914* (New York, London, 2005), pp. 197–8; S. A. Smith, *Russia in Revolution: An Empire in Crisis, 1890 to 1928* (Oxford, 2017), pp. 34–7, 92.
40 'Groziashchaia katastrofa i kak s nei borot'sia' (written 23–7 September), *PSS*, vol. 34, p. 191.
41 See, for example, 17 April speech at Bolshevik conference: *PSS*, vol. 31, pp. 110–11; 'Otsenka momenty' (written 21–6 April), vol. 31, p. 143; 7 May speech at Seventh Party Conference: vol. 31, pp. 355–6; 'Voina i revoliutsiia' (27 May), vol. 32, p. 83; 'Materialy po peresmotru partiinoi programmy' (20 May), vol. 32, p. 139; 'Groziashchaia katastrofa', vol. 34, pp. 168, 191–2; 'Uderzhat li bol'sheviki gosudarstvennuiu vlast'?' (written 14 October), vol. 34, p. 307; 'K peresmotru partiinoi programmy' (written 19–21 October), vol. 34, p. 373.
42 'Rech' v zashchitu rezoliutsii o tekushchem momente', *PSS*, vol. 31, pp. 443–5. See also Lenin's comments on Aleksei Rykov in his 7 May speech: vol. 31, p. 363. I believe this belies James White's (*Lenin*, p. 133) and Read's (*Lenin*, pp. 166–7) view that Lenin's confidence in the prospects of socialism in backward Russia was underpinned by purely political and no economic considerations.
43 *PSS*, vol. 33, p. 38.
44 Ibid., pp. 42–3. See also p. 116.
45 For example, 17 April speech: *PSS*, vol. 31, p. 108; 'S"ezd krest'ianskikh deputatov' (29 April), vol. 31, p. 273.
46 See, for example, 17 April speech: *PSS*, vol. 31, p. 108; 'O dvoevlastii' (22 April), vol. 31, p. 146; 'Nashi vzglaidy' (1 May), vol. 31, p. 280; 'Gosudarstvo i revoliutsiia', vol. 33, pp. 42–3, 48, 109, 114.

Notes

47 'Neminuemaia katastrofa i bezmernye obeshchaniia', second instalment (30 May), *PSS*, vol. 32, p. 111.
48 'Gosudarstvo i revoliutsiia', *PSS*, vol. 33, p. 50.
49 'Uderzhat li', *PSS*, vol. 34, pp. 312, 320.
50 *PSS*, vol. 33, pp. 108–9.
51 Ibid., p. 50.
52 Ibid., p. 101. Also pp. 97, 100.
53 'Groziashchaia katastrofa', *PSS*, vol. 34, p. 192.
54 'Uderzhat li', *PSS*, vol. 34, p. 307.
55 'Gosudarstvo i revoliutsiia', *PSS*, vol. 33, p. 101.
56 'Uderzhat li', *PSS*, vol. 34, pp. 306–7.
57 See for the disastrous conditions and the workers' response: Christopher Read, *War and Revolution in Russia, 1914–22* (Basingstoke, New York), 2013, pp. 96–7; Geoffrey Swain, *The Russian Revolution* (London, New York, 2017), pp. 29, 33, 58–9, 96–100, 105–13; Smith, *Russia*, ch. 3; Tsuyoshi Hasegawa, *Crime and Punishment in the Russian Revolution: Mob Justice and Police in Petrograd* (Cambridge, London, 2017), pp. 109–66.
58 See, for example, 12 May speech, *PSS*, vol. 31, p. 446; 'Otkrytoe pis'mo k delegatam vserossiiskogo s"ezda krest'ianskikh deputatov' (24 May), vol. 32, p. 47; 'Partiia proletariata na vyborakh v raionnye dumy' (26 May), vol. 32, p. 69; 'Grozit razrukha' (27 May), vol. 32, pp. 75–6; 'Neminuemaia katastrofa' (29 May), vol. 32, pp. 106–7; second instalment of this article: vol. 32, pp. 109–10; 'Ischezlo li dvoevlastie?' (2 June), vol. 32, p. 129; 'Materialy', *PSS*, vol. 32, p. 143; 'Rezoliutsiia ob ekonomicheskikh merakh bor'by s razrukhoi' (7 June), vol. 32, pp. 195–7; 13 June speech at first Petrograd conference of factory committees: vol. 32, pp. 239–40; 'Melkoburzhuaznaia pozitsiia v voprose o razrukhe' (14 June), vol. 32, p. 248; 17 June speech at First Congress of Soviets: vol. 32, pp. 267–8; 'Razrukha i proletarskaia bor'ba s nei' (17 June), vol. 32, pp. 293–4; 'Groziashchaia katastrofa', vol. 34, pp. 156–64.
59 'Gosudarstvo i revoliutsiia', *PSS*, vol. 33, p. 102.
60 'Russkaia revoliutsiia i grazhdanskaia voina' (29 September), *PSS*, vol. 34, p. 223; 'Uderzhat li', vol. 34, pp. 308–9.
61 'Pis'ma' (22 March): *PSS*, vol. 31, p. 33; third letter: vol. 31, pp. 42–4; 'Zadachi proletariaia v nashei revoliutsii' (23 April), vol. 31, p. 165; 'Pozabyli glavnoe' (18 May), vol. 32, p. 26.
62 Lih, *Lenin*, p. 136. For Lenin on the need of a *tverdaia* authority: 'O tverdoi revoliutsionnoi vlasti' (19 May): *PSS*, vol. 32, pp. 30–2; 'Rech' po agrarnomu voprosu' (4 June), vol. 32, p. 172.
63 'Pis'ma', third letter, *PSS*, vol. 31, p. 40; 'Zadachi proletariata', *PSS*, vol. 31, p. 163; 'O proletarskoi militsii' (3 May), vol. 31, p. 288; 'Gosudarstvo i revoliutsiia', vol. 33, pp. 42–9, 100–2, 116; 'Odin iz korennykh voprosov revoliutsii' (27 September), vol. 34, p. 202; 'Uderzhat li', vol. 34, pp. 315–16.
64 'Gosudarstvo i revoliutsiia', *PSS*, vol. 33, pp. 44, 49, 78, 100–1; 'Russkaia revoliutsiia', vol. 34, p. 224; 'Uderzhat li', vol. 34, p. 308.
65 'Uderzhat li', *PSS*, vol. 34. p. 315.
66 Ibid., p. 307.
67 Ibid., pp. 313, 316.

68 See for this argumentation: 'Gosudarstvo i revoliutsiia', *PSS*, vol. 33, p. 102. The withering away of the state was mainly about the ultimate demise of classes, which would make repression, even ordinary police work, and therefore the state, superfluous: vol. 33, pp. 89–91.
69 Lenin's thesis that, together with the state, democracy too would fade away meant no more than there would no longer be minority to be repressed by the majority: vol. 33, pp. 19, 82–3, 89.
70 See, for example, 'Gosudarstvo i revoliutsiia', *PSS*, vol. 33, pp. 17, 102.
71 For references to the state of soviets, see, for example, 17 April speech: *PSS*, vol. 31, pp. 107–9; 'O dvoevlastii', vol. 31, p. 148; 'Doklad o tekushchem momente i ob otnoshenii k Vremennomu pravitel'stvu' (27 April), vol. 31, p. 244; 'Gosudarstvo i revoliutsiia', vol. 33, p. 97; 'Uroki revoliutsii' (19 September), vol. 34, p. 60; 'Odin iz', vol. 34, p. 202.
72 'Pobeda kadetov i zadachi rabochei partii' (1906), *PSS*, vol. 12, p. 317.
73 He referred to the project of a Soviet state even in January–February 1917 notes, when soviets were nowhere to be seen: *PSS*, vol. 33, p. 230.
74 'Bürgerkrieg', *MEW*, vol. 17, p. 342.
75 17 April speech, *PSS*, vol. 31, p. 111.
76 Lenin used the term 'direct democracy' only very sporadically. See, for example, 'Uderzhat li', *PSS*, vol. 34, p. 305.
77 'Gosudarstvo i revoliutsiia', *PSS*, vol. 33, p. 24.
78 Ibid., p. 97.
79 See, for example, 'Nashi vzgliady', *PSS*, vol. 31, p. 280; 'O proletarskoi militsii', vol. 31, p. 287.
80 'Pis'ma', third letter, *PSS*, vol. 31, p. 42.
81 'Gosudarstvo i revoliutsiia', *PSS*, vol. 33, pp. 46–8.
82 'Bürgerkrieg', *MEW*, vol. 17, p. 339.
83 'Gosudarstvo i revoliutsiia', *PSS*, vol. 33, pp. 46–8.
84 See, for example, Marx's first draft of 'Bürgerkrieg', *MEW*, vol. 17, p. 546; 'Von der Autorität', vol. 18, p. 308; Marx's 1874–5 notes on Bakunin, vol. 18, p. 630.
85 'Die Klassenkämpfe in Frankreich 1848 bis 1850', *MEW*, vol. 7, p. 33.
86 For a full overview of the known twelve occasions of use of the term, see Hal Draper, *The 'Dictatorship of the Proletariat' from Marx to Lenin* (New York, 1987), pp. 22–39.
87 'Zur Kritik', *MEW*, vol. 22, p. 235.
88 1891 introduction to Marx's 'Bürgerkrieg', *MEW*, vol. 17, p. 625.
89 *MEW*, vol. 4, p. 481.
90 'Gosudarstvo i revoliutsiia', *PSS*, vol. 33, p. 26. For Lenin's definition of the state as 'special detachments (*otriadakh*) of armed people', see ibid., p. 9. See also 'Ursprung', *MEW*, vol. 21, p. 166.
91 'Gosudarstvo i revoliutsiia', *PSS*, vol. 33, p. 7.
92 Ibid., p. 89.
93 For example, 'Zadachi proletariata', *PSS*, vol. 31, p. 181; 'Ischezlo', vol. 32, pp. 128–9; 'Vsia vlast' sovetam!' (18 July), vol. 32, p. 408.

Notes

94 'Ischezlo', *PSS*, vol. 32, p. 129.
95 'Materialy', *PSS*, vol. 32, p. 141.
96 'Gosudarstvo i revoliutsiia', *PSS*, vol. 33, p. 83; also p. 25.
97 Draper, *'Dictatorship of the Proletariat'*, p. 80.
98 Ibid., p. 90.
99 'Doklad ob uchastii sotsial-demokratii vo vremennom revoliutsionnom pravitel'stve', *PSS*, vol. 10, p. 129.
100 'Pobeda kadetov', *PSS*, vol. 12, p. 318.
101 Ibid., p. 320.
102 Ibid., p. 318.
103 Ibid., p. 321.
104 Draper, *'Dictatorship of the Proletariat'*, p. 92. Ryan (*Lenin's Terror*, p. 36) suggests Lenin was mainly referring to the need of extralegal violence during the establishment of the new state, not to the form of the new state. In my reading, Lenin was characterizing the functioning of the revolutionary dictatorship throughout its existence.
105 'O dvoevlasti', *PSS*, vol. 31, pp. 145–6.
106 'Zadachi proletariata', *PSS*, vol. 31, p. 155.
107 Ibid., p. 354.
108 'Epidemiia doverchivosti', *PSS*, vol. 32, p. 315.
109 At one point Lenin defined 'democratic' as 'acting in the interests of the majority of the people and not of a clique (*kuchki*) of the rich': 'Groziashchaia katastrofa', *PSS*, vol. 34, p. 164.
110 Lenin indicated in so many words that corrupted workers too would be placed under dictatorship: 'Gosudarstvo i revoliutsiia', *PSS*, vol. 33, p. 102.
111 *PSS*, vol. 33, p. 26. Throughout the months preceding the revolution Lenin was advertising the Bolshevik party's willingness to seize power *alone*. See, for example, 17 June speech, *PSS*, vol. 32, p. 267; 'O kompromissakh' (written 14–16 September), vol. 34, p. 134; 'Uderzhat li', *PSS*, vol. 34, p. 290.
112 See Claude Nicolet, 'Dictatorship in Rome', in Baehr and Richter (eds), *Dictatorship in History*, pp. 263–78.
113 John P. McCormick, 'From constitutional technique to Caesarist ploy: Carl Schmitt on dictatorship, liberalism, and emergency powers', in Peter Baehr and Melvin Richter (eds), *Dictatorship in History and Theory: Bonapartism, Caesarism, and Totalitarianism* (Cambridge, 2004), p. 209.

Chapter 2

1 See Peter Kenez, *The Birth of the Propaganda State: Soviet Methods of Mass Mobilization, 1917–1929* (New York, 1985).
2 John Rae, *Contemporary Socialism* (New York, 1884), pp. 127–9.
3 Friedrich Engels, 'The Prussian military question and the German Workers' Party', in Marx and Engels, *Collected Works* 20 (New York, 1975–2004), pp. 77–8.

Notes

4   For a more detailed discussion of Lassalle's contribution, see Lars T. Lih, *Lenin Rediscovered* (Chicago, 2006), pp. 53–61; all Lassalle citations are taken from this source.
5   Vernon Lidtke, *The Alternative Culture: Socialist Labor in Imperial Germany* (New York, 1985); Kevin J. Callahan, *Demonstration Culture: European Socialism and the Second International* (Leicester, 2010).
6   Lenin's *Left-Wing Communism*. Available at https://www.marxists.org/archive/lenin/works/1920/lwc/index.htm.
7   Lidtke, *Alternative Culture*.
8   Marc Angenot, *Place au prolétariat conscient et organisé!* (Montréal, 1992).
9   William J. McGrath, *Dionysian Art and Populist Politics in Austria* (New Haven, 1974), p. 222.
10 Callahan, *Demonstration Culture*, p. 134.
11 Ibid., p. 159.
12 Ibid.
13 For a full discussion of Kautsky's role as mentor to Russian Social Democracy in the 1890s, see Lih, *Lenin Rediscovered*, pp. 74–101. All citations from Kautsky are taken from this source.
14 Lenin, *Polnoe sobranie sochinenii* [*PSS*], 3rd ed., vol. 2 (Moscow, 1926–35), p. 616.
15 Martov, *Proletarskaia bor'ba v Rossii* (St. Petersburg, 1904), p. 80.
16 For a detailed discussion of Kuskova's *Credo*, see Lih, *Lenin Rediscovered*, pp. 221–40.
17 K. M. Takhtarev, *Rabochee dvizhenie v Peterburge 1893–1901 gg.* (Leningrad, 1924), pp. 179–81.
18 Lenin, *PSS*, 5th ed., vol. 7 (1958–65), p. 133.
19 Lenin, *PSS*, vol. 7, pp. 139–40.
20 Lenin *PSS*, vol. 22, p. 199 (unpublished article of November 1912); 'radical change in the entire political system' is a euphemism for 'revolution' that was used to get past the censor.
21 The concept of Erfurtianism is discussed at length in Lih, *Lenin Rediscovered*.
22 Moissaye J. Olgin, *The Soul of the Russian Revolution* (New York, 1917), pp. 282–91.
23 'Partiinaia organizatsiia i partiinaia literatura' in Lenin, *PSS*, vol. 12, pp. 99–105.
24 Kenez, *Propaganda State*, pp. 36–7.
25 For discussion of a similar argument from Lenin in *What Is to Be Done?*, see Lih, *Lenin Rediscovered*.
26 Bukharin, *Program of the Communists* (this work was written to express party consensus and not the views of the Left Communist faction). Bukharin's *Program of the Communists (Bolsheviks)* (1918) is available online under the title *Programme of the World Revolution*: http://www.marxists.org/archive/bukharin/works/1918/worldrev/index.html (accessed 12 June 2018).
27 Draper, *The 'Dictatorship of the Proletariat' from Marx to Lenin* (New York, 1987), p. 142.
28 John Riddell (ed.), *Workers of the World and Oppressed Peoples, Unite! Proceedings and Documents of the Second Congress, 1920*, vol. 1 (New York, 1991), p. 153.
29 Besides Kenez, *Propaganda State*, see Victoria E. Bonnell, *Iconography of Power Soviet Political Posters under Lenin and Stalin* (Berkeley, 1997); James von Geldern, *Bolshevik Festivals, 1917–1920* (Berkeley, 1993); Karen Petrone, *Life Has Become More Joyous*,

Notes

Comrades: Celebrations in the Time of Stalin (Bloomington, 2000); Jeffrey Brooks, *Thank You, Comrade Stalin!: Soviet Public Culture from Revolution to Cold War* (Princeton, 2000); Nina Tumarkin, *Lenin Lives!: The Lenin Cult in Soviet Russia* (Cambridge, MA, 1983); Jan Plamper, *The Stalin Cult: A Study in the Alchemy of Power* (New Haven, 2012); Kevin Morgan, *International Communism and the Cult of the Individual Leaders, Tribunes and Martyrs under Lenin and Stalin* (Cham, Switzerland, 2017).

30 Lenin, 'Partiinaia organizatsiia'.

31 For Lunacharskii's account of First of May, see *A. V. Lunacharskii o massovykh prazdnestvakh, estrade, tsirke* (Moscow, 1981), pp. 80–4.

32 For a more detailed comparison of the two international congresses, see my review of Callaghan's *Demonstration Culture* in *The International Newsletter of Communist Studies* 19/26 (2013).

33 Riddell, *Workers of the World*, pp. 4–5. I had the opportunity to annotate a wide range of photographs from the Comintern's visit to Petrograd; see Andre Liebich and Svetlana Yakimovich (eds), *From Communism to Anti-Communism: Photographs from the Boris Souvarine Collection at the Graduate Institute, Geneva* (Geneva, 2016). Von Geldern, *Bolshevik Festivals* devotes a chapter to the second congress in 1920.

34 John D. Littlepage and Demaree Bess, *In Search of Soviet Gold* (London, 1939), p. 222. For an important case study of campaignism during the 1930s, see John McCannon, *Red Arctic: Polar Exploration and the Myth of the North in the Soviet Union, 1932–1939* (Oxford, 1998).

35 Olga Velikanova uses such campaigns as an organizing device in Velikanova, *Popular Perceptions of Soviet Politics in the 1920s: Disenchantment of the Dreamers* (Cham, Switzerland, 2013); *Mass Political Culture under Stalinism: Popular Discussion of the Soviet Constitution of 1936* (Cham, Switzerland, 2018).

Chapter 3

1 Gosudarstvennyi arkhiv Rossiiskoi Federatsii (hereafter GARF), f. R141, op. 10, d. 1, l. 169; Gosudarstvennyi arkhiv Sverdlovskoi oblasti (hereafter GASO), f. R1196, op. 1, d. 4, l. 115.

2 Lars T. Lih, *Bread and Authority in Russia, 1914–1921* (Berkeley, 1990), p. 60.

3 'Zhurnal No. 13', *Bor'ba*, No. 13, 13 July 1917.

4 Ibid., l. 497.

5 GASO, f. 62, op. 1, d. 620, l. 484.

6 Ibid., l. 175.

7 GASO, f. R1573, op. 1, d. 28, ll. 72–4.

8 GASO, f. 62, op. 1, d. 620, l. 613.

9 Hasegawa, *Crime and Punishment in the Russian Revolution*, p. 2.

10 'Krazhi', *Ural'skaia zhizn'* (*UV*), No. 75, 9 April 1917; 'Nanesenie ran', *Zaural'skii krai* (*ZK*), No. 153, 14 July 1917; 'Ubiistvo', *UV*, No. 142, 4 July 1917; 'Publichnoe nakazanie', *UV*, No. 115, 31 May 1917.

11 GASO, f. 62, op. 1, d. 620, l. 170.

12 'Eshche odin samosud', *ZK*, No. 147, 7 July 1917; 'Napadenie na F.G. Shcherbakova', *ZK*, No. 117, 31 May 1917; 'Soldaty-vory', *ZK*, No. 115, 28 May 1917.

13 'Nashi zadachi', *Bor'ba*, No. 7, 1 May 1917.
14 'Achinskii eshelon', *Dumy Urala* (*DU*), No. 14, 28 April 1917.
15 'Sobitiia 26 aprelia', *UV*, No. 90, 28 April 1917.
16 GASO, f. R1573, op. 1, d. 28, l. 115; d. 4, l. 162.
17 'Na ulitsakh goroda', *ZK*, No. 93, 29 April 1917; 'Ekaterinburgskaia Gorodskaia Prodovol'stvennaia Uprava', *ZK*, No. 100, 7 May 1917.
18 GASO, f. R1573, op. 1, d. 28, l. 126.
19 'Protokol obshchevo sobraniia S.R. i S.D., 27 April 1917', *Bor'ba*, No. 8, 6 May 1917.
20 I.V. Orlov, *Kommunal'naia strana: Stanovlenie sovetskogo zhilishchno-kommunal'nogo khoziastva (1917–1941)* (Moscow, 2015), p. 65.
21 GASO, f. R1196, op. 1, d. 4, l. 115.
22 GASO, R1573, op. 1, d. 22, l. 2.
23 Ibid., l. 36.
24 Ibid., l. 34.
25 Orlando Figes and Boris Kolonitskii, *Interpreting the Russian Revolution: The Language and Symbols of 1917* (New Haven, CT, 1999), p. 43.
26 Sarah Badcock, *Politics and the People in Revolutionary Russia: A Provincial Study* (Cambridge, 2007), p. 55.
27 GASO, f. R1573, op. 1, d. 28, l. 84.
28 'Partii na vyborakh v raionnye dumy Petrograda', in V. I. Lenin (ed.), *Polnoe sobranie sochinenii*, 5th Printing, vol. 32 (Moscow, 1969), 191.
29 *Bor'ba*, No. 14, 29 July 1917; Tsentr dokumentatsii obshchestvennykh organizatsii Sverdlovskoi oblasti (hereafter TsDOO SO), f. 41, op. 1, d. 75, l. 6.
30 TsDOO SO, f. 41, op. 1, d. 76, l. 181.
31 'Platforma Sotsialistov-Revoliutsionerov pri vyborakh v Ekaterinburgskuiu Gorodskuiu Narodnuiu Dumu', *DU*, No. 33, 11 July 1917; 'Munitsipal'naia platforma Ekb. Komiteta R. S.-D. Rab. Partiia', *UV*, No. 146, 8 July 1917.
32 GASO, f. 62, op. 1, d. 620, l. 473.
33 'Munitsipal'naia platforma Ekb: Komiteta R. S.-D. Rab. Partiia', *UV*, No. 146, 8 July 1917.
34 A. Paramonov, 'Svoboda slova', *Bor'ba*, No. 8, 6 May 1917.
35 'Resul'taty vyborov v Ekaterinburgskuiu Gorodskuiu Dumu', *DU*, No. 55, 2 August 1917; TsDOO SO, f. 41, op. 1, d. 70, l. 24.
36 GASO, f. 62, op. 1, d. 620, ll. 524–5.
37 Ibid., ll. 524–8.
38 L. A. Obukhov, *Sovety Urala v 1917 godu* (Perm', 1992), p. 27; 'Protokol obshchego sobraniia No.1 S.R. i S.D.,' *Bor'ba*, No. 10, 5 June 1917.
39 V. Vorob'ev, *Oktiabr'skie dni v Ekaterinburge: Ocherk* (Sverdlovsk, 1927), p. 25; Donald J. Raleigh, *Revolution on the Volga: 1917 in Saratov* (Ithaca, 1986), p. 201.
40 'Sobranie R. i S. Deputatov, 25-go oktiabria', *UV*, No. 174, 28 October 1917.
41 Vorob'ev, *Oktiabr'skie dni v Ekaterinburge*, p. 30.
42 'Istoricheskii den'' v Ekaterinburge', *Bor'ba*, No. 16, 28 October 1917.
43 TsDOO SO, f. 221, op. 2, d. 212, l. 183.

Notes

44 TsDOO SO, f. 41, op. 2, d. 154, l. 33.
45 'Istoricheskii den'' v Ekaterinburge', *Bor'ba*, No. 16, 28 October 1917; TsDOO SO, f. 41, op. 2, d. 154, l. 44.
46 Vladimir P. Anichkov, *Ekaterinburg-Vladivostok (1917–1922)* (Moscow, 1998), p. 61.
47 'V Soviet R. i S. Deputatov', *UV*, No. 174, 28 October 1917.
48 Ibid.
49 'Chestnaia koalitsiia', *Ural'skii rabochii* (*UR*), No. 26, 1 November 1917.
50 TsDOO SO, f. 41, op. 1, d. 70, l. 6.
51 'Zasedanie Isp. Komiteta 29 okt.', *UR*, No. 26, 1 November 1917.
52 'Ot Oblastnogo Komiteta Sovetov Rabochikh i Soldatskikh Deputatov Urala', *UR*, No. 25, 31 October 1917; 'Revoliutsionnyi komitet', *UV*, No. 182, 10 November 1917.
53 'Za delo', *UR*, No. 25, 31 October 1917; 'Pervye shagi Soveta R. i S. D.', *UV*, No. 174, 28 October 1917.
54 'Vtorichnye vybory v Gorodskuiu Dumu', *UV*, No. 159, 11 October 1917.
55 TsDOO SO, f. 41, op. 1, d. 61, l. 30.
56 'Vybory v gorodskuiu dumu', *UV*, No. 181, 9 November 1917.
57 'Akkordy zhizni', *UV*, No. 182, 10 November 1917.
58 'Novaia gorodskaia uprava', *UV*, No. 191, 21 November 1917.
59 'V gorodskom uprave', *UV*, No. 188, 17 November 1917.
60 'Pervoe sobranie Ekaterinburgskoi gorodskoi dumy', *ZK*, No. 185, 23 November 1917.
61 TsDOO SO, f. 41, op. 2, d. 430, ll. 32, 88.
62 Lev Krol', *Za tri goda: Vospominaniia, vpechatleniia i vstrechi* (Vladivostok, 1921), p. 10.
63 TsDOO SO, f. 41, op. 1, d. 70, l. 6.
64 Hasegawa, *Crime and Punishment in the Russian Revolution*, p. 192.
65 'Vypusk spirta', *UV*, No. 179, 7 November 1917.
66 TsDOO SO, f. 41, op. 2, d. 28, ll. 24–5.
67 TsDOO SO, f. 41, op. 1, d. 102, l. 8.
68 'Ob''iavlenie', *Izvestiia* (Ekaterinburg), No. 8, 20 January 1918.
69 'K naseleniiu', *Izvestiia*, No. 59, 9 April 1918; GASO, f. R64, op. 1, d. 6, ll. 5–12.
70 'Mekhanicheskaia khlebopekarniia', *ZK*, No. 181, 17 November 1917.
71 'Sobranie gorodskoi dumy', *UV*, No. 217, 23 December 1917.
72 'V prodovol'stvennom komitete', *Izvestiia*, No. 7, 19 January 1918.
73 GASO, f. 62, op. 1, d. 620, l. 357.
74 GASO, f. 62, op. 1, d. 624, l. 4, 34.
75 'Gorodskie finansy', *Zaural'skii krai*, 195, 5 December 1917.
76 'Finansovanie goroda', *Zaural'skii krai*, 206, 19 December 1917.
77 'Finansovaia pomoshch' gorodu' *Ural'skaia zhizn'*, 16, 20 January 1918.
78 GASO, f. 62, op. 1, d. 624, l. 34.
79 TsDOO SO, f. 4, op. 1, d. 42, l. 206.
80 TsDOO SO, f. 41, op. 2, d. 23, l. 98.

81 GASO, f. 62, op. 1, d. 62, l. 13.
82 GARF, f. R393, op. 2, d. 7, l. 14.
83 GASO, f. 62, op. 1, d. 624, l. 34.
84 Anichkov, *Ekaterinburg-Vladivostok*, p. 80.
85 'Rospusk gorodskoi dumy', *UV*, No. 38, 2 March 1918.
86 GARF, f. R393, op. 2, d. 7, l. 88.
87 GASO, f. 62, op. 1, Predislovie, l. 6.
88 GASO, f. 62, op. 1, d. 624, l. 10.
89 TsDOO SO, f. 41, op. 2, d. 79, l. 5; 'Pokhorony Krasnogvardeitsev', *UV*, No. 26, 18 February 1918.
90 TsDOO SO, f. 41, op. 1, d. 102, ll. 43–4.
91 TsDOO SO, f. 41, op. 1, d. 70, l. 45a.
92 'Reorganizatsiia militsii', *Izvestiia*, No. 43, 21 March 1918.
93 Alexander Rabinowitch, *The Bolsheviks Come to Power: The Revolution of 1917 in Petrograd* (New York, 1976).

Chapter 4

1 Transcript of 'Direct Line with Putin', 7 June 2018, from the official Kremlin website http://en.kremlin.ru/events/president/news/57692 (accessed 1 December 2018).
2 Ibid.
3 Maureen Perrie, *Pretenders and Popular Monarchism in Early Modern Russia: The False Tsars of the Time of Troubles* (Cambridge, 1995); Daniel Field, *Rebels in the Name of the Tsar* (London, 1989).
4 See Lara Douds, *Inside Lenin's Government: Ideology, Power and Practice in the Early Soviet State* (London, 2018).
5 Edward L. Keenan, 'Muscovite political folkways', *The Russian Review* 45/2 (April 1986), pp. 115–81; V. Kozlov, 'Sheila Fitzpatrick: Russian context', in Golfo Alexopoulos, Julie Hessler and Kiril Tomoff (eds), *Writing the Stalin Era: Sheila Fitzpatrick and Soviet Historiography* (New York, 2011), p. 222. See also Lewin, *The Making of the Soviet System* and R. V. Daniels, 'Russian political culture and the post-revolutionary impasse', *Russian Review* 46/2 (1987), pp. 165–75.
6 Alfred J. Rieber, *Stalin and the Struggle for Supremacy in Eurasia* (Cambridge, 2015); R. Tucker, *Stalin in Power: The Revolution from Above, 1928–41* (W.W. Norton, 1990).
7 J. Arch Getty, *Practicing Stalinism: Bolsheviks, Boyars, and the Persistence of Tradition* (New Haven, 2013), pp. xi, 19.
8 Horace Dewey and Ann Kleimola, 'The Petition (chelobitnaia) as an Old Russian literary genre', *Slavic and East European Review* 14 (1970), pp. 284–301; Barbara Alpern Engel, *Breaking the Ties That Bound: The Politics of Marital Strife in Late Imperial Russia* (Ithaca, 2011); Andrew Verner 'Discursive strategies in the 1905 revolution: Peasant petitions from Vladimir Province', *The Russian Review* 54/1 (January 1995), pp. 65–90; O. G. Bukhovets, 'The political consciousness of the Russian peasantry in the revolution of 1905–1907: Sources, methods, and some results', *The Russian Review* 47/4 (October 1988), pp. 357–74;

Notes

Golfo Alexopoulos, *Stalin's Outcasts: Aliens, Citizens and the Soviet State, 1926–36* (Ithaca, NY, 2003); Golfo Alexopoulos, 'The ritual lament: A narrative of appeal in the 1920s and 1930s', *Russian History-Histoire Russe* 24/1–1 (1997), pp. 117–29; Sarah Davies, 'The cult of the vozhd: Representations in letters, 1934–41', *Russian History-Histoire Russe* 24/1–1 (1997), pp. 131–47; Sheila Fitzpatrick, 'Signals from below: Soviet letters of denunciation of the 1930s', *Journal of Modern History* 68/4 (1996), pp. 831–67; Sheila Fitzpatrick, 'Supplicants and citizens: Public letter writing in Soviet Russia in the 1930s', *Slavic Review* 55/1 (1996), pp. 78–105; Lewis Siegelbaum, 'Introduction' in *Stalinism as a way of life: A Narrative in Documents* (New Haven, 2000), pp. 1–27; Stephen Bittner, 'Local soviets, public order, and welfare after Stalin: Appeals from Moscow's Kiev Raion', *Russian Review* 62/2 (2003), pp. 281–93; Kristy Ironside, '"I Beg You Not to Reject My Plea": The late Stalinist welfare state and the politics of one-time monetary aid, 1946–1953', *Journal of Social History* 51/4 (June 2018), pp. 1045–68; Alexey Tikhomirov, 'The regime of forced trust: Making and breaking emotional bonds between people and state in Soviet Russia, 1917–1941', *The Slavonic and East European Review* 91/1 (January 2013), pp. 78–118.

9   Figes and Kolonitskii, *Interpreting the Russian Revolution*: 'there was no real cultural or social foundation for the liberal conception of democracy in Russia', p. 123.

10 See the following works for 'peasantization': Lewin, *Making of the Soviet System*; Worobec *Peasant Russia: Family and Community in the post-Emancipation Period* (Princeton, 1991); Stephen Frank, *Crime, Cultural Conflict and Justice in Rural Russia* (Berkeley, 1999); Ben Eklof, *Russian Peasant Schools: Officialdom, Village Culture, and Popular Pedagogy, 1861–1914* (Berkeley, 1986); John Bushnell 'Peasants in uniform: The tsarist army as a peasant society', *Journal of Social History* 13/4 (Summer 1980), pp. 565–76; Robert Johnson, *Peasant and Proletarian: The Working Class of Moscow in the Late Nineteenth Century* (New Brunswick, 1979); Joseph Bradley, *Muzhik and Muscovite: Urbanization in Late Imperial Russia* (Berkeley, 1985); David Moon, 'Peasants into Russian citizens? A comparative perspective' *Revolutionary Russia* 9/1 (1996), pp. 43–81; Aaron B. Retish, *Russia's Peasants in Revolution and Civil War: Citizenship, Identity and the Creation of the Soviet State, 1914–1922* (Cambridge, 2008).

11 Peter Kolchin, *Unfree Labor: American Slavery and Russian Serfdom* (Cambridge, MA, 1987), p. 274.

12 Lindsay Hughes, *Peter the Great* (New Haven, 2004), p. 120.

13 V. P. Kozlov et al. (eds), *Gosudarstvennost' Rossii*, vol. 2 (Moscow, 1996), pp. 198–9, 228–9, 322–4. See also N. P. Eroshkin and D. I. Raskin (eds), *Vysshie i tsental'nye gosudarstvennye uchrezhdeniia Rossii 1801–1917 gg.* (St. Petersburg, 1998), pp. i, 31 and 164–6; N. P. Eroshkin, *Istoriia gosudarstvennykh uchrezhdenii dorevoliutsionnoi Rossii* (Moscow, 2008), pp. 161, 220. The papers of the second and third of these bodies are both in fond 1412 at the Rossiiskii gosudarstvennyi istoricheskii arkhiv (RGIA). See S. N. Valk and V. V. Bedin (eds), *Tsentral'nyi gosudarstvennyi istoricheskii arkhiv SSSR v Leningrade: Putevoditel'* (Leningrad, 1956), pp. 319–20.

14 Isabel de Madariaga, 'Catherine II and the serfs: A reconsideration of some problems', *The Slavonic and East European Review* 52/126 (January 1974), pp. 34–62.

15 S. N. Pisarev, *Uchrezhdenie po priniatiiu i napraveleniiu proshenii i zhalob, prinosimykh na Vysochaishee imia, 1810–1910 gg: Istoricheskii ocherk* (St Petersburg, 1909), p. 13 and M. V. Klochkov, *Ocherki pravitelstvennoi deiatel'nosti vremeni Pavla I* (Petrograd, 1916), p. 119.

16 Richard Wortman, *Scenarios of Power: Myth and Ceremony in Russian Monarchy*: Volume 2: *From Alexander II to the Abdication of Nicholas II* (Princeton, 2000).

17 Corinne Gaudin, *Ruling Peasants: Village and State in Late Imperial Russia* (DeKalb, 2007), p. 28.
18 A. V. Remnev, 'Kantseliariia proshenii v samodarzhavnoi sisteme pravleniia kontsa XIX stoletiia', *Istoricheskii ezhegodnik* (1997), pp. 17–19.
19 Pisarev, *Uchrezhdenie po priniatiiu i napraveleniiu proshenii i zhalob*, pp. 178–89; Engel, *Breaking the Ties That Bound*.
20 For discussion of late-Imperial petitions for material assistance, see Hubertus Jahn, 'Voices from the lower depths: Russian poor in their own words', in Beate Althammer, Lutz Raphael and Tamara Stazic-Wendt (eds), *Rescuing the Vulnerable: Poverty, Welfare and Social Ties in Modern Europe* (New York, 2016), pp. 335–55.
21 A. P. Chekov (trans. Constance Garnett), *The Horse Stealers and Other Stories* (Fairfield, 2005), pp. 240–7.
22 V. I. Lenin, '"Our Father the Tsar" and the Barricades', in V. I. Lenin, *Collected Works*, vol. 8 (Moscow, 1962), pp. 101–23.
23 M. N. Skrypnik, 'Krest'iane-khodoki y Il'icha v smol'nom' in *Vospominaniia o Vladimire Il'iche Lenine*, vol. 2 (Moscow, 1957), pp. 89–92.
24 V. D. Bonch-Bruevich, *Izbrannie sochinenii*, vol. 3 (Moscow, 1963), p. 166. See also A. F. Ilyin-Zhenevskii (trans. Brian Pierce), *The Bolsheviks in Power: Reminiscences of the Year 1918* (London, 1984), pp. 7, 28.
25 Alexandra Kollontai, *The Autobiography of a Sexually Emancipated Communist Woman* (New York, 1975), p. 37.
26 See Natalie Zemon Davis, *Fiction in the Archives: Pardon Tales and Their Tellers in Sixteenth-Century France* (Stanford, 1987) on how petitions can be understood not as truth or falsity, but as narratives crafted to elicit a positive response from the authorities.
27 See permission passes to visitors to the Soviet government HQ in Gosudarstvennyi arkhiv Rossiiskoi Federatsii (hereafter GARF), f. 130, op. 1, d. 99 (Trebovatel'naia vedomost' na bydachu zhalovaniia sluzhashchim Upravleniia delami Sovnarkoma, 25 October 1917–1 March 1918). Also see E. K. Koksharova, 'V.I. Lenin v sovnarkome v 1917 godu', in *Lenin v 1917 godu: Vospominaniia* (Moscow, 1967), p. 291 and Bonch-Bruevich 'Pervye dni sovnarkomovskogo apparata' in *Lenin v 1917 godu*, p. 275.
28 E. K. Koksharova, 'V.I. Lenin v sovnarkome v 1917 godu', in *O Vladimir Il'iche Lenine: Vospominaniia, 1900–22 gody* (Moscow, 1963), pp. 310–14.
29 V. I. Lenin, *Polnoe Sobranie Sochinenii*, 5th ed. (Moscow, 1958–65) (hereafter *PSS*), vol. 35, pp. 62–3.
30 *Izvestiia*, No. 219, 8 November 1917.
31 Koksharova, 'Lenin v Sovnarkome v 1917 gody', p. 296.
32 M. N. Skrypnik, 'Krest'iane-khodoki y Il'icha v smol'nom', p. 76.
33 Bonch-Bruevich, *Izbrannye sochineniia*, vol. 3, p. 167.
34 GARF, f. 130, op. 2, d. 347, l. 70.
35 Bonch-Bruevich, *Izbrannye sochineniia*, vol. 3, p. 166.
36 L. A. Fotieva, *Iz zhizni V. I. Lenina* (Moscow, 1967), p. 90.
37 Bonch-Bruevich, *Izbrannye sochineniia*, vol. 3, pp. 166–72. See also N. P. Gorbunov, 'V Leninskoi Priemnoi', in *Vospominaniia, stat'i, dokumenty* (Moscow, 1986), p. 56.
38 Bonch-Bruevich, *Izbrannye sochineniia*, vol. 3, pp. 167–9.

Notes

39 Ibid., pp. 169–71.
40 E. B. Genkina, *Gosudarstvennaia deiatel'nost' V. I. Lenina 1921–1923* (Moscow, 1969), pp. 389, 396, Bonch-Bruevich, *Izbrannye sochineniia,* vol. 3, p. 173.
41 Kenez, *Birth of the Propaganda State*, pp. 61–4.
42 Sheila Fitzpatrick, *Everyday Stalinism: Ordinary Life in Extraordinary Times: Soviet Russia in the 1930s* (New York and Oxford, 1999), ch. 7 'Writing to the Government'.
43 'Nabrosok pravil ob upravlenii sovetskmi uchrezhdeniiami', 12 December 1918 in Lenin, *PSS*, vol. 37, pp. 366–7.
44 Rossiiskii gosudarstvennyi arkhiv sotsial'no-politicheskoi istorii (hereafter RGASPI), f. 5, op. 1, d. 1806, ll. 26–70.
45 Ibid., l. 38.
46 *Kratkaia kharacteristika deiatel'nosti VTsIK i SNK (BSNK, MSNK i STO)* (Moscow, 1921), p. 126.
47 V. I. Lenin (trans. Robert Service), *State and Revolution* (London, 1992), p. 79.
48 Bonch-Bruevich, *Izbrannye sochineniia,* vol. 3, p. 166.
49 Gorbunov, 'V Leninskoi Priemnoi', p. 56.
50 Fotieva, *Iz zhizni V. I. Lenina,* pp. 89–91.
51 Lenin, *PSS*, vol. 44, p. 268.
52 Ibid., 91.
53 V. I. Lenin, *PSS*, vol. 50 (Moscow, 1958–65), p. 245.
54 Fotieva, *Iz zhizni V. I. Lenina,* pp. 89–90.
55 Lenin, *PSS*, vol. 51, pp. 108, 400.
56 Bonch-Bruevich, *Izbrannye sochineniia,* vol. 3, p. 171.
57 Fotieva, *Iz zhizni V. I. Lenina,* p. 93.
58 Ibid.
59 S. B. Brichkina, 'Maloe v velikom', in *O Vladimire Il'iche Lenine- Vospominaniia 1900–1922 gg.* (Moscow, 1963), pp. 468–80.
60 T. F. Remington, 'The rationalization of state *kontrol*'' in D. Koenker, W. G. Rosenburg and R. G. Suny (eds), *Party, State and Society in the Russian Civil War: Explorations in Social History* (Bloomington, 1989), pp. 220–21.
61 Ibid., p. 221.
62 Ibid.
63 Dekreta SNK RSFSR, 'Ob ustranenii volokity', 30 December 1919, *Dekrety sovetskoi vlasti*, t. 7, 10 dekabriia 1919 g. -31 marta 1920 g (Moskva, 1975).
64 Lenin, *PSS*, vol. 54, pp. 108–9.
65 Ibid., p. 593.
66 James C. Scott, *Domination and the Arts of Resistance* (New Haven, 1990), p. xii.
67 Stephen Kotkin, *Magnetic Mountain: Stalinism as Civilization* (Berkeley, 1995) and the 'Soviet subjectivity' issue of *Russian Review* 60/3 (2001), pp. 307–59; Eric Naiman 'On Soviet subjects and the scholars who make them'; Igal Halfin 'Looking into oppositionists' souls: inquisition communist style'; and Jochen Hellbeck 'Working, struggling, becoming: Stalin-era autobiographical texts'.

68 Natalia Mamonova, 'Naive monarchism and rural resistance in contemporary Russia', *Rural Sociology* 81/3 (2016), p. 322.

69 Mamonova, 'Naive monarchism and rural resistance in contemporary Russia', pp. 316–42.

Chapter 5

1 Peter H. Solomon, *Soviet Criminal Justice under Stalin* (Cambridge, 1996), p. 191; Adam B. Ulam, *Stalin: The Man and His Era* (London, 2007), p. 402; Robert Conquest, *The Great Terror: A Reassessment* (Oxford, 2008), p. 79.

2 J. Arch Getty, 'State and society under Stalin: Constitutions and elections in the 1930s', *Slavic Review* 50/1 (1991), pp. 18–35; idem, '"Excesses are not permitted": Mass terror and Stalinist governance in the late 1930s', *The Russian Review* 61/1 (2002), 113–38; idem, *Practicing Stalinism*, pp. 206–36; Wendy Z. Goldman, *Terror and Democracy in the Age of Stalin: The Social Dynamics of Repression* (Cambridge, 2007), pp. 133–62; Gábor Tamás Rittersporn, *Stalinist Simplifications and Soviet Complications: Social Tensions and Political Conflicts in the USSR, 1933–1953* (Reading, 1991); Ellen Wimberg, 'Socialism, democratism and criticism: The soviet press and the national discussion of the 1936 draft constitution', *Soviet Studies* 44/2 (1992), pp. 313–32.

3 Lenin, 'Gosudarstvo i Revoliutsiia', pp. 18–22 (from now on: *PSS*).

4 Ibid., p. 91.

5 Ibid., p. 102.

6 Lenin, 'Uderzhat li bol'sheviki gosudarstvennuiu vlast'?', in *PSS* 34, pp. 287–339.

7 Ibid., pp. 315–16.

8 Ibid., p. 333.

9 Ibid., p. 329.

10 Lenin, 'Ocherednie zadachi Sovetskoi vlasti', in *PSS* 36, pp. 165–208, 173–4.

11 Ibid., p. 194.

12 Ibid., p. 196.

13 Ibid., p. 201.

14 Ibid., pp. 203–6.

15 Iu. S. Kukushkin and O. I. Chistiakov, *Ocherk Istorii Sovetskoi Konstitutsii* (Moscow, 1987), p. 246.

16 Donald J. Raleigh, *Experiencing Russia's Civil War: Politics, Society, and Revolutionary Culture in Saratov, 1917–1922* (New Haven, 2002), pp. 142–73.

17 Retish, *Russia's Peasants in Revolution and Civil War*, pp. 130–1, 155, 209.

18 David Priestland, 'Soviet Democracy, 1917–91', *European History Quarterly* 32/1 (2002), pp. 111–30, 116–17.

19 Isaac Deutscher, *The Prophet Unarmed: Trotsky 1921–1929* (London, 2003), pp. 218–19; Lars T. Lih, 'Zinoviev: Populist Leninist', *The NEP era: Soviet Russia, 1921–1928* 2 (2008), pp. 1–23.

20 *Pravda*, 29 October 1926.

Notes

21 John B. Hatch, 'The "Lenin Levy" and the social origins of Stalinism: Workers and the Communist Party in Moscow, 1921–1928', *Slavic Review* 48/4 (1989), pp. 558–77.

22 William Chase, *Workers, Society and the Soviet State: Labor and Life in Moscow, 1918–29* (Urbana, 1987).

23 *Pravda,* 19 August 1928.

24 Kotkin, *Magnetic Mountain,* p. 37.

25 I. V. Stalin, 'Otchetnii doklad XVII s'ezdu partii o rabote TSK VKP (b), 26 Ianvaria 1934 g.,' in *Sochninenia* 13 (Moscow, 1949), pp. 282–379, 309.

26 Ibid., p. 347. Even the implacable Trotsky had little to object to regarding the economic performance of the USSR. L. D. Trotskii, 'Nakanune s'ezda', *Biulleten' Oppozitsii* 38–9, 1934 g.

27 Stalin, 'Otchetnii', p. 349.

28 'Novaia epokha v razvitii sovetskoi demokratii', *PZM* 1 (1935), pp. 9–19, 10.

29 Ibid., p. 15.

30 James Hughes, *Stalinism in a Russian Province: Collectivization and Dekulakization in Siberia* (Basingstoke, 1996), pp. 33–51.

31 N. Kumikin, 'Zakonodatel'stvovanie v usloviakh proletarskoi demokratii', *SG* 3 (1935), pp. 34–42, 48.

32 Getty, 'State and society', p. 20; Samantha Lomb, *Stalin's Constitution: Soviet Participatory Politics and the Discussion of the 1936 Draft Constitution* (London, 2017), p. 23.

33 Ibid., pp. 19–33.

34 Gosudarstvenii arkhiv Rossiskoi Federatsii (hereafter GARF), f. 3316, op. 40, d. 7, l. 43. I am obliged to Samantha Lomb for sharing with me her copies of the constitutional drafts.

35 GARF, f. 3316, op. 8, d. 3, l. 11.

36 Wimberg, 'Socialism'; Lomb, *Stalin's Constitution,* pp. 63–81.

37 *Pravda,* 5 March 1936.

38 *Pravda,* 28 November 1936.

39 R. Vol'skii, 'Stalinskaia Konstitutsiia i polozhenie o viborakh v Verkhovnii Sovet SSSR', *SG* 3–4 (1937), pp. 52–61, 54–5.

40 'Peredovaia', *PZM* 9 (1937), pp. 1–9. For more examples of such articles, see issues of 9–12 of the same year.

41 Getty, *Practicing Stalinism,* p. 208.

42 Ibid., pp. 211–12.

43 Wendy Z. Goldman, 'Stalinist terror and democracy: The 1937 union campaign', *The American Historical Review* 110/5 (2005), pp. 1427–53.

44 James Harris, *The Great Fear: Stalin's Terror of the 1930s* (Oxford, 2016), pp. 171–4.

45 Getty, *Practicing Stalinism,* p. 263.

46 Single-candidacy was not codified in law. Regulations published the following year for elections to republic-level Soviets retained provisions for competing candidacies suggesting that the leadership still viewed the practice as an ad-hoc measure. *Pravda,* 17 February 1938.

47 *Pravda,* 19 January 1938.

48 Wendy Z. Goldman, *Inventing the Enemy: Denunciation and Terror in Stalin's Russia* (Cambridge, 2011), pp. 81–139.

49 Indicatively, *Pravda,* 25 January, 3 February, 29 March, 7 August 1938.

50 *Pravda*, 15, 24 April 1938; *Pravda Severa*, 27 November 1938.
51 *Pravda*, 1–2 February 1939.
52 Rossiiskii gosudarstvennii arkhiv sotsial'no-politicheskoi Istorii (hereafter RGASPI), f. 17, op. 21, d. 2705, l. 3.
53 *Krasnii Sever*, 17 February 1939, *Pravda*, 7 February 1939, *Pravda Severa* 11 February 1939, *Vostochno-Sibirskaia Pravda*, 15 February 1939.
54 *Pravda*, 13 February 1939.
55 *Pravda*, 19 February 1939.
56 *Pravda*, 7 February 1939.
57 *Pravda*, 8 February 1939.
58 *Pravda*, 7 February 1939.
59 *Pravda*, 9 March 1939.
60 *XVIII S'ezd VKP (b): Stenograficheskii Otchet* (Moscow, 1939), pp. 10–12.
61 Ibid., pp. 32–6.
62 Ibid., p. 144.
63 Ibid., p. 511.
64 Ibid., pp. 515–20.
65 Ibid., p. 526.
66 Ibid., p. 527.
67 RGASPI, f. 17, op. 21, d. 2703, ll. 3–5; RGASPI, f. 17, op. 21, d. 2705, l. 3.
68 Rossiiskii gosudarstvennyi arkhiv voenno-morskogo flota, f. r-852, op. 5, d. 15, ll. 29, 111; op. 8, d. 19, ll. 1–2.
69 Tsentral'nyi gosudarstvenyi arkhiv istoriko-politicheskikh dokumentov, f. 1012, op. 2, dd. 1467, 1954; op. 1, d. 1287.
70 Erik van Ree, *The Political Thought of Joseph Stalin: A Study in Twentieth Century Revolutionary Patriotism* (London, 2002), pp. 3–5.

Chapter 6

1 Isaac Deutscher, *The Prophet Armed* (Oxford, 1954); *The Prophet Unarmed* (Oxford, 1959); *The Prophet Outcast* (Oxford, 1963).
2 To cite just a few examples: Tony Cliff's multi-volume biography published by Bookmarks (1989, 1990, 1991, 1993); Paul Le Blanc, *Leon Trotsky* (London, 2015); Vadim Rogovin, *Byla li Al'ternativa?* (Moscow, 1992); Ronald Segal, *The Tragedy of Leon Trotsky* (Harmondsworth, 1979).
3 Leon Trotsky, *History of the Russian Revolution* (London, 1977), p. 17.
4 Leon Trotsky, *The Permanent Revolution & Results and Prospects* (New York, 1969), p. 115.
5 Leon Trotsky, *Dnevniki i Pis'ma* (Moscow, 1994), p. 103.
6 This interpretation was prominent in the very first histories of the Russian Revolution, beginning with Pavel Miliukov's three-volume *The Russian Revolution* (Gulf Breeze, FL, 1978, 1984, 1987).
7 See, for example, William Henry Chamberlain, *The Russian Revolution I* (Princeton, 1987), p. 100.

Notes

8   See, for example, Smith, *Russia in Revolution*, p. 375.
9   These points are made most forcibly by Trotsky in his anti-Kautsky polemic of the Civil War, *Terrorism and Communism* (London, 1975).
10 Leon Trotsky, *Social Democracy and the Wars of Intervention: Russia 1918–1921* (London, 1975), pp. 85, 92–5; Trotsky, *Terrorism and Communism*, p. 123.
11 James D. White, *The Russian Revolution 1917–1921: A Short History* (London, 1994), p. 240.
12 Leon Trotsky, *How the Revolution Armed 4: 1921–1923* (London, 1981), pp. 283–91.
13 Trotsky, *Social Democracy and the Wars*, p. 84.
14 Rex A. Wade, 'The October revolution, the constituent assembly, and the end of the Russian revolution,' in I. D. Thatcher (ed.), *Reinterpreting Revolutionary Russia* (London, 2006), pp. 72–85.
15 Trotsky, *Terrorism and Communism*, pp. 64–6.
16 Trotsky, *Social Democracy and the Wars*, pp. 90–1.
17 Trotsky, *Terrorism and Communism* p. 177.
18 Leon Trotsky, *History of the Russian Revolution to Brest-Litovsk* (London, 1919).
19 Trotsky, *Terrorism and Communism*, pp. 121–2. This quote in which Trotsky gives a central role to the party in preserving the class hegemony of the proletariat comes close to his statement at the Thirteenth Party Congress in May 1924 that 'the Party is the sole historical instrument that the working class possesses for the solution of its fundamental tasks'. Robert Daniels claims that Trotsky intended these words to be 'sarcastic', but they appear to me to be a continuation of his thinking of the post-1917 period more generally. See Robert V. Daniels, *Trotsky, Stalin, and Socialism* (Boulder, CO, 1991), p. 101.
20 Leon Trotsky, *The Challenge of the Left Opposition (1923–1925)* (New York, 1975), pp. 152–3.
21 Valentina Vilkova, *The Struggle for Power: Russia in 1923* (New York, 1996), p. 56.
22 See, for example, 'A lesson in democracy I did not receive,' in Leon Trotsky (ed.), *Writings of Leon Trotsky [1929]* (New York, 1975), pp. 100–7.
23 'The class nature of the Soviet State', in Leon Trotsky (ed.), *Writings of Leon Trotsky [1933–34]* (New York, 1975), p. 105, 115.
24 'Stalinism and Bolshevism', in Leon Trotsky (ed.), *Writings of Leon Trotsky [1936–37]* (New York, 1978), p. 423.
25 'The Workers' State, Thermidor and Bonapartism', in Leon Trotsky (ed.), *Writings of Leon Trotsky [1934–35]* (New York, 1974), p. 183.
26 Leon Trotsky, *Stalin* (London, 2016), p. 6.
27 Ibid., pp. 82–3, 667.
28 Ibid., p. 68.
29 Ibid., pp. 623, 628.
30 Leon Trotsky, *Our Political Tasks [1904]* (London, nd), p. 77.
31 See also, for example, 'How did Stalin defeat the opposition?', in *Writings of Leon Trotsky [1935–36]* (New York, 1977), pp. 171–9.
32 Trotsky, *Stalin*, p. 673.
33 Ibid., p. 663.
34 Ibid., p. 680.
35 Leon Trotsky, *Literature and Revolution* (London, 1991), p. 284.
36 Leon Trotsky, *Their Morals and Ours* (New York, 1973), pp. 39–42.

Chapter 7

1. Leon Trotsky, *My Life* (New York, 1930), ch. 40 'Conspiracy of the epigones'; Isaac Deutscher, *Stalin: A Political Biography* (Oxford, 1949; Leonard Schapiro, *The Origins of the Communist Autocracy: Political Opposition in the Soviet State: First Phase: 1917– 1922* (London, 1955); Deutscher, *The Prophet Unarmed: Trotsky, 1921–1929* (Oxford, 1959); Robert V. Daniels, *Conscience of the Revolution: Communist Opposition in Soviet Russia* (Cambridge, MA, 1960). For more recent works based on archival sources that fundamentally reproduce the old story, see Valentina Vilkova, *The Struggle for Power: Russia in 1923* (London, 1996); O. G. Nazarov, *Stalin i bor'ba za liderstvo bol'shevistskoi partii v usloviiakh NEPa* (Moscow, 2000); Simon Pirani, *The Russian Revolution in Retreat, 1920–1924* (London, 2008); Alexander Reznik, *Trotskii i tovarishchi: levaia oppozitsiia i politicheskaia kul'tura RKP(b), 1923–1924* (St Petersburg, 2017).
2. Very little has been written that has specifically focused on the Trotsky–Stalin relationship, but almost every political history of the Soviet interwar period and every biography of Stalin and of Trotsky addresses it to some extent. See, for example, Daniels, *Conscience of the Revolution*, ch. 9 'The new course controversy'; Louis Rapport, *Stalin's War against the Jews* (New York, 1990), pp. 24–40, ch. 3 'Stalin's rivalry with Trotsky'; Dmitrii Volkogonov, *Trotskii*, vol. 2 (Moscow, 1999) 'Duel "vydaiushchikhsia vozhdei"', pp. 44–9; Service, *Stalin*, ch. 20 'The opportunities of struggle'.
3. T. H. Rigby, *Communist Party Membership in the USSR, 1917–1967* (Princeton, 1968), p. 52.
4. I discuss this in greater depth in 'Stalin as general secretary: The appointments process and the nature of Stalin's power', in Sarah Davies and James Harris (eds), *Stalin: A New History* (Cambridge, 2005), pp. 63–82. See also Christopher Monty, 'The Central Committee Secretariat, the Nomenklatura, and the politics of personnel management in the Soviet Order, 1921–1927', *The Soviet and Post-Soviet Review* 2 (2012), pp. 166–91; Getty, *Practicing Stalinism*, esp. chs. 3–4. M. V. Zelenov, A. V. Krylova, N. Iu, Pivovarov and A. A. Chernobaev published a useful selection of documents on the theme under the title 'Stalin i "konstruirovanie" partiinoi vlasti' *Istoricheskii arkhiv* 1, 2, 3 and 6 (2017).
5. Sheila Fitzpatrick and others have argued that the civil war centralized and militarized the party and made it intolerant of dissent. While this is intuitively compelling, this chapter argues that the emergence of the party dictatorship was substantially driven by practical imperatives of leadership and administration after the civil war. Sheila Fitzpatrick, 'The civil war as a formative experience', Woodrow Wilson International Center for Scholars; Kennan Institute Occasional Paper Series #134, 1981, 55 pages.
6. See the resolutions of the 10th Party Congress in March 1921. Lenin was particularly critical of Trotsky's ideas for trades unions in the context of labour militarization. V. I. Lenin 'The trade unions, the present situation and Trotsky's mistakes', *Collected Works*, vol. 32 (Moscow, 1965), pp. 19–42.
7. Large-scale industry was at 15 per cent of pre-war levels in 1920, was at 17 per cent in 1921 and 20 per cent in 1922. Rural and artisanal manufacture recovered faster, reaching 54 per cent of pre-war levels by 1922, but the net effect of that faster recovery was relatively insignificant. State industry employed more than forty times the workforce of small-scale leased enterprises as of September 1922. E. H. Carr, *The Bolshevik Revolution, 1917–1923*, vol. 2 (London, 1952), ch. 19.
8. In 1922, 197,000 workers participated in strikes. That figure fell marginally in 1923 to 165,000. Vladimir Buldakov, *Utopiia, agressiia, vlast': Psikhosotsial'naia dinamika postrevoliutsionnogo vremeni Rossiia, 1920–1930 gg.* (Moscow, 2012), pp. 215, 220.

Notes

9   A version of Trotsky's theses can be found in Rossiiskii Gosudarstvennyi Arkhiv Sotsial'no-politicheskoi Istorii (hereafter RGASPI), f. 558, op. 1, d. 3419, ll. 1–13.

10 Stalin dwelt on these points in his speech to the 12th Party Congress, without referring explicitly to Trotsky. *XII S"ezd RKP(b): Stenograficheskii otchet* (Moscow, 1968) pp. 62–6. Nogin's speech on behalf of the Revizionnaia Komissiia addressed these matters too. See esp. pp. 72–4.

11 RGASPI, f. 558, op. 1, d. 3419, l. 5.

12 *XII S"ezd RKP(b)*., pp. xi, 816–20.

13 Ibid., p. 116.

14 Ibid., pp. 101–5. Iurii Lutovinov, a Trades Union official who broadly sympathized with the Workers' Opposition but was not a member, criticized the Politburo for presenting itself as a 'sinless pope'. He argued that shutting down criticism would only drive criticism underground, pp. 115–16.

15 Ibid., p. 110.

16 Buldakov, *Utopiia, Aggressiia, Vlast'*, pp. 210–15; Pirani, *The Russian Revolution in Retreat*, pp. 192, 201.

17 On Southern Metallurgy and on reducing administrative costs in Trusts (16 July); on the fuel plan (27 July); on the Putilov factory (2 August); Rykov commission on wage policy (9 August); Kalinin commission on grain prices (20 September); Kuibyshev commission on international trade (2 October); Dzerzhinskii commission on the Scissors; Iaroslavskii commission on Donbas (13 November). G. M. Adibekov, K. M. Anderson and L. A. Rogovaia (eds), *Politbiuro TsK RKP(b) – VKP(b): Povestki dnia zasedanii: Tom 1: 1919–1929. Katalog* (Moscow, 2000), pp. 231–48.

18 RGASPI, f. 17, op. 3, d. 351, l 32. (10 May 1923).

19 RGASPI, f. 17, op. 3, d. 362, l. 18. 'O Rabochei Pravde' (3 July 1923).

20 RGASPI, f. 17, op. 3, d. 381, l. 13 (18 September 1923); f. 558, op. 3, d. 72, ll. 7–14.

21 RGASPI, f. 17, op. 3, d. 288, l. 7 (12 April 1922); Vilkova, *The Struggle for Power*, p. 46.

22 The most useful discussion of the economic crisis remains E. H. Carr, *The Interregnum, 1923–1924* (London, 1954), ch. 3.

23 The story of Trotsky's departure from the Plenum appears in Boris Bazhanov, *Avec Staline dans le Kremlin* (Paris, 1930), pp. 76–7 and Max Eastman, *Since Lenin Died* (London, 1925). His dramatic departure from the Plenum was also connected with a ham-fisted effort by the Politburo to dilute Trotsky's power in the Revolutionary Military Council (Revvoensovet). Vilkova, *The Struggle for Power*, pp. 43–5, 62–6.

24 RGASPI, f. 17, op. 2, d. 685, ll. 53–68. The document was translated and published in Vilkova, *The Struggle for Power*, pp. 46–57.

25 An internal investigation indicated that the leaks could not have originated in the Central Committee apparatus RGASPI, f. 17, op. 2, d. 685, l. 99.

26 RGASPI, f. 17, op. 2, d. 685, ll. 91–2, 96–7; Vilkova, *The Struggle for Power*, pp. 67, 74–5, 79–81.

27 At the request of the Politburo and the Presidium of the TsKK, Trotsky 'tried' to halt the distribution of the Declaration, but that proved impossible. RGASPI, f. 17, op. 3, d. 388, l. 11.

28 RGASPI, f. 51, op. 1, d. 21, ll. 50–50ob.

29 *Izvestiia TsK KPSS* 7 (1990), pp. 176–89; 10 (1990), pp. 167–81; Vilkova, *The Struggle for Power*, pp. 105–26, 139–65.

30 RGASPI, f. 17, op. 34, d. 102, l. 36.
31 The schedule of presentations (*poriadok dnia*) was agreed on 29 November 1923. RGASPI, f. 17, op. 3, d. 397, l. 18.
32 See, for example, the letter of G. Magidov, Secretary of the Poltava Gubkom to Stalin on 10 November 1923. RGASPI, f. 558, op. 1, d. 2565, ll. 2–8; Vilkova, *The Struggle for Power*, pp. 202–3, 213, 216, 218.
33 RGASPI, f. 558, op. 1, d. 2571, ll. 5–12; *Izvestiia TsK* 10 (1990), pp. 170–1; Vilkova, *The Struggle for Power*, pp. 205–10.
34 Bukharin called Trotsky's letter 'a declaration of war'. *Izvestiia TsK* 12 (1990), p. 173. See also pp. 165–6, 168.
35 The battle in the national party press began on 14 December 1923 and continued up to and indeed beyond, the 13th Party Conference in mid-January 1924.
36 See, for example, Derzhavnyi arkhiv Vinnitskoi oblasti (hereafter DAVO), f. 1, op. 1, d. 39 (Materials of the Podol'skii gubkom); Tsentrdokumentatsii obshchestvennykh organizatsii Sverdlovskoi oblasti (hereafter TsDOO SO), f. 6, op. 1, d. 8. Materials of Sverdlovskii okruzhkom, both from early January 1924.
37 DAVO, f. 1, op. 1, d. 41, l. 130.
38 TsDOO SO, f. 4, op. 2, d. 6, l. 68.
39 'The press is wholly in our hands', he added. *Izvestiia TsK* 3 (1991), pp. 201–2.
40 DAVO, f. 1, op. 1, d. 29, l. 44. From a file marked 'Secret correspondence on internal party matters.'
41 Even Iurii Larin, one of the most outspoken and independent members of the political elite and no obvious ally of the majority, observed how the 'opposition' now recognized they had lost the argument. *Trinadtsataia Konferentsiia Rossiiskoi Kommunisticheskoi Partii (Bol'shevikov)* (Moscow, 1924), p. 63.
42 He referred specifically to the low levels of literacy, to the threats presented by foreign governments hostile to the revolution and the danger of 'degeneration' (*pererozhdenie*) within the party while capitalist relations between town and countryside prevailed.
43 *Trinadtsataia Konferentsiia*, pp. 92–103. The speech was reprinted in Stalin, *Sochinenii* t. 6 (Moscow, 1952), pp. 5–26.
44 See, for example, the speeches of Lominadze, Riazanov and Mel'nichanskii. *Trinadtsataia Konferentsiia*, pp. 113–18, 120–3, 133–5.
45 This conference marks the first time the term 'opposition' was used consistently to describe Trotsky's group. It is sometimes argued that the term was applied by Stalin as a verbal weapon to strengthen his position and weaken his rivals. But in this meeting, Trotsky's group seems to have accepted the term and willingly used it to describe themselves and their position.
46 There were only three votes against among the 128 delegates.
47 *Trinadtsataia Konferentsiia*, pp. 198–204.
48 TsDOO SO, f. 4, op. 2, d. 12, ll. 3–5, 151, 262–4; f. 4, op. 2, d. 59, ll. 11, 15; f. 4, op. 2, d. 146, ll. 20–6; DAVO, f. 2, op. 1, d. 136, l. 1; f. 2, op. 1, d. 163, l. 33.
49 See, for example, TsDOO SO, f. 1, op. 1, d. 41, ll. 72, 220.
50 See, for example, DAVO, f. 1, op. 1, d. 47, ll. 54–5.

Notes

Chapter 8

1. Mark D. Steinberg, *Voices of Revolution, 1917* (New Haven, 2001), p. 20.
2. Ibid., p. 18.
3. The Cheka ('Extraordinary Commission for Struggle with Counterrevolution and Sabotage') was the first Soviet political police, founded at the end of 1917 and coming into operation in early 1918. It was replaced by the GPU ('State Political Administration') in 1922. In 1923, with the formation of the USSR, it became the OGPU ('United State Political Administration'). In 1934, the OGPU was transformed into the NKVD ('People's Commissariat of Internal Affairs'). Recalling its early days, political police officials were called 'chekists' for many years even after the Cheka was dissolved.
4. George Leggett, *The Cheka: Lenin's Political Police* (Oxford, 1981), p. 53.
5. Arno Mayer, *The Furies: Violence and Terror in the French and Russian Revolutions* (Princeton, 2000), pp. 128, 137. Mayer argues that the line between official justice and revenge was always a blurry one: 'State justice was not entirely free of the avenging logic, nor was revenge pure savagery [...]. vengeance is anything but unwitting, blind, and dark: the selection of victims is not haphazard, nor is the place, time, and method of revenge and re-revenge.' p. 127.
6. Isaac Babel (trans. Walter Morton), *Collected Stories* (New York, 1955), p. 106.
7. Dietrick Beyrau, 'Brutalization revisited: The case of Russia', *Journal of Contemporary History* 50/1 (2015), pp. 15–37, 18–19, 36.
8. Nathalie Babel (ed.), *The Complete Works of Isaac Babel* (New York, 2002), pp. 293, 359.
9. See Ryan, *Lenin's Terror*.
10. Leggett, *Cheka*, p. 111.
11. A. K. Goncharov, I. A. Doroshenko, M. A. Kozichev and N. N. Pavlovich (eds), *Iz istorii vserossiiskoi chrezvychainoi komissii, 1917–1921 g.g: Sbornik dokumentov* (Moscow, 1958), pp. 142–3.
12. A. I. Kokurin and N. Petrov (eds), *Lubianka: VChK-OGPU-NKVD-NKGB-MGB-MVD-KGB: 1917–1960: Spravochnik* (Moscow, 1997), p. 9.
13. Soviets looked up to the All-Russian Central Executive Committee (VTsIK) and the Russian People's Commissariat of Internal Affairs (RNKVD) rather than the Council of People's Commissars (SNK).
14. Kokurin and Petrov, *Lubianka: Spravochnik*, pp. 159–61.
15. Ibid., p. 167.
16. These chaotic inter-agency arrests continued into the 1920s, requiring Moscow to constantly sort them out. See J. Arch Getty, *Practicing Stalinism: Bolsheviks, Boyars, and the Persistence of Tradition* (New Haven and London, 2013), pp. 147–53.
17. Leggett, *Cheka*, pp. 123–30.
18. Ibid., pp. 131, 134.
19. V. N. Khaustov, V. P. Naumov and N. S. Plotnikov (eds), *Lubianka: Stalin i VChK-GPU-OGPU-NKVD: Ianvar' 1922–dekabr' 1936* (Moscow, 2003), pp. 11–12, 64–6, 90. Justice officials N. Krylenko and his successor A. Vyshinskii would continue to joust with Dzerzhinskii and his successors V. Menzhinskii and G. Iagoda on this question, arguing that the police should be deprived of the right to inflict extrajudicial punishment and that all cases should be adjudicated by regular courts according to a strict application of law.

See Solomon, *Soviet Criminal Justice under Stalin* and G. T. Rittersporn, 'Extra-judicial repression and the courts: Their relationship in the 1930s', in Peter Solomon (ed.), *Reforming Justice in Russia, 1864–1996* (Armonk, NY, 1997), pp. 207–227.

20 Krylenko rightly observed that these conditions were a meaningless sop. He lost. Khaustov, Naumo and Plotnikov, *Lubianka 1922–1936*, pp. 65–6.

21 Ibid., p. 16.

22 Paul M. Hagenloh, *Stalin's Police: Public Order and Mass Repression in the USSR, 1926–1941* (Baltimore, 2009), p. 40.

23 Kokurin and Petrov, *Lubianka: Spravochnik*, p. 179.

24 Rossiiskii gosudarstvennyi arkhiv sotsial'no-politicheskoi istorii (hereafter RGASPI), f. 17, op. 17, d. 579, ll. 6, 17.

25 *Izvestiia*, 11 July 1934, p. 1 and Kokurin and Petrov, *Lubianka: Spravochnik*, pp. 183–5.

26 RGASPI, f. 17, op. 3, d. 939, ll. 1–2.

27 Kokurin and Petrov, *Lubianka: Spravochnik*, p. 168.

28 Leggett, *Cheka*, pp. 135, 149–50.

29 RGASPI, f. 17, op. 162, d. 6, l. 118.

30 Khaustov, Naumov and Plotnikov, *Lubianka 1922–1936*, p. 275; RGASPI, f. 17, op. 3, d. 840, l. 9 and f. 17, op. 162, d. 10, l. 108.

31 RGASPI, f. 17, op. 3, d. 877, l. 77.

32 For this and other statistics on party weakness in the countryside, see J. Arch Getty, *Origins of the Great Purges: The Soviet Communist Party Reconsidered, 1933–1938* (Cambridge, New York, 1985), pp. 29–31.

33 Nicholas Werth, 'L'OGPU en 1924: Radiographie d'une institution à son niveau d'étiage', *Cahiers Du Monde Russe* 42/2–4 (2001), pp. 397–421, 406.

34 On the changing 'moods' of the population in the 1920s, see A. N. Sakharov et al. (eds), *'Sovershenno sekretno:' Lubianka-Stalinu o polozhenii v strane (1922–1934 gg.)* (Moscow, 2002).

35 In 1923, there were 240 bandit attacks on trains, a number that increased to 280 in 1924. In that year, 2,337 bandits were shot and 10,663 captured and 388 regular police and 76 OGPU officers were killed in armed combat with bandits. Werth, 'L'OGPU', pp. 413–15.

36 Some years ago in a Soviet-era museum, I was shown the revolver pocket sewn into S. M. Kirov's 1930s-era jacket. Kirov was secretary of the relatively 'safe' Leningrad party organization.

37 V. Danilov, R. Manning, L. Viola et al. (eds), *Tragediia sovetskoi derevni: Kollektivizatsiia i raskulachivanie: Dokumenty i materialy v 5 tomax: 1927–1939*, vol. 5, kn. 1 (Moscow, 2004), p. 38.

38 V. Danilov, R. Manning, L. Viola et al. (eds), *Tragediia sovetskoi derevni: Kollektivizatsiia i raskulachivanie: Dokumenty i materialy v 5 tomax: 1927–1939*, vol. 1 (Moscow, 1999), p. 39.

39 RGASPI, f. 558, op. 11, d. 63, l. 34.

40 RGASPI, f. 17, op. 162, d. 7, ll. 158, 171.

41 On kulak 'terror' and peasant resistance in general, see L. Viola, V. Danilov, N. Ivnitskii and D. Kozlov (eds), *The War against the Peasantry, 1927–1930: The Tragedy of the Soviet Countryside* (New Haven and London, 2005), pp. 150–1; Lynne Viola, *Peasant Rebels under Stalin: Collectivization and the Culture of Peasant Resistance* (New York: Oxford, 1996) and Solomon, *Criminal Justice*, p. 83.

Notes

42 Danilov et al., *Tragediia* I, p. 714; RGASPI, f. 17, op. 3, d. 761, l. 17. Emphases mine.
43 Danilov et al., *Tragediia* I, p. 732.
44 RGASPI, f. 558, op. 11, d. 86, ll. 51–2.
45 'By the time the Politburo issued specific instructions on dekulakization in early February, the process had been under way in nearly all areas for weeks.' Hagenloh, *Stalin's Police*, pp. 54–5.
46 Viola et al., *The War against the Peasantry, 1927–1930*, pp. 219–21, 237. Iagoda's complaint about arrests 'by anyone who felt like it' would be repeated almost word for word by Stalin in his May 1933 decree (see below) suggesting that this chaotic practice would continue for more than three years after Iagoda's warning.
47 *Pravda*, 2 March 1930.
48 Viola et al., *The War against the Peasantry, 1927–1930*, p. 266.
49 V. Danilov, R. Manning, L. Viola et al. (eds), *Tragediia sovetskoi derevni: Kollektivizatsiia i raskulachivanie: Dokumenty i materialy v 5 tomax: 1927–1939*, vol. 2 (Moscow, 2000), p. 174.
50 Danilov et al., *Tragediia* II, p. 313.
51 Khaustov, Naumov and Plotnikov, *Lubianka 1922–1936*, p. 113.
52 RGASPI, f. 17, op. 162, d. 8, l. 17. The Moscow Political Commission seems to have been somewhat more lenient than provincial instances. In the six months of 1932 for which we have evidence, the Commission found the local death sentences in half (39) to be excessive and reduced them to terms in prison. See RGASPI, f. 17, op. 162, d. 12, ll. 69–70, 91, 71–4, 145–6, 190; Ibid., d. 13, ll. 27, 74.
53 RGASPI, f. 17, op. 3, d. 822, l. 7.
54 RGASPI, f. 17, op. 162, d. 10, l. 108.
55 Solomon, *Criminal Justice*, pp. 158–9.
56 Gosudarstvennyi arkhiv Rossiiskoi Federatsii, f. 9401, op. 1, d. 4157, ll. 201–3, 205.
57 RGASPI, f. 17, op. 162, d. 14, l. 61.
58 Ibid., l. 123.
59 RGASPI, f. 17, op. 3, d. 922, l. 50.
60 RGASPI, f. 558, op. 11, d. 27, l. 63.
61 RGASPI, f. 17, op. 3, d. 922, l. 16.
62 Ibid., ll. 50–5.
63 RGASPI, f. 17, op. 162, d. 15, ll. 2, 27.
64 RGASPI, f. 17, op. 162, d. 17, l. 43.
65 RGASPI, f. 17, op. 3, d. 948, l. 95.
66 RGASPI, f. 82, op. 2, d. 886, ll. 55–6.
67 The interpretation is alive and well in Moscow, represented by the leading historian of Stalin there: Oleg V. Khlevniuk, *Master of the House: Stalin and His Inner Circle* (New Haven, 2008); Oleg V. Khlevniuk, *Stalin: New Biography of a Dictator* (New Haven, London, 2015).
68 David Shearer and Vladimir N. Khaustov, *Stalin and the Lubianka: A Documentary History of the Political Police and Security Organs in the Soviet Union, 1922–1953* (New Haven, London, 2015), pp. 2–3.

69 In a purely fanciful claim Shearer and Khaustov suggest that Dzerzhinskii 'died before coming into serious conflict with Stalin.' There is no evidence suggesting any past or potential conflict between the two. Ibid., p. 3.

70 Lars Lih, Oleg Khlevniuk and Oleg Naumov (eds), *Stalin's Letters to Molotov, 1925-1936* (New Haven, London, 1995), pp. 44, 190.

71 Feliks Ivanovich Chuev, Vyacheslav Mikhaylovich Molotov and Albert Resis, *Molotov Remembers: Inside Kremlin Politics: Conversations with Felix Chuev* (Chicago, 1993), p. 257.

72 I have analysed this elsewhere. See Getty, '"Excesses are not permitted:" Mass terror and Stalinist governance in the late 1930s', pp. 113–38; J. A. Getty, 'Pre-election fever: The origins of the 1937 mass operations', in James R. Harris (ed.), *The Anatomy of Terror: Political Violence under Stalin* (Oxford, 2013), pp. 216–235. For detailed statistical information on the mass operations, see M. Junge and R. Binner, *Kak terror stal 'bol'shim': Sekretnyk prikaz No. 447 i tekhnologiia ego ispolneniia* (Moscow, 2003); Junge, Bordiugov and Binner, *Vertikal' Bol'shogo Terrora: Istoriia operatsii po prikazu NKVD No. 00447* (Moscow, 2008) and R. Binner, M. Junge and B. Bonvech (eds), *Stalinizm v Sovetskoi provintsii: 1937–1938 gg: Massovaia operatsiia na osnove prikaza No. 00447* (Moscow, 2009).

73 Feliks Ivanovich Chuev, *Sto sorok besed s Molotovym* (Moscow, 1991), p. 296. The regional secretary was Nikita Khrushchev.

74 'The initiative for expanding the scale of repression came from below – from secretaries of kraikoms and obkoms.' V. N. Khaustov and Lennart Samuelson, *Stalin, NKVD i repressii: 1936–1938 gg.* (Moscow, 2009), p. 270.

75 Junge, Bordiugov and Binner, *Vertikal' Bol'shogo Terrora*, p. 46. See also Danilov et al., *Tragediia* I, pp. 97–8, 603.

76 Lynne Viola, *Stalinist Perpetrators on Trial: Scenes from the Great Terror in Soviet Ukraine* (New York, 2017), ch. 1.

77 Danilov et al., *Tragediia* II, pp. 824–5.

78 'Faced with the devastating effects of mass repressions, the Party leadership tried to regulate terror and to keep it within controllable limits.' Oleg V. Khlevniuk, 'The Politburo, penal policy, and "legal teforms," in the 1930s', in Solomon (ed.), *Reforming Justice in Russia*, p. 192.

Chapter 9

1 Getty, 'State and society under Stalin', pp. 34–5; idem., *Practicing Stalinism: Bolsheviks, Boyars, and the Persistence of Tradition* (New Haven, CT, 2013), p. 206; Sheila Fitzpatrick, *Stalin's Peasants: Resistance and Survival in the Russian Village after Collectivization* (Oxford, 1994), p. 281.

2 Nicholas Timasheff, *The Great Retreat: The Growth and Decline of Communism in Russia* (New York, 1946).

3 David Hoffmann, 'Was there a "Great Retreat" from soviet socialism? Stalinist culture reconsidered'; Evgeny Dobrenko, 'Socialism as will and representation', *Kritika* 5/4 (2004), pp. 651–74, 675–708.

4 The doctrine that will is a fundamental factor in the individual or the universe. Stalin insisted, for example, that 'realisation (of the First Five-Year Plan) depends exclusively on ourselves, on our ability and our will to use the very rich possibilities we have.' I. V. Stalin, *Sochinenia*, vol. 13 (Moscow, 1951), p. 367.

Notes

5   Hoffmann, 'Was there a "Great Retreat?",' p. 656.
6   Stalin, *Sochinenia*, vol. 13, p. 67.
7   Khlevniuk and Favorov, *Stalin*, p. 141.
8   *British Foreign Office–Russia Correspondence, 1781–1945* (Wilmington, DE, 1975), F.O. 371/1936, vol. 20351, p. 75.
9   O. V. Khlevniuk, *Khoziain: Stalin i Utverzhdenie Stalinskoi Diktatury* (Moscow, 2010). pp. 117, 212.
10 Alexei Yurchak, *Everything Was Forever, until It Was No More* (Princeton, 2005), p. 21; Brooks, *Thank You, Comrade Stalin!*, p. xvi.
11 Dobrenko, 'Socialism', pp. 685, 702; Stephen Kotkin, 'Will Putin ever leave?' *The Wall Street Journal*, 10–11 March 2018, p. 11.
12 Marquis de Custine, *Letters from Russia* (London, 1991).
13 Dobrenko, 'Socialism,' p. 707.
14 Sarah Davies and James Harris, *Stalin's World: Dictating the Soviet Order* (New Haven, CT, 2014), p. 11.
15 Stalin, *Sochinenia*, vol. 13, p. 366.
16 Reader W. Bullard, *Inside Stalin's Russia: The Diaries of Reader Bullard, 1930–1934* (Charlbury, UK, 2000), p. 211.
17 Stalin, *Sochinenia*, vol. 13, pp. 69–73.
18 Ibid., Report to the January 1933 TsK Plenum 'Results of the First Five-Year Plan', p. 208.
19 Secret Politburo Decree, 10 May 1933. Khaustov, Naumov and Plotnikova (eds), *Lubianka.*, p. 436.
20 Rossiiskii gosudarstvennyi arkhiv sotsial'no-politicheskoi istorii (hereafter RGASPI), f. 667, op. 1, d. 10, ll. 15–21, 22–4.
21 Stalin, *Sochinenia*, vol. 13, pp. 308, 314, 369.
22 RGASPI, f. 558, op. 11, d. 1119, ll. 8–10.
23 Ibid., op. 1, d. 5388, ll. 209–10; L. Kosheleva et al. (eds), *Pis'ma I. V. Stalina V.M. Molotovu 1925–1936* (Moscow, 1995), pp. 253–4.
24 David L. Hoffmann, *Cultivating the Masses: Modern State Practices and Soviet Socialism, 1914–1939* (Ithaca, NY, 2011), pp. 13–14, 286; Hoffmann, 'Was there a "Great Retreat?",' pp. 661, 672.
25 Stalin, *Sochinenia*, vol. 13, pp. 56–7, 342–3; Khlevniuk, *Khoziain*, pp. 248–9.
26 NKVD circulars 19 April 1935; 5 August 1935; 20 June 1936 in V. Danilov, R. Manning and L. Viola (eds), *Tragediia sovestskoi derevni: Kollektivizatsiia i raskulachivanie; Dokumenty i materialy*, vol. 4 (Moscow, 2002), pp. 468–9, 560, 794.
27 Bullard, *Inside Stalin's Russia*, p. 52.
28 Véronique Garros, Natalia Korenevskaya and Thomas Lahusen (eds), *Intimacy and Terror: Soviet Diaries of the 1930s* (New York, 1997), pp. 130, 144.
29 R. W. Davies, *The Industrialisation of Soviet Russia, Volume 6, The Years of Progress: The Soviet Economy, 1934–1936* (Basingstoke, UK, 2014), p. 321.
30 Garros et al., *Intimacy and Terror*, p. 209.
31 A. Y. Livshin, I. B. Orlov and O. V. Khlevniuk (eds), *Pis'ma vo Vlast', 1928–1939* (Moscow, 2002), pp. 312–13.

32 Davies, *Industrialisation*, pp. 347, 349.
33 David Shearer, *Policing Stalin's Socialism: Repression and Social Order in the Soviet Union, 1924-1953* (New Haven, 2009), pp. 131-3.
34 Khaustov, *Lubianka: 1922-1936*, pp. 410-13, 439, 748.
35 Fitzpatrick, *Stalin's Peasants*, pp. 240, 365; Danilov, *Tragediia*, vol. 4, pp. 553, 721.
36 N. N. Pokrovskii, V. P. Danilov, S. A. Krassil'nikov and L. Viola (eds), *Politburo and Krestianstvo: Vysylka, Spetsposelenie, 1930-1940*, vol. 2 (Moscow, 2006), p. 661.
37 Khlevniuk, *Khoziain*, p. 246.
38 Olga Velikanova, *Mass Political Culture under Stalinism: Popular Discussion of the Soviet Constitution of 1936* (London, 2018), pp. 116-18.
39 Khlevniuk, *Khoziain*, p. 243.
40 Khaustov, *Lubianka: 1922-1936*, p. 721.
41 S. Wheatcroft, 'Towards explaining the changing levels of Stalinist repression in the 1930s: Mass killings' in S. Wheatcroft (ed.), *Challenging Traditional Views of Russian History* (London, 2002), p. 125; Oleg Khlevnyuk and R. W. Davies, 'The end of rationing in the Soviet Union, 1934-1935', *Europe-Asia Studies* 51/4 (1999), pp. 557-609.
42 Danilov, *Tragediia*, vol. 4, pp. 752-3.
43 Giorgio Agamben, *State of Exception* (Stanford University Press, 2005), p. 5.
44 Lewin, *The Making of the Soviet System*, pp. 281-84. Getty suggests opposite argument in this volume.
45 Wheatcroft, 'Mass killings', p. 123; Khlevniuk, *Khoziain*, p. 242; V. Khaustov and L. Samuelson, *Stalin, NKVD i repressii, 1936-1938 gg.* (Moscow, 2010), pp. 101-2.
46 See Getty's article in this collection.
47 Lewin, *The Making of the Soviet System*, pp. 282-3.
48 Solomon, *Soviet Criminal Justice under Stalin*, pp. 153-73; Gabor T. Rittersporn, 'Terror and soviet legality: Police vs judiciary', in James Harris (ed.), *The Anatomy of Terror: Political Violence under Stalin* (Oxford, 2013), p. 180.
49 In 1934-631; in 1935-3,447; in 1936-23,279 persons. Khaustov and Samuelson, *Stalin*, p. 93.
50 Danilov, *Tragediia*, vol. 4, pp. 387-8, 417, 550, 339, 508-9, 550-1. More than 134,000 people were deported in the first half of 1935. Seventy per cent of the targets were kulaks and the disenfranchised, but they also included foreign nationals. Social origin and status were a reason for arrests, exile and discrimination at workplace.
51 David Priestland, Review of *Policing Stalin's Socialism*, by David Shearer. *The American Historical Review* 115/5 (2010), pp. 1553-5.
52 David Shearer, 'Elements near and alien: Passportization, policing, and identity in the Stalinist state, 1932-1952', *The Journal of Modern History* 76/4 (2004), p. 854.
53 Ibid., pp. 854-5.
54 Harris defines the period of 'moderation' as 1931-3. He called it coherent, radical, short-lived and influenced mostly by social and faction tensions within senior officialdom and perceived international complications. Harris, *Great Fear*, p. 103.
55 Danilov, *Tragediia*, vol. 5, kn. 1 (Moscow, 2004), pp. 40, 42, 260, 287, 303.
56 Khlevniuk, *Khoziain*, pp. 317, 389-90.

Notes

57 Stephen Kotkin, *Stalin: Waiting for Hitler: 1929-1941* (New York, 2017), p. 433; Khlevniuk, *Khoziain*, p. 307.

58 Fitzpatrick, *Stalin's Peasants*, p. 281.

59 However, this insecurity was perpetual and caused repressions already in 1927. Olga Velikanova, 'The first Stalin mass operation (1927)', *The Soviet and Post-Soviet Review* 40 (2013), pp. 64-89.

60 Harris, *Great Fear*, p. 177.

61 Peter Whitewood, 'The purge of the Red Army and the Soviet Mass Operations 1937-1938', *Slavonic and East European Review* 93/2 (2015), pp. 286-314.

62 Getty, 'Pre-election fever: the origins of the 1937 mass operations', p. 234.

63 Ibid., p. 224.

64 Leonid Maksimenkov, 'Rezoliutsia kak sistema.' *Kommersant.ru.* 3 July 2017. Available at https://www.kommersant.ru/doc/3336286?from=doc_vrez (accessed 16 January 2018); Khlevniuk, *Khoziain*, p. 300.

65 See Getty, *Practicing Stalinism*, chs. 6, 7.

66 Stalin, *Sochinenia*, vol. 13, p. 314.

67 *Pravda* 13 June; 7 July; 15 January 1936.

68 See Velikanova, *Mass Political Culture*, chs. 9, 10; Danilov, *Tragediia*, vol. 5, kn. 1, pp. 85, 247, 524; kn. 2, pp. 84-5; Khaustov, *Lubianka: 1922-1936*, p. 775; Getty, *Practicing Stalinism*, pp. 219-21;

69 A. A. Kulakov and A. N. Sakharov, *Obschestvo i Vlast': Rossiiskaia Provintsiia*, vol. 2 (Moscow, 2005), p. 428; Gosudarstvennyi arkhiv Rossiiskoi Federatsii (hereafter GARF), f. 3316, op. 41, d. 126, l. 147.

70 GARF, f. 3316, op. 41, d. 86, ll. 2a, verso, 2b, verso.

71 Similar comments see GARF, f. 3316, op. 8, d. 225, ll. 92-3; f. 3316, op. 40, d. 40, l. 103; d. 15, l. 121; RGASPI, f. 89, op. 4, d. 55, l. 19; f. 17, op. 120, d. 232, l. 71; Tsentral'nyi gosudarstvennyi arkhiv istoriko-politicheskikh dokumentov Sankt- Peterburga (TsGAIPD SPb), f. 4000, op. 7, d. 1176, ll. 13, 24.

72 Velikanova, *Mass Political Culture*, chs. 2, 6.

73 Stalin, *Doklad o proekte konstitutsii SSSR* (Moscow, 1947), p. 30.

74 Among many, in October 1936 North-Caucasus UNKVD reported protests responding to the constitution against *kolkhozes*, taxes and demands for opening the churches, welfare provisions and calls 'to prepare for elections' to outvote the Bolsheviks. Khaustov, *Lubianka: 1922-1936*, pp. 773-6.

75 'February-March Plenum TsK VKPb', 23 February 1937, *Voprosy Istorii* (1992) 4-5, pp. 33-4.

76 Mikhail Prishvin, *Dnevniki, 1936-1937* (Saint-Petersburg, 2010), pp. 298, 382.

77 *Pravda*, 5 March 1936. Stalin's interview to Roy Howard.

78 Khlevniuk, *Khoziain*, p. 320.

79 *Pravda*, 2 January 1937.

80 Catherine Merridale 'The 1937 census and the limits of Stalinist rule', *The Historical Journal* 39/1 (1996), pp. 226, 232.

81 Karl Schloegel, *Moscow, 1937* (Cambridge: 2012), pp. 118-19.

82 Khaustov, *Lubianka: 1937-1938*, pp. 96, 104, 106.

83 The Communist Party numbered 2 million members.
84 Kotkin, *Stalin*, pp. 383, 391 cites RGASPI, f. 17, op. 71, dd. 43, 44, 45, 46.
85 See Kokosalakis' article in this volume.
86 Khaustov, *Lubianka: 1937–1938*, pp. 273–4.
87 Operations against anti-Soviet elements in summer 1927, speculators and bandits. Olga Velikanova, *Popular Perceptions of Soviet Politics in the 1920s* (Basingstoke, 2013).
88 Yuri Zhukov, *Narodnaia Imperia Stalina* (Moscow, 2009).
89 Secret Politburo decree 10 May 1933. Khaustov, *Lubianka: 1922–1936*, p. 436.

Chapter 10

1   Francine Hirsch, *Empire of Nations: Ethnographic Knowledge and the Making of the Soviet Union* (Ithaca, 2005), p. 8 (Italics in the original).
2   Terry Martin, *The Affirmative Action Empire: Nations and Nationalism in the Soviet Union, 1923–1939* (Ithaca, 2001), p. 1; Yuri Slezkine, 'The USSR as a communal apartment, or how a socialist state promoted ethnic particularism', *Slavic Review* 53/2 (1994), p. 415.
3   V. I. Lenin, 'The war and Russian social-democracy', in Vladimir Lenin, *Collected Works*, 2nd ed., 45 vols. (Moscow, 1963-73), vol. 21, p. 28.
4   V. I. Lenin, 'The socialist revolution and the right of nations to self-determination. Theses', in Vladimir Lenin, *Collected Works*, vol. 22, p. 151.
5   Taras Hunczak (ed.), *The Ukraine, 1917–1921: A Study in Revolution* (Cambridge, MA, 1977), p. 382.
6   *Tretii Vserossiiskii S"ezd Sovetov rabochikh, soldatskikh i krestianskikh deputatov* (Petrograd, 1919), pp. 72–8.
7   Ibid., p. 78.
8   *Vos'moi S"ezd RKP(b): Mart 1919 goda: Protokoly* (Moscow, 1959), p. 425.
9   Lev Yurkevych, 'Iesuits'ka polityka', in Taras Hunchak and Roman Solchanyk (eds), *Tysiacha Rokiv Ukrains'koi Suspil'no-Politychnoi Dumky*, vol. 6 (Kyiv, 2001), pp. 184–90; Lev Yurkevych, 'Rosiiski sotsial-demokraty ta natsional'ne pytannia', in *Tysiacha rokiv*, vol. 6, pp. 220–37.
10 Serhii Mazlakh, Vasyl Shakhrai, *Do Khvyli: Shcho Diiet'sia na Ukraini i z Ukrainoiu?* (New York, 1954); *On the Current Situation in the Ukraine* (Michigan, 1970).
11 On the early history of the Bolsheviks in Ukraine, see Moisei Ravich-Cherkasskii, *Istoria Kommunisticheskoi Partii (bov) Ukrainy* (Kharkov, 1923); M. Popov, *Narys istorii Komunistychnoi partii (bil'shovykiv) Ukrainy* (Kharkiv, 1929).
12 Stephen Velychenko, *Painting Imperialism and Nationalism Red: The Ukrainian Marxist Critique of Russian Communist Rule in Ukraine, 1918–1925* (Toronto, 2015), p. 122.
13 *Borot'ba* (Kyiv), 20 February 1919.
14 *Borot'ba* (Vienna), 7–8 April 1920.
15 *Chervonyi Prapor* (Kyiv), 22 January 1919.
16 'Resoliutsiia pro Vidnoshennia Fraktsii Nezalezhnykh do Rosiis'koi Komunistychnoi Partii i do Komunistychnoi Partii (bol'shevikiv)', in Pavlo Khrystiuk, *Zamitky i Materiialy do Istorii Ukrains'koi Revoliutsii 1917–1920*, vol. IV (New York, 1969), p. 56.

Notes

17 'Memorandum Ukrains'koi Komunistychnoi partii (borot'bystiv) Vykonavchomu Komitetovi II-ho Komunistychnogo Internatsionaly (serpen' 1919 r.)' in *Tysiacha rokiv*, vol. 6, pp. 403–4.

18 *Chetverta Konferentsiia Komunistychnoi Partii (Bil'shovykiv) Ukrainy 17–23 bereznia 1920 r.* (Kyiv, 2003), pp. 173–7.

19 V. I. Lenin, 'Proekt rezoliutsii ob ukrainskoi partii Borot'bistov', in Lenin, *Polnoe Sobranie Sochinenii*, vol. 40, p. 122.

20 'Rezoliutsiia TsK RKP(b) o Sovetskoi Vlasti na Ukraine', in Lenin, *Polnoe Sobranie Sochinenii*, vol. 39, pp. 334–7.

21 Lenin, *Polnoe Sobranie Sochinenii*, vol. 40, p. 42.

22 Ivan Maistrenko, *Istoriia Komunistychnoi Partii Ukrainy* (Munich, 1979), p. 74; Popov, *Narys*, p. 219.

23 M. Frolov, *Kompartiino-Radians'ka Elita v Ukraini (1923–1928 rr): Osoblyvosti Isnuvannia ta Funktsionuvannia* (Zaporizhzhia, 2004), p. 175.

24 In October 1922–March 1924, the Narkomos was headed by the Bolshevik Volodymyr Zatons'kyi.

25 'Politika partii po natsional'nomu voprosu', *Pravda*, 10 October, 1920; I. V. Stalin, *Sochineniia*, vol. 4 (Moscow, 1947), p. 351.

26 Quoted from Elena Borisenok, *Fenomen Sovetskoi Ukrainizatsii, 1920–30-e gody* (Moscow, 2006), p. 67.

27 Slezkine, 'USSR as a communal apartment, p. 423.

28 Quoted from ibid., pp. 417–18.

29 'Politika partii po natsional'nomu voprosu', Stalin, *Sochineniia*, vol. 4, p. 358.

30 Leon Trotsky, *Literature and Revolution* (Chicago, 2005 [1925]), p. 61.

31 Bohdan Krawchenko, *Social Change and National Consciousness in Twentieth-Century Ukraine* (Basingstoke, 1986), p. 101.

32 George Liber, *Soviet Nationality Policy, Urban Growth, and Identity Change in the Ukrainian SSR 1923–1934* (Cambridge, 2002), p. 88.

33 Liber, *Nationality Policy*, pp. 87–103.

34 Krawchenko, *Social Change*, p. 9.

35 On social and ethnic composition of Ukraine's urban areas see Liber, *Nationality Policy*; Krawchenko, *Social Change*.

36 Tsentral'nyi derzhavnyi arkhiv hromads'kykh ob'iednan' Ukrainy (TsDAHO), f. 1, op. 1, spr. 208; *Kul'turne Budivnytstvo v Ukrains'kii RSR: Vazhlyvishi rishennia Komunistychnoi partii Radians'koho uriadu 1917–1959 rr: Zbirnyk dokumentiv*, vol. 1 (Kyiv, 1959), pp. 312–18.

37 TsDAHO, f. 1, op. 6, spr. 88, ark. 129–zv.

38 Ibid.

39 TsDAHO, f. 1, op. 20, spr. 2248, ark. 1–7; Stalin, *Sochineniia*, vol. 8, pp. 149–54.

40 Stalin, *Sochineniia*, vol. 8, p. 152.

41 On challenges for proletarian Ukrainization, see Martin, *Affirmative Action*, p. 97.

42 Liber, *Nationality Policy*, p. 77.

43 George Liber, 'Language, literacy, and book publishing in the Ukrainian SSR, 1923–1928', *Slavic Review* 41/4 (1982), pp. 673–85.

44 V. I. Lenin, *What Is to Be Done?* (c. 1901).
45 James Mace, *Communism and the Dilemmas of National Liberation* (Cambridge, MA, 1983), p. 230.
46 *Kul'turne Budivnytstvo*, 1, pp. 282–6.
47 Matthew D. Pauly, *Breaking the Tongue: Language, Education, and Power in Soviet Ukraine, 1923–1934* (Toronto, 2014), pp. 153, 165.
48 Quoted from Martin, *Affirmative Action*, p. 225.
49 Iurii Shapoval, '"On Ukrainian separatism" A GPU circular of 1926', *Harvard Ukrainian Studies* XVIII 3/4 (1994), pp. 292–3.
50 Pauly, *Breaking the Tongue*, 249.
51 Volodymyr Prystaiko and Iurii Shapoval, *Sprava 'Spilky Vyzvolennia Ukrainy': Nevidomi Dokumenty i Fakty* (Kyiv, 1995), p. 44.
52 James Harris, *The Great Urals: Regionalism and the Evolution of the Soviet System* (Ithaca; London, 1999); Teresa Rakowska-Harmstone, 'The dialectics of nationalism in the USSR', *Problems of Communism* 23/5–6 (1974), pp. 1–22.
53 Hirsch, *Empire of Nations*, p. 146.
54 *XV S"ezd VKP (b): Stenograficheskii otchet* (Moscow, 1928), pp. 133–4.
55 Bohdan Somchynsky, 'National communism and the politics of industrialization in Ukraine, 1923–28', *Journal of Ukrainian Studies* 25 (1988), pp. 52–69.
56 H. Hryn'ko, 'Narys ukraiins'koi ekonomiky', *Chervonyi Shliakh* 6 (1926), pp. 120–36; Mykhailo Volobuiev, 'Do Problem Ukrains'koi Ekonomiky', *Bil'shovyk Ukrainy*, 30 January, 1928; 15 February, 1928; *Dokumenty Ukrains'koho Komunizmu* (New York, 1962), pp. 132–230.
57 Volobuiev, *Do Problem*, pp. 137–40.
58 Quoted from Inna Kochetkova, *The Myth of the Russian Intelligentsia: Old Intellectuals in the New Russia* (London and New York, 2010), p. 23.

Chapter 11

1 See, for instance, Oleg Khlevniuk, 'The objectives of the great terror, 1937–1938', in J. Cooper et al. (eds), *Soviet History, 1917–53: Essays in Honour of R. W. Davies* (Basingstoke, 1995), pp. 258–276; Peter Whitewood, *The Red Army and the Great Terror: Stalin's Purge of the Soviet Military* (Kansas, 2015); Harris, *The Great Fear*.
2 For an exception, Olga Velikanova examined the importance of the foreign threat to the Soviet Union in the 1920s and the impact of popular mobilisation campaigns. See *Popular Perceptions of Soviet Politics in the 1920s* (Basingstoke, 2013).
3 V. I. Lenin, *Collected Works*, vol. 32 (Moscow, 1973), pp. 436, 454, 478.
4 See Józef Borzęcki, *The Soviet-Polish Peace of 1921 and the Creation of Interwar Europe* (New Haven, 2008).
5 Jan Jacek Bruski, *Between Prometheism and Realpolitik: Poland and Soviet Ukraine, 1921–1926* (Krakow, 2016), p. 13.
6 Lenin, *Collected Works*, vol. 32, pp. 114–15.

Notes

7   A. A. Plekhanov and A. M. Plekhanov (eds), *F. E. Dzerzhinskii – Predsedatel' VChK–OGPU, 1917–1926: Dokumenty* (Moscow, 2007), pp. 248–9.

8   Tsentral'nyi derzhavnyi arkhiv vyshchykh orhaniv vlady ta upravlinnia Ukraïny (hereafter TsDAVO), f. 4, op. 1, d. 14, l. 23.

9   Arkhiv vneshnei politiki Rossiiskoi Federatsii (hereafter AVPRF), f. 4, op. 32, p. 210, d. 52511, ll. 13–17.

10 Quoted in Michael Carley, *Silent Conflict: A Hidden History of Early Soviet–Western Relations* (Maryland, 2014), p. 55; Harris, *Great Fear*, p. 43, fn. 14.

11 Rossiiskii gosudarstvennyi voennyi arkhiv (hereafter RGVA), f. 33987, op. 1, d. 460, ll. 54–5.

12 David R. Stone, 'The prospect of war? Lev Trotskii, the Soviet army, and the German revolution in 1923', *The International History Review* 25/4 (2003), p. 815.

13 See Dzerzhinskii's letter to V. N. Mantsev, 11 November 1921. Plekhanov and Plekhanov, *Dzerzhinskii*, pp. 344–5.

14 See note to Konstanty Skirmunt, TsDAVO, f. 4, op. 1, d. 31, l. 3. See also *Dokumenty vneshnei politiki SSSR*, vol. 5 (Moscow, 1961), pp. 145–7.

15 *Odinnadtsatyi s'ezd RKP(b): Protokoly* (Moscow, 1936), p. 637.

16 Rossiiskii gosudarstvennyi arkhiv sotsial'no-politicheskoi istorii (hereafter RGASPI), f. 558, op. 1, d. 2326, l. 1.

17 M. Ul', V. Khaustov and V. Zakharov (eds), *Glazami razvedki: SSSR i Evropa, 1919–1938 gody: sbornik dokumentov iz rossiiskikh arkhivov* (Moscow, 2015), p. 58.

18 Ibid., p. 64. On the movement of Polish troops reported in July 1922, see RGVA, f. 25899, op. 3, d. 515, l. 118ob.

19 Ul', Khaustov and Zakharov, *Glazami razvedki*, p. 83.

20 TsDAVO, f. 4, op. 1, d. 591, l. 2. Oleksandr Shumskyi, Soviet Ukraine's Ambassador to Poland, also sent a warning to Frunze in September about Polish 'systematic preparations' for war. See Bruski, *Prometheism and Realpolitik*, p. 194 (fn. 11).

21 RGVA, f. 25899, op. 3, d. 536, l. 1.

22 On the Bolsheviks' enthusiasm for the revolutionary events in Germany, see Stone, 'Prospect of war'.

23 RGASPI, f. 558, op. 11, d. 789, l. 2.

24 Stone, 'Prospect of war', p. 802.

25 *Dvenadtsatyi s'ezd RKP(b): stenograficheskii otchet* (Moscow, 1968), p. 16.

26 See intelligence report from January 1923, RGVA, f. 33988, op. 2, d. 533, l. 3.

27 RGVA, f. 25899, d. 3, d. 565, l. 120; Ul', Khaustov and Zakharov, *Glazami razvedki*, p. 108. Some intelligence presented a more moderate picture, noting that Foch believed that Poland and France should pressure the Bolshevik government into collapse, however, not going as far as armed intervention. RGVA, f. 33988, op. 2, d. 533, l. 89.

28 RGVA, f. 25899, op. 3, d. 536, l. 34ob.

29 Derzhavnyi haluzevyi arkhiv sluzhby bezpeky Ukraïny (hereafter DHASBU), f. 13, ark. 162, tm. 12, l. 34.

30 RGVA, f. 25899, op. 3, d. 536, l. 30.

31 RGVA, f. 25899, op. 2, d. 556, l. 206.

32 RGASPI, f. 76, op. 2, d. 17, l. 86.

33 Plekhanov and Plekhanov, *Dzerzhinskii*, pp. 486–7.
34 In a report to the Politburo two years later Frunze described this as a 'sudden transition' towards military preparations. N. S. Simonov, '"Strengthen the defence of the land of the Soviets": The 1927 "war alarm" and its consequences', *Europe-Asia Studies* 48/8 (1996), pp. 1359–60.
35 RGASPI, f. 17, op. 162, d. 1, l. 12.
36 Stone, 'Prospect of war', p. 804.
37 Ibid.
38 TsDAVO, f. 2, op. 2, d. 905, l. 8.
39 RGASPI, f. 17, op. 87, d. 177, l. 95.
40 DHASBU, f. 13, ark. 162, tm. 7, l. 2.
41 RGVA, f. 308, op. 3, d. 39, l. 25.
42 On Polish politics in 1923, see Bruski, *Prometheism and Realpolitik*, pp. 73–4.
43 Pirani, *The Russian Revolution in Retreat, 1920–24*, pp. 55–7.
44 Lenin, *Collected Works*, vol. 32, p. 53. At a speech to Moscow metal workers shortly after, Lenin argued that dictatorship was necessary because the entire bourgeois world was against Russia. See ibid., p. 108.
45 Ibid., pp. 167–9.
46 Ibid., p. 495.
47 Ibid., p. 505.
48 Lenin, *Collected works*, vol. 33 (Moscow, 1973), pp. 322–4.
49 *Odinnadtsatyi s'ezd RKP(b)*, p. 138.
50 Ibid., p. 603.
51 *Dvenadtsatyi s'ezd RKP(b)*, p. 6.
52 Ibid., pp. 198–200.
53 Valentina Vilkova, *RKP(b): Vnutripartiinaia bor'ba v dvadtsatye gody: Dokumenty i materialy: 1923* (Moscow, 2004), p. 267.
54 On the discussion about party democracy after October 1923, see Robert V. Daniels, *The Conscience of the Revolution: Communist Opposition in Soviet Russia* (New York, 1969), pp. 220–35. See also James Harris, 'Discipline vs democracy: the 1923 party controversy' in this volume.
55 I. V. Stalin, *Collected Works*, vol. 6 (Moscow, 1953), p. 23.
56 See, for instance, Boris Souvarine, *Stalin: A Critical Survey of Bolshevism* (New York, 1939); Daniels, *Conscience of the Revolution*; Ulam, *Stalin: The Man and His Era* (New York, 1979); David R. Stone, *Hammer and Rifle: The Militarization of the Soviet Union, 1926–1933* (Kansas, 2000).
57 RGASPI, f. 76, op. 2, d. 58, l. 3.
58 Iu. V. Ivanov, *Ocherki istorii rossiisko(sovetsko)-pol'skikh otnoshenii v dokumentakh: 1914–1945* (Moscow, 2014), pp. 154, 160.
59 DHASBU, f. 13, ark. 445, l. 1.
60 A meeting of leaders from the political police, foreign ministry and military noted that the threat of war had significantly increased with Piłsudski's return to power. RGASPI, f. 76, op. 3, f. 364, l. 72.

Notes

61 Ivanov, *Ocherki*, p. 151.
62 Stone, *Hammer and Rifle*, pp. 20–22.
63 Stephen Kotkin, *Stalin: Paradoxes of Power* (New York, 2015), p. 589.
64 RGASPI, f. 76, op. 3, d. 364, l. 57; f. 558, op. 11, d. 726, ll. 55–60b.
65 Iu. Shapoval, V. Prystaiko and V. Zolotar'ov (eds), *ChK –GPU–NKVD v Ukraïni: Osoby, fakty, dokumenty* (Kyiv, 1997), p. 254.
66 RGASPI, f. 76, op. 3, d. 364, l. 71.
67 A military intelligence report from June 1926 argued that Piłsudski would break with the efforts of his predecessors to improve relations with the Soviet Union. See Ivanov, *Ocherki*, p. 153.
68 RGASPI, f. 76, op. 2, d. 58, ll. 156, 158.
69 Stalin, *Collected Works*, vol. 8 (Moscow, 1954), pp. 276–7.
70 Carley, *Silent Conflict*, p. 257; Kotkin, *Paradoxes*, p. 623. Litvinov conveyed a similar message in January 1927 at a meeting of the foreign affairs commissariat. Here he argued that some intelligence reports were fantasy and that it was a mistake to see the malevolent hand of the British government everywhere. Ibid., p. 622.
71 L. S. Gatagova, L. P. Kosheleva and L. A. Rogovaia (eds), *TsK RKP(b) – BKP(b) i natsional'nyi vopros, kniga 1 1918–1933 gg.* (Moscow, 2005), pp. 486–93.
72 RGASPI, f. 558, op. 11, d. 71, l. 2.
73 In a speech following the raids in London, Voroshilov claimed that the next logical step was a British attack on the Soviet Union. RGASPI, f. 74, op. 2, d. 49, l. 42.
74 Stalin, *Collected Works*, vol. 9 (Moscow, 1954), pp. 328–69.
75 RGASPI, f. 558, op. 22, d. 726, ll. 55–60b. Dzerzhinskii was not totally off the mark. The Polish press reported on the ongoing internal struggle and the inability of the party majority to do anything about this. See Gosudarstvennyi arkhiv Rossiiskoi Federatsii, f. 4459, op. 2, d. 158, l. 45.
76 Stalin, *Collected Works*, vol. 9, p. 318.
77 Ibid., pp. 336–7.
78 Stalin, *Collected Works*, vol. 10 (Moscow, 1954), p. 62.
79 See Voroshilov's and Arkady Rosengolts's comments in 1927: RGASPI, f. 74, op. 2, d. 49, ll. 47, 77.
80 Igal Halfin, *Intimate Enemies: Demonizing the Bolshevik Opposition, 1918–1928* (Pittsburgh, 2007), p. 246.
81 Leon Trotsky, 'The "Clémenceau thesis" and the party regime', September 1927. Available at https://www.marxists.org/archive/trotsky/1927/09/clemenceau.htm (accessed 1 September 2018).
82 Trotsky, *The Challenge of the Left Opposition 1926–27* (New York, 1980), p. 245. Zinoviev was just as adamant about the inevitability of war. See Simonov, 'Strengthen the defence', p. 1359.
83 Trotsky, 'Platform of the joint opposition', 1927. Available at https://www.marxists.org/archive/trotsky/1927/opposition/ch09.htm (accessed 1 September 2018).
84 Trotsky, *The Challenge*, p. 248.

Chapter 12

1 A. V. Lunacharskii, 'Kommunisticheskaia propaganda i narodnoe prosveshchenie', *Izvestiia*, 26 March 1919.

Notes

2   Narkompros was in effect the government ministry for education and the arts after the October Revolution, subordinate to the Council of Ministers (Sovnarkom).
3   Leonard B. Schapiro, *The Origin of the Communist Autocracy: Political Opposition in the Soviet State: First Phase, 1917–1922* (New York, 1965), p. v.
4   Richard Pipes (ed.), *The Unknown Lenin from the Secret Archive* (New Haven, 1998), pp. 6–12; afterword to paperback edition, p. 181.
5   Victor Sebestyen, *Lenin the Dictator: An Intimate Portrait* (London, 2017), p. 335.
6   See Lars T. Lih, 'The great awakening', in Sebastian Budgen, Stathis Kouelakis and Slavoj Žižek (eds), *Lenin Reloaded* (Durham, NC, 2007), pp. 283–396.
7   Lars T. Lih, *Lenin Rediscovered: 'What Is to Be Done?' in Context* (Chicago, 2008).
8   'Significant Others' – meaning Lenin's intellectual interlocutors in the Russian Social Democratic moment before 1917 – is the title of part 2 of Lih, *Lenin Rediscovered*. Krupskaia is not included in the category.
9   N. K. Krupskaia, *Pedagogicheskie sochineniia*, 11 vols. (Moscow, 1957–63), vol. 2, p. 76.
10 Robert H. McNeal, *Bride of the Revolution: Krupskaya and Lenin* (Ann Arbor, 1972), pp. 30–3.
11 Maria Essen, 'Vstrechi na partiinoi rabote', in A. M. Arsenev, V. S. Dridzo and A.G. Kravchenko (eds), *Vospominaniia o Nadezhde Konstantinovne Krupskoi* (Moscow, 1966), p. 61.
12 *Narodnoe obrazovanie i demokratiia* (1915), text in Krupskaia, *Pedagogicheskie sochineniia*, vol. 1, pp. 249–350.
13 McNeal, *Bride*, p. 36.
14 N. K. Krupskaia, *Vospominaniia o Lenine* (Moscow, 1957), pp. 10–11. It took a while for Krupskaia to get over the negative impression this created in her, but she gradually came to realize that his harshness about anything that smacked of liberal do-gooding was related to the pain of his family's ostracism by respectable society after the arrest and execution for revolutionary activity of his older brother, Alexander Ulyanov.
15 As Deutscher comments, the late 1905 returnees like Lenin 'watched (the Petersburg Soviet) in suspense and bewilderment' but 'they had too much of the air of émigrés to gain a foothold in it.' Isaac Deutscher, *The Prophet Armed: Trotsky: 1879–1921* (London, 1970), pp. 135–6. His 'Two tactics of Social Democracy' (1905), in V. I. Lenin, *Polnoe sobranie sochinenii*, 5th ed., 58 vols. (Moscow, 1958–70), vol. 11, pp. 1–131, focused on leadership, while a retrospective appraisal of 1905 twelve years later gave pride of place to mass strikes and mutinies, with only a perfunctory paragraph on the soviets. 'Doklad o revoliutsii 1905 g.', in Lenin, *Polnoe sobranie sochinenii*, vol. 30, pp. 306–28.
16 See E. M. Kozhevnikov (ed.), *Vladimir Ilyich Lenin o vospitanii i obrazovanii v 2-kh tomakh*, vol. 1 (Moscow, 1980).
17 See the Table of Contents of *Vladimir Ilyich Lenin o vospitanii i obrazovanii*, vol. 1, pp. 541–2.
18 Krupskaia, *Vospominaniia*, p. 206.
19 The conversation of 1912 is related in Nikolay Valentinov (N. V. Volsky), *Encounters with Lenin*, in Paul Rosta and Brian Pearce (trans.) (London, 1968), pp. 48–9. It should be noted that Volsky strongly disliked Krupskaia and enjoyed pointing up any differences between her and Lenin.
20 McNeal, *Bride*, pp. 163–5. 'Fantastic' comes from Krupskaia, *Vospominaniia*, p. 270, as does the characterization of this as a possible money-making venture. The dryness with which she

Notes

recounts this episode (pp. 269–70) suggests a certain resistance to Lenin's moving in on her pedagogical work and trying to turn it to his advantage.

21 Krupskaia, *Vospominaniia*, p. 206.
22 Ibid., pp. 292–4.
23 See memoir by G. I. Petrovskii in Arsenev, Dridzo and Kravchenko (eds) *Vospominaniia*, p. 82, of a conversation in 1912 when Lenin became carried away by the idea of small partisan units and their potentially useful role 'disorganizing the existing order.' Krupskaia evidently felt that in real life this might not work out so well.
24 The origin of Krupskaia's alleged comment 'It seems that Lenin is out of his mind' is an unpublished memoir by George Denike, quoting the progressive educationalist Albert Pinkevich, then a member of the inter-district international group trying to reunite the social democrats (he would join the Bolshevik Party only in 1923) who was standing next to her at the Finland Station as Lenin delivered his April theses: McNeal, *Bride*, p. 171.
25 Quoted in ibid., p. 172.
26 Ibid., p. 182. For her dry account, see Krupskaia, *Vospominianiia*, pp. 313–14.
27 *Gosudarstvo i revoliutsiia*, in Lenin, *Polnoe sobranie sochinenii*, vol. 33, pp. 1–120.
28 Harding, *Lenin's Political Thought*, vol. 2, p. 118.
29 Lenin, *Gosudarstvo i revoliutsiia*, postscript to 2nd ed., loc. cit.
30 Vserossiiskii ispolnitel'nyi komitet s"ezdov sovetov RSFSR (VTsIK). This body was in fact set up, initially as a republican institution, but played only a secondary role in the new government, A corresponding Soviet organ (TsIK, later renamed the Supreme Soviet) was added after the creation of the Soviet Union in 1924.
31 Rigby, *Lenin's Government*.
32 *Lenin's Government* is the classic work on this. For a recent work developing Rigby's insights, see Douds, *Inside Lenin's Government*.
33 Lenin 'Ocherednye zadachi sovetskoi vlasti'(1(14) October 1917), *Polnoe sobranie sochinenii*, vol. 36, pp. 126–64.
34 In *State and Revolution*, Lenin had written sanguinely that commune (soviet)-type institutions could easily take over administrative tasks, avoiding becoming bureaucratized by the principles of election, easy recall and constant rotation of officials. A few weeks later, still before the seizure of power, Lenin had described the soviets as the new form of state apparatus and insisted that the 'class conscious workers and soldiers' – if not yet the toiling masses as a whole – were ready to take over the administrative burden. 'Uderzhat li Bol'sheviki gosudarstvennuiu vlast'?' (1(14) October 1917) in Lenin, *Polnoe sobranie sochinenii*, vol. 34, pp. 287–339. By the spring, after four months in power, 'We must learn to combine the "meeting" democracy of the toiling masses – turbulent, surging, overflowing its banks like a spring flood – with *iron* discipline while at work, with *unquestioning obedience* to the will of one person, the Soviet leader, while at work.' 'Ocherednye zadachi', loc. cit.
35 Lenin dismissed soviet participatory democracy with the rather patronizing comment that 'holding meetings is the real democracy of the toilers, it is their way of unbending their backs, their awakening to new life, their first step along the road which they themselves have cleared of reptiles (the exploiters, the imperialists, the landlords and capitalists) and which they want to learn to lay down themselves, in their own way.' Ibid., loc. cit.
36 Ibid., loc. cit.
37 On the withering of the soviets as revolutionary institutions and their 'mobilization' by the Bolsheviks after October, see John H. L. Keep, *The Russian Revolution: A Study in Mass*

Mobilization (London, 1976). For an illuminating discussion of the local as well as central pressures that made 'bureaucratization' of the soviets (the emergence of a quasi-professional, quasi-permanent group of officeholders) virtually inevitable, see Marc Ferro, *Des soviets au communisme bureaucratique* (Paris, 1980).

38 Sheila Fitzpatrick, *The Commissariat of Enlightenment: Soviet Organization of Education and the Arts, October 1917–1921* (Cambridge, 1970), pp. 27–8. Lunacharskii, the Commissar, took the most radical position against the very existence of appointed education departments in 1918, while Krupskaia was readier to accept them if they operated under the supervision of educational soviets. But over the long term, it was Krupskaia who was the most persistent supporter of educational soviets.

39 'O sovetakh narodnogo obrazovaniia' (1918), in Krupskaia, *Pedagogicheskie sochinenii*, vol. 2, pp. 75–7.

40 See Fitzpatrick, *Commissariat*, pp. 28–9. Parents were notable by their absence, as such, from the educational soviets, for Narkompros – and current thinking in general in the Bolshevik Party – at this point regarded them as a 'bourgeois' element whose influence over their children's upbringing needed to be contested by the socialist state.

41 In 'Polozhenie ob organizatsii dela narodnogo obrazovaniia v Rossiiskoi Respublike', 26 June 1918: Krupskaia, *Pedagogicheskie sochinenii*, vol. 2, pp. 696–7 (note).

42 For draft, see V. I. Lenin, *Vladimir Il'ich Lenin o vospitanii i obrazovanii v 2-kh tomakh*, ed. E. M. Kozhevnikov, vol. 2 (Moscow, 1980), pp. 81–2.

43 Par. 6 of Section on Education, 'Programme of the Communist Party of Russia adopted at the Eighth Party Congress held 18 to 23 March 1919', published in English translation as an appendix to N. Bukharin and E. Preobrazhenskii, *The ABC of Communism* (Harmondsworth, 1969), p. 444.

44 'Ocherednye zadachi sovetskoi vlasti' in Lenin, *Polnoe sobranie sochinenii*, vol. 36, pp. 124–64.

45 Krupskaia, *Vospominaniia*, p. 322.

46 Krupskaia to Pokrovskii, letter of June 1920, in her *Pedagogicheskie sochineniia*, vol. 10, p. 47 ('my hobbyhorse'); Larry E. Holmes, *The Kremlin and the Schoolhouse: Reforming Education in Soviet Russia, 1917–1931* (Bloomington, 1991), p. 30, notes Krupskaia's stubbornness through the 1920s sticking to her ideals, 'tirelessly keeping alive the idea of educational soviets'.

47 Fitzpatrick, *Commissariat*. This does not mean that he supported Narkompros across the board: there were disagreements with Lunacharskii about support for elite cultural institutions like the Bolshoi Ballet, Proletkult and other matters, but on basic educational matters – schools, universities, literacy and adult education– he was solidly behind the Commissariat, although he was inclined to want 'less talk of innovative methods and more concern for traditional content' and to urge Narkompros to do better in timely provision of syllabi, lesson plans and textbooks for schools: Holmes, *Kremlin*, p. 23.

48 See Lenin, *O vospitanii i obrazovanii*, vol. 2: the contents of the volume for 1918–21 include eleven drafts of decrees and resolutions and nine speeches at educational and teachers' conferences. Even when sidelined by illness in 1922, Lenin sent greetings to a teachers' congress.

49 The only occasion Lenin's support for Krupskaia's educational stand wavered was in the debate over general versus specialized professional education at the end of 1920, when in an unpublished commentary on a draft intervention of Krupskaia's he made more concessions than she had done to the professional lobby. But he worried about this and marked his

Notes

comments 'Private. Draft. *Not for publication*. I have to think this over a couple more times.' Lenin, 'O politekhnicheskom obrazovanii: Zametki na tezisy Nadezhdy Konstantinovny', in his *Polnoe sobranie sochinenii*, vol. 42, pp. 228–30.

50 For specific instances of Lenin's support of Narkompros, see Fitzpatrick, *Commissariat*, pp. 72–5, 82, 196–200, 210–15, 221–6 and 248 (policy questions) and 204, 248, 276 and 285 (budget and personnel). After the Tenth Congress of Soviets mandated the introduction of school fees, to Narkompros' bitter disappointment, in 1922, Krupskaia wrote to a colleague that the measure would 'probably not have passed' had Lenin not been out of commission through illness: letter to Z. G. Grinberg, 9 January 1923, in Krupskaia, *Pedagogicheskie sochineniia*, vol. 11, p. 224.

51 For cultural analysis, see the articles written in 1923–4 published as L. Trotsky, *Voprosy byta* and *Literatura i revoliutsiia*. For Lenin's proposal, see Leon Trotsky, *My Life* (New York, 1960), pp. 478–9.

52 In the Politburo in 1920, Bukharin took the party agitprop side against Narkompros (and Lenin) in debate on *politprosvet*: Fitzpatrick, *Commissariat*, p. 185. The previous year, in an argument over theatre policy, Lunacharskii had called him an advocate of 'absolutely primitive Communism': quoted in A. Gozenpud, *Russkii sovetskii opernyi teatr (1917–1941)* (Leningrad, 1963), p. 26.

53 For conflicts between Lunacharskii and Narkompros in Moscow on the one hand and Lilina and Zinoviev on the other, see Fitzpatrick, *Commissariat*, pp. 46, 190 and 276.

54 Fitzpatrick, *Commissariat*, p. 200.

55 From a 1928 letter to comrade Chistov of the Central Committee's agitprop department, in 'Letters of N. K. Krupskaia', *Sovetskaia pedagogika*, 11 (1961), pp. 143–5. On the *politprosvet* battles of 1920–1, see Fitzpatrick, *Commissariat*, pp. 243–55.

56 See Fitzpatrick, *Commissariat*, p. 251.

57 Lenin, 'Stranichki iz dnevnika' (1923) in his *Polnoe sobranie sochinenii*, vol. 45.

58 See particularly Moshe Lewin, *Lenin's Last Struggle* (New York, 1968). For a recent recapitulation, Slavoj Žižek (ed.), *Lenin 2017: Remembering, Repeating, and Working Through* (London, 2017).

59 See, for example, V. T. Ermakov, *Istoricheskii opyt kul'turnoi revolutsii v SSSR* (Moscow, 1968). In the West, the cultural theme was picked up by Carmen Claudin-Urondo, *Lénine et la revolution culturelle* (Paris, La Haye, 1974).

60 Lenin, 'O kooperatsii' (6 January 1923) *Polnoe sobranie sochinenii*, vol. 45, pp. 369–77.

61 Ibid., p. 369–77.

62 'O nashei revoliiutsii (po povodu zapisok N. Sukhanova)', in Lenin, *Polnoe sobranie sochinenii*, vol. 45, pp. 378–82.

63 Lenin, 'Stranichki iz dnevnika', *Pravda* (4 January 1923), 1 in Lenin, *Polnoe sobranie sochinenii*, vol. 45.

64 See Lewin, *Lenin's Last Struggle*, pp. 119–21 (workers' control) and Sheila Fitzpatrick, *The Cultural Front* (Ithaca NY, 1994), p. 6 (specialists).

65 E. H. Carr, *Socialism in One Country 1924–1926*, vol. 2 (London, 1959), pp. 304–9.

66 Lenin, letter to G. I. Miasnikov, 5 August 1921, in his *Polnoe sobranie sochinenii*, vol. 44, pp. 78–83.

67 After Lenin's death, an attempt at soviet revitalization with respect to the countryside was made by Zinoviev in the 'Face to the countryside' campaign launched in the autumn of 1924.

Carr, *Socialism*, vol. 2, pp. 318–34, 320. This initiative had the full approval of Krupskaia (who was to become a member of the Zinoviev faction in the succession struggle), but it soon foundered along with Zinoviev's own political fortunes.

68 Robert Service, *Lenin: A Biography* (Cambridge, MA, 2000), p. 463.
69 See Lewin, *Lenin's Last Struggle*, pp. 65–103.
70 For the long-running conflict with Stalin that this entailed, see V. A. Kumanev and I. S. Kulikova, *Protivostoianie: Krupskaia-Stalin* (Moscow, 1994). The Opposition made its first formal appearance in October 1925, when Krupskaia signed a letter with Zinoviev, Kamenev and Sokolnikov complaining about peasant policy. Her departure from the Opposition was announced by Stalin in early November 1926 in his closing remarks to Fifteenth party conference and confirmed by Krupskaia in a letter published in *Pravda* 20 May 1927. Daniels, *The Conscience of the Revolution*, pp. 255, 282.
71 Krupskaia, *Vospominaniia*, pp. 321–3.
72 For example, on *edinonachalie*, of which Lenin was a strong advocate on efficiency grounds (see above, n. 34).
73 See quotation above, p. 190.

Chapter 13

1 Tat'iana M. Goriaeva, *Politicheskaia tsenzura v CCCP 1917–1991* (Moscow, 2002), p. 191.
2 Ibid., p. 5.
3 Herman Ermolaev, *Censorship in Soviet Literature, 1917–1991* (London, 1997), p. 1.
4 Yuri Slezkine, *The House of Government: A Saga of the Russian Revolution* (Princeton, 2017), p. 30.
5 Stephen Kotkin, Stalin, *Vol II: Waiting for Hitler 1928–1941* (London, 2017), p. 2.
6 V. I. Lenin, *The Re-Organisation of the Party & Party Organisation and Party Literature* (London, 1905), p. 16.
7 Ibid., p. 19.
8 D. Strovsky and G. Simons, 'The Bolsheviks' attitude towards the press in Russia: 1917–1920', *Arbetsrapporter Working Papers* 109 (January 2007), p. 4.
9 John Keep (ed.), *The Debate on Soviet Power: Minutes of the All-Russian Central Executive Committee of Soviets – Second Convocation, October 1917–January 1918* (Oxford, 1979), p. 69.
10 Ibid., pp. 74–5.
11 Lenin, *The Re-Organisation of the Party*, p. 18.
12 Samantha Sherry, 'Censorship in Translation in the Soviet Union in the Stalin and Khrushchev eras' (University of Edinburgh PhD thesis, 2012), pp. 38, 46.
13 Beate Müller, 'Censorship and cultural regulation: Mapping the territory', in Beate Müller (ed.), *Censorship and Cultural Regulation in the Modern Age* (Amsterdam, 2004), pp. 4–5.
14 I. Kollárová, 'The reading ideal and reading preferences in the age of Joseph II', *Human Affairs* 23/3 (2013), p. 354.

Notes

15 R. A. Houston, *Literacy in Early Modern Europe* (London, 2002); Annabel Patterson, *Censorship and Interpretation: The Conditions of Writing and Reading in Early Modern England* (Madison, WI., 1984); Richard Dutton, *Licensing, Censorship and Authorship in Early Modern England: Buggeswords* (Basingstoke, 2000).

16 Patterson, *Censorship and Interpretation*, p. 3.

17 Kevin Birmingham, *The Most Dangerous Book: The Battle for James Joyce's Ulysses* (London, 2014), p. 63.

18 Ibid., pp. 2–3.

19 Müller, *Censorship and Cultural Regulation*, p. 11.

20 Patterson, *Censorship and Interpretation*, p. 21.

21 *Dekret SNK o likvidatsii bezgramotnosti sredi naseleniia RSFSR*, 26 December 1919, Gosudarstvennyi arkhiv Rossiiskoi Federatsii (GARF). Available at http://www.rusarchives.ru/projects/statehood/08-41-dekret-bezgramotnost-1918.shtml (accessed 31 October 2017).

22 Pergament, L. I, *Massovyi pokhod za likvidatsiiu negramotnosti v Vologodskoi gubernii (1918–1922)* (Vologda, 1973). Available at https://www.booksite.ru/education/main/likvid/2.htm (accessed 31 October 2017).

23 Ermolaev, *Censorship in Soviet Literature 1917–1991*, pp. 2–3.

24 Ibid., p. 3.

25 Kotkin, *Magnetic Mountain*, p. 368.

26 Stuart Finkel, *On the Ideological Front: The Russian Intelligentsia and the Making of the Soviet Public Sphere* (New Haven, 2006), p. 118.

27 Tat'iana M. Goriaeva, *Istoriia sovetskoi politicheskoi tsenzury: dokumenty i kommentarii* (Moscow, 1997), pp. 29–32.

28 L. V. Maksimenkov (ed.), *Bol'shaia tsenzura: pisateli i zhurnalisty v strane sovetov 1917–1956* (Moscow, 2005), p. 18.

29 Ibid., pp. 18–19.

30 Finkel, *On the Ideological Front*, pp. 117–18.

31 Ibid., p. 121.

32 Maksimenkov (ed.), *Bol'shaia tsenzura*, p. 33.

33 Ibid., p. 50.

34 Ibid., p. 92.

35 Ibid., p. 120.

36 G. V. Zhirkov, *Istoria tsenzuru v Rossii XIX–XX vv* (Moscow, 2001), p. 257.

37 Ibid., p. 256.

38 M. N. Glazkov, *Chistki fondov massovykh bibliotek v gody sovetskoi vlasti* (Moscow, 2001), p. 8.

39 Goriaeva, *Politicheskaia tsenzura*, p. 190.

40 Ibid., p. 42.

41 Ibid., p. 56.

42 Ibid., p. 70.

43 Zhirkov, *Istoria tsenzuru v Rossii XIX–XX vv* (Moscow, 2001), p. 257.

44 Ibid., p. 259.

45 Ibid.
46 Maksimenkov, *Bol'shaia tsenzura*, p. 39.
47 Ibid., p. 46.
48 Julie Fedor, *Russia and the Cult of State Security: The Chekist Tradition from Lenin to Putin* (London, 2011), ch. 1.
49 Maksimenkov, *Bol'shaia tsenzura*, p. 66.
50 E. L. Varustina, 'Zapretnye knigi epokhi repressii', in T. S. Iur'evoi (ed.), *Terror i kul'tura: sbornik statei* (Saint Petersburg, 2016), pp. 51-2.
51 The website http://www.alexanderyakovlev.org/db-docs allows the reader to search all the documents published by the Alexander Yakovlev foundation in their document collections. When the search term 'запретный' is used, for the dates 1921-30, one document is returned, on the subject of free movement of former White officers. When the search term 'запрещённый' is used for the same date range, nineteen documents are returned, including six that are directly to do with questions of censorship. For the same date range, the word 'цензура' (censorship) returns thirteen documents. (All words searched as they appear here and using each appropriate word ending.)
52 Maksimenkov, *Bol'shaia tsenzura*, p. 93.
53 Lewis Sieglebaum and Andrei Sokolov (eds), *Stalinism as a Way of Life: A Narrative in Documents* (New Haven, 2000), p. 148.

Chapter 14

1 V. I. Lenin, *Polnoe sobranie sochinenii*, 5th ed., vol. 33 (Moscow, 1958-62), pp. 86-95; Lewis H. Siegelbaum, *Soviet State and Society between Revolutions, 1918-1929* (Cambridge, 1992), pp. 9-10; Neil Harding, *Lenin's Political Thought: Theory and Practice in the Democratic and Socialist Revolutions*, vol. 2 (London, 1983), pp. 91-2; Alfred B. Evans, 'Rereading Lenin's State and Revolution', *Slavic Review* 46 (1987), pp. 1-19.
2 Siegelbaum, *Soviet State and Society*, p. 10.
3 The most complete list of 'social organisations' has been catalogued in Irina N. Il'ina, *Obshchestvennye organizatsii Rossii v 1920-e gody* (Moscow, 2000), pp. 174-214.
4 Il'ina, *Obshchestvennye organizatsii*, pp. 110-12.
5 Stephen Lovell, *Russia in the Microphone Age: A History of Soviet Radio, 1917-1970* (Oxford, 2017), esp. pp. 27-8.
6 Il'ina, *Obshchestvennye organizatsii*; Joseph Bradley, 'Subjects into citizens: Societies, civil society, and autocracy in tsarist Russia', *The American Historical Review* 107/4 (October 2002), pp. 1084-123; Yasuhiro Matsui (ed.), *Obshchestvennost' and Civic Agency in Late Imperial and Soviet Russia: Interface between State and Society* (London, 2015), esp. intro.; Karl Loewnstein, 'Obshchestvennost' as key to understanding soviet writers of the 1950s: *Moskovskii Literator*, October 1956-March 1957', *Journal of Contemporary History* 33 (2009), pp. 473-92, esp. p. 475; Catriona Kelly and David Shepherd (eds), *Constructing Russian Culture* (Oxford, 1998), esp. pp. 26-7.
7 N. Bukharin, *Teoriia istoricheskogo materializma* (Moscow-Petrograd, 1923), p. 229; cited in Zenji Asaoka, 'Nikolai Bukharin and the *Rabsel'kor* movement: *Sovetskaia Obshchestvennost'* under the 'Dictatorship of the Proletariat'', in *Obshchestvennost' and Civic Agency*, pp. 85-6.

Notes

8   Ibid., p. 86.
9   Ibid., esp. pp. 90–5.
10 N. Bukharin, *K novomu pokoleniiu: doklady, vystupleniia i stat'i, posviashchennye prolemam molodezhi* (Moscow, 1990), pp. 498–9; also cited in Matthias Neumann, *The Communist Youth League and the Transformation of the Soviet Union, 1917–1932* (London, 2011).
11 Matsui, 'Introduction' in *Obshchestvennost' and Civic Agency in Late Imperial and Soviet Russia: Interface between State and Society*, p. 3.
12 Sandra Dahlke, 'Kampagnen für Gottlosigkeit: Zum Zusammenhang zwischen Legitimation, Mobilisierung und Partizipation in der Sowjetunion der zwanziger Jahre', *Jahrbücher für Geschichte Osteuropas* 50 (2002), pp. 174–5; Neumann, 'Communist youth league and *obshchestvennost*", p. 94.
13 Cf. Matsui, 'Introduction'.
14 Lenin, 'Gosudarstvo i revoliutsiia', p. 101.
15 A. S. Tumanova (ed.), *Samoorganizatsiia rossiiskoi obshchestvennosti v poslednei treti XVIII–nachale XX v.* (Moscow, 2011), pp. 9–12.
16 See Ronald Grigor Suny and Terry Martin (eds), *A State of Nations: Empire and Nation-Making in the Age of Lenin and Stalin* (New York, 2001).
17 Michael David-Fox, 'Review: Obshchestvennye organizatsii Rossii v 1920-e gody', *Kritika* 3/1 (2002), pp. 173–81, 174.
18 Bradley, 'Subjects into citizens,' p. 1096.
19 Adele Lindenmeyr, *Poverty Is Not a Vice: Charity, Society, and the State in Imperial Russia* (Princeton, NY, 1996), ch. 6, esp. pp. 120–1.
20 Bradley, 'Subjects into citizens', p. 1114; Tumanova, *Obshchestvennye organizatsii i russkaia publika v nachake XX veka* (Moscow, 2003).
21 David-Fox, 'Review: Obshchestvennye organizatsii Rossii', p. 176.
22 Matsui, 'Introduction'.
23 Volkov, 'Obshchestvennost'', p. 77.
24 David-Fox, 'Review', p. 174.
25 Volkov, 'Obshchestvennost'', pp. 77–9; Tumanova, *Samoorganizatsiia rossiiskoi obshchestvennosti*, p. 9.
26 Ilya V. Gerasimov, *Modernism and Public Reform in Late Imperial Russia: Rural Professionals and Self-Organization, 1905–30* (Basingstoke, 2009), esp. chs. 1–2.
27 Daniel Beer, *Renovating Russia: The Humane Sciences and the Fate of Liberal Modernity, 1880–1930* (Ithaca, NY, 2008).
28 David-Fox, 'Review', p. 176.
29 Oleg Kharkhordin, 'Reveal and dissimulate: A genealogy of private life in Soviet Russia', in Jeff Weintraub and Krishan Kuman (eds), *Public and Private in Thought and Practice: Perspectives on a Grand Dichotomy* (Chicago, IL, 1997), pp. 333–63. Cf. Laura Engelstein, 'Combined underdevelopment: Discipline and the law in Imperial and Soviet Russia', *American Historical Review* 98/2 (April 1993), pp. 338–53.
30 David-Fox, 'Review', p. 176.
31 Matsui, 'Introduction', pp. 6–7.
32 Loewnstein, 'Obshchestvennost'', p. 475.

Notes

33 Oleg Kharkhordin, *The Collective and the Individual in Russia: A Study of Practices* (Berkley, CA, 1999), p. 313.
34 Loewnstein, 'Obshchestvennost'', p. 481.
35 David-Fox, 'Review', p. 178.
36 Il'ina, *Obshchestvennye organizatsii*, p. 174.
37 David-Fox, 'Review'; a key point also noted in Loewnstein, 'Obshchestvennost'', p. 476.
38 Also see Matsui, 'Introduction', p. 3.
39 David-Fox, 'Review', p. 180.
40 Neumann, 'Communist youth league and obshchestvennost'', p. 104; Il'ina, *Obshchestvennye organizatsii*, esp. p. 142
41 *Iunyi kommunist* 5 (1926), pp. 34–6; cited in Neumann, 'Communist', pp. 104–6.
42 Ibid., pp. 106–7.
43 Ibid., p. 106.
44 Ibid.
45 A. S. Balezin, F. B. Glinkina, E. G. Zak and I. A. Podol'nyi, *Stepan Afanas'evich Balezin, 1904–1982* (Moscow, 1988), pp. 9–10.
46 *Muzei istorii Rossiikii gosudarstvennyi pedagogicheskii universitet im A. I. Gersena* (hereafter MRGPU im. Herzen), d. B-5 ll. 19–17. For more on Balezin, see Andy Willimott, *Living the Revolution: Urban Communes & Soviet Socialism, 1917–1932* (Oxford, 2017), esp. pp. 62–5.
47 'Universal "plug"'. *Komsomol'skaia pravda*, Thursday 8 April, No. 80 (1926), p. 5.
48 'Kak vesti bor'bu s khuliganstom', *Komsomol'skaia pravda*, Thursday 20 September, No. 225 (1926), pp. 2–3.
49 E. Petrov, 'Akademizm i obshchestvennost'', *Krasnyi student*, No. 6 (1925), p. 12.
50 MRGPU im. Herzen, d. B-5 ll. 19–17.
51 MRGPU im. Herzen, d. B-5 ll. 16–15.
52 Chlen kommuny, 'Kommuna studentov-vodnikov', *Krasnyi student*, No. 4–5 (1924), pp. 44–5.
53 Iu. Ber, *Kommuna segodnia, Opyt proizvodstvennykh i bytovykh kommun molodezhi* (Moscow, 1930), pp. 64–5.
54 Iu. Verber, 'Krasnovorotskaia', *Krasnoe studenchestvo*, No. 6 (1929), pp. 20–1.
55 Ibid.
56 N. Krupskaia, *O Bytovykh vorposakh* (Moscow, 1930), p. 35.
57 Cf. Anne E. Gorsuch, *Youth in Revolutionary Russia* (Bloomington, IN, 2000), p. 49.
58 Willimott, *Living the Revolution*, esp. pp. 90–1.
59 Ibid., pp. 59, 99–104.
60 Chlen kommuny, 'Kommuna studentov-vodnikov', pp. 44–5; Willimott, *Living the Revolution*, ch. 4.
61 S. Samuelii, 'Rabotu proizvodstvennykh kommun i kollektivov – na novye rel'sy', *Partiinoe stroitel'stvo*, No. 15–16 (1931), pp. 12–18.
62 Klaus Mehnert, (trans. Michael Davidson), *Youth in Soviet Russia* (London, 1933), pp. 88–9.
63 Ibid. pp. 108–9.
64 David-Fox, *Revolution of the Mind*, p. 104.

Notes

65 Gorsuch, *Youth*, p. 82.
66 Rossiikii gosudarstvennyi arkhiv sotial'no-politicheskoi istorii (RGASPI), f. M. 1, op. 4, d. 41, ll. 143–52 (Meeting of the Central Committee of the Komsomol, 18 December 1929); Willimott, *Living the Revolution*, pp. 122–4. Cf. Peter Gooderham, 'The komsomol and the worker youth: the inculcation of "communist values" in Leningrad during NEP', *Soviet Studies* 4 (1982), pp. 506–28.
67 Neumann, 'Communist youth league and obshchestvennost", p. 112.
68 Gorsuch, *Youth*, p. 50.
69 Il'ina, *Obshchestvennye organizatsii*, pp. 82–5.
70 Asaoka, 'Bukharin', p. 99.
71 Neumann, 'Communist youth league and obshchestvennost", p 119. Cf. David-Fox, 'Review', p. 180.
72 Yasuhiro Matsui, 'Obshchestvennost' in residence: community activities in 1930s Moscow', in *Obshchestvennost' and Civic Agency*, p. 110.
73 Ibid., pp. 123–4.
74 Ibid., p. 119.
75 Mie Nakachi, 'What was obschestvennost' in the time of Stalin?' in *Obshchestvennost' and Civic Agency*, esp. pp. 129, 130–3, 146.
76 David-Fox, 'Review', p. 181.

Chapter 15

1 There was no similar campaign to struggle with male prostitution. Soviet authorities in certain regions turned their attention to male prostitution when sodomy was recriminalized in 1934. Anti-sodomy law in the Ukrainian SSR included a clause that men found to be having sex with men 'for payment, as a profession or in public' would receive additional penalties. This law was not adopted in other regions of the USSR. Dan Healey, *Russian Homophobia from Stalin to Sochi* (London, 2018), p. 159.
2 Gosudarstvennyi arkhiv Rossiiskoi Federatsii (GARF hereafter), f. R6983, op. 1, d. 79, l. 95.
3 Ibid., l. 91.
4 On the regulation of prostitution in imperial Russia, see Siobhán Hearne, 'To denounce or defend? Public participation in the policing of prostitution in the late Russian empire', *Kritika: Explorations in Russian and Eurasian History* 19/4 (2018), pp. 717–44.
5 Laurie Bernstein, *Sonia's Daughters: Prostitutes and Their Regulation in Imperial Russia* (Berkeley and Los Angeles, 1995), pp. 189–232.
6 For Marx, prostitution was a manifestation of the exploitation of workers under capitalism, as he noted in the Economic and Philosophic Manuscripts of 1844 that 'prostitution is only a specific expression of the general prostitution of the labourer', Karl Marx and Friedrich Engels, *Collected Works*, vol. 3 (Moscow, 1975), p. 295.
7 Lenin criticized the 'aristocratic-bourgeois' delegates at anti-prostitution congresses in the late imperial period for ignoring the social and economic causes of prostitution, Vladimir I. Lenin, 'Fifth International Congress Against Prostitution', *Rabochaia Pravda* (13 July 1913), available via Marxist Internet Archive https://www.marxists.org/archive/lenin/works/1913/jul/26.htm (accessed 21 February 2019).

Notes

8   Several historians have touched on questions of who could be 'reforged', such as Tricia Starks, *The Body Soviet: Propaganda, Hygiene and the Revolutionary State* (Madison, 2008); Steven A. Barnes, *Death and Redemption: The Gulag and the Shaping of Soviet Society* (Princeton, 2011).

9   Elizabeth Waters, 'Victim or villain: Prostitution in post-revolutionary Russia', in Linda Edmondson (ed.), *Women and Society in Russia and the Soviet Union* (Cambridge, 1992), pp. 175–6, n. 25.

10 'Raskryt priton', *Pravda*, 24 April 1935; 'Raskryt priton', *Pravda*, 3 December 1935.

11 Frances Bernstein, 'Envisioning health in revolutionary Russia: The politics of gender in sexual-enlightenment posters of the 1920s', *Russian Review* 57/2 (1998), pp. 208–9.

12 The transmission of venereal diseases remained a crime for the entire Soviet period. A. A. Sizov and S. J. Zavalishina, 'Russian criminal legislation in the prevention of sexually transmitted diseases in the territory of the Russian Federation', *Biology and Medicine* 7/5 (2015), p. 2.

13 Alissa Klots, 'The kitchen maid as revolutionary symbol: Paid domestic labour and the emancipation of Soviet women, 1917–1941', in Melanie Ilic (ed.), *The Palgrave Handbook on Women and Gender in Twentieth-Century Russia and the Soviet Union* (Basingstoke, 2017), pp. 83–100; Wendy Z. Goldman, *Women at the Gates: Gender, Politics, and Planning in Soviet Industrialisation* (Cambridge, 2002), pp. 31–2.

14 Bernstein, 'Envisioning health in revolutionary Russia', pp. 205–8.

15 Elizabeth A. Wood, *The Baba and the Comrade: Gender and Politics in Revolutionary Russia* (Bloomington and Indianapolis, 1997), p. 115. On juvenile prostitution, Alan Ball, *And Now My Soul Is Hardened: Abandoned Children in Soviet Russia, 1918–1930* (Berkeley and Los Angeles, 1996), pp. 56–60.

16 This figure does not include women who slipped under the radar of the authorities, so we can assume that numbers were higher in reality. Statistics from 1920 in Stanislav Panin, 'Prodazhnaia liubov v sovetskoi Rossii (1920-e gody)', *Vestnik Evrazii*, 1 (2005), p. 81; for 1922 Richard Stites, *The Women's Liberation Movement in Russia: Feminism, Nihilism and Bolshevism, 1860–1930* (Princeton, 1978), p. 372.

17 Panin argues that the famine gave prostitution a 'second wind' due to the 'threat of death from starvation', Panin, 'Prodazhnaia liubov', p. 81.

18 The poster was entitled 'The struggle with famine – The struggle with prostitution' and can be found in GARF, f. R9550, op. 4, d. 8997.

19 Goldman, *Women at the Gates*, p. 11.

20 Wendy Z. Goldman, 'Working-class women and the "withering away" of the family: Popular responses to family policy', in Shelia Fitzpatrick, Alexander Rabinowitch and Richard Stites (eds), *Russia in the Era of NEP: Explorations in Soviet Society and Culture* (Bloomington and Indianapolis, 1991), p. 131.

21 Goldman, *Women at the Gates*, pp. 17–20.

22 Ibid., p. 17.

23 GARF, f. A413, op. 2, d. 327, ll. 4–6.

24 Ibid., l. 5.

25 Barbara Evans Clements, 'Working-class and peasant women in the Russian revolution, 1917–1923', *Signs* 8/2 (1982), p. 225; Jane McDermid and Anne Hillyar, *Women and Work in Russia, 1880–1930: A Study in Continuity Through Change* (London and New York, 1998), pp. 27–8, 122.

Notes

26 GARF, f. A413, op. 2, d. 327, l. 6.

27 The perception that lower-class women were naïve and vulnerable was at the heart of the rescue campaigns of the Russian Society for the Protection of Women, who focused on rescuing women from prostitution through moral education and material support. See chapter 4 of Siobhan Hearne, 'Female Prostitution in Urban Russia, 1900–1917', PhD dissertation (University of Nottingham, 2017).

28 Tsentral'nyi gosudarstvennyi arkhiv Sankt-Peterburga (TsGASPb hereafter), f. 4370, op. 1, d. 409, l. 193.

29 GARF, f. R6983, op. 1, d. 79, l. 12.

30 Fannina Halle, *Women in Soviet Russia* (London, 1933), p. 257.

31 TsGASPb, f. 142, op. 1, d. 9, l. 325.

32 B. M. Bronner, 'Zamaskriovannye pritony', *Rabochaia Moskva*, 12 January 1923, p. 3. See also 'U domashnikh khoziaek', *Zhilishchnoe Tovarishchestvo*, 20 March 1927, p. 25. With thanks to Deirdre Ruscitti Harshman for providing me with this reference.

33 S. Danishevskii, 'Zabytyi front', *Pravda*, 13 March 1927.

34 Halle, *Women in Soviet Russia*, pp. 233–62; Anna Haines, *Health Work in Soviet Russia* (New York, 1928), pp. 118–19.

35 'Amerikanskie vrachi v Moskve', *Pravda*, 18 June 1935; 'Delegaty kongressa komiterna i kongressa fiziologov v parke kul'tury im. gor'skogo', *Pravda*, 19 August 1935.

36 A questionnaire is reproduced in Halle, *Women in Soviet Russia*, pp. 262–6.

37 'Zabytyi front'.

38 Domestic workers were symbols of revolutionary transformation in the early Soviet Union and were the face of many propaganda campaigns about ending gender inequality. See Alissa Klots, 'The Kitchen Maid That Will Rule the World: Domestic Service and the Soviet Revolutionary Project, 1917–1941', PhD dissertation (Rutgers, The State University of New Jersey, 2017).

39 GARF, f. 5452, op. 12, d. 7, l. 57. I am grateful to Alissa Klots for providing me with this reference. The decree of the All-Russian Central Executive Committee from 8 February 1926 gave domestic workers the right to their previous living space for up to two weeks following their dismissal.

40 GARF, f. R6983, op. 1, d. 79, l. 92.

41 S. Borogad, 'Gde perevospityvaiutsia prostitutki', *Pravda*, 25 November 1935; Halle, *Women in Soviet Russia*, pp. 245–7.

42 Halle, *Women in Soviet Russia*, pp. 246–7.

43 GARF, f. R6983, op. 1, d. 79, l. 11.

44 Halle, *Women in Soviet Russia*, p. 248.

45 GARF, f. R6983, op. 1, d. 79, ll. 10, 31.

46 For example, one woman had to travel from her hometown of Rostov-Iaroslavskii to Ivanovo-Voznesensk, a distance of 130 kilometres. GARF, f. R6983, op. 1, d. 205, l. 1.

47 Haines, *Health Work in Soviet Russia*, p. 119.

48 Siobhan Hearne, 'The "black spot" on the Crimea: venereal diseases in the Black Sea fleet in the 1920s', *Social History* 42/2 (2017), p. 194.

49 TsGASPb, f. 1000, op. 11, d. 606, l. 3.

50 Tsentral'nyi gosudarstvennyi arkhiv istoriko-politicheskikh dokumentov Sankt-Peterburga (TsGAIPDSPb hereafter), f. R598(k), op. 1(1), d. 1764, l. 16.

Notes

51 'Gde perevospityvaiutsia prostitutki'.
52 'Bor'ba s prostitutsiei', *Izvestiia*, 6 November 1925.
53 N. B. Lebina and M. V. Shkarovskii, *Prostitutsiia v Peterburge (40e gg. XIXv. – 40e gg. XX v)* (Moscow, 1994), pp. 158–62.
54 Klots, 'The kitchen maid as revolutionary symbol', p. 87.
55 Clara Zetkin, 'My recollections of Lenin, an interview on the woman question', in Vladimir I. Lenin, *The Emancipation of Women: From the Writings of V. I. Lenin* (New York, 1972), p. 101. On the Council of Police-Controlled Girls of Hamburg-Altona (founded 1920), see Julia Roos, *Weimar Through the Lens of Gender: Prostitution Reform, Woman's Emancipation and German Democracy, 1919–1933* (Ann Arbor, 2010), pp. 78–9.
56 Alexandra Kollontai, 'Prostitution and ways of fighting it', in Alix Holt (ed.), *Alexandra Kollontai: Selected Writings* (New York and London, 1977), p. 266.
57 The Venereal Council for the Struggle with Prostitution was established in 1918. The committee was renamed the Petrograd/Leningrad Committee for the Struggle with Prostitution in 1922.
58 TsGASPb, f. 142, op. 1, d. 3, ll. 25–6. This was the most frequently used term for a brothel in the pre-revolutionary period.
59 TsGAPSb, f. 142, op. 1, d. 3, ll. 25–6.
60 Sexual relations between women were not a crime in Soviet law, even after the criminalization of sex between men in 1934. Dan Healey, *Homosexual Desire in Revolutionary Russia: The Regulation of Sexual and Gender Dissent* (Chicago, 2001), p. 199.
61 Anna Bek, *The Life of a Russian Woman Doctor: A Siberian Memoir, 1869–1954*, in Anne D. Rassweiler (ed. and trans.) (Bloomington and Indianapolis, 2004), p. 100.
62 TsGASPb, f. 3299, op. 1, d. 480, l. 15.
63 TsGASPb, f. 142, op. 1, d. 3, l. 26. The theory of the prostitutes' innate deviance was popularized by Italian criminologist Cesare Lombroso in the late nineteenth century. In Russia, dermatologist and venereologist Veniamin Tarnovskii published widely on the theme of degeneracy in prostitutes. Kollontai argued that 'Marxists and the most conscientious scholars, doctors and statisticians have shown clearly that the idea of "inborn disposition" is false'. Kollontai, 'Prostitution and ways of fighting it', p. 264.
64 In the 1950s and 1960s, new articles were added to the criminal code criminalizing the refusal to engage in productive labour and persistent vagrancy. Neither article mentioned prostitution explicitly but they made earning a living solely from prostitution a criminal offense. John Quigley, 'The dilemma of prostitution law reform: Lessons from the Soviet Russian experiment', *American Criminal Law Review* 29/4 (1992), p. 1222. In mid-1987, prostitution was made an administrative offense. Elizabeth Waters, 'Restructuring the "woman question": *perestroika* and prostitution', *Feminist Review* 33 (1989), p. 12.
65 Tsentral'nyi gosudarstvennyi arkhiv goroda Moskvy (hereafter TsGAgM), f. 1488, op. 1, d. 62, l. 1.
66 'Bor'ba s prostitutsiei', *Pravda*, 14 August 1921.
67 Quigley, 'The dilemma of prostitution law reform', p. 1211.
68 'O merakh bor'by s prostitutsiei', *Ezhenedel'nik Sovetskoi Iustitsii*, 16 (26 April 1923), pp. 381–2.
69 Quigley, 'The dilemma of prostitution law reform', p. 1213.
70 Lebina and Shkarovskii, *Prostitutsiia v Peterburge*, p. 143.
71 GARF, f. R393, op. 43a, d. 1124, l. 3.

Notes

72 GARF, f. R6983, op. 1, d. 79, l. 8.
73 TsGASPb, f. 7384, op. 11, d. 1, l. 125.
74 TsGASPb, f. 4370, op. 1, d. 409, l. 193.
75 Ibid.
76 Halle, *Women in Soviet Russia*, pp. 248–9.
77 Ibid., p. 250.
78 TsGASPb, f. 7384, op. 11, d. 1, l. 126.
79 Hearne, 'The "black spot" on the Crimea', pp. 193–6.
80 'Zabytyi front'.
81 TsGASPb, f. 7384, op. 11, d. 1, l. 125.
82 TsGAIPDSPb, f. R598(k), op. 1(1), d. 1764, ll. 11–12.
83 Bernstein, 'Envisioning health in revolutionary Russia', pp. 205–6.
84 Hearne, 'The "black spot" on the Crimea', p. 195.
85 Wendy Goldman describes the committee as 'the last bastion of organised and effective feminism' after the liquidation of the Women's Department (*Zhenotdel*) in 1930. Goldman, *Women at the Gates*, p. 63.
86 GARF, f. R6983, op. 1, d. 205, l. 1.
87 Halle, *Women in Soviet Russia*, p. 231.
88 Ibid., pp. 231–2.
89 'Bor'ba s prostitutsiei', *Izvestiia*, 9 May 1923.
90 GARF, f. R6983, op. 1, d. 79, l. 4.
91 Elena Zubkova, 'Les exclus: le phénomène de la mendicité dans l'Union soviétique d'après-guerre', *Annales HSS* 68/2 (2013), p. 364.
92 GARF, f. R6983, op. 1, d. 79, l. 8.
93 Ibid., l. 100.
94 Ibid., l. 10.
95 This would have been the equivalent of between ten and twenty-three days' pay for an unskilled male worker. Goldman, *Women at the Gates*, p. 17.
96 GARF, f. R6983, op. 1, d. 79, ll. 91–3.
97 Ibid., l. 94.
98 Shearer, 'Elements near and alien', p. 851.
99 Healey, *Homosexual Desire in Revolutionary Russia*, pp. 177–8, p. 327n86.
100 Shearer, 'Elements Near and Alien', pp. 850–1.
101 TsGAIPDSPb, f. R598(k), op. 1(1), d. 1764, l. 47.

Chapter 16

1 Helena Goscilo, 'Luxuriating in Lack: Plenitude and Consuming Happiness in Soviet Paintings and Posters, 1930s–1953', in *Petrified Utopia: Happiness Soviet Style*, ed. Marina Balina and Evgeny Dobrenko (London: Anthem Press, 2009), pp. 54–78.

Notes

2   See François-Xavier Nérard, 'Variations on a Shchi theme: Collective dining and politics in the early USSR', *Gastronomica: The Journal of Critical Food Studies* 17/4 (2017), pp. 36–47.

3   Harvard Project on the Soviet Social System, schedule A, vol. 5, case 54 (interviewer M. F., type A3). Male, 57, Cossack, Peasant. Widener Library, Harvard University.

4   On the first wave of canteen construction during the civil war, see Mauricio Borrero, *Hungry Moscow: Scarcity and Urban Society in the Russian Civil War, 1917–1921* (New York, 2003) or Mary McAuley, *Bread and Justice: State and Society in Petrograd, 1917–1922* (Oxford, New York, 1991). See also my article on the Urals, François-Xavier Nérard, 'The Sisyphean opening of the first soviet canteens in the Urals: Successes and failures (1918–1925)', *Quaestio Rossica* 5/4 (2017), pp. 1063–72.

5   See Davies and Khlevnyuk, 'The end of rationing in the Soviet Union, 1934–1935', pp. 557–609.

6   The well-known formula was first coined by Stalin in a speech given on 13 April 1928 during a meeting of Moscow communists. I. V. Stalin, 'O rabotakh aprel'skogo ob'edinennogo plenuma TsK i TsKK', *Sochineniia*, vol. 11 (Moscow, 1949), p. 58. He used it a second time, more widely quoted in propaganda, on 4 February 1931 before an audience of industrial managers. I. V. Stalin, 'O zadachakh khoziaistvennikov', *Sochineniia*, vol. 13 (Moscow, 1951), p. 41.

7   The first *fabrika kukhnia* (factory kitchen) was opened in the industrial town of Ivanovo in March 1925. The one in Nizhnii Novgorod was the second, before Dneprostroi, Moscow and Leningrad.

8   Italics are mine.

9   The photo was published in *Pravda* on 4 May 1927, No. 98, p. 6. The original may be found at the Gosudarstvennyi arkhiv audiovizual'noi dokumentatsii Nizhegorodskoi oblasti (hereafter GArkhADNO), f. R-5, ed.khr. 556.

10 What was called 'dish' in official statistics is actually very different: it may have been a soup, a kacha plate or a glass of kisel. The main aim was to produce highly impressive figures even, if needed, by mixing apples and oranges.

11 Gosudarstvennyi obshchestvenno-politicheskii arkhiv Nizhegorodskoi oblasti (hereafter GOPANO), f. 30, op. 1, d. 41, l. 44 and Julie Hessler, *A Social History of Soviet Trade: Trade Policy, Retail Practices, and Consumption, 1917–1953* (Princeton, 2004), p. 177.

12 Rossiiskii gosudarstvennyi arkhiv sotsial'no-politicheskoi istorii (hereafter RGASPI), f. 17, op. 3, d. 841, ll. 12–17.

13 A collection of his negatives is kept in the Gosudarstvennyi arkhiv Saratovskoi oblasti, f. F-1.

14 Some pictures were published in *Pravda* on 4 May 1927. Others can be found in the GArkhADNO archive, f. R-5, ed. khr. 557 or 558.

15 On the reality of Stalinist canteens, see Nérard, 'Variations on a *Shchi* theme', pp. 36–47.

16 RGASPI, f. 17, op. 163, d. 1005.

17 The campaign began in 1930 with a series of articles in *Bol'shevik*, the party journal. 'Iskusstvo partiinogo rukovodstva', *Bol'shevik* 5 (1930), p. 10. See Sarah Davies and James Harris, *Stalin's World. Dictating the Soviet Order* (New Haven, 2015), pp. 44–9.

18 *Stalinets*, No. 247, 26 October 1932, p. 1.

19 GOPANO, f. 2, op. 1, d. 670, l. 59.

20 *Ural'skii rabochii*, 19 September 1931, p. 6.

Notes

21 Tsentr dokumentatsii obshchestvennykh organizatsii Sverdlovskoi oblasti (hereafter TsDOOSO), f. 1020, op. 1, d. 142, ll. 111–17.
22 GOPANO, f. 2, op. 1, d. 1877, l. 8.
23 Ibid., l. 5.
24 On this case, see TsDOOSO, f. 1071, op. 1, d. 2, ll. 85–7.
25 These books were established in April 1935. On the drawbacks of the system, see GARF, f. 7511, op. 1, d. 145, ll. 27–31.
26 Gosudarstvennyi arkhiv Rossiiskoi Federatsii, f. 7511, op. 1, d. 145, ll. 27–31.
27 Rossiiskii gosudarstvennyi arkhiv ekonomiki (hereafter RGAE), f. 7971, op. 1, d. 394, l. 206.
28 Poem quoted by Sergei Ikonnikov, *Sozdanie i deiatel'nost' ob'edinennikh organov TsKK-RKI v 1923–1934* (Moscow, 1971), p. 239.
29 RGASPI, f. 17, op. 163, d. 1005.
30 GOPANO, f. 3, op. 1, d. 1064, l. 84.
31 RGAE, f. 7971, op. 1, d. 394.
32 Olski was arrested on 30 May 1937. He was shot in Novembre 1937. See http://stalin.memo.ru/names/index.htm.
33 Ibid., l. 101.
34 Ibid., l. 102.
35 RGAE, f. 7971, op. 1, d. 394, l. 34.
36 Tsentral'nyi arkhiv Nizhegorodskoy oblasti (hereafter TsANO), f. 2209, op. 3, d. 4960.
37 Eduard Karlovich Pramnek (1899–1938) was appointed First Secretary of the Gorkii region (krai) in 1934 after Andrei Zhdanov. He was transferred to Donetsk in May 1937 and then arrested in April 1938 and shot in July of that year.
38 GOPANO, f. 30, op. 1, d. 1929, l. 9.
39 GOPANO, f. 30, op. 1, d. 1745, l. 33. These were the names of all the top leaders of the province.
40 TsANO, f. 2209, op. 3, d. 4960.
41 GOPANO, f. 30, op. 1, d. 1929.
42 GOPANO, f. 30, op. 1, d. 1929, l. 3.
43 Ibid., l. 74.
44 Ibid., l. 68.
45 Ibid., l. 11.
46 Ibid., l. 75.

SELECT BIBLIOGRAPHY

Bruski, Jan Jacek, *Between Prometheism and Realpolitik: Poland and Soviet Ukraine, 1921–1926* (Krakow, 2016)
Buldakov, Vladimir, *Utopiia, agressiia, vlast': Psikhosotsial'naia dinamika postrevoliutsionnogo vremeni Rossiia, 1920–1930 gg.* (Moscow, 2012)
Carr, E. H., *The Interregnum, 1923–1924* (London, 1954)
Daniels, Robert V., *The Conscience of the Revolution: Communist Opposition in Soviet Russia* (Cambridge, MA, 1960)
David-Fox, Michael, *Revolution of the Mind: Higher Learning among the Bolsheviks, 1918–1929* (Ithaca, NY, 1997)
Davies, Sarah and James Harris, *Stalin's World: Dictating the Soviet Order* (New Haven, CT, 2014)
Davies, Sarah and James Harris (eds), *Stalin: A New History* (Cambridge, 2005)
Deutscher, Isaac, *The Prophet Unarmed: Trotsky 1921–1929* (Oxford, 1959)
Douds, Lara, *Inside Lenin's Government: Ideology, Power and Practice in the Early Soviet State* (London, 2018)
Fainsod, Merle, *How Russia Is Ruled* (Cambridge, MA, 1954)
Figes, Orlando and Boris Kolonitskii, *Interpreting the Russian Revolution: The Language and Symbols of 1917* (New Haven, CT, 1999)
Fitzpatrick, Sheila, *The Commissariat of Enlightenment: Soviet Organization of Education and the Arts, October 1917–1921* (Cambridge, MA, 1970)
Fitzpatrick, Sheila, 'The civil war as a formative experience' in Abbott Gleason, Peter Kenez and Richard Stites (eds), *Bolshevik Culture: Experiment and Order in the Russian Revolution* (Bloomington, 1985), pp. 57–76.
Fotieva, L. A., *Iz zhizni V. I. Lenina* (Moscow, 1967)
Friedrich, Carl and Zbigniew Brzezinski, *Totalitarian Dictatorship and Autocracy* (Cambridge, MA, 1956)
Getty, J. Arch, '"Excesses are not permitted:" Mass terror and Stalinist governance in the late 1930s', *Russian Review* 61/1 (2002), pp. 113–38
Getty, J. Arch, *Practicing Stalinism: Bolsheviks, Boyars, and the Persistence of Tradition* (New Haven, CT, 2013)
Goldman, Wendy Z., *Women at the Gates: Gender, Politics, and Planning in Soviet Industrialisation* (Cambridge, MA, 2002)
Goriaeva, Tat'iana M., *Politicheskaia tsenzura v CCCP 1917–1991* (Moscow, 2002)
Hasegawa, Tsuyoshi, *Crime and Punishment in the Russian Revolution: Mob Justice and Police in Petrograd* (Cambridge, MA, London, 2017)
Hearne, Siobhán, 'The "black spot" on the Crimea: Venereal diseases in the Black Sea fleet in the 1920s', *Social History* 42/2 (2017)
Hessler, Julie, *A Social History of Soviet Trade: Trade Policy, Retail Practices, and Consumption, 1917–1953* (Princeton, NJ, 2004)
Hirsch, Francine, *Empire of Nations: Ethnographic Knowledge and the Making of the Soviet Union* (Ithaca, 2005)
Il'ina, Irina N., *Obshchestvennye organizatsii Rossii v 1920-e gody* (Moscow, 2000)

Select Bibliography

Kenez, Peter, *Birth of the Propaganda State: Soviet Methods of Mass Mobilization 1917–29* (Cambridge, MA, 1985)
Khlevniuk, Oleg V., *Stalin: New Biography of a Dictator* (New Haven, London, 2015)
Klots, Alissa, 'The kitchen maid as revolutionary symbol: Paid domestic labour and the emancipation of Soviet women, 1917–1941', in Melanie Ilic (ed.), *The Palgrave Handbook on Women and Gender in Twentieth-Century Russia and the Soviet Union* (Basingstoke, 2017), pp. 83–100.
Kotkin, Stephen, *Magnetic Mountain: Stalinism as Civilization* (Berkeley, 1997)
Kotkin, Stephen, *Stalin: Paradoxes of Power, 1878–1928* (London, 2014)
Krupskaia, N. K., *Vospominaniia o Lenine* (Moscow, 1957)
Lewin, Moshe, *The Making of the Soviet System: Essays in the Social History of Interwar Russia* (London, 1985)
Liber, George, *Soviet Nationality Policy, Urban Growth, and Identity Change in the Ukrainian SSR 1923–1934* (Cambridge, MA, 2002)
Lih, Lars T., *Lenin* (London, 2001)
Lomb, Samantha, *Stalin's Constitution: Soviet Participatory Politics and the Discussion of the 1936 Draft Constitution* (London, 2017)
McNeal, Robert H., *Bride of the Revolution: Krupskaya and Lenin* (Ann Arbor, 1972)
Nérard, François-Xavier, 'The Sisyphean opening of the first Soviet canteens in the Urals: Successes and failures (1918–1925)', *Quaestio Rossica* 5/4 pp. 1063–72
Pirani, Simon, *The Russian Revolution in Retreat, 1920–1924* (London, 2008)
Plekhanov, A. A. and A. M. Plekhanov (eds), *F. E. Dzerzhinskii – Predsedatel' VChK–OGPU, 1917–1926: Dokumenty* (Moscow, 2007)
Rabinowitch, Alexander, *The Bolsheviks Come to Power: The Revolution of 1917 in Petrograd* (New York, NY, 1976)
Raleigh, Donald J., *Revolution on the Volga: 1917 in Saratov* (Ithaca, 1986)
Rigby, T. H., *Lenin's Government: Sovnarkom, 1917–22* (Cambridge, MA, 1979)
Ryan, James, *Lenin's Terror: The Ideological Origins of Early Soviet State Violence* (London, New York, 2012)
Schapiro, Leonard, *The Origin of the Communist Autocracy: Political Opposition in the Soviet State, First Phase, 1917–1922* (London, 1955)
Service, Robert, *The Bolshevik Party in Revolution: A Study in Organizational Change, 1917–1923* (London, 1979)
Siegelbaum, Lewis H., *Soviet State and Society between Revolutions, 1918–1929* (Cambridge, MA, 1992)
Solomon, Peter H., *Soviet Criminal Justice under Stalin* (Cambridge, MA, 1996)
Steinberg, Mark D., *Voices of Revolution, 1917* (New Haven, 2001)
Stone, David R., *Hammer and Rifle: The Militarization of the Soviet Union, 1926–1933* (Kansas, 2000)
Timasheff, Nicholas, *The Great Retreat: The Growth and Decline of Communism in Russia* (New York, 1946)
Ul', M., V. Khaustov and V. Zakharov (eds), *Glazami razvedki: SSSR i Evropa, 1919–1938 gody: sbornik dokumentov iz rossiiskikh arkhivov* (Moscow, 2015)
Velikanova, Olga, *Popular Perceptions of Soviet Politics in the 1920s: Disenchantment of the Dreamers* (Cham, Switzerland, 2013)
Vilkova, Valentina, *RKP(b): Vnutripartiinaia bor'ba v dvadtsatye gody: Dokumenty i materialy: 1923* (Moscow, 2004)
Viola, L., V. Danilov, N. Ivnitskii and D. Kozlov (eds), *The War against the Peasantry, 1927–1930: The Tragedy of the Soviet Countryside* (New Haven and London, 2005)
Willimott, Andy, *Living the Revolution: Urban Communes & Soviet Socialism, 1917–1932* (Oxford, 2017)

INDEX

accounting and control 23
Adibekov, G. M. 276 n.17
Adler, Viktor 35
Agamben, Giorgio 147
agricultural and industrial prices 115–16, 118
Akhmatova, Anna 209
alcohol pogroms 57
Alexander III 66
All-Russian Central Executive Committee (VTsIK) 278 n.13
All-Union Communist Party. *see* Communist Party
The Alternative Culture: Socialist Labor in Imperial Germany (Lidtke) 34–5
anarchism 20
Anderson, Kevin 17
Andronnikov, Vladimir 59
Anichkov, Vladimir P. 55, 59
anti-Bolsheviks 97
Anti-Duhring (Engels) 20
anti-Leninist 121, 123
anti-stigmatization
    brothel keepers 238
    engaging in debauchery 238
    illiberal administrative measures 241
    Leningrad Committee 240
    liberation and authoritarianism 237
    morality 238
    prejudices 238
    professional beggars 241
    prostitutes 237
    social patronage scheme 239
    socially harmful element 242
    stigmatization of prostitutes 239
    struggle campaign 237
    venereal disease transmission 240
    waged labour 237
    welfare and repression 237
appointmentism 117, 122
aristocratic-bourgeois 300 n.7
Armand, Inessa 20
Artuzov, Artur 181
Arzhilovskii, Andrei 145
Asaoka, Zenji 217, 228
authoritarianism 2, 7, 205
    liberation and 237
    Soviet 11

Babel, Isaac 129
Badcock, Sarah 52
Balezin, S. A. 222, 224, 226–8
batiushka myth 64
Bebel, August 36
Bednyi, Dem'ian 251
Beer, Daniel 220
Bek, Anna 238
Beria, Lavrentii 90
Besancon, Alain 18, 24
Blium, Arlen 204
Bogdanov, Alexander 191, 195
Bolshevik programme 79
Bolshevik theory 160
Bolsheviks 1, 39, 42, 55, 110
    as administrators 59
    approach to censorship 212
    authoritarian DNA 49
    authoritarian order 1
    bourgeois state, smashing 6
    capitalist powers 13
    chaos of 1917 111
    City Duma elections 56
    and civil war 158–63
    democratic development 2
    foreign policy 174
    full autonomy 53
    and Kadets 56
    mobilization 292 n.37
    municipal platform 61
    political agenda 52
    political freedom 45
    progressive taxes 53
    revolutionary dreaming 6
    social conception of citizenship 84
    socialist revolution 64
    state monopoly campaignism 32
    state power, collapse 43
    struggle against disorder 57
Bolshevism 34, 49, 57, 81, 83
    foundations of 123
    and Menshevism 37
    organizational principles of 100
    revolutionary traditions 105–6
    Trotsky's 100–3
Bonaparte, Louis 19
Bonch-Bruevich, V. D. 70

Index

bourgeois-anarchist individualism 202
bourgeois democracy 3–4, 65, 100
bourgeois freedom 33
bourgeois parliamentarism 18
bourgeois philanthropists 232
bourgeois wartime state 18
Bradley, Joseph 219
Brezhnev, Leonid 74
Bri-Bein, Maria Feliksovna 245
Brichkina, S. B. 72
Brooks, Jeffrey 143
Brzezinski, Zbigniew 1
Bukharin, Nikolai 18–21, 42, 86, 216–17
Bulgakov, Mikhail 210
bureaucracy 12
    Bolshevism–Leninism, defeat 101
    rule of 99
    Trotsky's fight against 100
bureaucratic-military state machine, smashing 22
bureaucratic organization 20
bureaucratism 9, 13, 80
bureaucratization 12, 193, 293 n.37
Burov, Aleksei 250

Callahan, Kevin J. 34, 36
campaignism 11, 32
    aim of 33
    life in Soviet Union 44–5
    Marxism and 33
    and political freedom 36–40
    state monopoly 40–4
canteens 245
    directors 252
    disappearance of food 246
    dysfunction 249
    and fortresses 248
    at Gorky automobile plant 247
    illegitimacy 248
    industrialization 247
    inspections 250
    kitchen factory 251
    narpit 249
    penury 247, 248
    quantitative approach 248
    scandals, resilience and violence 249–52
capitalist culture 4
censorship 201, 297 n.51
    elements of 202
    as freedom 214
    linguistics of 211–12
    policy of state 203
    and political police 210–11
    into practice 207–10
    pre-revolutionary 202
    in principle 205–7
    and Soviet censorship 203–5
    tsarist system 202
Central Control Commission (TsKK) 116–20, 122–3
centralisation 127
    arrests and 132–3
    jurisdiction and 130–2
    legality and repression 139
    of political police 132, 139
    self-determination *vs.* party 158–63
chaos
    Bolsheviks 111
    mass operations and centralized 138–9
    political and social 170
    revolutionary events 58
Cheka(s) (political police) 130
    control of local 130
    draft statute 130
    Ekaterinburg 60
    into GPU 131
    quasi-religious role 211
chelobitnyi prikaz 66
Chicherin, Georgii 175, 182
Chubar, Vlas 166
Chutskaev, Sergei 56, 58–9
civil war 112
    Bolsheviks and 158–63
    re-igniting 138
Civil War (1918–21) 128–30
Clemenceau, Georges 184
Cohen, Stephen F. 1
Cold War 1–2
    scholarship 2
collective catering system 247–8, 253–4
    ever-failing system 252
    portrait 249
    repression 252
    sabotage 252
    Soviet 248
collectivization 133–6, 141
    lethal force 137
Comintern 103
Commissariat of Finance (Narkomfin) 116
Committee for Public Safety (KOB) 50
commune-state 25, 215, 217, 228–9
communism 4, 106
    self-administered society 5, 7
    Soviet 10
Communist Manifesto (Marx & Engels) 19–20, 26
Communist Party 1, 77
    Bolshevism of 1917 and 102
    bureaucratization 99
    commune-state to party-state 78–83
    18th Congress and new party rules (*see* 18th Congress and new party rules)

Index

constitutional provisions 84
democratic politics 86
democratization campaign 86–7
elections 85–6
industrialization process 83
one-party dictatorship and 98
one-party rule 85
under proletarian revolution 98
remnants of capitalism 83
socialist legislative process 84
society and state 85
workers and toilers unite 84
Communist Party of Western Ukraine (KPZU) 168
18th Congress and new party rules
    amendments to Rules 88–9
    democratization campaign 87, 90
    function of military repression 89
    Marxism-Leninism 88, 92
    multi-candidate rule 91
    over-vigilance 87, 89
    party life 87
    phases 89
    principle of electability 88
    recruitment 88
    social transformations 90
    socialism and defence 90
    TsK resolution 87
Credo (Kuskova) 37
crisis pragmatism 145
cultural revolution 9, 13

Das Erfurter Programm (Kautsky) 40
David-Fox, Michael 219–21, 229
Declaration of the 46 118–23
'A Defenceless Creature' (Chekhov) 67
degeneration 277 n.42
democracy 2, 79, 127
    Bolshevism and Stalinism (1929–40) 100–3
    conceptions 128
    defence of 9
    establishment of 19
    inner-party 8
    and liberalism 2
    majority rule 26
    most extensive 17
    party 12
    premodern 2
    and unavoidable civil war 55
    vision of 4
democratic centralism 160
democratic transition 10
democratization 12, 52, 77, 100
Demonstration Culture: European Socialism and the Second International (Callahan) 34
Denikin, Anton 161–2

Dewey, John 191
dictatorship
    capitalist encirclement and 178–81
    and democracy in Soviet State (1917–22) 96–8
    question of agency, Stalin 103–6
    state of intense war 178
dictatorship, unlimited
    class dictatorship 26
    intense struggle 27
    limitation 29
    revolutionary people 27
    scientific concept 27
    workers' party 28
dictatorship of the proletariat 25
discursive referent 221
Dmitriev, Maksim 248
Dobrenko, Evgeny 141, 143
Draper, Hal 26–7, 42
Duma, City 50
    after February Revolution 53
    ambitious programme 57
    democratic elements 52
    fiscal management 59
    KOB 50
    people's militia 50
Dutov, Ataman Aleksandr 60
Dzerzhinskii, Feliks 72, 116, 130–2, 137, 177, 183, 211

Egorov, Aleksandr 182
Ekaterinburg 49
    anti-Bolshevik forces 61
    Bolsheviks (*see* Bolsheviks)
    Cheka 60
    City Duma (*see* Duma, City)
    city management 59
    civil war 61
    commissariat system in 60
    counter-revolutionary uprising 60
    food purchasing areas 50
    Food Supply Committee 58
    food supply question 51
    guberniia administration 54
    limited franchise 54
    liquidation of institutions 60
    local self-government 59
    municipal platform 53
    privatized monopoly 58
    proletariat dictatorship 60
    Provisional Government 50
    Revkom 57
    SRs 54
    traditional institutions 49
    unstable financial situation 59
Engels, Friedrich 4, 17, 19–22, 24–6, 32–3

Index

enlightenment
- agitation 195
- bourgeois influences 195
- bureaucratism 197–8
- bureaucratization 193
- controlling and advisory 194
- cultural revolution 196, 198
- education 189–90
- educational reform 194–5
- educational soviets 194
- grassroots democracy 199
- hobbyhorse 194
- intellectual readjustments 193
- labour school 191
- Lenin's enthusiasms 192
- one-man-management 198
- *politprosvet* (political enlightenment) 194, 196
- progressive pedagogical theory 190, 192
- proletarian culture 191
- radical modification 196
- radicalism 192
- revolutionary working class 193
- tsarist education 191–2

The Erfurt Program (Kautsky) 36
Erfurtian underground 40
Erfurtianism 263 n.21
European Social Democracy 31, 43
evangelistic enthusiasm 44
Ezhov, Nikolai 138, 150

factionalism 12, 114, 122, 180, 183
factory committees 23
factual *kontrol* 73
The Fatal Eggs (Bulgakov) 210
February Revolution 49–52, 58, 61, 64, 110, 128, 157, 192
female unemployment and poverty 232
- commissariat 234
- demobilized soldiers 233
- dispensaries 235–6
- domestic workers 235
- dominance, women 233
- and economic instability 236
- economic vulnerability 237
- inspection brigade 234
- preventing 234
- prostitutes 234
- resources and funding 236
- special cadre of inspectors 234

Ferdinand, Franz 183
First Five-Year Plan (FYP) 77, 83
first phase of communism 85, 89, 144
Fitzpatrick, Sheila 13–14, 149

Foch, Ferdinand 176
France
- Enlightenment in pre-Revolutionary 36
- political freedom in 33
- revolutions of 1848 19
- suffrage 3, 257 n.15

Frank, Stephen 268 n.10
French revolutionary Declaration of the Rights of Man and the Citizen (1789) 85
Friedrich, Carl 1
Frolov, Sergei 74
Frunze, Mikhail 176

Garasko, K. 250
Georgian movement 103
Gerasimov, Ilya V. 219
Germany
- political freedom in 33
- Social Democratic movement 35
- suffrage 3
- *Waffen- und Munitionsbeschaffungsamt* 18

Getty, J. Arch 64, 86, 150, 152
Gitis, Israel 252
Glavlit 203, 206–7, 209–10, 214
Gorkii, Maksim 40, 150
Gorsuch, Anne E. 227
Great Terror (1937–8) 141, 148, 152, 252
Great War 21
Gubernia, Samara 74
gublit 210–11
Guesde, Jules 35
Gumilev, Nikolai 209

Habermas, Jurgen 220
Haines, Anna 235
Halle, Fannina 235
hardened prostitutes 234–5, 237, 242
Harding, Neil 17
Harris, James R. 148
Hasegawa, Tsuyoshi 50–1, 57
Hilferding, Rudolf 18
Hill, Christopher 18
Historical Materialism (Bukharin) 216
History of the Russian Revolution to Brest-Litovsk (Trotsky) 95
Hoffmann, David 141, 145
hooligans 57
Howard, Roy 85
Hryn'ko, H. 163, 169

Iagoda, G. 134, 137, 143, 146, 148, 181
illiberal liberation 2
illiteracy, campaigns 8
The Immediate Tasks of Soviet Power (Lenin) 80

Index

international situation 173
    capitalist encirclement and dictatorship 178–81
    Piłsudski coup and war scare 181–3
    renewed pressure on opposition 183–5
    renewed war (1921–3), fear 174–7
International Social Democracy 19, 35
invasion, fear of
    capitalist encirclement and dictatorship 178–81
    renewed war (1921–3) 174–7
Ioffe, Adolf 174
Ispolkom 54–6, 59
Iurovskii 57
Iushin, V. 72

Jesuits' policy 160
Joyce, James 205

Kaganovich, Iulii 253–4
Kaganovich, Lazar 134, 165–6, 168–9, 182
Kalinin, Mikhail 70
Kamenev, L. B. 98, 121, 131, 163
Kamenev, Sergei 175
Karpinskii, V. A. 72
Kautsky, Karl 20, 22, 36, 40, 96
Kerschensteiner, Georg 191
Kharkhordin, Oleg 221
Khlevniuk, O. V. 142–3, 148–50
Khrushchev, Nikita 74
Kirov, S. M. 135
Klimovich 88
Kokosalakis, Yiannis 143
Kollontai, Alexandra 20, 68, 179, 237–8
Komissiia proshenii (1810–84) 66
Komsomol 13, 215–16
    cultural mission 216
    Eighth Congress 217, 227
    ideological imperatives 216
    obshchestvennaia nomenklatura 221–2
    social and cultural initiatives 227
    subbotniki 216
konspiratsia underground 40
korenizatsiia policy 13, 158
    anti-Ukrainian chauvinism 166
    bilingualism 167
    Bolshevik ideology 170
    comprehensive national programme 164
    economic decentralization 169
    governmental employees 167
    indigenous populations 164
    industrial working class 165
    industrialization 169, 171
    modernization and economic equalization 164
    objectives 169
    rural-to-urban migration 165
    socialism 164
    success of 170
    Ukrainian-Polish Army 163
    Ukrainization (*see* Ukrainization)
    unity 163
    working-class mobilization 167
Kosheleva, L. 282 n.23
Kosior, Stanislav 114
Kotkin, Stephen 149, 153, 207
Krasnaia Niva 210
Krausz, Tamàs 18, 22
Krawchenko, Bohdan 165
Krestinskii, Nikolai 174
Krol', L. A. 57–8
Kronstadt rebellion 97
Krupskaia, N. K. 189, 206, 209, 225
Krylenko, N. 148
Kulygin, V. 151
Kuskova, Elena 37–8
KUTB 231, 235, 240
Kviring, Emanuil 161

labour armies 112
Lander, Karl 73
Lassalle, Ferdinand 33–6, 44–5
leadership, Communist Party 80, 82
Lebedev-Polianskii, Pavel 201, 203, 207, 210, 213
Lebina, N. B. 237
Left Opposition 12
Left Socialist Revolutionaries 81
Left-Wing Communism (Lenin) 34
Lenin, V. I. 173, 237
    election proposal 5
    Ilyich, Vladimir 195, 198
    living link 74
    parenthetical qualification 34
    parliamentarism 25
    petitioning 68
    proletariat dictatorship 5, 9
    radical-democratic credentials 18
    revolutionary censorship 14
    self-administered society 7, 9
    social conception of citizenship 81
    socialism 23
    socialist revolution 18
    The State and Revolution (Lenin) 4–7, 13, 17, 19, 22–3, 26, 28, 49, 61
    state monopoly capitalism 21
    unlimited government 29
    view of workers 38
    workers' control 24
Lenin Levy 82
Leninism 1, 107
    departure from 122
    foundations of 123
Lensch, Paul 21

Index

liberal democracy 2
liberal universalism 19
Lidtke, Vernon 34–5
Lih, Lars T. 18, 23, 189–91
Lindenmeyr, Adele 219
liquidation schools 206
Litvinov, Maksim 175, 182
living link 71, 74
Loewenstein, Karl 220
Lunacharskii, A. V. 43, 189, 206–8

Maiakovskii faction 209
malicious prostitutes 237
maliciously diseased prostitutes 240
Mandelstam, Osip 209
Martov, Iulii 37
Marx, Karl 4–5, 17, 19–20, 24–6, 32–3, 78–9, 192–3, 215, 220
Marxism 5, 31, 97, 143
    and campaignism 33
    and Stalinism 102
Marxism–Leninism 111
Marxist Draper 26
Marxist project 24
Marxist revolution 201
mass literacy 203
mass operations and centralized chaos 138–9
mass repressions 149–50, 154, 281 n.78
mass violence 138–9
    Bolshevik leadership 133
    civilization and class vengeance, breakdown 129
    controlling 130
    dekulakization campaign 134
    grain crisis 135
    in judicial order 134
    lethal violence 133
    Lower Volga communists 133
    mass repression 135
    monopoly on death sentences 135
    OGPU plenipotentiaries 134
    orgy of arrests 136
    Red Terror of 1918 128–9
    On Revolutionary Legality order 135
    spontaneous violence 129
The Master and Margarita (Bulgakov) 210
Matsui, Yasuhiro 220, 228
Mazlakh, Serhii 160, 167
Mehnert, Klaus 226
Mensheviks 4, 53, 110
Menshevism 37
Miasnikov, G. I. 197
Mikoian, Anastas 252
military censorship 207
military dictatorship 7

moderation, Stalinist 141
    adjustments 149
    agricultural workforce, lack 146
    anti-Soviet elements 153
    'care about technical cadres' 144
    Constitution (1936) 142–3
    contradictions 142
    Cossacks 147
    crisis pragmatism 145
    decisive force 143
    developments 150
    election law and changes 144–5
    explosions of fury 150
    figurative power system 142
    franchise, expansion 151
    historians as 147
    investments, industry 146
    legality and extralegality 147–8
    liberal constitution 150–2
    mobilization campaigns 153
    New People in the Stakhanovites 150
    objective conditions 143
    pattern of duality 141–2
    repressions 145, 148–9, 154
    sabotaging procurement 146
    socialism 143, 145, 152
    socialist offensive 143
    state of exception 147
modern capitalism 24
modern communism 19
Molotov, Vyacheslav Mikhaylovich 77, 83, 121, 137, 143, 182
most malicious prostitutes 241
Mother (Gorkii) 40
Muller, Beate 205
municipalization 59

Nagorskii, M.V. 55
Narkomos 163, 168–9
Narkompros 13, 189, 194–8, 293 n.40, 293 n.47
Narodnaia volia 36
Neumann, Matthias 221–2, 228
New Economic Policy (NEP) 8, 109, 111–16, 119, 122, 227–8, 233
Nicholas II 96
Novgorod, Nizhnii 52, 247–8, 251, 253

Obscene Publications Act of 1857 205
obshchepit system 253
obshchestvennaia sfera 219
obshchestvennost', Soviet 216
    collectivism 224
    commune life 225–6
    cultural-enlightenment activities 225
    development 217

Index

drunkenness 223
hooliganism 223
as identity 220
loyal critique 223
managed 227–9
Mutual Aid 222
notion 221, 228
obshchestvennaia nomenkaltura 222
radical-democratic vision 218
revolutionary state management 218
samokritika (self-criticism) 225
scientific approach 226
self-motivated 222
social work 222–4, 226
student population 224
obshchvestvennaia rabota 229
October Revolution 3, 12, 49, 54–6, 59–61, 95, 101, 106, 128
    interruption 193
    in *kontrol* 73
    liquidation of exploitative classes 89
    and Soviet regime 157
OGPU 131–2, 210
Okruzhkom, Vinnistkii 121
Olgin, Moissaye J. 40
Olski, Ian 252–3
one-party dictatorship 180
OSOAVIAKhIM 216, 228

Palko, Olena 12–13
Paris Commune of 1871 19, 22, 27
    democratic republic 25
    government of the working class 24
Parliamentarianism (Kautsky) 36
parliamentarism 25
Parti Ouvrier Francais (Guesde) 35
party discipline 124
Patterson, Annabel 205
Paul I. 66
Pedagogical Dictionary 192
permanent campaign 31
    campaignism and life in Soviet Union 44–5
    Lassalle and SPD 33–6
    Marxist origins 32–3
    and political freedom 31
    Russian social democracy 36–40
    to state monopoly campaignism 40–4
personal audience 64
petitions/petitioning, rulers 64
    de-bureaucratizing tool 68
    government and people 74
    Great Reforms 66
    kontrol' 70
    negative effects 73
    political culture 67

political participation 74
proshenie 68, 75
serfs 66
tsar and peasants 66, 69
tsarist administration 67
Petliura, Symon 175
Petrograd
    All-Russian Congress of Soviets 54
    mob violence in 50
    radical transformations 56, 60
    seizure of power 54
    unavoidable civil war 55
Petrov, E. 223–4, 228
Petrovskii, G. I. 130
Pipes, Richard 189
Piłsudski, Jozef 163, 175, 177
Piłsudski coup and war scare
    anti-Soviet coalition 182
    foreign imperialism 182
    Polish militarism 182
    Sarajevo 183
    Soviet Union and Poland 181
    Voikov's murder 182
planned economy 45
pluralism 95, 107
Pod Znamenem Marksizma (PZM) 83, 86
Polan, A. J. 18
Politburo
    economic crisis 117
    economic policy 116
    economic recovery 113
    electoral principle 117
    factional dictatorship 117
    illegal arrests, specialists 132
    Party organizations 113
    series of commissions 113, 115
    systematic struggle 116
    troikas 136
    Trotsky and 109
Politburo majority 12
political campaign 31
political freedom
    betrayal 39
    Bolsheviks 45
    campaignism and 36–40
    in Germany and France 33
    role of 37
political *kontrol* 73
political police/policing 131, 289 n.60
    censorship and 210–11
    Cheka (*see* Cheka(s) (political police))
political systems 3
politprosvet (political enlightenment) 194, 196
powerless feign deference 74
Pramnek, Eduard 253

Index

Pravda 77, 82, 87–8, 120, 178, 183, 208–9, 212, 232, 235, 240
Priemnaia 68
primitive democratism 22
Primo de Rivera, Miguel 7
Prishvin, Mikhail 152
professional prostitutes 242
Program of the Communists (Bukharin) 42
proletarian democracy 11, 70
   living link 11
   openness and responsiveness 11
   Soviet 14
   workers' control 17
proletarian dictatorship 5, 19
proletarian public 44
proletarian revolution 160
Proletkult movement 6
prostitutes 233, 237, 239
   hardened 234–5, 237, 242
   malicious 237
   professional 242
   repression 242
   stigmatization 242–3
   theory of 303 n.63
prostitution 231, 239, 300 n.6
   campaign to eradicate 240
   as economic problem 238
   law reform: 303 n.64
   male 300 n.1
   as necessary evil 232
Public Education and Democracy (Krupskaia) 190
public-worker activists 225
Putin, Vladimir 63–4

Rabinowitch, Alexander 61
Rabkrin 73
Radek, Karl 176
radical-democratic utopianism 28
Rae, John 32
Read, Christopher 17–18
Red Guards 6, 57
Red Terror of 1918 128–9
redeemable woman 242
renewed war (1921–3)
   anti-Soviet border-states 175
   French and Belgian troops 176
   military attack 175
   Polish intervention 176
   Red Army 175–7
   Soviet intelligence 176–7
   Soviet–Polish War 174
   trade agreements 177
repression of 1937–8 245
revisionists 1
Revolution (1905) 65
revolutionary dictatorship 262 n.104

revolutionary people 27
Revolutionary Salvation Committee *(Revkom)* 55, 57
revolutionary social democracy 31, 36
Rieber, Alfred J. 64
Rodchenko, Aleksandr 248
Ruhr crisis 179
Russia
   capitalist elements 179
   crisis 7
   electrification 6
   managed democracy 74
   political culture 75
Russian People's Commissariat of Internal Affairs (RNKVD) 278 n.13
Russian Revolution 12, 26, 96–7, 106, 161, 163
Russian social democracy 36–40, 103
   anti-tsarist revolution, abandonment 39
   bourgeoisie 37
   Iskra group, critics 37
   Kautsky writings 36
   konspiratsia 40
   liquidationists 39
   Mensheviks and Bolsheviks 39
   political freedom 36–7
   political liberty 37
   praktiki 39–40
   proletarian workers 38
   revolutionary social democracy 36
   Social Democratic campaignism 38
   socialist realism 40
   SPD model 37–8
   underground 40
Russian Social Democratic party 41
Russian Social Democratic Worker Party 37
Ryan, James 18
Rykov, Aleksei 121, 137

sabotage, liquidation of consequences 252–5
scandals
   desensitization 251
   public 249–50
   public denunciation 250
Schapiro, Leonard 189
Schmitt, Carl 29
Scissors Crisis 114–15
Scott, James C. 74
security threats 82
seizure of power 4, 6, 292 n.34
self-administered society 5, 7, 9
self-governing commune-state 83
Semashko, Nikolai 236, 241–2
serious political error 118
Shakhrai, Vasyl 167
Shakhty Affair 137
Shearer, David 148

Index

Shelomovich, V. 88
Sherry, Samantha 204
Shkarovskii, M. V. 237
Shliapnikov, Aleksander 7, 179
Shums'kyi, Oleksander 163, 167–9
Shvernik, Nikolai 86
Siegelbaum, Lewis H. 215
single-party rule 81–2
Skrypnik, M. N. 166–7
Skrzyński, Aleksander 181
social democracy
    permanent campaign 36
    pre-war 32, 42, 45
    revolutionary 31, 36
    Russian (*see* Russian social democracy)
    SPD 34
Social Democratic movement 20, 35–6
social democratic thinking 19–20
social ownership 4
social revolution 32
socialism 20–1, 28, 232, 259 n.42
    attainment of 141, 145
    construction 80–1, 85, 90
    as efficient hierarchy 22–4
    realization 143
socialist regulation 18
socialist revolution 23, 189
Socialist Revolutionaries (SRs) 4, 53–4
    tactical blunders 56
Sosnovskii, Lev 51, 55
Soviet censorship
    historical parallels 204–5
    post-revolutionary censorship 203
    pre-revolutionary censorship 203
    quotidian reality 213
    speech regulation 204
Soviet-civil society
    associational public activity 219
    component aspect 220
    imagined community 220
    obshchestvennost' 218–19
    professionalization 221
    public sphere 220–1
    regime's dysfunctions, loyal critique 221
Soviet democracy
    commune-state 25
    parliamentarism 25
    proletarian state 25
    pyramid of soviets 24
Soviet governments
    petitions or denunciations 65
    Reception 70
    tsarist and 74
Soviet nationalities policy
    implementation 158
    korenizatsiia (*see korenizatsiia* policy)

moderation 163
resolution 162
Tsentral'na Rada 159
Soviet political system
    democratization 86
    fundamental traits 80
    over bourgeois parliamentarism 85
Soviet Union 2
    campaignism and life in 44–5
    internal and external threats 184
Soviet–Polish War 174
Sovnarkom Reception 69–71
    complaints and statements 72
    illiberal liberation 71
    as living link 71–2
Sozialdemokratische Partei Deutschlands (SPD) 34, 37–8
Spanish Civil War 153
Spectacle of Two Worlds 44
speech regulation 14
Spilka Vyzvolennia Ukrainy (SVU) 168
Stakhanovite movement 44–5, 145
Stalin, I. V.
    capitalist powers 183
    censorship 207
    criticisms 120
    cult of personality 136
    dictatorship and question of agency 103–6
    Dizziness from Successes 142
    grouping victims 138
    moderation (*see* moderation, Stalinist)
    opposing mass operations 138
    political police, control 137
    revolutionary movement 103
    Secretariat 111
    tactical manoeuvre 122
Stalin, Joseph 91
Stalinism 1, 32, 100–3
    Bolshevism and 102
    Marxism and 102
The State and Revolution (Lenin) 4–7, 13, 17, 19, 22–3, 26, 28, 49, 61, 71, 78–80, 89, 143, 192, 215
    tiny minority of exploiters 80
state apparatus, smashing 20
state capitalism 21
state monopoly campaignism 32
    impact of 45
    permanent campaign to 40–4
state monopoly capitalism 21
State Planning Committee (Gosplan) 116
State Political Administration (GPU) 206
state power 7, 79
    revolutionary 84
struggle with prostitution, campaign 231
Struve, Petr 37

Index

Takhtarev, K. M. 38
Tarasevich, Piotr Adamovich 253
Thaw 221
Third Party Congress 26
Timasheff, Nicholas 141
To the Rural Poor (Lenin) 38
totalitarian censorship 207
totalitarian model 1
transitional dictatorship 10
Treaty of Brest-Litovsk 161
Treaty of Riga 174–5
Trotsky, Leon 8–10, 12, 82, 95, 109, 164, 175–6, 178–80, 184, 208, 212, 274 n.19
   attack on TsK 120
   capitalism and socialism 113
   capitalist exploiters 96
   centralization of economy 97–8
   class dictatorship 98
   Commission on State Industry 113
   committeemen 105
   criticisms 114, 120
   December 5 resolution 119–20, 122–3
   decline of democracy 124
   degeneration 119
   democratic concerns (1923–9) 98–100
   democratically elected Constituent Assembly 97
   disagreements with Politburo 116–17
   electoral principle 119
   endorsement of future war 185
   extremism and opportunism 104
   flagrant violation of party discipline 123
   internal party, critique 118
   par excellence 96, 103
   party bureaucratization 100
   party majority, criticism 110
   permanent revolution 95
   persistent factional attacks 121
   and Politburo 109
   skloki 113, 119
   social imperialists 96
   socialism and capitalism 101
   socialist democracy 103
   state industry report 114–15
   substitutionism 105
Tsiurupa, Alexander 72
TsK (Central Committee) 77, 161
   February-March plenum 87, 90
   initiatives 88
   resolution 87
   sanction 135
   and TsKK 117–18, 120, 122–3
Tucker, R. 1
Tukhachevskii, Mikhail 175, 182
Tumanova, A. S. 219

Ukraine
   anti-Ukrainian attitude 162
   autonomy and cultural development 163
   Bolshevik approach 158
   Borot'bysty 161–3
   claims for independence 160–1
   German occupation of 160
   korenizatsiia (*see korenizatsiia* policy)
   self-determination 159
   social democrat 160
Ukrainization
   cultural work 168
   demographic character 165
   Gosplan 169
   hostile forces 168
   KPZU programme 168
   objectives 169
   proletarian 165–6
   re-identification 166
   reinforcing comprehensive 165
   Soviet culture and society 168
   spontaneous 168
   success of 167
   SVU trial 168
Ulitsa, Mokhovaia 70
ultra-democratic model 17
unemployment 6–7, 112, 120. *see also* female unemployment and poverty
Uprava 52, 57
   Budget-Finance Committee 58
   commissariat system 60
   compulsory regulations 58
Urals Bolsheviks 56–7
Urals Oblast 56
Uryvaev, M. E. 114

Valentinov, Nikolay 192
Val'ter, F. A. 238
van Ree, Erik 10, 91, 190, 218
Vandervelde, Emile 36
vanguard party 18
Vareikis, I. M. 121
Velychenko, Stephen 161
violence 246, 250, 255
   mass violence (*see* mass violence)
Virginia Declaration of Rights (1776) 85
Voikov, Petr 182
Volkov, Vadim 219, 221
Volobuev, Mykhailo 169
Vol'skii, R. 85
Vyshinskii, Andrei 148

Waffen- und Munitionsbeschaffungsamt 18
War Communism 7, 233
war socialism 21

Index

What Is to Be Done? (Lenin) 39
Witte, Sergei 21
workers' control 23–4
workers' democracy 119, 122
Workers' Opposition 7, 112–13
Workers' Opposition and Democratic Centralist 81, 178
Workers' Opposition and Workers' Truth 114, 116
Wrangel, Petr 175

Yenukidze, Avel 143–4
Yurchak, Alexei 143

Zemliatcha, Rosalinda 251
Zhdanov, Andrei 86–8, 90–2
Zhukov, N. 222, 227–8
Zhurova, Natalia 63
Zhvachkin, Sergei 63
Zinoviev, G. 42, 82, 98, 129, 176